From the Ivory Tower

GITA
DENECKERE

# FROM THE IVORY TOWER

## 200 YEARS OF GHENT UNIVERSITY

TIJDSBEELD Publishing

Dedicated to Benn Deceuninck (1960-2017) in the silence of light

Contents

Prologue

> From Bildung to Bologna 6

1. Inter utrumque: between science and society 11
2. Pluralism, religion and science 57
3. Industry and valorisation 91
4. Caring for body and mind 115
5. Society as laboratory 145
6. Language 165
7. War and peace 185
8. Democratisation 211
9. Gender and sexuality 231
10. Colonialism and development cooperation 261
11. Environment and biotechnology 287

Epilogue

> Measuring the clouds 321

Bibliographical essay 333

Acknowledgements 342

Useful acronyms 344

Index of names 346

Prologue

# FROM BILDUNG TO BOLOGNA

This book is an ode to my alma mater. In 2017, Ghent University celebrated its 200th birthday, but thanks to its students it remains eternally young. A beacon of light in the city. As an author, the great thing about writing a jubilee book is that you don't have to be shy about emphasising all the marvellous and compelling stories. Of course, I do so under the motto of the university — 'Dare to think'. Therefore, I will also not neglect to hold up the university's past and present to a critical light and even express a contrary view from time to time, as an expression of my commitment to the fortunes of my university.

The title of the book suggests an active call to the university to stand up and strive for social impact. This is not new. Since the nineteenth century, universities have been compared to ivory towers. The tower symbolises the haughty distance they supposedly take from the hustle and bustle of the outside world. The image of protected solitude originally comes from the biblical Song of Songs. In the Middle Ages, however, the 'ivory tower' had less negative connotations. The medieval university was sometimes depicted as a tower that the student climbed step by step, from the *artes liberales* to theology, a metaphor for individual growth. During his climb he could see the world around him grow smaller through the narrow windows as he became more spiritual. The nineteenth-century founder of the modern secular university, Wilhelm von Humboldt, considered the search for philosophical truth a process that had to be removed from daily reality. The 'pure' scholar entrenched himself in *Freiheit und Einsamkeit*, far from practical worries and shabby power struggles. This academic freedom enabled him to reflect impartially and endowed the scholarly class with social prestige and authority.

Gradually, however, seclusion from 'real life' was considered in a less positive light. Today, if a scholar is said to live in an ivory tower, he or she is implicitly being denied the right to speak about concrete social problems. The authority derived from isolation from the hustle and bustle of everyday life is thereby swept away. The modern world demands of its academics that they live with both feet on the ground rather than 'hovering' unworldly above. Better a tower of concrete than of ivory.

## Bildung, scholarship and society

Most universities in the nineteenth century answered to Humboldt's ideal much less than the association with the ivory tower suggests. At the beginning of the century, universities were mainly oriented towards the formation of an elite that would become doctors, lawyers, magistrates, engineers or professors. To put it rather unfairly, the university offered an elevated form of vocational education for the professions, the civil service and industry. As government and industry diversified, the variety of higher vocational education also expanded, with university diplomas for engineers, architects, veterinarians, dentists, pharmacists, diplomats, business administrators and teachers.

In addition to the transfer of knowledge, an initiation or rite of passage in the social and cultural world of bourgeois life took place. In this way, the university upheld the social barriers of the intellectual and governing elites. The acquisition of social and cultural status at the university meant that degree programmes had to be more than merely professional. The *artes liberales* or the seven liberal arts from the Middle Ages were an integral part of the university *Bildungsideal*. The difficult-to-translate *Bildung* refers to the general development and self-realisation of the bourgeois elites. The nineteenth-century citizen spoke his languages and cared about art, politics and science. Part of his status consisted in knowing the classics of world literature and the literature of his own country, but familiarity with astronomy, botany and national history was an additional plus. The individual development of the citizen benefited society and the nation. The modern world needed intellectually independent citizens who offered their critical and independent contribution to the progress of humanity.

The academic freedom and greater autonomy of the universities with respect to the state ensured the increasing importance of scientific research at the end of the nineteenth century. The university had not only to pass on directly usable knowledge and educate critical citizens, but also, increasingly, to stimulate a scientific attitude among its students. In many disciplines, this led to major scientific breakthroughs around 1900. This was certainly not limited to 'pure' science in the ivory tower. Even though academic freedom and independence were necessary conditions for the development of scientific thought, the scientists themselves were not necessarily other-worldly weirdos. On the contrary, they were often connected with industry, politics and society in the broadest sense through diverse personal and social networks.

Since 1998, societal engagement has been expressly included in the mission statement of the Ghent University as its first and most important selling point. But the university's social involvement goes back much further in time. More than that: the genealogy of the university itself is closely intertwined with the major societal issues that have determined European history since the nineteenth century. 'The history of science is the history of mankind, wrote historian of science George Sarton when he founded *Isis: The International Review Devoted to the History of Science and its Cultural Influences* in 1913. Social history meets history of science in my story of 200 years of Ghent University. A story that shows how the work of scientists with both feet planted firmly in society cannot be captured in mere quantitative indicators or output. The utilitarian approach to universities is too restrictive when it comes to societal added value and impact.

# A history for the future

As a historian, if you study the *longue durée* of 200 years, you have a much clearer view of continuity and discontinuity in history. Since the 1980s, public universities have been under pressure from market-driven or utilitarian logic. Fundamental research is suppressed in favour of applied research and shrinking government subsidies make the university more dependent on financing from industry and the private sector. The 'useless' humanities may end up paying the price. The 'twenty-first-century skills' that universities promote today increasingly conjure up a nostalgic longing for the 'old-speak' of *Bildung*, enlightenment and civilisation, with universities as refuges where better people and alert citizens are formed. In the US, this position is powerfully expressed by Martha Nussbaum in her book *Not for Profit: Why Democracy Needs the Humanities* (2010). Since the Bologna Declaration of 1999 brought about the creation of a European higher education area, it is gradually becoming apparent in Europe that education driven by profit and added value creation, international rankings and efficiency is not the same as education aimed at *Bildung* and democracy. The humanities, literature and art pay the greatest price for this shift. The cultivation of the imagination is not profitable. Or at least, yields nothing that can immediately be valorised in economic terms. Individual development and the cultivation of critical citizenship are at risk of being sacrificed to multiple-choice exams, the writing of fragmented minute papers and an oppressive system of near-permanent evaluation and increasingly flexible degree programmes.

The answer to increasing criticism of this system seems to lie in the past, or in a return to that which was lost in the 'great leap forward': the ideal of *Bildung*. Universities around the world are currently reinventing this ideal, less out of nostalgia than out of necessity, refreshed and adapted to the questions and challenges of the twenty-first century. The future itself offers no alternative …

I did not write this book out of nostalgia, but precisely because history offers inspiration for the times to come. The past is not a distant, foreign country where people did things differently; through all kinds of surprising and tortuous paths, we are more closely bound to it today than we think. I would therefore like to take you as a reader by the hand along the highways, byways and escape routes of 200 years of university history.

I have deliberately chosen not to write a chronological narrative. A jubilee history of a single university always runs the risk of being little more than an uncritical list of successes. Moreover, there is also the risk of teleology, in which the finishing point 'anniversary' forms the triumphal outcome of a history of growth (of students), increase (of knowledge) and acceleration (of technology).

Instead of a purely chronological and linear narrative, I have chosen to relate the 200-year history of Ghent University through eleven themes. These eleven chapters do not tell the whole story and do not cover all the socially relevant areas of research conducted at the university today. To write a book of comprehensible size, I have inevitably had to make choices that do not do justice to all the interesting things that could not be covered within this framework. For a more complete picture, I refer the reader to UGentMemorie.be, the constantly growing virtual memory of the university. Everyone is free to contribute. Since 2008, a close-knit team of historians in the History Department has been working to shape the collective memory of the university in word and image, with societal impact as the leading thread running throughout the whole. Without the treasure trove of stories that UGentMemorie has meanwhile become, I simply could not have written this book.

Per theme, I try to sketch the broad outlines of events from 1817 to 2017, ending each chapter with a provocative question or polemical point of contention for the future. In doing so I have tried not to lose sight of the role of individuals and their *petites histoires*. For contemporary history, oral history has given me recourse to the rich memory of a broad range of privileged witnesses. The bird's-eye-view of the *longue durée* becomes interwoven with the frog's-eye-view of the people who have made UGent what it is today. In addition, I focus not only on professors with an international reputation, but also on the less-familiar names of men and women who risk falling into oblivion. Hence, this book is conceived not as an encyclopaedic but as a kaleidoscopic history of the university. Like a viewer in which the various figures are multiply reflected and show different patterns with every minute shift in movement: a dynamic history with many nuances, coincidences and changes of perspective. All in the hope that 200 years of Ghent University will also be an exciting voyage of discovery for you, dear reader.

Gita Deneckere, July 2017

Jan Fabre,
*The Legs of Reason Skinned*, 2000
During the citywide exhibition *Over the Edges* in 2000, Jan Fabre covered the columns of the Aula with ham. An incarnation of the slogan 'Dare to Think'.
(Ghent, Universiteitsarchief, Angelos bvba, photo Hilde Christiaens)

Chapter 1

# INTER UTRUMQUE: BETWEEN SCIENCE AND SOCIETY

The original motto of Ghent University — *inter utrumque* — indicates that it did not come into being in a social vacuum. *Inter utrumque* means 'between the two': between striving for wisdom through the practice of science and service to king and country. In today's terms, you might translate it as: a university 'between science and society'. On the coat of arms of the university is Minerva, goddess of wisdom and knowledge, depicted between branches of orange and laurel. The orange branch refers to William I of Orange-Nassau, founder of the university. The laurel is a symbol of peace and victory. The golden head of Minerva is said to have been drawn by the famous painter Jacques-Louis David, best known for his painting of *Minerva Fighting Mars* (1771), which now hangs in the Louvre in Paris.

**The university's coat of arms**
From 1817 to 1988, the head of Minerva was the official logo of the university.
(The Hague, Nationaal Archief)

In 1817, the goddess of wisdom triumphed over the god of war, Mars, in what is now Belgium. The French Revolution of 1789 had pushed Europe into a turbulent period of war and destruction that ended in 1815. After the Battle of Waterloo, Napoleon was finally defeated and exiled to St Helena. At the Congress of Vienna, it was agreed that the great powers would preserve eternal peace. The United Kingdom of the Netherlands was a means to this end. The Southern Netherlands were separated from France for fear that the French would invade Great Britain via Antwerp. The 'amalgam' of North and South formed a sturdy buffer, a *boulevard de l'Europe contre la France*. The British viewed William I as a trump card. He was a descendant of the illustrious forefather of the Dutch stadtholders, William of Orange. The cult of the stadtholders, recollections of the Dutch Golden Age and the solidarity between the House of Orange and Great Britain were ideal foundations on which to establish a new royal house, focused on the greater goal of keeping peace and order in Europe. It was to be a monarchy with a constitution, where the revolutionary principle of popular sovereignty had no place. William I governed his kingdom autocratically and bureaucratically, from behind his desk. He is still popular in Ghent today. He will even receive a neo-nineteenth-century statue on the Bisdomplein. Nevertheless, the king rarely visited the city during his fifteen-year reign over the unified Northern and Southern Netherlands.

On the coat of arms, Minerva is protected by the crown of the Netherlands and the lion of Ghent. After the Revolution of 1830, to the great dissatisfaction of many inhabitants of Ghent, this crown was replaced by the crown of Belgium. The new kingdom of Belgium took over the protective function in 1835. The university continued to exist in Ghent, along with its sister university in Liège. The investments that the city made in its university were an important argument in favour of its remaining there. Thus, the protection by the lion of Ghent has been a constant throughout the 200-year history of the university. Although the Belgian flag still flutters over the main university buildings, the 'State' in 'State University of Ghent' has in the meantime been expunged. Higher education has become the purview of the Flemish government, yet it is also inextricably bound up in European integration and globalisation.

In this introductory chapter, I sketch the broader social-political context in which the university has developed, with attention to its interaction with local, national and international areas of tension.

## A new university, but where?

In 1816, the Southern Netherlands was a virtual desert in terms of education, particularly higher education. The old university of Leuven was abolished in 1793 under the French revolutionary regime. The universities were but servants of 'aristocracy and barbarism' and were moreover completely useless, according to the French revolutionaries. Only a handful of institutions survived the fall of Napoleon. Many French professors left the country. It was an international phenomenon: the French Revolution and Napoleon left behind them a trail of destruction. In 1789, there were 143 universities in Europe; in 1815, only 83 remained.

Initially, William I contemplated founding just one new university in the South. Leuven fired the starting shot in a bitter struggle between several Belgian cities over the question of where that university should be located. In a veritable charm offensive directed at the Dutch crown, mayors, city councils and governors outdid themselves with all manner of appeals and petitions. In November 1814, the city council of Ghent sent William a petition. History was trotted out. Was it not in Ghent that the famous Pacification was concluded in 1576, against the tyranny of the Duke of Alva? Was it not under the illustrious House of Orange that a Calvinist university was founded in the Pand, unfortunately destroyed in the godless Eighty Years War? The conclusion was obvious: 'the city of Ghent [asks] therefore only the return of that which arose from the will of the ancestors of the magnanimous prince, who was called by the allied powers to the greater good of our region'.

The commission that advised the king deemed that one university was more than enough for the potential student population of the Southern Netherlands. That one university, which 'would be able to teach all subjects of human science to even greater perfection', would thus be able to compete with the best universities in Europe. The aged canon and renowned antiquarian Martin De Bast was the only member of the commission who was from Ghent. He assumed that Ghent would have no chance if only one university was established. And so he argued in favour of several universities. Healthy competition could moreover avert a situation in which one complacent university lulled itself to sleep. It was a thinly disguised sneer at Leuven, which had already lost its scientific lustre in the eighteenth century. But no one else shared De Bast's vision.

As befits an enlightened despot, William ignored the advice of the commission. He established not one, but three universities in the Southern Netherlands: in Leuven, Liège and Ghent. The trio formed a reflection of the three universities in the Northern Netherlands at the time: Leiden, Utrecht and Groningen. In this way, the king wanted to bring the two parts of the country closer together and ensure balance. The risk that elites in the South would feel disadvantaged if they only had one university was too great.

In a hefty document, drawn up in June 1816, Ocker Repelaer van Driel, minister of education, arts and sciences, refuted the arguments of the commission one by one. He stood by his 'long-cherished idea' that it was more useful to invest in several universities: 'It may be true that in the management of several colleges one acquires more reputation and fame than another, but this is exactly what proves that competition is necessary and should be cultivated, because the one whose reputation is in decline finds precisely herein new stimulus to encouragement, with the goal of regaining its renown and becoming the equal of its competitors.'

The minister did not even think it necessary inquiring into the establishment of a single university in Leuven. The reasons for this were 'either very easy to refute or indeed add too little weight to the balance to be applicable here'. Trepidation with respect to a Leuven monopoly on higher education had ideological grounds: 'the rightly feared resurrection of the former college of Leuven, in many respects as disadvantageous as it is dangerous to the state and to education'. History had shown that it was not a good idea to expand too greatly the power of a single university. If no resistance was offered, its power could be abused. Repelaer was also of the opinion that Brussels had major disadvantages as a location for a single university: too many diversions and distractions for young people; moral turpitude in the capital was bad for students 'in the first throes of youth to be exposed to'. In Brussels, the cost of living was higher and with the rapidly increasing population, it was more difficult to secure university buildings and the accommodations provided for students was more expensive.

Not one, then, but three universities. William had already determined in 1815 that in such case there would certainly be a university in Leuven. Liège was an obvious choice for other reasons: its location, its attractiveness to German students and the contacts with German intellectual culture. Ghent was more difficult. Only canon De Bast was in favour of it; the five other members of the commission deemed Bruges far preferable to rebellious Ghent. The recruitment of English students so close to the coast, the lower cost of living, the greater control over students in a smaller city ... These were all arguments in favour of Catholic Bruges, which moreover had a library and a (rudimentary) chemistry and physics cabinet. But on this point as well, Repelaer van Driel would follow De Bast's line of reasoning: 'The available means for higher education are in my opinion more abundant in Ghent than in Bruges, such as the fine Herbal Garden, the Agricultural Society, the Medical School, the Hospitals, the Library.' Moreover, English students who undertook a journey by sea would surely be willing to continue on to Ghent. The 'reviving Dutch spirit of the people' (Ghent was an Orangist bulwark), 'the good taste of the inhabitants' and the importance attached by the citizens of Ghent to the arts and sciences made Ghent more suitable as a university town than the more parochial Bruges, in the minister's view.

William did indeed give preference to Ghent, where he had visited the library at the Baudelo Abbey in 1815. At the end of 1817, it was to be transferred to the university.

**The library in the Baudelo Abbey on the Ottogracht**
The collection of Ghent bibliophile Charles Van Hulthem forms the basis of the Universiteitsbibliotheek, which moved to the Book Tower in 1942.
(Ghent, Universiteitsbibliotheek)

Under the motto 'increasing knowledge, combating ignorance', the Ghent bibliophile Charles Van Hulthem had saved from destruction the rich collections of manuscripts, books, paintings and art treasures from the abolished monasteries and assembled them in the Baudelo Chapel. Van Hulthem was positively disposed towards the United Kingdom of the Netherlands and undoubtedly influenced the final decision to establish a university in Ghent.

On 25 September 1816, William issued his *Reglement op de Inrigting van het Hooger Onderwijs in de Zuidelijke Provinciën van het Koningrijk der Nederlanden*, the 'birth certificate' of the three universities. The battle of the cities was won; Ghent rejoiced. But the triumph came at a price. Since the establishment of a university within the walls of Ghent, Leuven and Liège was a 'considerable advantage', Repelaer van Driel found it 'not unreasonable' that each city provide the buildings needed for academic education. This meant considerable savings for the Dutch treasury: 'In this way the national state would be saved a not inconsiderable expense.' A Dutchman wouldn't be a Dutchman if he couldn't count. And so it was.

## 177 bottles of wine and 12 bottles of champagne

Ghent University was inaugurated on 9 October 1817 by Prince William Frederick. That is, not by King William I himself. The throne in the well-known painting by Matthias van Bree in the Rijksmuseum in Amsterdam is indeed empty. A painted portrait of William I under the canopy of the throne was meant as compensation.

In his speech to the prince, Orangist mayor Philippe De Lens expressed his gratitude towards the king as 'benefactor' and heir to 'Le Grand Guillaume', father of the

Matthias van Bree, *Official Founding of Ghent University in the Town Hall on 9 October 1817.* Crown prince William Frederick listening to a speech by Ocker Repelaer van Driel, the Dutch minister of education. On the right are the dignitaries of the city.
(Amsterdam, Rijksmuseum)

fatherland and founder of Leiden University. Rector Jan Van Rotterdam reported to The Hague that the best rapport and harmony prevailed at the new university: 'Everyone is active with such great diligence, motivated as we are by grateful recognition of our good king, to whom our city and we in particular owe so much.'

The lion of Ghent honoured its prominent place in the university coat of arms from the outset. As stipulated in the Regulations of 1816, the city was to provide buildings for the university and assume the financial burden thereby entailed. In the first phase, these were the Pakhuis on the Korenmarkt (for the faculty of Medicine), the old Jesuit monastery in Voldersstraat (for Arts and Philosophy), the Baudelo Library (for Law) and the St Eligius Chapel in the Geldmunt (for Sciences and Anatomy). But the Ghent city council did more than just reallocate existing buildings for education. In November 1816, architect Louis Roelandt was commissioned to design a prestigious 'palace of the university' as a location for academic and civic ceremonies, and as a landmark in the city.

Ghent envisioned something grand: the Aula Academica had to reflect the new university's prestigious glow over the city. The local Pantheon for the glorification of enlightened science clearly showed that the city held the university close to its heart. Ten years after its foundation, on 3 October 1826, the Aula was officially inaugurated. The striking building in the heart of the city exceeded all expectations. The Aula impressed; it was included in travel guides and provoked great admiration far beyond the borders of the kingdom. There were passers-by who stopped to stare in 'dumb amazement' at the splendid neoclassical creation.

Ange de Baets, *Interior view of Aula Academica, 1827*
With the Aula, Ghent puts itself on the European map as a city of arts and sciences.
(Ghent, Universiteitsarchief)

Ghent was happy with its university, this much was clear. The papers reported ecstatically on the official installation on 9 October 1817. During the banquet and the ball afterwards, it was rumoured that 177 bottles of wine and 12 bottles of champagne had been consumed — by a limited gathering of 78 guests. But it was not only the city hall that celebrated: the entire city was lit up and the pubs were allowed to remain open the whole night through. Mayor De Lens understood very well that the university would provide the city with 'inestimable benefits' and 'a new lustre'. The city was willing to do a great deal in return.

The lectures commenced on 3 November 1817. Students were able to enrol at four faculties: Arts and Philosophy, Law, Sciences, and Medicine. There were sixteen professors, including nine foreigners; the administrative staff consisted of thirteen employees. The first academic year witnessed the enrolment of 190 students. The official language of the six universities in the Netherlands was Latin. Like the high financial threshold, this language barrier created social exclusivity and exclusion.

## The first professors

For William, the education of a social, political and cultural elite could only be entrusted to reliable and competent professors. They were servants of the state and appointed directly by the king. Many of them praised the modern spirit of William, who as an enlightened monarch appreciated the importance of the arts and sciences. In his view, the aura of a university depended on having professors worthy of the name. Men — there would be no question of women for quite some time — who, by virtue of

**Ermine, gown and beret**
The official dress of professors and rectors at the two state universities in Ghent and Liège was established by royal decree in 1838.
(Ghent, Universiteitsbibliotheek)

**Johannes Schrant**
(Ghent, Universiteitsbibliotheek, lithograph, Anicet Lemonnier)

**Jacques-Joseph Haus**
(Ghent, Universiteitsbibliotheek, lithograph, Anicet Lemonnier)

their genius, placed themselves far above their contemporaries, opened new avenues for science or cast unexpected light on existing paths. But the glory of a university was also fostered by the teaching ability of the professors: sharing enthusiasm, actively influencing the minds of young people in order to lead them to beauty and goodness. These elements were also highly valued by the Dutch government.

William appointed almost exclusively (broad-minded) Catholics and Liberals in the South. He assumed that they would enjoy the confidence of the local populations and have a favourable influence on public opinion. For example, there was the Nieuwpoort medical doctor Jacob Lodewijk Kesteloot, who had studied in Leiden and had been a director of the Catholic poor in The Hague. Kesteloot would turn out to be an advocate of the Dutch language as an instrument of civilisation, also at the university. The Dutch priest Johannes Schrant was more difficult to convince to accept a professorship. As a candidate for the chair of Dutch Literature and Eloquence, he shied away from 'French morals' and prejudices against the Netherlands in highly Frenchified Ghent. The king also appointed well-regarded and loyal citizens of Ghent, such as the young lawyer Pierre De Ryckere, who, during William's visit to Ghent on 11 July 1817, wrote an ode to *Wilhelmo I, Belgarum regi*.

The king also recruited actively abroad, particularly in Germany and France. The extremely young professor of Criminal Law Jacques-Joseph Haus, for example, belonged to the original corps of professors. Haus would occupy his chair for 63 years, an absolute record. Rather remarkably, it was the king himself who persuaded foreign professors to actually settle in Ghent.

William's appointment policy was widely criticised, precisely because so many chairs in the South had been given by preference to foreign scholars. More than half (nine of the sixteen professors in Ghent) came from abroad. The government defended itself with the argument that 25 years of war and occupation had created a serious shortage of people with the scientific background, erudition and culture needed to assume a professorship. A small country like the United Kingdom of the Netherlands was moreover surrounded by large nations where civilisation had reached a high level of development. It would lag behind these great nations if it isolated itself and withdrew from modern scientific and literary influences. This too justified the recruitment of foreign professors. That they were mainly Germans was related to the desire to strengthen ties between the Southern Netherlands and Germany. French literature was so dominant that it had practically become the national literature of what is now Belgium. What better way to restore equilibrium than to disseminate deeper knowledge of and about Germany than through German professors? In any case, it was assumed that eventually the government would no longer have to go abroad to attract good professors. Foreign professors would become an exception in the future, in rare cases of 'extraordinary and recognised merit'.

## A final charm offensive

Johan Thorbecke
(Ghent, Universiteitsarchief)

Johan Thorbecke, who became professor of Contemporary Political History of Europe in Ghent in 1825, was fervently convinced that Dutch as a language of higher education could make the connection between North and South. He consistently gave his lectures on statistics and political economics in Dutch, and repeated them in Latin for the French-speaking students.

His brief tenure in Ghent afforded the great liberal statesman, who laid the basis for parliamentary democracy in the Netherlands, important insights. It is no coincidence that Thorbecke studied both constitutional law and the 'influence of machines on the composition of social and civil relations' in the industrial hotspot of Flanders. He also sent confidential reports to The Hague on recently graduated doctors in law. This was done on behalf of the government, which sought to recruit reliable Belgians for public office. After all, there were increasing complaints in the South about the preference for Northern Netherlanders.

In April 1828, the king established a new higher education commission to advise him on the necessary course of action. Thorbecke was part of it. He wrote a detailed memorandum on behalf of the faculty of Arts on the planned university reform. At the time, the United Kingdom of the Netherlands was already under considerable pressure from the growing opposition movement in the South. William ignored the complaints, including those concerning higher education. His goal was to modernise the universities and make them more scientific according to the German Humboldt model, and to centralise the institutions as in France. The king saw the universities in his realm as anything but ivory towers. For example, there was the explicit question of their societal role: Were the universities in the first place scientific and literary centres focused on the increase of knowledge? Or were they government institutions whose mission was the education of good civil servants and enlightened citizens? Did university education adequately meet the needs of society? Was it necessary for practical knowledge of trade, agriculture and industry to be offered at every university? Or was the development of a spearhead policy *avant la lettre* preferable? Industry in Ghent and Leiden, mining and political science in Liège, agriculture in Utrecht and so on? The question of the desirability of a polytechnic institution for engineers and architects was stated explicitly. The training of the industrial class would be more efficient if knowledge was concentrated in one or two universities. Other universities could then develop other faculties. After all, not every course of study could be equally good at every university. Leuven had good philologists at the beginning of the nineteenth century; Liège excelled in modern and political history; and Ghent, as a city of the fine arts, displayed a close link between art and science with its superb Aula and cabinets filled with unique collections.

Bust of King William I
(Ghent, photo Benn Deceuninck)

The advisory commission concluded its activities in 1829. As a result of the Belgian Revolution of 1830, however, its findings remained a dead letter. In June 1829, William visited Ghent University during his tour of the South, a final charm offensive. The king wished to make himself personally aware of the mood among the population and to show his fatherly, responsible side. In the Aula, he gave a speech before the students of Ghent, and through his minister of Domestic Affairs he informed the academic authorities afterwards that he was extremely satisfied with 'the good spirit that animates the youngsters of Your College'. The king appreciated this all the more, because it provided 'the surest guarantee' that the students of Ghent 'will, in their future destiny, answer to what is expected of them by King and Fatherland'.

This did not help. About a year later, the revolution was a fact. The Latin inscription *Auspice. Gulielmo. I. Acad. conditore. Posuit. S.P.Q.G. MDCCCXXVI*, which honours William as patron, was promptly removed by insurgents from the frieze of the Aula. A year later, the students' new fatherland received a new monarch.

## A mutilated university in independent Belgium

After 1830, the universities in the North and South developed along separate paths. In the North, the regulations of 1815 were maintained until 1876 and the unification of university culture was a success. In newly independent Belgium, a period of chaos and uncertainty broke out. The provisional government not only announced the complete freedom of education, it abolished by provisional decree of 16 December 1830 no less than five faculties at the three universities. In Ghent, two of the four faculties were closed: Arts & Philosophy and Sciences, which served as preparatory courses for Law and Medicine. The city protested vehemently against this 'disastrous mutilation': two densely populated provinces were not only cut off from *l'étude de tous les arts et de toutes les professions savants* but the students were henceforth forced to move to Leuven or Liège in order to acquire the necessary candidate diplomas. Moreover, the city had invested huge sums of money in buildings and scientific cabinets. The neglect of the jewel in the city's crown naturally added fuel to the fire in an Orangist city that had had the wind in its sails under William I and now dug in its heels against the new Belgian state. The figurehead of the Orangists was Hippolyte Metdepenningen, who graduated in 1818 as the first doctor in law in Ghent and was well established in university and Masonic circles.

In 1831 the provisional government set up a new committee to work out new permanent regulations for higher education. The Regulations of 1816 were torn to pieces: they had resulted in education without practical use and did not answer to existing societal needs. The courses were from another age, oriented towards the education of a 'learned class', at least according to the committee. Once again, a vehement struggle broke out among the cities. The quality of higher education did not benefit from the persistent malaise, not least because many erudite (foreign) professors were dismissed after the revolution and replaced by extremely young successors without experience. Student enrolment dropped sharply.

Adolphe Quételet, one of the first Ghent alumni in mathematics (class of 1819), was a member of the committee. At the time, he was connected with the Musée des Sciences et des Lettres in Brussels, which he had founded, and was director of the Observatory there. This is an indication that Quételet did not necessarily represent the interests of his hometown, Ghent. As expected, the committee argued for a single, central university situated in the capital, one that would bring the small nation of Belgium international renown. In addition, a modern polytechnic would be established along French lines. Not surprisingly, this two-part structure met fierce resistance and a storm of criticism from the existing university towns.

Ghent, too, made a fervent plea to the first Belgian king, Leopold I, for the maintenance of its university. Upon his last visit to the city, wrote the moderate Orangist mayor Joseph Van Crombrugghe hopefully, hadn't the king taken the trouble to view the splendid university buildings, the well-stocked library, the Botanical Garden and cabinets, and promised his patronage? The city offered comfortable rooms to students at reasonable prices and had for many years supported the promotion of the arts and sciences in Belgium. The Aula had cost the city a great deal of money and the building was impossible to repurpose. A population of more than 85,000 souls ensured a daily rate of 200 to 250 patients in the Bijloke, the civil hospital. For students of medicine, this was an ideal place for clinical observation and practical instruction. Students of law could become proficient at various courts, including the Court of Appeals of East and West Flanders. While Ghent had known great prosperity thanks to industrial development under Dutch rule, it now suffered under the stagnation of industry. The loss of its university would only aggravate the city's condition. As a commercial and industrial city, Ghent rivalled Brussels in terms of civilisation and knowledge.

Leopold understood that he could only bind Ghent to Belgium by breaking down the Orangist connection as much as possible. And that could only be accomplished by

Joseph Van Crombrugghe
Mayor of Ghent during the turbulent revolutionary period 1825-1836. Surrounding him are his achievements in the city, including the peristyle of the Aula and the library on the Baudelo.
(Ghent, Universiteitsarchief)

Coat of arms of Leopold I and Louise in the Golden Book, 1834
The first King of the Belgians, Leopold I, was not to be outdone by William I as patron of the university. Jules Van Praet and Edward Conway, his most important advisers, studied at the Ghent law faculty.
(Ghent, Universiteitsarchief)

promoting Ghent's interests as much as William had. The first King of the Belgians also cultivated a much more active politics of presence in the rebellious city than his predecessor. It is striking to note how, throughout the 1830s, almost the entire Coburg clan came to adorn the university's Golden Book with their coat of arms. On 16 September 1843, Queen Victoria of Great Britain and Prince Albert, Leopold's niece and nephew, concluded the royal family procession. Albert had already been in Ghent in 1836, together with his brother Ernst, Duke of Saxe-Coburg. The Belgian Coburg dynasty has remained favourably inclined to the (State) University of Ghent ever since.

## Free universities in Leuven and Brussels

In the background of the struggle between the cities, an ideological conflict was playing out that had been crucial in the run-up to the Belgian revolution. Paradoxically, it would prove to be the salvation of the two state universities in Ghent and Liège. Because of their awkward locations, neither one of them was eligible to become the *only* state university in the country. In 1831, moreover, freedom of education was laid down in the constitution. For both the clerical and anticlerical factions, this offered interesting perspectives for development — in the area of higher education as well. Their mutual aim of having a free university of their own was rewarded even before parliament made the definitive decision concerning the fate of the two state universities. Not that Leuven was ready to admit defeat. On the contrary, it threw all claims based on its age-old tradition and reputation into the arena. The preservation of Ghent and Liège would create a gap between Flemings and Walloons. A single, centrally located state university in Leuven, where Flemish and Walloon youth — both Catholic and Liberal — could study: this was the way to cultivate real Belgians.

Despite all the pleas for a concentration of talent and resources, a Catholic university was established in Mechelen in November 1834. Several days later, the anticlerical Université Libre de Bruxelles (ULB) would also see the light of day. In December 1835, the Catholic university moved from Mechelen to Leuven. The state university there had meanwhile been abolished, and the historical line to the old medieval university could be restored. Finally, the basic structure of university education in Belgium had taken shape: two state universities, in Ghent and Liège, and two free universities, in Brussels and Leuven. In The Hague, William I turned up his nose at the 'so-called Free Colleges', which 'were maintained not by state funds, but by private means, and are therefore likely to be subject to different supervision'.

To reconcile freedom of education and the ideological diversity of the four universities with national interests, however, the young Belgian state built in government control over the degrees. A central jury, appointed by the government and with equal representation from the four universities, administered exams and awarded diplomas until 1876. In this way, the Belgian state retained control over the curriculums and 'final attainment levels' of higher education and continued to guard the gateway to civil service and the liberal professions.

## A Belgian compromise

The law of 27 September 1835 on university education was the result of a typically Belgian compromise. The preservation of ideological and community equilibrium would dominate university politics until well into the twentieth century. The government acknowledged that the number of universities had to be limited. For a small country with a well-developed transportation network, a single, central state university offered indisputable advantages in terms of promoting science and developing national sentiment. In a country that had to be built from scratch, public education was of utmost importance for the formation of national spirit among young people. Moreover, quality education in all branches of science would attract many foreign students, while an overabundance of universities could generate mediocrity. The concentration of talent and resources in one location could allow Belgium to rival foreign universities. With fewer resources, it would thus be possible to achieve more and perform better. But this logic — which also played a role in 1816 — clearly did not weigh against the political disadvantages associated with the establishment of a state university in Brussels and the dangers and temptations to which students would be exposed in the capital.

The consolidation of Ghent and Liège had a major advantage in this respect: the Flemish and Walloon provinces each retained their university as a powerful instrument of civilisation. An industrial or polytechnic faculty could also be added seamlessly to both universities: in Ghent, focused on the construction of bridges and roads; in Liège, on mining. Of course, two public universities cost more, but that extra expense was more than compensated by the immense added value that was created for the entire country.

The new Belgian nation resolutely chose Belgians over foreigners for the post of professor. Moreover, it was now possible to recruit from its 'own' alumni. In 1835, for example, Joseph Guislain was appointed to the Human and Comparative Physiology chair at the re-established medical faculty. He graduated in 1819 as one of the first doctors in medicine and made a name for himself as the father of psychiatry. Joseph Plateau, for his part, had studied in Liège. First Arts and Law, then Sciences, with a

**Joseph Guislain**
(Ghent, Universiteitsarchief)

**Joseph Plateau**
(Ghent, Universiteitsarchief)

PhD on the after-effects of light on the eye. He, too, as an inventor of the phenakistiscope and founder of cinematography, would make an enormous contribution to the outreach of Ghent University.

The university of 1835 was less closely connected to the city than that of 1817. The administrative bond that existed with the governing board, chaired by the mayor, was cut. The annually changing rector was from then on flanked by an executive director, who was appointed by the government and ensured continuity. He had great power within the university, much greater in any case than that of the rector (and of the government commissioner today). The city was still responsible for the university buildings, but this was difficult to sustain when the university's mission was radically adapted to modern times.

## The introduction of modern science

When the academic year opened in 1880, rector Albert Callier was ill. The departing dean of the faculty of Medicine, Nicolas Du Moulin, gave the rector's speech, entitled *L'esprit scientifique et les universités*. He had thought about it long and hard. The sciences did not make enough progress in comparison to neighbouring countries and were not at the level of the arts in Belgium. Young Belgians rarely showed originality and intellectual independence in scientific questions. This had to do with the practical orientation of the Belgian nation, which mainly focused on industry and trade — or rather, on making a fortune. The 'Flemish race' was traditionally more focused on feeling than on the development of reason. In the domain of the arts, this would have led it to reach great heights. But centuries of oppression and a poor educational system that served the interests of blind faith had smothered the scientific spirit. In addition, the excessive importance attached by the Belgian government since 1830 to overloaded study programmes and difficult theoretical exams only inhibited the development of a scientific mind. The system of the central exam jury encouraged learning by rote and encyclopaedic studies, and hindered the drive to scientific research. Belgium should

Disc with dancing figure for a phenakistiscope, invented by Joseph Plateau, ca. 1832
A moving image is suggested by a play of optical illusions.
(Ghent, Ghent University Museum)

finally take note of how things were done in Germany: now there was a place where science was really cultivated! By introducing research-driven education, the modest Belgian and the humble Fleming could turn historical submission into activity and creativity. In Germany, the dissertation required to become a doctor or master was an *oeuvre de création*. In Belgium, the dissertation as 'master piece' no longer existed due to an error of ill-inspired legislation.

Du Moulin was certainly not the first to denounce the lack of scientific spirit and point an accusing finger at the government. Ever since university education was more or less up and running in Belgium in the mid-nineteenth century, it was an oft-repeated complaint.

## The footprint of Wilhelm von Humboldt

Towards the end of the nineteenth century, the French model of higher education, with its centrally organised state control of specialised Collèges, Écoles and Instituts Polytechniques, was superseded throughout Europe. It had been eroded by the striking success of the German model, which was based on academic freedom and original scientific research. The foundation of a university in Berlin in 1810 by the liberal Prussian statesman and linguist Wilhelm von Humboldt marks the most important intervention in eight hundred years of university history. It was then that the fusion of education and research came about. The German model was definitively introduced across Europe in 1870 and still exists as the university ideal today.

The scientific orientation of the universities was the result of the greater academic freedom and autonomy of the institutions. The modern world needed intellectually independent citizens who made their critical, unrestrained contributions to the progress of mankind. The university could not become a pedantic clearing house of authorised and directly usable knowledge; it must stimulate a scientific attitude among its students. The professor was no longer a walking, talking textbook; he gave small groups of students in laboratories and seminars the tools they needed to grasp a subject scientifically, so that they would be able to arrive at knowledge and truth themselves.

The only trouble was that the idealistic Humboldt model, with its limited role for the government, was much more difficult to implement than the centralised French model. The introduction of students to scientific research through seminars and laboratories was undertaken only with reluctance. But while Paris was still a mecca for students and scientists from all over the world at the beginning of the nineteenth century, the liberal German model represented the modern university by the end of the century. Not only in Europe, but also in the US and Japan. The victory of Germany in the Franco-Prussian War of 1870-1871 was after all generally attributed to its scientific and technological superiority thanks to the academic freedom of its professors.

With the central examination juries of 1835, Belgium had opted for a compromise between Paris and Berlin. In 1876, the Delcour Law abolished central examinations. The universities were henceforth allowed to award degrees and issue diplomas themselves, a milestone in the history of Belgian universities on the path to greater scientific orientation and experimental research. Professors were given the freedom to integrate new findings into their lessons and to add their own emphases when preparing examinations. Nevertheless, the Belgian government retained control of the curriculums — for example, by providing extra guidelines on the organisation of scientific research and practical exercises.

The Delcour Law was initially received enthusiastically in Ghent, but disenchantment soon followed. In 1881, in the heat of academic battle, the anticlerical rector Albert Callier declared freedom of education difficult to reconcile with the interests of science and public universities. After all, there was no guarantee of the quality and scientific competence of the institution that issued the diplomas. Those who graduated from a free university were eligible to apply for public office. Although the state demanded guarantees from the graduates who would serve the state, it could no longer determine those guarantees and was obliged to rely on private institutions for its choice of civil servants. The political interest of the Catholic government in this operation was clear, according to the rector. In this way, it was easier to populate the government machinery with Catholic officials. In any case, true academic freedom was not observed by the Delcour Law, let alone established.

Belgian universities did not do badly in Europe in terms of higher professional education, rector Callier continued. But their mission — even then — was broader than just educating doctors, lawyers and engineers. The Belgian government seemed to lose sight of the fact that higher education also had the noble task of shaping people, of developing the intellectual and moral capacities of younger generations, as Oxford or Cambridge did. Not to mention the vigorous universities that gave Germany so much grandeur. Every German university was both an educational institution and a scientific workshop, both a school and an academy. A professor was not just a teacher, but also and especially a scholar. By this was meant not just an erudite man, but also a researcher, a creator. Hence, the student learned less *science faite,* and more of the way science was actually practised. He followed the example of his master in verifying and questioning everything, of relying solely on his own experience and searching for the truth himself. In Germany it was understood that only one form of education was really fruitful, that of emulation: the professor who took students into his mental world and showed them how science was practised, stirring up the students' zeal (in the good sense of the word), their desire to equal and even surpass their professor.

Why couldn't this happen in Belgium? Were Belgians unable to elevate themselves to the cult of pure science? Callier refused to believe that. On the contrary: the liberal rector was even convinced that Ghent was well prepared to introduce teaching methods based on the personal work of the student. But introducing the seminar system also meant increasing the duration of study. The new educational system required more time than the classic lectures and rehearsals. Nevertheless, the great majority of students were more attracted to practice than to research. They wanted to become doctors and lawyers — not necessarily scientists. Callier therefore argued in favour of setting up Special Schools for the intellectual aristocracy, with a system of seminars analogous to Germany's. While now only the *Brodstudium* was available, also for the elite, Callier saw the wisdom of combining professional and scientific education. By the same logic, it was also possible to organise a separation between state entrance exams for the civil service and the liberal professions, on the one hand, and the scientific exams of the university itself on the other.

## August Kekulé's cabinet of curiosities

In Ghent the way had already been paved for the introduction of a more scientific approach to education. The city had financed a well-equipped laboratory for applied chemistry. The laboratory's two incinerators even received a bronze medal at the Paris World Exhibition in 1867. There was a cabinet for photography with a three-metre-long dialytic enlarger, which Wunderkind and recent graduate Désiré Van Monckhoven had patented in 1863. The observations and experiments carried out there were ahead of their time.

The general chemistry lab was a success thanks to the appointment of August Kekulé as professor. The promising *Privatdozent* from Heidelberg was 'headhunted' on the orders of the Liberal Minister of the Interior, Charles Rogier, who grasped the importance of scientific research for the development of the Belgian nation and industry. The government was not disappointed. Kekulé wrote his *Lehrbuch der Organischen Chemie oder der Chemie der Kohlenstoffverbindungen* (1859-1866) in Ghent. In his study at Veldstraat 72, he had his legendary daydream of dancing atoms in the form of a snake biting its own tail. The cyclical structure of benzene formed the foundation of aromatic chemistry.

When Kekulé published his discovery in 1865, the laboratory in Ghent, which had been specially equipped for him, was already world-famous. Upon arriving in Ghent, the renowned chemist had complained to a friend about the lamentable state of the university's infrastructure, which looked like a palace from the outside, but inside excelled in lack of space. At the time, nearly the entire university was housed in the buildings along the Lange Meer (now Universiteitstraat). Kekulé's chemistry lab was in fact reasonably well endowed with a room measuring 8 by 8 metres. His colleague Charles Poelman in Anatomy had to be content with a few mansard rooms in the building's attic. The dissection of large animals created a horrible stench, especially in the summer.

From his window, Kekulé could see a sort of 'kennel', a 'dark hole' where the engineering students did their *Manipulationen*. His own laboratory more closely resembled a perfectly tidy cabinet of curiosities than an actual workplace, leading him to ask himself *'was, wie, wo und wann haben die Leute hier gearbeit?'* The endless procedures — for example, in the purchase of new equipment — made everything that much more difficult. First, the executive director had to receive a budget; the supplier had to draw up his invoice in quadruplicate using carbon paper. Kekulé would immediately modernise the infrastructure of his laboratory, starting with 'small improvements' such as the installation of gas lines and the provision of running water.

Upon his arrival in Ghent, the Catholic press had stirred up the students against the 'foreigner' appointed by the Liberal Rogier government instead of the Catholic candidate, François Donny. Kekulé wrote that at his first lecture the audience made as much noise at the beginning as the 'rabble' at the opera. The harassment was short-lived, however. During his *Vorlesung*, the jaws of his audience dropped in amazement.

**August Kekulé and students in his laboratory, ca. 1865**
The discoverer of the benzene ring attracted a multitude of brilliant young researchers, such as Adolph von Baeyer (Nobel Prize in Chemistry 1905). The term 'barbiturates' could be traced back to his time in Ghent. When he discovered 'barbituric acid' in 1863, it was reportedly St Barbara's Day, name day of the patron saint of the artillery officers who met the chemists every afternoon in a nearby restaurant.
(Ghent, Universiteitsarchief, photo Beernaert Frères)

**Sint-Pietersnieuwstraat, mid-nineteenth century**
Professor of Applied Chemistry François Donny was an amateur photographer,
and in the pioneering period of photography made a series of cityscapes,
some of which have been preserved.
(Ghent, Universiteitsarchief)

Kekulé was the first in Ghent to change the system of official instruction. He also managed to get permission to use the second floor of the building on the Lange Meer from 1861 onwards. The teaching laboratory was a majestic, state-of-the-art classroom with a built-in space for incinerators and a large coal stove in the middle, among other things. The city made serious investments in the building, the machinery and the equipment.

In addition to the discovery of the benzene ring, Kekulé's great contribution was that he was the first to allow students to take the initiative by experimenting and making their own observations in order to develop scientific insight. This was unique in Belgium at the time. In Liège, the time was not yet ripe, but the Ghent physicists were also denied practical instruction in their discipline. Rector Joseph Roulez, a classical philologist, nonetheless emphasised in his address of 14 October 1862 how obvious it was that innovative education should be offered in the industrial city of Ghent. Prosperity and even the very survival of industry would be jeopardised if the train of progress, driven by science, were missed.

Kekulé's reputation ensured that he attracted a group of brilliant young researchers from abroad to Ghent, such as Adolph von Baeyer, who won the Nobel Prize for Chemistry in 1905. But no matter how great the scientific success of the clutch of star students around him, Kekulé was rather lonely and bored in Ghent. He worked day and night and there was little variety, except Sundays, when he dutifully took a walk in order to stay fit.

In June 1862 he married Stephanie Drory, a native of Ghent. She died in childbirth only a year later. His work held him together. But even though he had the wallpaper in his house rehung, 'as a form of superstition', he did not want to die in Ghent as a 'forgotten German'. When he accepted a long-hoped-for appointment at the hypermodern Chemisches Institut in Bonn in 1867, he was succeeded by his assistant Théodore Swarts, an excellent teacher who continued the tradition of training chemists through laboratory practice.

## Modernisation with state aid

Education in the medical sciences was also subjected to a complete overhaul. One of the main pioneers was Richard Boddaert, who after his studies in Ghent had learned the importance of the experimental method in London with Claude Bernard. From 1868 onwards, he personally introduced students to the fascinating world of the microscope in his course on General Human Anatomy. The students learned how to use the delicate instrument and observed histological details that even the best pen would have been unable to describe. When Boddaert became dean, he argued for the extension of hands-on experimental exercises to other branches of science. Rector Charles Andries was also of the opinion that the government couldn't encourage research-driven instruction enough.

The steady expansion of laboratory instruction to other disciplines created an urgent problem in terms of scientific infrastructure and assisting staff to facilitate research. It was only in 1878 under the anticlerical government of Frère-Orban and Van Humbeeck that the Belgian state was ready to invest in new university buildings.

Physics Laboratory, Institute for the Sciences, ca. 1900
(Ghent, Universiteitsbibliotheek)

The government appointed August Wagener as executive director. Wagener, who had been alderman of Public Education and Fine Arts in Ghent since 1863, would manage the university with flair for twenty years and guide it through a crucial transition period. Wagener profiled himself as a liaison officer between the city and the Belgian state, and succeeded in steering Ghent University 'in a modern direction'. The Belgian government was happy to go along with this. The new Ministry of Education drew up a one-time budget for new buildings. In 1882 the function of assistant was created by royal decree in order to accommodate the growing number of laboratory courses. In 1883 there were ten assistants working in Ghent; in 1914 their number had risen to fifteen.

The Liberal Frère-Orban–Van Humbeeck government (1878-1884) was convinced that only the flourishing of higher education could ensure the nation an intellectual culture of the highest quality. Minister of Education Pierre Van Humbeeck emphasised from the very beginning how much importance he attached to expanding and reinforcing the sciences and educating *'une jeunesse instruite, patriotique, profondément attachée à nos institutions, et dont un jour les travaux augmentent la prospérité du pays et affirment sa réputation à l'étranger'* (a learned youth, patriotic and profoundly attached to our institutions, whose labours will one day increase the country's prosperity and confirm its reputation abroad). The cultivation of patriotism and a love for the just, the true and the good was an important goal in the minister's eyes.

Hence, the Liberal government was prepared to invest more in modern university infrastructure and buildings. The city adhered to the legal obligations at hand, but its means were too limited to support the excellent, research-driven education that the university was striving for. This was certainly the case in the faculty of Sciences and in the Special Schools, where the importance of practical exercises was beyond doubt.

In the first place, there were too few laboratories, and their infrastructure was abysmal. The chemistry lab had moreover become too small: the professor had to reject students. In the physics amphitheatre and in botany, the same lament could be heard. The problem was only less dire in medicine. In the fine, new Bijloke hospital, a new amphitheatre and several operating rooms had been added. But it was not suitable for laboratory research. And during the winter, it was simply too dark to conduct lessons after three o'clock in the afternoon.

## The architecture of the modern university

The Liberal government understood that the needs of the university transcended local interests. City architect and professor Adolphe Pauli, who had also build the new Bijloke clinic, was commissioned to design a new Institute for the Sciences. His colleague, architect Lambert Noppius of Liège, was entrusted with a similar project. Around Christmas 1881, three hundred families from the notorious quarter of Batavia on the Blandijnberg received news that they would have to make way for the expansion of the university. The slum clearance was carried out under the guise of public health. Three small passages gave access to the 117 dwellings of Batavia, divided across four narrow lanes. An open sewer in the middle of the neighbourhood was used to dispose of waste. It was a stinking cesspool and breeding ground for epidemics. The price per square metre of land was notably lower than elsewhere in the city, and the demolition yielded a huge surface area of 14,700 square metres.

On 16 April 1883 the first stone was laid for the foundation of the new Sciences building and the Special Engineering Schools. Rector Albert Callier waxed lyrical. Book knowledge had made way for real science. The cabinet of the armchair scholar was replaced by a laboratory with ever more ingenious instruments that would unravel the secrets of nature.

Pauli signed off on plans for what would be one of the largest buildings in Belgium, made to measure for the 850 students of which Ghent could now boast. In November 1890 it was ready. All the natural and engineering sciences were gathered under one roof, with a majestic entrance for the engineers as its crowning glory. Four allegorical sculptures adorned the imposing façade: Bridges and Highways, Civil Engineering, Arts and Manufacturing, and Architecture. Five inner courtyards and windows several metres high ensured optimal natural lighting on the drafting tables.

In 1890 and 1891 the parliament approved new laws that consolidated the new scientific approach to education and ensured increasing specialisation. This mainly had an effect on education in the Arts and Philosophy, which was completely reorganised. For the Humanities, this was the run-up to a second Belgian 'renaissance'. The number of professors increased considerably thanks to integration with the normal schools. Qualified teachers for the upper grades of secondary school were henceforth trained at the university. With the official creation of seminars and practical exercises, the government sought to give the courses a sounder basis. The two faculties that had traditionally functioned as a preparation for Law and Medicine, Arts and Sciences, were split into different sections with their own programmes. In this way, students

**Institute for the Sciences, laying the foundation stone, 1883**
In an exuberant atmosphere, the foundation stone of the Institute for the Sciences was laid with a certificate and coins on 16 April 1883. (Ghent, Stadsarchief)

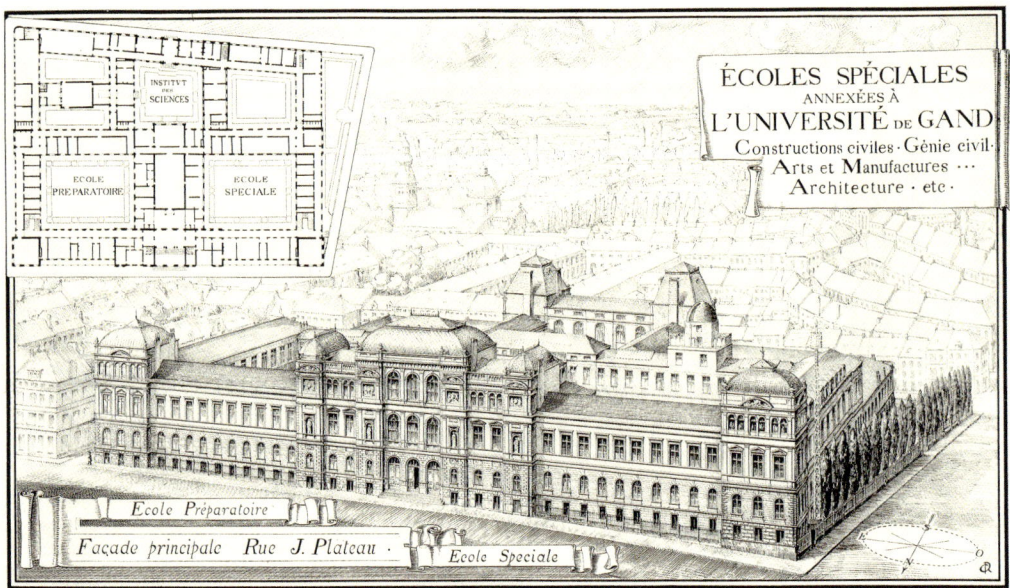

**The Institute for the Sciences**
The Plateau Building was the second largest building in Belgium at the time. Three hundred families of the Batavia slums had to make way for students in natural sciences and engineering. (Ghent, Universiteitsarchief)

could specialise as soon as they were candidates. Sciences included Mathematics, Physics, Chemistry, Botany, Zoology and Geology; Arts comprised History, Philosophy and Classics, Romance and Germanic Philology. In order to earn the degree of doctor, the dissertation, which had been abolished in 1849, was reintroduced. Students were required to conduct personal, original research and were initiated into scientific method and critical discussion.

These were the golden years of seminar education, in which eminent professors such as Paul Fredericq and Henri Pirenne taught a small group of students to interpret original historical sources. And in which the equally famous classical philologist Franz Cumont inducted his students into the mysteries of the Persian god Mithra with a sense of historical criticism. The rich collections and libraries further piqued the curiosity and discernment of dedicated students.

In the study of Law, the laws of 1890 had a much less pronounced effect. There was less emphasis on the development of a scientific mind, and the faculty of Law has traditionally remained a highly vocational course of study.

## Scientific revolutions

Even in the seminars of the cultural sciences, the spirit of modern times was demonstrably present. The past was a distant foreign country, just like the exotic languages and primitive cultures that were studied. Outside, progress raced by increasingly faster, louder and overwhelmingly. These were vertigo years of unprecedented possibilities for the sciences and a worldwide expansion in broad swaths of society. The *fin de siècle* was characterised in turns by expectant excitement and bottomless fear. Thanks to the pioneering work of Joseph Plateau, ordinary people could gaze in awe at the first moving images as a fairground attraction. Plateau gradually went blind because of the experiments he conducted in his laboratory, but the popularisation of his invention ensured that the eyes of hundreds of people were glued simultaneously to the silver screen.

Richard Vankenhove in the Seminar on Geology, 1913
From the end of the nineteenth century onwards, students in all branches of science were initiated in original research and critical method.
(Ghent, Universiteitsarchief)

At Ghent University, science and technology shifted into a higher gear. In this context, serendipity was never far away. Who still remembers that the laws of the Austrian monk Gregor Mendel were (re)discovered in the Botanical Garden of Ghent? Mendel had published his findings on the dominant and recessive traits of genetic material in 1866 in a fairly obscure scientific journal and presented them to Charles Darwin. The article remained in a stack of unread material for years, an intellectual tragedy. Mendel's experiments on several generations of peas in his monastery garden went unnoticed for four decades.

Perhaps the time was not yet ripe. Forty years later, in 1900, three botanists arrived at the same results independently of one another, which confirmed the laws of inheritance: Hugo De Vries in Amsterdam, Carl Correns in Tübingen and … Erich von Tschermak-Seysenegg in Ghent. The Austrian *Pflanzenzüchter* got to know Professor Julius Mac Leod in Ghent and received his permission to conduct test crosses in the Botanical Garden. He was also advised to read Charles Darwin's work on *The Effects of Cross- and Self-Fertilisation in the Vegetable Kingdom*.

Chance worked in Tschermak's favour. If he had continued experimenting on the wallflower, he might never have become world-famous. But because he would not be staying in Ghent for very long, he tried using peas because of their short growing period. As luck would have it, several sorts of peas were grown in the cold room of the Botanical Garden. Tschermak made good use of them. He did not even have time to wait for the results of his test crosses, and so left them to the garden assistant. The latter sent him the pods and seeds — not even by registered mail — to Vienna via parcel post. 'A true happiness that this shipment reached me', writes Tschermak in his autobiography. 'Otherwise I would not have been one of the rediscoverers of Mendel's laws of genetic inheritance.' In 1899 he himself was astonished by the wonderful laws of numerical proportion in his cultivated peas: one green pea to three yellow peas, and one wrinkled pea to three smooth ones. Not long afterwards, he found the reference to Mendel's 1866 publication and the key to this mystery of nature. With a jealous sigh he admits that in the second year of his research, he thought that he had discovered *'etwas ganz neues …'*.

Investment in the development of modern science led to unexpected innovation in other domains as well. For example, it was a native of Ghent who developed long-distance telephony. The meteorologist François Van Rysselberghe, appointed to the Special School to teach a course on Applied Electronics in 1882, lent his name a few years later to the telephone system that would connect not only several Belgian cities, but also New York and Chicago. Bell Telephone would only equal this feat seven years later! The name Van Rysselberghe was known worldwide for about as long. In 1905 his alma mater had six telephones. By then Van Rysselberghe had already been dead for twelve years, having died unexpectedly at the age of forty-six; he is now completely forgotten.

The engineer Jules Meuwissen perfected the technique of colonial packet boats. Jules Boulvin applied himself with untiring diligence to increasing the efficiency of steam engines, the motor of industrialisation. Filled with awe, Ghent's engineers embraced the new inventions of the second industrial revolution: the diesel motor, the turbine, the automobile … The *nouveautés scientifiques* were displayed and won prizes at World Exhibitions, which reflected the *merveilles* of modernity like mirror palaces.

In 1913, the World Exhibition was held in Ghent. The university wanted to be represented there in a dignified manner. There was no separate Hall of Science, as there would be in Chicago twenty years later, but science was everywhere and nowhere: in the Machine Hall, in the Palace of Light, with the *électricité* (group V), the *génie civil, moyens de transport* (group VI), *industrie chimique* (group XIV) and *hygiène, bienfaisance* (group XVII). The emphasis lay on the industrial applications of science, not on science itself.

Not even a month after the triumphant publication of the discovery by Wilhelm Conrad Röntgen of what he called 'X-rays', the professor of Forensic Medicine Charles De Visscher and his young assistant, Jules De Nobele, made an X-ray of the hand of a young man who had been brought to the Bijloke hospital. The hand had been pierced by shot at close range. This was at the end of January 1896. The fascination with this new sort of mysterious radiation was immense and widely shared in amateur photography circles and in the popular press throughout Europe. The press in Ghent reported on it — not always accurately — and at a 'photography festival' in the Ghent opera house, X-ray demonstrations were shown: a hand, a compass in its box, a wallet full of coins, a pair of spectacles in their case. Science and wonder met on common ground. The magical effect of the X-rays held the general public in thrall and grew into an unprecedented medical-scientific hype.

Jules De Nobele experimented with the exposure time of X-ray images in the laboratory of Henri Schoentjes, professor of Experimental Physics. He passed round his prints as *jetons de présence* to those present at the meeting of the Ghent section of the Association belge de photographie. With Daniël Van Duyse, professor of Pathological Anatomy, he was the first to use X-rays for the diagnosis of tuberculosis, fractures and dislocations, and the detection of foreign objects. Van Duyse would study ophthalmology and developed new radiographic techniques for detecting metal fragments in the eye. Although he only became an instructor with the title of professor in 1908

**Centre for Oncology, 1926**
Jules De Nobele became head of the first department of radiology in 1906 with a laboratory in a new wing of the Bijloke. He only had one laboratory assistant, who made X-rays under his supervision and conducted radiotherapy sessions in between. Twenty years later, the Centre for Oncology was opened in the presence of Queen Elisabeth. In the photo, she signs the university's Golden Book. Director Jules De Nobele looks on benevolently. In the foreground is rector Georges Van den Bossche.
(Ghent, Universiteitsarchief)

(attached to the Higher Institute of Physical Education), De Nobele established an impressive department before the First World War, in which diagnostic radiology, radiotherapy and electrology were subsumed.

In 1900, when he was still an assistant, De Nobele was the first to employ radiotherapy in Belgium, just two years after the discovery of radium by Marie and Pierre Curie. Like the first female Nobel Prize winner, De Nobele was mainly interested in the therapeutic characteristics of radioactivity. In 1926, as director of the Centre for Oncology (Centrum voor Gezwelziekten) at the Bijloke, he had the honour of opening the facility with Queen Elisabeth of Belgium. It was a multidisciplinary centre *avant la lettre*, where he spent most of his time in the X-ray and brachytherapy department.

Although Pierre Curie had expressed both his hope and his fear concerning the use of radium in human hands when he accepted the Nobel Prize, progress seemed to know no bounds in the turbulent years leading up to the First World War. The prestige of Ghent University shot up like an arrow. The built surface area quadrupled in twenty years, and the number of students doubled: from 788 in 1890 to 1,315 in 1914, including 365 students of 'foreign' origin. Brazilians, Russians and Chinese may have been more of an administrative burden, but they were cherished as ambassadors of Belgian higher education, particularly the engineering programme. 'It is due to superiority in the intellectual domain that Belgium is known far beyond its borders', announced Hector Leboucq in his farewell speech as rector. The national rhetoric of unbridled expansion and pride in one's own knowledge and capabilities during the unusually rich and creative years between 1900 and 1914 is difficult to separate today from the heated battle of nations that followed. With the dark shadow of the First World War, the progressive optimism of the *belle époque* came to be viewed in an entirely different light. After the war, the US took over from Germany, snatching the belief in science from the flames unharmed.

## The US, heartland of science

In December 1919 rector Henri Pirenne awarded an honorary doctorate via the American ambassador to Herbert Hoover, who would become president of the United States ten years later. Hoover was delighted with the recognition. He had already hinted in 1916 to the Belgian minister of Finance in exile, the Catholic Aloys Van de Vyvere, that the surplus of funds that he had collected with the Commission for Relief in Belgium should be used after the war to stimulate scientific and industrial research.

The powerful businessman Emile Francqui also received an honorary doctorate from Ghent University in 1919. He had been chairman of the National Committee for Aid and Food (Nationaal Comité voor Hulp en Voeding), which had kept the people of Belgium supplied with victuals. Through the international tentacles of the Société Générale, the most important bank in Belgium, he had launched the Poor Little Belgium solidarity movement in the US, where Hoover had taken over the ropes. The reconstruction of Belgium was near and dear to his heart. After the war, the Commission for Relief in Belgium did indeed have a surplus of more than 35 million dollars (approximately 500 million Belgian francs). Ghent received the first instalment of

20 million Belgian francs in 1919. In order to manage this generous gift, Pirenne ensured that the university was granted the status of legal entity (law of 5 July 1920). Another part of the American money was intended for the establishment of the Belgian-American Educational Foundation (BAEF) and the University Foundation (Universitaire Stichting), which would grant scholarships and loans to less affluent students until 1955.

The US introduced a new channel for financing basic scientific research. In 1915 the National Research Council was established, an example of a public-private partnership under the impulse of Andrew Carnegie and John Rockefeller. It was imitated worldwide. The Belgian king Albert I had the American model in mind when he prepared his famous address to industrialists on the occasion of the centenary of metal giant Cockerill. The speech that the king gave in the impressive factory hall in Seraing on 1 October 1927 is still a guiding light for science policy in Belgium: 'Our public is insufficiently aware that pure science is the essential condition for applied science, and that the nations that neglect science and scholars are marked by fate for decline.'

**The address at Seraing, 1927**
King Albert's speech to the industrial elite at the Cockerill factory hall on 1 October 1927 is still regarded as a beacon for the basis of research in Belgium.
(Brussels, Archive of the Royal Palace)

The speech did not fall on deaf ears. Seven months later, on 28 April 1928, the founding acts of the National Fund for Scientific Research (Nationaal Fonds voor Wetenschappelijk Onderzoek, or NFWO) were signed. Two bankers, Emile Francqui and Félicien Cattier, had succeeded in a very short time in raising a starting capital of 109,330,626.60 Belgian francs. Eighty per cent came from major industrial players in Belgium. It was a question of recruiting a scientific elite corps that would increase the international prestige of Belgian research. Brilliant students, regardless of their social background, were selected by scientific committees, in which the four universities were represented along with figures from industry and finance. On the board of directors, the financial-industrial elite and the two free universities, Leuven and Brussels, held sway.

The crucial role of king Albert in the establishment of the NFWO confirmed the close ties between dynasty and science, a connection that would remain as long as the unitary (and later federal) state of Belgium determined science policy. But notwithstanding the express importance that king Albert attached to fundamental research in his speech, science was primarily at the service of national interest, and hence of industrial reconstruction and development. Fundamental and applied research were on uneasy terms from the beginning. In particular, industry leaders had trouble with the idea that their money would be spent on 'useless' projects, such as the excavation of a Roman metropolis in Syria.

## The flip side of Dutchification

The interwar period in Ghent was particularly influenced by the troubles around the Dutchification of the university. In 1923, legislation regarding the splitting of the university into a Dutch- and French-speaking division, known as the Nolf Law, was approved. At the same time, minister Pierre Nolf wanted to thoroughly reorganise higher education. It would take five years before academic and political circles were in agreement. The law of 1929 introduced the titles of licentiate and qualified teacher (for secondary school). The doctorate in Arts and Philosophy and in the Sciences was from then on reserved for a scientific elite that, after attaining a licentiate (similar to a master's degree), defended a dissertation. The law was accompanied by an extensive reform of the training programme and the introduction of specialised optional courses. This was carried out in a rigid, uniform way across the four universities. The subject matter followed the same pattern everywhere.

The energy needed for reconstruction and Dutchification, combined with the economic crisis of the 1930s and the Second World War, meant that a small country like Belgium (and by extension an even smaller region, like Flanders) could hardly keep up with the US. The State University of Ghent lost its lustre as well as foreign students. The major scientific breakthroughs in the areas of quantum mechanics and nuclear physics passed Ghent by, while the Solvay conferences at the ULB (Université Libre de Bruxelles) were both an important witness and significant agent in this respect. The career of Jules Verschaffelt, the only physicist from Ghent who took part in the Solvay conferences, is an illustration of this trend. Verschaffelt was a Ghent native who attained the grade of doctor in the sciences in 1893. He was an assistant with the

renowned geologist Alphonse Renard and, thanks to a travel scholarship, had the opportunity to study physics in Amsterdam and Leiden with no less than four Nobel Prize winners. Exactly one month before the German invasion of Belgium on 4 August 1914, Verschaffelt became a professor at the ULB, where he had taught experimental physics since 1906. During the war, he fled with his family to the Netherlands, where he worked as an assistant at the Physics Laboratory (Natuurkundig Laboratorium) in Leiden. After the war, he was opposed at the ULB because of his pro-Flemish stance. In 1923, Verschaffelt was appointed to a chair in experimental physics at the partially Dutchified University of Ghent. The half-hearted language regime, however, hindered the development of Dutch-language instruction, with all that this implies for the research of someone of Verschaffelt's calibre. In the meantime, the eminent physicist had a solid international reputation with his publications on the equations of state of pure substances and thermomechanics. While Verschaffelt was having considerable difficulty starting up his physics laboratory in Ghent, Einstein's theory of relativity took hold at the ULB. Ghent remained behind to such an extent that the theory of relativity would only be taught from the 1980s onwards — at least according to a witticism of André De Leenheer, who, as the first rector of the twenty-first century, would give research at his university a hefty boost.

**Homage to Jules Verschaffelt, 1934**
On 25 April 1934 a festive gathering was held in honour of Ghent physicist Jules Verschaffelt (fifth from the right). His scientific merits were highlighted by his pupil Julien Verhaeghe, but it was also Verschaffelt the Flamingant who was honoured, by the Ghent Student Corps and Frans Daels (with glasses, diagonally behind Verschaffelt), among others.
(Ghent, Universiteitsarchief)

## 'Big Science'

In 1947, under the direction of Julien Verhaeghe, a student of Jules Verschaffelt, a Laboratory of Nuclear Physics would be established in Plateaustraat. The great heights to which nuclear science had soared became all too clear at the end of the Second World War with the atom bombs dropped on Hiroshima and Nagasaki. Verhaeghe saw its importance for economic development and decided to reorganise the Physics Laboratory of his predecessor. From 1951 onwards, he would teach a course on 'Radioactive phenomena'. In spite of limited means, he and his team built the first linear electron accelerator (LINAC) in the mid-1950s. The danger of irradiation and lack of space in Plateaustraat prompted the university to seek a more suitable location. In 1965, a nuclear reactor and a LINAC of 90 MeV were installed at the Institute of Nuclear Sciences (Instituut voor Nucleaire Wetenschappen) in Proeftuinstraat. In accordance with Ghent tradition, this was primarily the work of the laboratory itself. It ensured a great deal of expertise in the area of particle accelerators and photonics, an atypical example of how research in the nuclear sciences could be built up relatively independently and on a small scale in the post-war period. Certainly in this domain, Belgium was, after 1945, drawn into the new Atlantic space ruled by the US.

As a European answer to the new challenges, the Conseil Européen pour la Recherche Nucléaire (CERN) was established in Geneva in 1954. In addition to Jean Willems, chairman of the Interuniversity Institute for Nuclear Science (Interuniversitair Instituut voor Kernwetenschappen), Julien Verhaeghe was appointed by king Baudouin at its foundation as the official Belgian delegate. In 2016 the Belgian universities nominated Dirk Ryckbosch of the department of Physics and Astronomy as their scientific representative on the CERN Council.

**Institute of Nuclear Sciences, 1967**
King Baudouin visits the Institute of Nuclear Sciences in Proeftuinstraat, built in 1965.
(Ghent, Universiteitsarchief, photo R. Masson)

**Ghent University celebrates 150 years, 1967**
Rector Jean-Jacques Bouckaert in conversation with queen Fabiola during celebrations on the occasion of the university's 150th anniversary.
(Ghent, Universiteitsarchief, photo R. Masson)

The immense scale of scientific research after the Second World War mobilised unprecedented financial, technological and human resources. The genius of the individual researcher was no longer the epicentre of science. The merging of science, technology and engineering created the figure of the engineer-entrepreneur, who could assemble resources and researchers from various disciplines and get them to collaborate.

The Ghent civil engineer Robert Cailliau was such an entrepreneur. Cailliau began working for CERN in 1974 and helped lay the foundations of what would become the internet. In 1987 he was group leader of Office Computing Systems in the department of Data Handling. With the goal of managing CERN documentation, he began to think about connecting information systems with hypertext, but he quickly realised that a similar project by his colleague Tim Berners-Lee had a more universal scope. They decided to work together: Berners-Lee devoted himself to the technical aspect, while Cailliau brought fresh talent to Geneva and was responsible for management. Together they came up with the name 'World Wide Web' in 1990. Starting in 1994, Cailliau organised the International WWW Conference at CERN. This conference brought together 380 internet pioneers and still meets today. In her acknowledgment speech upon accepting an honorary doctorate from Ghent University and the Catholic University of Leuven in January 2017, chancellor Angela Merkel referred to the contribution of Robert Cailliau to the first web-based project of the European Commission as an example of how universities shape the future.

## Large-scale research in a divided country

The 'useful, patriotic, social, pacifist, private patronage supported science' of funds such as the NFWO was no longer sufficient in scale after 1945. The American government pumped huge amounts of money and resources into the scientific race with the Soviet Union, which was in the first place an arms race. Big Science came to serve the increasing polarisation of East and West during the Cold War. At Expo 58 in Brussels, the close link between science and politics was symbolised in the Soviet Pavilion by a model of Sputnik I above a giant statue of Lenin. The new international context obliged national governments in Europe to adjust their science policy. To compete successfully on the world stage, drastic reorganisation of the way science was conducted would be necessary. Strategic cooperation in a global scientific space in which English was increasingly the lingua franca were the leitmotifs of progressive rectors, professors and politicians in a world dominated by American universities. The danger of brain drain to the US, or to top European universities, was a signal for the government to change course.

However, the political divisions between Catholics and Liberals on the one hand, and French-speaking and Flemish-speaking communities on the other, made the rescaling of research in Belgium very difficult. University expansion (read: the complex multiplication of half and whole universities in the context of Belgian 'compromise' politics) was at odds with the need to join forces. Beginning in the 1970s, the NFWO was forced by successive government reforms into conducting a regional rather than a national policy. The National Council of Science

Dirk Frimout, the first Belgian in space, 1992
Frimout obtained a PhD in applied physics from the University of Ghent in 1970. His alma mater awarded him an honorary doctorate in 1992.
(Ghent, Universiteitsarchief, photo NASA)

Policy (Nationale Raad voor Wetenschapsbeleid, or NRWB), founded in 1959 with the Ghent biochemist Lucien Massart as its first chair, was not strong enough to oppose these centrifugal forces. Moreover, the relationship between the NRWB and the NFWO was strained. Starting in 1970, the national Department for the Programming of Science Policy (Diensten voor Programmatie van het Wetenschapsbeleid, or DPWB) launched the Concerted Research Actions (Geconcerteerde Onderzoeksacties, or GOAs) between university and government. The goal was to develop (interuniversity) centres of excellence that integrated basic and applied research and aimed (even then) at the economic and social valorisation of the research results.

With their research on T-DNA in plants, Jeff Schell and Marc Van Montagu belonged to the Ghent elect, as did Walter Fiers with his biomedical DNA research. Gradually, more and more groups enjoyed the support of this funding, which also began to focus on research that could not be defined as Big Science, particularly in the humanities and social sciences.

The positioning of Belgium in the chosen domains of Big Science — nuclear energy and space travel — was increasingly dependent on European cooperation within the framework of CERN in Geneva, the European Space Agency (ESA, 1975) in Paris, or the European Synchotron Radiation Facility (ESRF, 1994) in Grenoble. Belgium played a crucial role in the creation of the ESA. The first Belgian in space, Dirk Frimout, was an alumnus of Ghent University. In 1989 he was selected by NASA for the STS-45 Space Shuttle mission, a stepping stone to the launching of the Atlantis in Florida on 24 March 1992. He was allowed to address the crown prince as 'Philippe' in an audio-visual contact that has since become legendary, because 'in space, there is absolutely no protocol'.

The new European structures that were established in the 1970s and afterwards to facilitate large-scale projects and networks increasingly gained in importance and impact, from the European Cooperation in Science and Technology (COST, 1971) to the European Community Action Scheme for the Mobility of University Students of ERASMUS (1987). At the same time, internal politics in Belgium went directly against the tendency towards scaling up: centrifugal forces ensured the opposite, a provincialisation of the university landscape.

## University expansion, Belgian style

'What I've been wanting to defend are the interests of the university-age youth in our country, of the youth that, regardless of social background, has the right to a high-quality university education that should allow it, tomorrow, in Greater Europe, to fulfil adequately the role society expects of it.' After a vain struggle that had lasted a year, rector Jean-Jacques Bouckaert had lost none of his caustic indignity when he addressed the university community.

This was 1 April 1965. A broad protest movement aimed at changing the mind of the Lefèvre–Spaak government, with the (Catholic) rector of Ghent as its unquestioned leader, was to no avail. The law of 9 April 1965 established two university centres, in Antwerp (Rijksuniversitair centrum Antwerpen) and Mons (Centre Universitaire Mons-Hainaut), raised the faculties of St Ignatius in Antwerp, the Facultés Saint-Louis

Protest in the Aula against university expansion, 1965
Along with rector Jean-Jacques Bouckaert, representatives of the academic staff and students took the floor at the protest meeting in the peristyle on 1 April 1965.
(Ghent, Universiteitsarchief)

in Brussels and the Facultés Notre-Dame de la Paix in Namur to the status of 'half universities' and allowed the free universities, specifically Leuven, to expand to Wavre, Sint-Lambrechts-Woluwe and Kortrijk.

Yet the government plan had been advised against by the NRWB. The arguments of the four rectors (including Leuven's) were compelling: expansion led to fragmentation, while the concentration of people and resources ensured better education and research. The major investment of the state in decentralisation could be better spent on reinforcing the existing universities. The growing student population gave rise to drastic adjustments to university infrastructure. On 22 May 1964, rector Bouckaert had already informed prime minister Theo Lefèvre, an alumnus of Ghent, that the expansion would mean a 'death sentence by slow and systematic suffocation' for his alma mater.

While borders in Western Europe faded, the government nevertheless chose regional education, under pressure from the bishops and under the guise of democratisation. 'Increasing quality is sacrificed to increasing numbers,' Bouckaert fulminated about this 'democratisation of education degraded by devaluation'. Moreover, in a typically Belgian way, the university expansion was clearly a delayed surge in the intense ideological battle over education in the 1950s. During a political meeting in Eeklo, Lefèvre openly accused the faculty of Arts and Philosophy in Ghent of not being 'neutral and objective'. Kortrijk campus would have had no reason for existing if Ghent had been neutral and objective, according to the prime minister. That the government sacrificed the state universities to the proliferation of the free universities was anything but an empty argument.

Bouckaert's speech on 1 April 1965 in the peristyle of the Ghent Aula was a 'last gesture of protest'. The massive audience of professors, assistants, students, and administrative and technical personnel overflowed onto Voldersstraat. Rarely was the Aula filled with such unity. There was applause for the Liège delegation; the two state universities were after all united by 'a deep solidarity' against the law permitting university proliferation. The rector announced that, as a consequence, he would tender his resignation to the king the Monday afterwards. He was applauded like a hero: 'Bouckaert: yes!, Theo: no!'

## Finance act and internal reorganisation

All the fuss surrounding the university expansion was symptomatic of the growing rivalry between the free and the state universities, on the one hand, and the permanence of the ideological divide between Catholics and Liberals and Socialists on the other, even after the School Pact of 1958. At the same time, the communitarisation of Belgium had a great impact on the further fragmentation of the university landscape. As a result of the protests around 'Leuven Flemish' (Leuven-Vlaams), the University of Leuven split in 1968. The Catholic University of Leuven (Katholieke Universiteit Leuven, or KUL) remained in Leuven, while the Université Catholique de Louvain-la-Neuve (UCL) moved to a new location in Ottignies. Two years later, the Dutch-speaking Free University of Brussels (Vrije Universiteit Brussel, or VUB) was established in Etterbeek, near the French-speaking Université Libre de Bruxelles (ULB). Antwerp received a pluralistic superstructure with the University Institution of Antwerp (Universitaire Instelling Antwerpen, or UIA). The three institutions in Antwerp were legally

**Demonstration against the finance act, 1970s**
The finance act of July 1971 elicited a wave of protests at Ghent University. Students and staff would suffer as a result of university expansion.
(Ghent, collection of Marc Van Montagu)

recognised as a university in 1971, as was the Université Mons-Hainaut. Henceforth, no province need feel neglected: Hasselt received the Limburg University Centre (Limburgs Universitaire Centrum), Aarlen something similar. For that matter, Ghent professors became rectors of the new institutions: Lucien Massart and Marie De Groodt of the RUCA (1965-1981), Aloïs Gerlo of the VUB (1969-1974) and Laurent Vandendriessche of the UIA (1971-1979).

A crucial result of the finance act of July 1971 was that the free and the state universities were placed on equal footing. The basic funding or subsidy was dependent on the number of students, with a flat-rate coefficient depending on the field of study. Bouckaert had already warned against this tendency six years earlier: 'A free university should never be entirely funded by the state, because, apart from the state allowances, it also has other sources of income that the state universities don't have.'

The law was decisive for how Belgian universities would function over the next two decades. It was primarily Ghent and Liège that paid the price for university expansion and decentralisation when the crisis years of the 1970s and the austerity measures of the 1980s took hold. The government froze subsidies, reduced the flat-rate cost per student and increased the registration fee. The constant savings measures put the core funding of the universities under great pressure until the 1990s. Only when the economy began to pick up again did it appear that the initial funding had also been structurally reduced.

In the meantime, Ghent University was also reorganised internally. The law of 28 April 1953 gave the state universities more autonomy and a new management structure. A board of governors, consisting of the rector-chairman, the deans and a representative from each faculty, could now make decisions on recruitment, appointments, credit distribution and so on. The executive director was replaced by a government commissioner in an advisory capacity. Outgoing executive director Edgard Blancquaert, the first government commissioner, was allowed to hold his post as professor of Dutch linguistics concurrently. The two subsequent government commissioners, Hans Van Acker (1957-1987) and Yannick De Clercq (1987-present), were exclusively civil servants with the task of checking the legality of the university board's decisions.

In 1959 the central administration of the university was moved from Voldersstraat to Sint-Pietersnieuwstraat, near the Vooruit. Yannick De Clercq was welcomed there thirty years ago by his predecessor with the inspired words: 'Welcome to the largest umbrella factory in the country.' It was typical of the bureaucratic mentality in the final days of the university as a 'state' institution. Nevertheless, there was a lot of movement, both inside the university and out. In 1967 an advisory college with twenty-six representatives from political, industrial and economic circles was called into being to make proposals for adapting research and education to societal change.

The societal transformations of the 1960s had not left Ghent untouched. Democratisation and public participation were the order of the day. The wave of protest in March 1969 turned against rector Bouckaert, who had resisted the expansion law so heroically and had had the students behind him. Five years later, they criticised the elitist and autocratic character of the university and demanded participation on the board. The Vermeylen–Dubois Law of 1971 met those demands to some extent.

The board of governors now included a broader selection of members: rector, vice-rector, nine representatives from political, social and economic circles, and twenty elected members from the university community: ten professors, four students, four members of the scientific personnel and two members of the administrative and technical staff. According to minister of education Piet Vermeylen, the new composition was a fine democratic reflection of society. But the students, who in the spirit of May 1968 had counted on more participation, reacted indignantly by boycotting the first elections.

## Basic funding under pressure

The university expansion took its toll. In its meeting of 15 September 1973 the advisory board pointed out that it was irresponsible to offer all specialties at all universities. Although everyone agreed in principle that a certain division of labour among the universities was needed, this proved to be very difficult to achieve in practice. Every faculty was 'very reluctant' to accept 'any tangible limitation'. If the universities themselves had not taken the initiative, an interuniversity system of consultation would be imposed on them from without. In 1976 the Flemish Interuniversity Council (Vlaamse Interuniversitaire Raad, or VLIR) was established. The government also had the impression that the funding for scientific research was highly fragmented. Available funds should rather be allocated in larger but 'less numerous packages' to larger research units 'for really valuable projects'. The central bodies of the university had no clear view of on-going research. Was it also possible for the university itself to conduct the evaluation and selection of scientific projects and research programmes?

In 1978 the universities were obliged by royal decree to establish a research council. This cannot be seen in isolation from the cost-cutting policy and increasing complaints from the universities about the shortage of basic funding. Not coincidentally, one of the first acts of the new Ghent Research Council was the intensification of co-operation between the university and industry. The austerity regime of the 1980s under Wilfried Martens freed up resources for this cooperation. The neoliberal tendency was becoming increasingly evident. The government would further withdraw and facilitate research funding from the private sector. The St Anne's Plan (Sint-Annaplan) of 1986 stipulated that science policy had to surrender 9%. The subsidies for the universities were frozen at 1985 levels. At the same time, the special projects to attract state-of-the-art technology received 25 million Belgian francs in subsidies over five years.

The new tendency in science policy coincided with the communitarisation of Belgium and the growing role of the regions and communities. Education became a community matter in 1988. Gaston Geens, the 'father' of Flanders Technology, found the division between basic and applied research artificial. He demanded that basic research also be considered a Flemish jurisdiction. In 1988 the NFWO split permanently into the Flemish FWO and the French-speaking FNRS.

# The mega-decree of 1991 and 'verzapping'

When Assyriologist and cuneiform scholar Leon De Meyer accepted the position of rector in 1985, the university found itself at a low point. Minister of education Daniël Coens had imposed a rigorous cost-cutting plan. Moreover, with a financial deficit of around 3.2 million Belgian francs, the Academic Hospital (Academisch Ziekenhuis, or AZ) was virtually bankrupt. There was a hiring freeze. Student enrolment was down: from 12,990 in 1984 to 12,343 at the lowest point of the crisis in 1987. After that, things gradually began to look up.

State University of Ghent becomes Ghent University, 1991
(Ghent, Universiteitsarchief, Fotoklas UGent)

De Meyer took up his post at a very difficult time in the history of the university and guided his institution through the most significant administrative transition since the Dutchification of 1930. The Special Decree of 26 June 1991 implemented the 'un-stating' of the University of Ghent. The RUG (Rijksuniversiteit Gent) became UGent, a public institution and legal entity. The removal of the letters 'Rijks' on the wall of the rectorial building was more than just a symbolic farewell to the rigid university of yesteryear. The mega-decree of 12 June 1991 concerning Flemish universities placed greater responsibility with the institutions themselves. In the meantime there were six: UGent, KULeuven (with Campus Kortrijk), VUB, UAntwerpen, LUC in Diepenbeek, and last but not least, the Catholic University of Brussels (Katholieke Universiteit Brussel, or KUB, formerly UFSAL).

The decree defined the three core tasks of the Flemish universities: education, research and services to society. Basic funding was adjusted; for the time being, the number of eligible students remained the starting point. The teaching staff of the universities were 'zapped' as of 1991: chairs disappeared and one was permitted to use the title of professor from the moment he or she was appointed as a lecturer. The professor lost his status and privileges and had to enter into a new context of departments with democratically elected chairpeople. Staff were divided into ZAP-ers (*zelfstandig*, or independent academic personnel), AAP-ers (assisting academic personnel) and ATP-ers (administrative and technical personnel). The entire 'zapping' operation caused a drastic rise in the number of professors in Ghent: from 348 in 1990 to 547 in 1991. Although the number of women professors had increased considerably (from 20 to 55), only 10% of the professorial staff were women. That percentage would only increase by small increments in the decades that followed.

Ghent University, est. 1817
Ghent University commits itself to the formation of a corporate identity. Rector Anne De Paepe, wearing a typical hoodie, poses with a student in 2016.
(Ghent, image bank UGent, photo Maxine Stevens)

In 1991 a new governance model was also introduced in Ghent. The board of governors now consisted of thirty-three voting members. It could formulate policy more independently and had greater jurisdiction than the former board, which could do little more than mind the shop. The Permanent Bureau (Vast Bureau) became the Executive Board (Bestuurscollege), a smaller, operational team assembled

**Proclamation, Economics and Business Administration, 2009**
Under rector Paul Van Cauwenberge, invented traditions have emerged, such as faculty colours, masters' gowns and student berets.
(Ghent, image bank UGent, photo Nic Vermeulen)

from the different segments of the university. To this day, a core four-person team is responsible for the day-to-day management of the university. Rector and vice-rector are elected offices, while an academic manager and a logistics manager ensure continuity. The managers form the link between the governing bodies and the central administration, which today consists of ten directors. Three of the ten central administrations — education, research and internationalisation — are run by academic directors. They operate as *de facto* vice-rectors of the university, although they have not been elected and have a renewable term of office of four years.

The governance of the UGent is presently in full transition (2018). One of the sore points in the governance of the University of Ghent is the gap between the central administration and the faculties. After the Second World War, the university expanded from four to eleven faculties. The faculty of Applied Sciences (1957), Economics (1968), Veterinary Medicine (1968), Psychological and Pedagogical Sciences (1969), Agricultural Science (1969), Pharmacy (1970), and finally Political and Social Science (1992) subsequently saw the light of day. The last faculty was split off from the faculty of Law. It was the merit of rector De Meyer to restructure the feudal tangle of tiny departments, known as seminars, into larger units: the departments. Achieving this was a real *tour de force*. Eminent professors who made their careers in another age predicted that the chances of the operation's success were particularly low, especially in the short time proposed. In 1992 the departments were a fact.

Ghent University not only renewed its confidence, it also adopted a new logo. In 1988, the sleek columns of the Aula replaced the head of Minerva. The importance of communication and PR became greater and would give the university an attractive profile and identity of its own. The corporate identity of the university took shape under the motto 'Dare to Think' (Durf Denken), a form of 'branding' entirely in line with the spirit of the times. The department of Communication was thoroughly professionalised and made into a new board in 2017.

## Uphill path to rationalisation

'To our great regret, this is only an opening speech and not a eulogy. We would have preferred to stand at the graveside of the neo-capitalist university.' The speaker is Luc Van den Bossche, president of the FaculteitenKonvent (Umbrella organisation that represented the different student faculty associations), at the official opening of academic year 1970-1971. As one of the first student representatives on the board of governors, Van den Bossche probably had no idea how prophetic his words would turn out to be. The finance act of 1971 did indeed open the way to the 'neo-capitalist university' of the twenty-first century.

Twenty-five years later, in 1995, that same Van den Bossche, now Flemish minister of education, was once again in the speaker's chair of the Aula for another opening speech. The rebellious socialist student had in the meantime made the language of neo-capitalism his very own. 'Time is running out', he said, and opined that the universities had done too little with the autonomy they had acquired in 1991. In fact, without actually saying it, the minister meant that the universities were now themselves responsible for the (financial) consequences of the university expansion between 1965 and 1971. The minister acknowledged that the universities had had to cope with insufficient means in recent years. But there was no room for additional government funding. He called for getting money, or at least more money, from 'the private sector', the world of industry and business. Moreover, the 'quality of the return for society' had to be sufficiently high for the government to continue financing the universities. 'The universities have to learn to take the consequences of evaluations and dare to implement the changes that arise as a result of those evaluations.'

At the end of 1995 the minister tasked the pro-rector of Leuven, Roger Dillemans, with researching the extent to which the educational programmes on offer in Flanders could be improved. Two weighty reports, submitted in 1997, homed in on drastic rationalisation and qualitative optimisation of the degree programmes. The years of academic proliferation were over, according to Dillemans. 'Regional or ideological interests no longer suffice for making another version of a course of study somewhere else.'

Luc Van den Bossche was extremely satisfied. At the start of academic year 1997-1998 in Ghent, he announced that only three large universities could continue to exist in Flanders. 'Universities that think they can base their identity and their survival on purely ideological grounds or regional considerations have gone astray and risk paying the price.' Interuniversity cooperation was necessary. Some degree programmes had to be discontinued, so that the government could invest in truly high-quality knowledge centres that could compete on a European scale.

In the meantime the number of students soared, particularly at Ghent University. After a dip in the 1980s, enrolment increased sharply from 13,983 students in 1991 to 20,222 in 1997. Thanks to a loophole in the university decree of 1991, however, the increase had no proportional impact on funding. All universities were entitled to a 'historical lump sum', a fixed amount that was intended to balance the effects of funding based on student enrolment figures. But it was not the regionally or ideologically driven smaller institutions that paid the price — UGent did. The university evolved into a mammoth, while the smaller institutions, such as those in Antwerp and Brussels, could continue to enjoy their traditional flat rate. This naturally had consequences for the degree programmes that, within a fixed framework, had to 'serve' an exponentially growing group of students. The small universities meanwhile offered the same subjects for much smaller groups, which were consequently better staffed.

Van den Bossche was well aware of the underfunding of his alma mater and remarked in 1997 that 'the balance of financing in the university decree of 1991 is disrupted to an inadmissible degree by the structural shift in the influx of students'. Rector André Oosterlinck of KULeuven was also aware of the problem. UGent was moreover catching up with his university in terms of enrolment figures. It was time to change direction. Already in 1996 the Leuven rector-entrepreneur argued for an increase in basic funding linked to a change in the financial distribution. The quality of education had to become more important than enrolment figures alone. But divvying up the government pie on the basis of 'quality' was not yet an option. After all, how was this quality to be measured? Flemish-Dutch education inspections were set up to try and answer this question. The (no longer extant) visitations made problems discussable within the degree programmes themselves. It was the intention — idealistic, and perhaps even naive — of the preparatory workgroup that the initial inspection of each study programme would have to be 'complete'; the second would then be just a marginal assessment. But the bureaucratic systems began to lead a life of their own. A rationalisation of the degree programmes on offer in Flanders never materialised, at least not in the drastic sense that Dillemans had envisioned. In 2008 a ministerial commission chaired by Luc Soete conducted a new exercise in this direction. The '115 norm' they proposed, in which bachelor's programmes with less than 115 students were discontinued or fused with other study programmes, remained a dead letter.

## Pioneer in European education

From the outset, Ghent University profiled itself in the context of European education and research. In 2004 the university even received accolades from Europe for the thoroughness with which the ECTS (European Credit Transfer System) was integrated into the administration. Since the approval of the Erasmus programme by the European Commission in 1987, student mobility had increased dramatically. This created the need for a uniform system of grading or credits for exchange students. Already in 1988, the first year Ghent students participated in Erasmus, a test was conducted in the History department. The ECTS would form the backbone of the European educational space created by the Bologna Declaration of 1999.

One of the spearheads of the Bologna Declaration was the harmonisation of study trajectories. The BaMa reform (that introduced Bachelor and Master's programmes), had far-reaching consequences, both for the degree programmes and for the internal operation of the universities as well as the formation of associations with the colleges. It obliged the degree programmes that traditionally offered instruction according to candidatures and licentiates to reorganise into a three-year Bachelor's and a one- to three-year Master's. This was more easily said than done. For example, students who went from a Bachelor's programme to a one-year Master's suddenly had to write their

Master's thesis in one year, while licentiates had always had at least two years to write their theses. Obviously this had consequences for the quality of the end result. Evidently 3+1 was not necessarily equal to 2+2, an Orwellian defect that one-year Master's programmes still have to struggle with more than ten years after the BaMa reform.

Rector Jacques Willems had warned from the beginning that the 3+1 structure would have undesirable side effects, but he was dead set against lengthening the duration of study. With the semester system, the concept of the 'academic year' also lost relevance and meaning. The increased flexibility of education, with complex, individualised study trajectories, resulted in a new kind of academic career in which the word '*bissen*' — to repeat a year — went out of use. Nowadays, students freely combine subjects from different academic years and think in terms of credits. Allowing subjects to 'migrate' into a new academic year is more acceptable to some parents than their son or daughter 'flunking' and having to take the whole year again. That students in practice take longer to complete their degrees in this way is usually not mentioned.

## 'Study at KULeuven. Also in Ghent'

The new BaMa structure was launched in 2004-2005. The decree of 2003 by minister of education Marleen Vanderpoorten and her shadow minister Marc Luwel determined that universities and colleges had to work together in associations in order to prevent fragmentation of the degree programmes on offer. There was a political agreement in the works that would allow these associations to be formed on a regional basis, but it was blocked by the imperialism of Leuven's rector, André Oosterlinck. He saw his chance to group the Catholic colleges under the umbrella of KULeuven on the basis of an ideological divide. Leuven's urge to expand spread from Ostend to Diepenbeek. The only exception to this rule is the Arteveldehogeschool, which together with UGent, Hogeschool Gent (HoGent) and Hogeschool West-Vlaanderen (HoWest) belongs to the University Association of Ghent (AUGent). An initial agreement to include Sint-Lieven in the AUGent was overturned. However, the bishop of Ghent, Arthur Luysterman, had no difficulty with the idea of merging all the colleges in Ghent with the university to form a unified whole, thereby tempering mutual competition. He did not have to be convinced that the time in which Ghent was considered 'a university of the devil' was now a thing of the past.

Oosterlinck's move was not preceded by any political negotiations. 'Thanks to Karel De Gucht (VLD), among others, an out-dated battle between freethinkers and Catholics was revived, with the result that the Catholic institutions closed ranks', said AUGent chairman Luc Van den Bossche in an interview with Oosterlinck in *Knack* (2006). 'The Flemish government provided an open goal without a goalkeeper and Leuven kicked the ball right in.' 'In this way — against all reason — not-regionally oriented associations were created,' wrote Stijn Baert, student representative on the board of governors, in the student newspaper *Schamper*. Baert mourned the fact that AUGent had become an empty shell, and that it suffered from a shocking lack of vision. In 2013, integration and 'acadcmisation' of the four-year college degrees followed. Since then, it has become a thorn in the side for many inhabitants of Ghent to see trams running through the city of Jacob van Artevelde with the slogan 'Study at KULeuven. Also in Ghent'. The marketing stunt only scratches the surface of how deeply ideological pillarisation has been ingrained in the university landscape.

It ended up being a university expansion in the Flemish style, with which UGent complied without offering much resistance. The time of rector Bouckaert, who was able to mobilise the entire university community against Belgian-style expansion forty years earlier, was clearly over.

## Output financing, distribution keys and allocation models

The formation of associations with the colleges was not really the main concern of rector André De Leenheer, a convinced Liberal. But De Leenheer did manage to take successful legal action against the historical underfunding of Ghent University. He filed suit at the Arbitration Court. 'I do not accept that a law student at the Catholic University of Brussels (KUB) receives a staffing and financing of 385,000 old Belgian francs and a law student at Ghent only 185,000 francs. Explain that to me, if you will', he is quoted as saying in *Schamper*. The Arbitration Court ruled in his favour. From 2006 onwards, Ghent University's funding was increased.

De Leenheer will mainly go down in history as the rector who revived the research drive at his university. Of his own generation of academics, he says unabashedly that in 95% of the cases, securing their own appointment was the most they ever achieved. When he began studying pharmacy in 1958, the average professor did not go to conferences and scarcely published at all, let alone internationally. There was not a strong research tradition in Ghent. Ambitious students who were research-minded went to the US to get their PhDs. Jacques Willems belonged to the first generation of engineers who did 'real' scientific research. After his studies, he went to America and after getting his PhD, went abroad again as a post-doc.

When they returned from the US, researchers brought with them not only knowledge, but also a new approach. By building up international connections and networks in all faculties, the seeds were planted of what would become high-performance research groups and success stories decades later.

At the beginning of the 1990s, Belgium was one of the worst-scoring countries in Europe in terms of public investment in research. In the meantime, the weight of science policy had shifted permanently to the regions. In 2001, Flanders spent four times as much on research as the French Community, and twice as much as the French Community, Wallonia and the Brussels-Capital Region together. The size of research funding tripled between 1993 and 2003, which was mainly reflected in an exponentially increasing group of temporary researchers, primarily doctoral students. UGent immediately jumped on the wagon of increasing Flemish research funding. Since 1994, every Flemish university has access to a Special Research Fund (Bijzonder Onderzoeksfonds, or BOF), financed by the Flemish government, to stimulate basic, pioneering research.

In the beginning, resources were limited and dependent on the number of students. There was little room for a research policy worthy of the name. One of De Leenheer's first achievements as rector was to increase the doctoral allowance for the

Procession in full regalia, 2004
At the forefront of the academic procession are the beadles with their fasces. They are followed by rector André De Leenheer, minister of education Frank Vandenbroucke, minister of state Willy De Clercq, vice-rector Marc De Clercq and mayor Frank Beke.
(Ghent, Universiteitsarchief, photo Hilde Christiaens)

supervisor to 10,000 euros per successfully completed doctorate. Previously, the department received an allowance of 25,000 Belgian francs (around 600 euros) per defended thesis. In 2003, the financial distribution key of the Special Research Fund (BOF) was adjusted and citations and publications in journals included in the citation indexing service of the Web of Science, the so-called A1 publications were also taken into account. Ghent University thus anticipated the new circumstances by linking payment of the doctoral allowance to publication conditions. Although this created a new dynamism in research, there was considerable grumbling on the work floor. The A1 metric privileged the exact scientists, who published short, English-language articles with several co-authors more frequently in the high-impact journals that were included in the Web of Science. Historian Bruno De Wever lashed out at the new doctoral regulations in *De Standaard*. In order to respond to the widely upheld complaints among the humanities and social sciences, the Flemish Academic Bibliography (Vlaams Academisch Bibliografisch Bestand, or VABB) was developed. Starting in 2011, the publications included in the VABB were also counted in the BOF distribution system. Nevertheless, the gap between the 'research faculties' and other, mainly 'alpha' faculties was not eliminated. It could hardly be otherwise: research and publication cultures exhibit such a degree of structural difference that they are impossible to 'adjust'. However, this does not change the fact that exponential growth in research output in esteemed channels can be observed across disciplines and departments.

The model of the private American research university, with a select student population that can afford to pay, is more and more the guiding principle in a totally different context of public education in Flanders. It makes for a difficult balancing act between the historically open, democratically accessible, broadly focused educational institutions, and the research-oriented university of the future, striving for top international rankings.

Minister of education Frank Vandenbroucke had in the meantime prepared a new funding decree adapted to the Bologna Declaration of 1999. Funding was no longer made dependent on the influx of students, but attuned to the results or the output of education and research. The decree came into effect in 2008. That the allocation model took the research results of a university into account for the first time gave rise to a great many academic reservations. Measurable parameters such as publications, citations and doctorates have since determined forty-five per cent of the subsidies of the universities. It is and remains problematic that the 'closed envelope' funding for research does not allow for the growth of resources in the absolute sense. In order to secure a bigger piece of the pie, one has to perform better than competing universities, which also do their utmost best. Training yourself to run faster than your previous record, in other words, only works if you also run faster than your competitors. One can compare it to the contest of the Red Queen, Alice's antagonist in *Through the Looking-Glass*. She explains to Alice the rules of chess, and how as a pawn she can become queen. 'Now here, you see, it takes all the running you can do, to keep in the same place.'

The new, result-driven system immediately gave rise to new, internal allocation models in which research output was calculated per faculty and even per department — within a closed envelope. Here too the Red Queen's race plays a role. The logical consequence: an unproductive battle between faculties. In particular, the standards used to measure the quality of research are controversial. Passion for science is converted into the 'scoring' of publications in the right high impact journals and the 'landing' of external, preferably large-scale European research funding. It makes for a malaise that affects all levels of the academic world. Not only in Flanders, but also within the broader European and even global context, this system is facing a growing chorus of critique.

## Not for profit

Looking back on the past two centuries, Ghent University was transformed profoundly in a neoliberal direction in a surprisingly short time. The still considerable public funding of higher education in the service of democratisation and the development of the knowledge economy justifies the demand for accountability from the universities. The taxpayer must literally get value for his or her money in terms of economic benefits. In this way, neoliberal ideas about public administration and good governance have silently taken hold of our alma mater as well. New public management has colonised the academic field with the language of economics. In the final analysis, it is an on-going attempt to quantify quality. This attempt is doomed to failure, but is not for that reason less compelling.

The logic of the financial distribution key at the Flemish level is extended all the way to the work floor and the level of individual careers through internal allocation models. The pressure of evaluation is omnipresent. All aspects of education and research are carefully monitored. The external inspections have in the meantime been replaced by the internal institutional review, a form of permanent self-evaluation. The bureaucracy of quality control is proliferating. The *nec plus ultra* of evaluations are the Shanghai or Times Higher Education rankings, in which the universities themselves compete against each other, and in which, according to critics, reputations are judged like restaurants on TripAdvisor.

In any case, Ghent University has changed since 1991 from a rigid state institution into a professionally run, dynamic concern with many chambers. Many, however, wonder whether academic freedom and the *Bildungsideal* of Wilhelm von Humboldt were not sacrificed along the way. Is the university becoming alienated from its historical roots and societal mission in the search for new finalities in the market?

Moreover, international organisations such as the Organisation for Economic Co-operation and Development (OECD) exercise above all a discourse of competition. Europe versus the US, Japan, and the BRIC nations (Brazil, Russia, India and China). Flanders against other countries or regions in Europe. Things might never have been any different. Science in the nineteenth and twentieth centuries was also a beacon of national pride and prestige.

Nevertheless, in the growing emphasis on the 'knowledge economy', a dimension has been lost. The example of the fading Belgian nation-state makes this clear. The federal government has had to loosen its grip on education and research, and the Belgian crown is now only a symbolic ornament. The Brabançonne is met at most with pitying smiles after a ceremony in the Aula. At the same time, The Lion of Flanders does not seem to arouse much national pride among the academic community either. Flemish nation-building is nonetheless strongly driven by science and technology as shapers of identity. Researchers should ideally be important ambassadors of Flanders, actively promoting and profiling 'Flemish' research within the space of Europe as an imaginary competitive model. For the time being, however, this model resembles a market more than an intellectual refuge.

'To be something we have to be Flemings. We want to be Flemings in order to become Europeans', wrote August Vermeylen in 1900. Perhaps those words will once again take flight in a Europe that wants to be not only an economic union, but also a social and cultural community.

**Leo Apostel**
Since the 1960s the Ghent philosophical school has played an important role in the secularisation of Flanders. Pluralism is deeply rooted in the history of Ghent University.
(Ghent, Universiteitsarchief, photo Stephan Vanfleteren)

# Chapter 2
# PLURALISM, RELIGION AND SCIENCE

Next to societal engagement, pluralism is the second most important core value in the mission statement of Ghent University. The university is open to all students and professors, regardless of their ideological or religious background. For two hundred years this has been an important asset for recruiting students. However, 'Ghent' also encountered a great deal of opposition from the Catholic side precisely for this reason.

Today, the university's teaching policy is explicitly framed around multiperspectivism. This concept, which was developed by vice-rector Freddy Mortier in 2015, blends seamlessly with the 'historical' pluralism of the institution — more specifically with the project of his mentors Leo Apostel and Jaap Kruithof. The leitmotif is a quote from the American literary theorist Kenneth Burke: 'Every way of seeing is also a way of not seeing. It is better to have a variety of models and archetypes so we stay flexible and open.'

As shown in the previous chapter, the state university's pluralism was more a liability than an asset in the broader context of the Belgian educational landscape. Nowadays, associations are formed with the colleges on the basis of ideology. The bellwether is KULeuven, where the 'K' in 'Katholiek' still stands for the university's distinctly Catholic identity, an important binding factor that should not be underestimated. The internal pluralism of the University Association of Ghent (AUGent), on the contrary, stands in the way of cooperation and clear profiling.

Within UGent itself, the ideological conflict usually only flares up during rectorial elections. For many at UGent, this is an anachronism — as if the university were stuck in the paradigms of the past. In terms of the university's core business, the pluralism of its mission statement and current vision of education, broadly supported by Catholics and freethinkers alike, is a plus point compared to universities that keep struggling with the conflict between religion and science.

## Pacification and tolerance in Ghent's DNA

In 1820, William I gave the university a telescope and a symbolically well-chosen painting of the city. The telescope is a top item of the Ghent University Museums (Gentse Universitaire Musea, or GUM); the painting still hangs today in the city hall of Ghent, near the entrance as one enters the Troonzaal (literally, the 'Throne Room'). It is by court painter Matthias van Bree and depicts William of Orange, who in 1578 argued before the Calvinist city administration for the release of Catholic prisoners. The memory of the Calvinist republic in Ghent (1576-1584) was a significant factor in William I's decision to choose Ghent instead of staunchly Catholic Bruges. City government's petitions never failed to mention the significance of the Pand, where, in the late sixteenth century, subjects taught in the Dominican monastery included ethics

Matthias van Bree, *Prince William Defending the Roman Catholics in Ghent*, 1578
During the Calvinistic Republic of Ghent (1576-1584) an embryonic university was established in the Pand. It formed the historical legitimation for the choice for Ghent in 1817. Like his ancestor, William of Orange, William I sought to play a conciliatory role between the Protestant North and Catholic South.
(Ghent, Stad Gent, Historic Huizen Gent, photo Dominique Provost)

and physics alongside theology, philosophy and languages, the basis for a fully fledged university.

William, of course, set great stock by his Orange family tree. In 1576, during the rebellion against Spain, his illustrious forefather was a driving force behind the Pacification of Ghent, a democratic alliance between the rebellious provinces against the religious policies of Philip II. The Calvinists in Holland and Zeeland were at the forefront. In the context of the Eighty Years War, the Pacification of Ghent is an icon of religious tolerance. William of Orange continued to act as a reconciler of Protestants and Catholics, against the intolerant Calvinist city administration of Jan van Hembyze. In a period during which Catholics in the South were protesting against his education and religious policies, William I's gift to the city was no mere matter of chance.

In the United Kingdom of the Netherlands, the six universities North and South were secular institutions administered by the state, not by the Church. In the run-up to the Revolution of 1830, this turned out to be a problem for Catholics and Liberals alike. For Roman Catholics, any state intervention in the spiritual realm constituted an infringement on the divine rights of the Church. Traditionally, the Church's close supervision of university institutions, the appointment of professors and the content of instruction was crucial; obedience and submission to ecclesiastical dogmas was necessary. A professor could not simply teach what he wanted, and was required to swear an oath of fidelity to the Catholic faith. At the beginning of the nineteenth century, the Liberals were already diametrically opposed to the Catholics on all these points. They rejected religious dogmas and fought against clericalism that was trying to re-conquer the machinery of government and education. Freedom was for them a struggle that went back to the Renaissance, the Reformation and the Enlightenment, with the Church as an obstruction to freethinking and Galileo as the greatest martyr of modern science. Hence, for the Liberals, secularisation of the university meant freedom from all dogmas. It was the task of the state to defend intellectual freedom. Nonetheless, in the Southern Netherlands, the Liberals would join forces with the Catholics, who fought for freedom of education against the state monopoly of William I.

The king ignored attacks on education as the exclusive right of the government. He was mainly interested in a speedy unification of the regulations of North (1815) and South (1816). The goal was further centralisation and modernisation of the universities, which riled the clerical factions even more. In the United Kingdom of the Netherlands, the clergy no longer had any influence on the appointment of professors. On the contrary: academic freedom opened the door to critical research. Dogmatically established religious truths were from now on subject to scientific investigation too. The three state universities in the South had the express task of spreading the intellectual spirit of the Enlightenment and sweeping away 'clerical obscurantism'. For the Church, this enlightened mindset was quite threatening. Even though most professors had kept their faith, there was no guarantee that this would remain so.

## 'No blasphemy at the state's expense!'

For the bishops one thing was clear: the three state universities in the South had to go. In 1829 the two vicars-general who governed the bishopric at the time sent around a pastoral letter at Lent in which they objected to a number of professors from Ghent.

Among them was the young German jurist Jacques-Joseph Haus. The stumbling block was a handbook on natural law from 1824, a work of minor importance that was moreover carefully phrased in order not to offend religious and political sensibilities. Nevertheless, the publication *Elementa doctrinae juris philosophicae sive juris naturalis* earned Haus the wrath of the Church. In 1829, five years after its publication, the treatise was placed on the *Index of Forbidden Books*.

The letter caused a huge commotion. Even Haus was taken by surprise. Although a convinced Liberal politically, in private he was a sincerely faithful Catholic. The vicars-general had clearly misunderstood one particular sentence in his book. The passage in question related to the obligations of adult children and the interpretation of the words *'stricto jure'*. To understand it required insight into the system of natural law and the distinction between legally enforceable duties, on the one hand, and moral duties on the other. That crucial distinction between law and morality was explained extensively in the discourse. Haus very clearly designated morality as the nobler and 'higher' of the two.

After Belgian independence, the university and the Church arrived at a fragile *modus vivendi*. The Liberals had been able to safeguard the state's right to organise higher education. The very survival of Ghent and Liège was proof. While the clergy had successfully recaptured primary and secondary education, the state universities managed to hold onto their academic freedom. No compulsory religious education

Liberal caricature, 1856
The caricature refers to the bishops' attacks on Ghent University during the controversy surrounding the 'godless' education of François Laurent and Hubert Brasseur. In 1857 the Liberals won the municipal elections.
(Ghent, Universiteitsbibliotheek)

was scheduled. It was the price that the bishops were prepared to pay for the establishment of the free Catholic university in Leuven in 1835.

The latent conflict between Ghent University and the Church would not flare up again until the 1850s. The unionism of Liberals and Catholics, which gave priority to Belgian unity in a climate of reconciliation, made way in 1847 for growing tensions between ultramontanists and anticlericals.

Until 1848, Jean-Baptiste d'Hane was executive director in Ghent. His policies gave the clergy nothing to complain about. But when he was replaced by Philippe Derote, a freethinking Liberal, the floodgates opened and incidents began to pile up. Several professors were put on a blacklist, and their publications on the *Index of Forbidden Books*. After a ferocious smear campaign, the charismatic philosophy professor François Huet was even forced to flee the university and the country in the wake of the February Revolution of 1848 in France. His utopian socialism exercised 'too dangerous [an] influence' on the students.

August Wagener had to endure the following clerical attack. Because of his brilliant results, he was appointed by the minister of domestic affairs Charles Rogier to teach ethics at the faculty of Arts and Philosophy in 1850. The young classicist made no effort to conceal his ideas about rational morality. He criticised dogmatic thinking and argued that in certain periods of history, official religion was no longer in agreement with the progress of science.

According to bishop Ludovicus Delebecque, Wagener was proclaiming a blasphemous 'bastard philosophy'; Ghent University had become a place of decadence. The bishop expressed his allegations at the beginning of academic year 1852-1853 in a caustic letter to the parish priests that caused a great commotion. When the Catholic Pieter De Decker took over governmental power and jurisdiction over education from Rogier in March 1855, Delebecque wasted no time in informing him of the professors who had 'gone astray' and the 'untenable' situation in Ghent.

The minister only gave the bishop partial satisfaction, as was soon evident from the sensational affairs surrounding François Laurent and Hubert Brasseur. Both professors were religious; that was not the problem. The problem was that, as professors of ideologically sensitive subjects, they did not start from Catholic dogmas, but from science. The publication of *Le Christianisme* by Laurent unleashed a storm of protest in the Catholic press, with the ultramontanist Ghent paper *Le Bien Public* at the forefront. Laurent saw Jesus as the most morally elevated person who ever lived, but not as God. God was for him an immanent aspect of humanity. He described Christianity as a phase in the development of religious consciousness and also argued that the Church had not contributed enough to the unification of humanity. A new rift was created between believers and non-believers, between orthodoxy and heresy.

In order not to exacerbate the situation, De Decker only reprimanded the professor in writing. Laurent had violated the trust of the parents as well as the good reputation of the university at home and abroad. From then on, the rector had to keep close watch on his courses and ensure that his bad ideas did not influence his teaching. Laurent answered that in Belgium, where there was strict separation between Church and state, the government did not have the right to intervene in religious discussions, let alone interfere with the religious beliefs of its officials.

Meanwhile, the affair concerning Laurent's young colleague Hubert Brasseur had erupted in full force. Even the pope intervened. The occasion was a course taught by Brasseur on how Christianity influenced the development of natural law. Four students objected to certain of his positions. They tipped off the brother-in-law of one of them, who wrote for *Le Bien Public*, and promptly gave their discontent a public forum: 'No blasphemy at the state's expense!'

Concerned parents filed complaints with rector Constant Serrure. Brasseur defended himself before his students, a large majority of whom sided with him. On 21 December 1855 a support committee even demanded in class that the 'informers' make themselves known. Tony Bergmann and Julius Vuylsteke, leaders of the freethinking student association 't Zal Wel Gaan asked the Academic Council to banish the four from the university because they slandered their professor. An internal investigation was launched, while *Le Bien Public* took up the defence of the four students. Once again the paper made a great to-do about godless education in Ghent. Brasseur responded by writing an open letter to *Le Bien Public* in which he invoked freedom of education and formally denied that he had repudiated the divinity of Christ. Like

Wagener a few years earlier, he explained that he approached Christianity not from a theological point of view, but from the perspective of philosophy, as a phase in the history of ideas. In doing so he showed that the Roman Catholic Church had gradually developed into an institution driven by power. And he had sung the praises of the Reformation as a 'liberation of the human spirit, suffocated by the yoke of the Church in the Middle Ages'. For *Le Bien Public* this was just one more proof that Brasseur's teaching was anticlerical. Between theology and philosophy there was no contradiction, according to the paper. The academic freedom of professors was not a dispensation for undermining the students' faith. The incident was used to discredit Ghent University even further in the eyes of Catholic parents. The teaching of the perfidious Brasseur was 'poison for the mind'.

Both the university administration and the government had to show their colours. On 3 January 1856, the Academic Council ruled unanimously that the four students' complaint against Brasseur was unfounded. He had made his remarks in 'good faith', and they had wrongly interpreted them; they were let off with a warning for displaying a negative attitude towards their professor. With this ruling issued by the Academic Council, government leader De Decker had little choice than to recognise the professor's philosophical immunity. Moreover, the moderate Catholic minister could not tolerate the idea that the Catholic *Index* would determine the choice of textbooks. The Liberal press triumphed and Brasseur was rehabilitated.

Still, the continuing incidents in and around the university were grist for the mill of *Le Bien Public*, which judged the anti-religious spirit of the university with increasing harshness. Bishop Delebecque involved the Vatican and asked his parish priests to warn parents of the dangerous influences to which their children were being exposed. His colleagues in Bruges and Tournai followed suit in an attempt to attract as many students as possible to Leuven and away from Ghent.

The *coup de grâce* came at the beginning of academic year 1856-1857. On Sunday, 14 September, a pastoral text was read out in all the churches of the bishopric on 'the teaching and education of our youth'. It took aim not only at the state university and its godless professors, but also at primary and secondary state and city schools. The clergy only accepted public education that was based on Catholic norms. A brief issued by Pope Pius IX to the Belgian bishops stressed that outside Catholic orthodoxy in Leuven, there could be no good education, and that intellectual freedom inevitably led to immorality and anarchy. Moreover, the pope condemned the literary almanac of 't Zal Wel Gaan, *Noord en Zuid* (North and South): *'Septentrio et Meridies, Miscellanea Academica, in lucem edita Gandavi ab alumnurom societate philologica vulgo dicta: "'t zal wel gaan", ex consensu alumnorum variarum Hollandiae et Belgii universitatum.'*

The homily and the papal ban only encouraged the radicalisation of anticlericalism in Ghent. It was the first time that public education had ever been attacked so openly. The Liberals won a clear victory in the city council elections that autumn. On a national level, the unionism that the De Decker government was trying to uphold was weakened. The two state universities were informed that their professors needed to refrain from any attack on recognised religions, not only in their courses, but also in their publications. In his speech at the opening of the parliamentary year, king Leopold I also referred to this point. In the Senate it was agreed that professors should honour the social, moral and religious principles that guarantee the peace and happiness of the state. Once again, a position subject to heavy debate. Finally the parliament arrived at a compromise: professors enjoyed academic freedom, but the government did not have to sit by and watch helplessly while they systematically undermined the religious principles to which the nation and its families attached so much importance. Belgium may not have had a state religion, but it was also not in favour of state rationalism at the state's expense, according to parliament in 1856. The University of Ghent had to find the right balance between Leuven, which operated in accordance with Catholic dogmas, and the ULB, where science was completely independent of any religious dogma whatsoever.

The Brasseur affair did not help Ghent's reputation. The moral authority of the Catholic clergy was still great in Flanders, and student enrolment figures dropped sharply: from 357 in 1855 to 291 in 1857. From then on, parents of students from Catholic schools and colleges sent their sons to Leuven. Hubert Brasseur's fortunes declined in the wake of the affair. During parliamentary discussions, it had come to light that he owed his first appointment in Liège to Catholic intervention. The Liberal students and papers promptly dropped him in the face of such servility. In 1857-1858, the Catholic Prosper de Haulleville took over the instruction of natural law from Brasseur. According to minister De Decker, this was not because of content, but because Brasseur had placed the university in a bad light. A year later, the young Haulleville also had to resign because his teaching was too religiously oriented. This was at any rate the view of Charles Rogier and the Liberals, who once again had the reins of government in hand. The politicisation of professorial appointments had become a fact.

## Anticlerical professors in the public forum

François Laurent refused to allow himself to be intimidated by the bishop and answered the charges with open letters in the style of Voltaire. He exchanged the academic register for a more polemical tone, with sharper attacks on the Church. He no longer eschewed controversy in the press. Catholics and Liberals alike found his uncompromising pleas for the state's re-conquest of the Church hard to swallow. According to Laurent, the separation of Church and state in the Belgian constitution of 1830 meant that the state had lost its power over the Church. At the beginning of the 1860s he conducted animated polemics in the newspapers on the budget for religious services, the cemetery question and the role of the Jesuits. His growing public renown gained him a seat on the city council of Ghent in 1863.

That same year he lost his colleague, kindred spirit and bosom friend Gustave Callier, who was only forty-four years old. Callier was elected as a city council member in 1856, and two years later he became alderman for Education. Like Laurent and Brasseur, he was on the bishopric's blacklist of professors, and was a leading figure in Liberal and freethinking circles. He was active in the Société Littéraire and the Association Libérale, and became the right hand of mayor Charles de Kerchove de Denterghem. On his deathbed, the Liberal alderman refused any manner of assistance from the Church. He was buried in a civil ceremony ... in consecrated ground. The clergy tried to prevent it, but had to bow to the will of the mayor. It was the time of the cemetery question. The priests would only permit civil funerals in unconsecrated ground. As a result, freethinkers were symbolically relegated to the distant corners of the cemeteries, next to the suicides, the mentally ill and criminals. Only with the establishment of municipal cemeteries was the power of the clergy broken on this point. The Westerbegraafplaats (Western Cemetery) at the Brugsepoort is still known in Ghent today as the 'Geuzenkerkhof', or 'Heretic's Resting Place'.

Callier's 'sacrilegious' burial coincided with a major international congress of the Association internationale pour le progrès des sciences sociales (International Association for Progress in the Social Sciences, or APSS), which descended upon Ghent with great pomp and circumstance. For bishop Delebecque, this was a gathering '*où les principes les plus sacrés ont été niés, outragés et blasphémés*' (where the most sacred principles were repudiated, insulted and blasphemed). François Laurent could not allow a fresh attack on science to go unanswered and sent an open letter to the bishop, fifty-six pages long. He accused the bishop of digging the Church's own grave with his pettiness. After his death in 1887, Laurent would be interred in Callier's crypt. This was more than just symbolic. The families Callier and Laurent were in the meantime intimately related. Albert and Hippolyte, Callier's sons, each married one of Laurent's daughters, Caroline and Marie.

In 1874, Laurent and his two sons-in-law founded the anti-Catholic weekly *La Flandre Libérale*. It became a mouthpiece for their social and political engagement. In 1876 the ambitious lawyer received the state prize for moral and political sciences for his monumental *Principes de droit civil* in thirty-three volumes. In 1882-1885, he also published an *Avant-projet de révision du Code civil*, an ambitious project for thoroughly improving Napoleon's Civil Law Code of 1804. He was so strongly opposed to the Church, however, that the Catholic electoral victory in 1884 literally planted a cross in his plans. In the meantime the project has been completely forgotten.

Leopold II would oppose the appointment of Laurent as rector of Ghent University because of the latter's rabid anticlericalism. His son-in-law Albert Callier did eventually become rector in 1879 under the anticlerical administration of Frère-Orban–Van Humbeeck. As a lecturer in the law faculty, he, too, had run-ins with Catholic opinion and students. In his lectures on the constitution, he discussed the separation of Church and state, which Pius IX had condemned in his *Syllabus errorum* of 1864. Callier's teaching, like that of his predecessors Haus, Wagener, Brasseur and his father-in-law Laurent, was denounced by the clergy as contrary to ecclesiastical rules.

The growing impact of the anti-modern, ultramontanist tendencies in Catholicism led to the so-called *Kulturkampf* throughout Europe in the 1870s and 80s. The moder-

**Funerary monument, Callier and Laurent families**
Liberal professor of Philosophy Gustave Callier was one of the figureheads of anticlericalism at the university. With his controversial civil funeral, he continued to stir feelings even after his early death. This family tomb at the Westerbegraafplaats points to the intimate ties between the families of leading Liberal professors in Ghent.
(Ghent, Universiteitsarchief)

ate Liberalism that respected the rights of the Church made room for a militantly positivist anticlericalism on the other side of the spectrum. Auguste Comte, one of the founders of sociology, posited three phases in the evolution of humanity that, according to the laws of progress, would lead to the triumph of reason. In this scheme of things, rationalism, materialism and modern science went hand in hand. This area of tension formed the context for a new ideological conflict at Ghent University at the beginning of the twentieth century.

## Religion and science: water and fire?

Charles Darwin first published his groundbreaking theory of evolution, *On the Origin of Species*, in 1859, two full decades after his expedition on the *Beagle*. In 1854 the dogma of the Immaculate Conception was proclaimed by Pius IX. Two near-simultaneous milestones in history that show how science and religion diametrically opposed one another in the second half of the nineteenth century. The ideological commotion at Ghent University in the 1850s did not mean that militant positivism ruled the roost. On the contrary, a figure like François Laurent combined his rationalist critique of the dogmas of the Church as a power institution with a spiritual notion of God and an unflinching critique of positivism. It is also worth noting that the bishops did not so much attack the development of the natural sciences as such, but rather the development of rational, religiously tinted philosophy and the vision of religion as a human creation. As a result, the conflict between science and religion primarily played out in the humanities.

However, after the Laurent–Brasseur affair it was the 'conversion' of Alphonse Renard that caused the biggest uproar. The famous mineralogist and oceanographer jumped ship in 1901. Not only did he marry a woman twenty years his junior, he also joined the progressive Brussels Freemasons' lodge, Les Amis Philanthropes. For the freethinkers, this was proof that science and religion were irreconcilable. Catholic opinion had maintained precisely the opposite until Renard's dramatic exit.

Alphonse Renard was educated at Maria-Laach Abbey in the Eifel region before studying philosophy and theology in Leuven. The volcanic mountains of the Eifel sparked his scientific interest in mineralogy. In 1877 he was not only consecrated as a priest, but also appointed as curator of Minerals at the Royal Museum of Natural Sciences in Brussels. In 1888 the Catholic administration appointed Renard as a professor in Ghent, in spite of the objections of August Wagener, who was executive director at the time. Renard's scientific merit was nevertheless undisputed, even though strictly speaking he did not have a doctorate. For example, he received the highly prestigious *laurea d'onore* from the University of Bologna, and the Bigsby Medal of the London Geological Society. Wagener feared, however, that as a priest, Renard would not possess the necessary freedom of mind in his scientific research. The incidents surrounding Haus, Laurent, Brasseur and, of course, Wagener himself were clearly still fresh in collective memory. Nor were the students very enthusiastic about the arrival of *l'abbé* Renard.

It was the minister who decided on appointments at the state universities. The

Alphonse Renard
(Ghent, Universiteitsbibliotheek, etching Wilhelm Rohr)

faculties had nothing to say. The appointment of Alphonse Renard, an in the meantime laicised priest, was in the first place a political appointment. He became a professor in the faculty of Sciences and turned out to be a highly dedicated and gifted teacher. He was the first to use a microscope to study rocks. He modernised laboratory education, introduced his students to fieldwork and organised excursions to the Ardennes. In the Institute for the Sciences (Instituut voor Wetenschappen), which was still under construction at the time of his appointment, he was responsible for the development of the mineralogical collections and new laboratories. The ambitious *Challenger* expedition in cooperation with Sir John Murray in the 1870s had opened the age of modern oceanography. A huge number of samples from all over the world supplied data for the geological map of the ocean floor. Renard would also be a fervent supporter of the exploratory voyage of the *Belgica*, led by Adrien de Gerlache. He was tasked with analysing the samples that the *Belgica* brought back from the expedition in 1899 — after being stuck in polar ice for over a year.

## Between faith and geology

Renard's passion for geology took him further and further away from the faith. His materialist and positivist world view conflicted with his religious beliefs. The dogma of papal infallibility, proclaimed in 1870, was occasion for the Jesuits to found the Société Scientifique de Bruxelles (Brussels Scientific Society), which was meant to promote complete harmony between science and religion. At Ghent University, the mathematician Paul Mansion was the driving force behind the Catholic revival, which, following Pius X and the Vatican Council, adhered to scientific anti-modernism. Mansion was utterly convinced of the dogmas of Pius X: '*L' hypothèse darwiniste, poussée aux extrêmes par les disciples du maître, ne le séduisit jamais*' (The Darwinian hypothesis, pushed to extremes by disciples of the master, never seduced him).

Initially, Renard published in the Jesuits' *Revue des questions scientifiques*, but he left the order in 1883. This did not yet mean that he had turned his back on the Church. From his personal archives, it seems that he had already lost his faith as a priest in the early 1880s, but was unwilling to leave the priesthood as long as his mother was alive. Her death at the end of 1898 coincided with the first signs that he had cancer. The scandal of his laicisation and marriage to young Henriette Van Gobbelschroy, a long-time friend, followed in 1901.

*Le Bien Public* dragged the apostate through the mud for days because he had left the Church for the pleasures of the flesh. *La Flandre Libérale*, by contrast, triumphantly announced that the eminent scientist had drawn his conclusions, and in this way had demonstrated the incompatibility of science and Catholicism. Renard himself enjoined the polemic with *Le Bien Public* and devoted the rest of his life to the popularisation of his scientific insights. In the Maison du Peuple (People's House) in Brussels,

John Murray
and Alphonse Renard,
*Report on Deep Sea
Deposits, based on
the Specimens collected
during the Voyage of
HMS Challenger in
1872-1876*, 1892
(Ghent, Universiteitsbibliotheek)

designed by Victor Horta, he started a series of lectures on the creation of the earth. In 1902 he translated Darwin's *Geological Observations on the Volcanic Islands visited during the Voyage of H.M.S. Beagle* into French. In his field, it was the first introduction to Darwinism in Belgium. In his foreword he recalled the *héros de la vérité*, whose only weapon was an intellect free from prejudice, and who, with enlightened reason and calm, diligent labour, at the cost of much bitterness, had caused human thought to advance a step forward. '*Entre eux, Darwin est des premiers.*'

Adrien de Gerlache and Ernest Solvay attended Renard's deathbed. His former Jesuit brethren and Catholic colleagues such as Paul Mansion still tried to get him to reconcile with the Church and repent. They tried in vain. In his will he had expressly stated that no priest was to be admitted to his presence at the hour of his death. Renard's civil burial was a public event, attended by numerous prominent freethinkers. In 1906 the mineralogist received a statue at his place of residence, Elsene, with the inscription *Scientia liberavit eum* — 'Science freed him'. Chairman of the Comité Alphonse Renard was Théodore Swarts, the successor of August Kekulé. The name of the famous mineralogist was also immortalised in Cape Renard, the projecting headland that towers over the ice in the Gerlache Strait, off the west coast of the Antarctic Peninsula.

## The Cumont affair

On 11 February 1910 the famous archaeologist Franz Cumont submitted his resignation to the minister of Sciences and Arts, Edouard Descamps. In a letter to the dean of his faculty, he expressed his regret and gratitude towards his colleagues, but also his bitterness about the fact that all efforts to advance higher education ran aground on an arbitrary clerical nomination policy.

The Catholics, who had had an absolute majority in Belgium since 1884, were not averse to political appointments at Ghent University. Between 1878 and 1883, the anticlerical government of Frère-Orban had appointed thirteen professors of Liberal persuasion, as opposed to only one Catholic. Between 1884 and 1907, a period of homogeneous Catholic governments, the balance was more than restored with the appointment of fifty-five Catholic professors. The anticlerical ascendancy had to be breached, especially in the faculties of Arts and Philosophy and Law, regardless of the candidates' scientific qualifications. The minister could effectively appoint whomever he wished; the faculties did not even have the right to advise. The rector and the executive director did, but the minister was not obliged to take their nominations into account. In 1905 the Ghent Liberal parliamentarian Albert Mechelynck, alumnus of the

**Cape Renard**
In 1898-1899, Adrien de Gerlache discovered Antarctica. There he named the 'most beautiful cape in the world' after Professor Alphonse Renard, a passionate promoter of his eventful voyage of discovery. In 1986 the Renard Centre of Marine Geology (RCMG) was founded in Ghent under the inspiring leadership of Jean-Pierre Henriet and Marc De Batist. In 1987 an RCMG team on board the icebreaker *Polarstern* sailed past Cape Renard. Since then the study of Antarctica has been back on the map.
(Creative Commons, photo Liam Quinn)

Franz Cumont (left) and Michael Rostovtzeff (right) in front of the altar of Mithra in Dura-Europos (Syria), 1933-1934
In 1933-1934 a small Mithraeum was discovered during the excavation of Dura-Europos in Syria. Franz Cumont had been away from Ghent for more than twenty years. Yale University called upon his expertise to explain historically the presence of Mithra in the Roman garrison town of Dura-Europos, at the crossroads of cultures.
(New Haven, Connecticut, Yale University Art Gallery, Dura-Europos Collection Archive)

law faculty, filed a bill for a new appointment system, but the Catholic majority rejected it.

Franz Cumont was a student of August Wagener and succeeded him in his courses on Roman antiquity. In 1894, Cumont published the first volume of his *Textes et Monuments relatifs aux Mystères de Mithra*, an innovative reference work that brought him world renown. This monumental sources edition (1894-1898) documented the origin and dissemination in the Roman Empire of the mystery cult surrounding the Persian deity Mithra. Cumont was already being attacked in the clerical press at the time, but his *Les Religions orientales dans le paganisme romain* (1906) shut the door for good. The brilliant antiquarian had broadened his gaze to encompass the other eastern religions that had laid the groundwork for Christianity from the second century AD onwards. But his historical and comparative approach to ancient religions was a thorn in the side of anti-modernist Catholics. For them, there was no connection whatsoever between Christianity and the pagan cults of the Near East. On the contrary, the two religious spheres had to be kept at a safe distance from one another. Reading the Bible as a text like any other text from antiquity was threatening to the Christian doctrine of revelation. Comparative religious research, unencumbered by confessional considerations, was thus actively resisted by the Catholics.

The entire affair started with one course, 'Political History of Rome'. What exactly was the problem? Adolf De Ceuleneer, the lecturer in charge, had lost credit with the students because of his increasing deafness and manifest incompetence. At the beginning of the academic year they had disrupted his class and refused to apologise afterwards. The problems dragged on until Cumont spontaneously offered to take over the course. It was a generous offer from a worldwide authority on the subject of Roman antiquity. This scenario seemed so self-evident as to need no further explanation — but this was without taking minister Descamps into account. He ignored the faculty's advice and appointed Alphonse Roersch instead, a Hellenist who had never even worked on Roman history — but was Roman Catholic.

The refusal of Cumont's offer unleashed a storm of protest against the clerical appointment policy. Internationally, colleagues took up their pens to defend academic independence. A unanimous faculty that had acted in the interests of the university was subjected to exposure in a way that was unheard of. A week after Cumont submitted his resignation, the students of Ghent sent a petition to the young king Albert I, asking that the appointment be reviewed. They collected 556 signatures: nearly half of the 1,177 students then enrolled at the university.

On 10 March 1910, Albert Mechelynck and Emile Vandervelde questioned the minister in parliament. Descamps's only defence was that the faculty had taken an illegal initiative by proposing Cumont for the course. He hid behind the appointment regulations and claimed that there were no political motives involved. According to Vandervelde, the scientific interests of Ghent University were sacrificed to religious prejudice.

Because of his refusal to seek a position at a foreign university, Cumont's reputation in the fight against administrative arbitrariness and for academic freedom only grew. Nevertheless, the new minister of Arts and Sciences, Frans Schollaert, would accept Cumont's resignation at the beginning of May 1911, all national and international protest to the contrary. A year later, without further ado, his cabinet chief Cyrille Van Overbergh would also eliminate the curatorial post that Cumont had held at the Royal Museums for Art and History in the Parc du Cinquantenaire since 1899. Embittered, the antiquarian left Belgium. Cumont continued to work on an impressive oeuvre as a private scholar in Paris and Rome. He died in Sint-Pieters-Woluwe in 1947. His *Lux Perpetua* (1949) was published posthumously, an investigation of the evolution of all representations of the afterlife in the Roman world and the relationship between religion, ancient philosophy and science. Like his analysis of Christianity in relation to the pagan religions of the East, Cumont's analysis was dialectic. He viewed astrology, for example, as an important historical fact that deserved a place in a comparative study of the history of religion and science. The humanist scholar was not only a pathfinder for the history of science project by his contemporary George Sarton, but also for a number of other important societal and philosophical discussions launched by Ghent philosophers in the 1960s.

## The arrival of Jaap Kruithof and Leo Apostel

Jaap Kruithof was thirty when he succeeded Edgar De Bruyne in 1959. The young Dutch philosopher was raised as a Protestant and, until his eighteenth birthday, was deeply religious. He had a degree in history and was an assistant in the Seminar for Contemporary History, led by the flamboyant professor Jan Dhondt. He owed his appointment largely to the socially engaged Dhondt, who ensured that philosophy

(left)
**Leo Apostel, 1958**
(Ghent, Universiteitsbibliotheek)

(right)
**Jaap Kruithof, 1959**
(Ghent, Universiteitsarchief)

and ethics in Ghent were entrusted to freethinking spirits. For subjects relating to the history of philosophy, De Bruyne received in addition to Kruithof an insignificant Catholic successor, Armand Janssens. In 1957, Leo Apostel, who came from the ULB, also became a lecturer thanks to Dhondt's efforts. Their appointment was, in Apostel's words, 'downright revolutionary' in the strongly pillarised Catholic Flanders of the 1950s. He had studied in Paris with Jean Piaget and had spent a year in the United States working with the famous philosopher of language, Rudolf Carnap. The influence of these two freethinking, atheist philosophers — Apostel and Kruithof — on the secularisation of Flanders can hardly be underestimated. When Etienne Vermeersch joined them in 1967, it became what he described as 'even more intense'.

At the time it was a tried and tested strategy to ensure pluralistic equilibrium by appointing both a Catholic and a freethinker to ideologically sensitive subjects. Apostel was in favour of this approach. At his insistence, in addition to Vermeersch, the German phenomenologist Rudolf Boehm was appointed, a scientific collaborator on the Husserl Archives in Leuven who had a Protestant background. Boehm would also turn out to be something other than a docile Christian. He did, however, represent the spiritualist branch of philosophy as a counterweight to the materialism and neo-positivism that would come to dominate the Ghent school. However incompatible their respective ideas about science and philosophy may have been, Vermeersch and Boehm shared with Kruithof and Apostel a strong sense of societal engagement. The enthusiasm of the four great Ghent philosophers ensured that 'the Blandijn' grew to be a freethinking, leftist bulwark in Flanders. With their progressive ideas, they not only reached thousands of students from all faculties, but also were very present in the public debate on numerous contemporary themes.

Their predecessors, the sensitive moral philosopher Gaston Colle and the neo-Thomist Edgar De Bruyne, were outspokenly Catholic. De Bruyne had fought as a volunteer on the Yser Front in 1918 before beginning his studies in Leuven. In the 1930s, he began

Edgar De Bruyne, *De universiteit in dezen tijd* (The university of today), 1934
Like many of his Flemish-minded contemporaries, philosopher Edgar De Bruyne published mainly in Dutch. As a result, he shut himself off to some extent from the international forum, even though the importance of his work on medieval aesthetics was highly appreciated by, for instance Umberto Eco
(Antwerp, Letterenhuis)

a political career within the Catholic Flemish People's Party (Katholieke Vlaamse Volkspartij). In 1945 he was involved in the creation of the Christian People's Party (Christelijke Volkspartij, or CVP). He was even briefly minister of Colonies in 1946.

Like his very unlike-minded successor Jaap Kruithof, De Bruyne was certainly not the sort of intellectual who shut himself up in an ivory tower. He was also extraordinarily erudite. His *Études d'esthétique médiévale* (1946) were a veritable treasure trove for Umberto Eco, who borrowed from it a 'cathedral of quotes' in *The Name of the Rose* (1980). In 2003, Eco was the high-profile keynote speaker at a tribute to De Bruyne organised by the Ghent jurist Marcel Storme. 'Everything written about medieval aesthetics before is incomplete, and everything written about it afterwards is in its debt.' The words Eco puts in the mouth of the aged Ubertino on the beauty of women's breasts is literally a medieval sermon about the Song of Songs recorded by De Bruyne. As a supporter of the Flemish movement, however, the Ghent professor was deeply committed to publishing in Dutch, so a considerable amount of his work remained inaccessible to the Italian writer.

But De Bruyne made much less of an impression on his students and the general public, in contrast to Apostel, Kruithof and Vermeersch. He was not exactly a rhetorical prodigy either, recalls Storme: '(He was) more of a thinker who slowly dictated his thoughts to us.'

That Kruithof ended up taking over from De Bruyne was only due to the intervention of fate — if one could call it that. In fact, the chair had been reserved for Johan Grooten, but De Bruyne's young assistant died tragically in his bath.

Jaap Kruithof graduated under De Bruyne and studied in Paris with the Hegel expert Jean Hyppolite, phenomenologist Maurice Merleau-Ponty and political philosopher Erich Weil. Here he became a self-declared Marxist. His dissertation was about *Het uitgangspunt van Hegels ontologie* (The starting point of Hegel's ontology) (1958). His inaugural address, however, dealt with *De moraal in onze samenleving* (Morality in our society), and would soon turn out to be a bank on the future.

## The academic as public intellectual

Apostel and Kruithof were classic examples of the new type of public intellectual of the 1960s. Their impact was huge, and this also had to do with a new manner of teaching. Etienne Vermeersch recalls the immense difference between the didactic approach of his professors in Classical Philology, on the one hand, and Philosophy on the other. The classicists in Ghent were not accustomed to students asking questions; at best, they were able to translate classical texts beautifully. A pedantic atmosphere prevailed. Boys and girls were seated separately and did little else than diligently take down what the professor dictated.

How different things were in the open and progressive atmosphere of Philosophy! During seminar exercises, the students were given assignments concerning a range of

(left)
**Etienne Vermeersch**
(Photo Saskia Vanderstichele)

(centre)
**Freddy Mortier**
(Ghent, Universiteitsarchief)

(right)
**Koen Raes**
(Ghent, Universiteitsarchief)

themes (the death penalty, suicide, euthanasia, asceticism …) that would be discussed extensively the following week. Thorough preparation was required. The students were challenged to engage in discussion with their young and highly motivated professors. The rigid, stiff hierarchy melted away; students were equals. Leo Apostel really did believe that his students had read as much as he had, and set the bar for his courses 'inhumanly high', as he chivalrously admitted later. But during exams he left the auditorium, so that the students could write to their heart's content. Apostel was too shy to teach large groups, but in smaller groups one could interrupt him constantly and in interviews he quickly impressed with his superior knowledge. 'A fantastic teacher', recalls Freddy Mortier, who can speak from experience. He describes how Apostel referred to himself as a 'walking encyclopaedia'. 'After ritually excusing himself for his "bad memory" — Apostel had a formidable memory — he spouted off dozens of references to all kinds of publications that we had to read as quickly as possible.' The Socratic wisdom of 'I know that I know nothing' was convincingly demonstrated each time afresh. But it worked. Apostel was also extraordinarily generous with his time. Since he only had two hours of logic exercises on Mondays, he divided the students into workgroups so that after a while, he could spend more or less the whole day, from 8 o'clock in the morning until evening, discussing with them in a pub.

Yet it was mainly Jaap Kruithof who convinced the young Mortier that he was in the right place studying philosophy and ethics. 'A man who conducted a sort of "jihad of reason" against the conventions and trite beliefs of the public at large, that's how it seemed to me.' Kruithof did not teach classes about his subject *per se* and sent all the histories of philosophy back to the library. Students could go and read them there for themselves. He refused to speak in front of the students about his own specialisation, Hegel. Instead, he took up all kinds of current topics in a completely unconventional way: the abortion issue, the Bilderberg conference, the revolution in Iran … it led to classes that made students think and understand *why* cultural resistance against the shah could lead to the rise of the ayatollahs. Kruithof simply wanted to show his students the world. He got them reading foreign newspapers: *Le Monde* and *Newsweek*, but also *Afrique-Asie*, for different ways of looking at the same things.

Kruithof could also be particularly harsh when he wanted to make something clear. Once, for example, he forced students to say 'Allah is great' when handing in

**The Primrose Museum, or Dealing (Differently) with Things, 2009**
Lateral thinker Jaap Kruithof left behind not only an extensive oeuvre, but also a remarkable collection of thousands of found objects, the result of his passion for collecting. The collection is a moving indictment of our utilitarian throwaway society.
(Ghent, Huis van Alijn, exhibition on Jaap Kruithof)

their exams in order to test the limits of their docility. Or he flung open the windows of the classroom in the depth of winter to let the (elitist) law students feel what it was like to be poor in the freezing cold.

As critical and socially engaged professors, Apostel and Kruithof also made themselves heard outside the walls of the Blandijn. Publications like *Jeugd voor de muur* (Youth against the wall) — which dealt frankly with sex and sexuality — and notable television appearances resonated far and wide. Jaap Kruithof in particular liked to provoke, and shocked the bourgeois mainstream with his blunt views on sexuality and moral conventions. Kruithof's ideas about the role of the academic as a public intellectual were as simple as they were powerful: 'There is a time for pure, professionally oriented production, and a time for making that production relevant to a wider community' — something he certainly did with flair.

When he retired, Kruithof deposited a detailed typed bundle entitled *Personalia* at the Ghent University Library. Like his collection — Museum Primrose — we can read the stirring stocktaking of his life story as the 'ultimate plea for a different way of dealing with things', in this case a different way of dealing with an academic career.

From the time he moved to Mortsel in 1974, Kruithof travelled about 'town and country, especially the Marolles in Brussels, to save cheap stuff from destruction', as he describes it. In this way, he built up a collection of thousands of objects from the period

1850-1940. When Kruithof passed away in 2009, the House of Alijn in Ghent exhibited the collection for the first time. This curious 'museum' is now part of the collection of the MAS in Antwerp. Kruithof's *Personalia* also invite reflection on the judgement of intrinsic value, especially at a time when quality control of academic production is primarily based on quantitative criteria and societal 'valorisation' is translated in mere economic terms. For every object that he brought home from the flea market, Kruithof made an index card with descriptive information and a number. In his study was a card catalogue filled with detailed information about his public appearances. His own publications took up three shelves of his bookcase, all neatly arranged in chronological order.

Kruithof rarely wrote scholarly articles, but he did write books, countless occasional pieces, opinions, editorials and interventions on urgent issues of the day. In addition, he gave more than a hundred interviews, of which most have been preserved in their entirety. Between 1954 and 1996 he gave more than 2,000 lectures. The audience ranged from 15 to 300 and was highly diverse: students, women, senior citizens, doctors, nurses, teachers, service clubs, environmental groups, trade unions … In addition, Kruithof supported a variety of think tanks, such as Charta 91 and Gaia, and was a member of numerous social organisations and associations, including the Protestant student club, the Liberal Flemish Students Association (Liberaal Vlaams Studentenverbond, or LVSV), the Humanist Association (Humanistisch Verbond, or HV), the Belgian Socialist Party (BSP, from 1956 to 1965), the Union Belgium-DDR, the Masereelfonds and Peace (Vrede). He was never a member of a Masonic lodge. He was asked twice, but refused on principle, knowing full well that it would mean that certain doors would always be closed to him.

## Moral sciences and organised freethinking

In the early years, Kruithof and Apostel were both active in the Humanist Association (Humanistisch Verbond, or HV), which was founded in 1951. The binding element of the HV was free thought in the broadest sense. Freethinking had cast off the rabid anticlericalism of the nineteenth century and sought to establish its own institutions and organisations parallel to the Church for people who had meanwhile rejected religious morality. Thanks to ideological segregation, pillarisation and subsidised freedom, the Catholic religion had no problem maintaining itself on all levels of (public) education. But in times of accelerated secularisation after the Second World War, the Church was reluctantly forced to accept philosophical pluralism. In the School Pact of 1958 a course in non-denominational ethics was made possible as a general 'elective' intended for students who did not want to take the course on (Catholic) religion. In 1961, 30 to 40% of the students took ethics instead of religion. The subject had no official status, however, and the teachers were not specifically trained for it. In the humanities, anyone with the equivalent of a master's degree (licentiate) could teach ethics. The growing demand in secondary education for university-trained ethics teachers increasingly made itself felt.

Kruithof and Apostel took advantage of this need to make ethics, 'that second-class substitute for religion', into a fully fledged subject. They were the driving force behind the degree programme in Moral Sciences in Ghent, which was meant to give teachers of non-denominational ethics a specific scientific, philosophical and pedagogical education. They viewed morality as something universal and wanted to give it a scientific basis, independent of dogmas or supernatural influences.

The programme was very broadly conceived and interdisciplinary, with many optional courses from other faculties. To analyse moral problems, it was necessary to have contemporary scientific approaches. Kruithof pointed to the importance of sociology for ethics; Apostel emphasised epistemology, logic and psychology, and kindred spirits Lucien De Coninck, William De Coster and Philip Polk contributed insights from biology, psycho-pedagogy and ecology.

Thanks to the support of the HV and good contacts with the socialist ULB professor Henri Janne, who became minister of National Education and Culture in 1963, the programme of Moral Sciences was put on the map relatively quickly, after only two years of preparation. It was a big boost for free thought in Flanders, which could now rely on expert teachers. When the Parents' Association for Ethics (Oudervereniging voor de Moraal, or OVM) and the Union of Freethinking Associations (Unie van Vrijzinnige Verenigingen, or UVV) claimed the right to appoint ethics teachers, it tempered the prevailing enthusiasm. It was feared that a freethinking Church was in the making. Etienne Vermeersch, for example, was not in favour of an 'episcopacy of ethics'. For similar reasons, Kruithof and Apostel took distance from the HV and organised freethinking, which reinforced the walls of ideological segregation instead of breaking them down.

The philosophers of Ghent lost the round. In 1994, Flemish minister of education Luc Van den Bossche institutionalised non-denominational ethics as an ideological subject in public education. At the same time, he recognised the Council for Inspection and Guidance of Non-Denominational Ethics (Raad voor Inspectie en Begeleiding niet-confessionele Zedenleer, or RIBZ), with UGent alumnus Karel Poma as its first president. The RIBZ had exactly the same function as the bishops' conference, but of course less power. Freddy Mortier confirms the historical foresight of his teachers. He describes organised freethinking as 'a small chapel' that acts as the biggest public lackey of the Church. 'In our system of subsidised freedom, freethinking in this way simply upholds the dominance of the Catholic Church in terms of subsidies.' Patrick Loobuyck's plea for an independent, obligatory and generally formative course on Ideology, Ethics and Philosophy (Levensbeschouwing, Ethiek en Filosofie, or LEF) in all educational networks can be seen in this context. It is a good example of progressive thinking in times of secularisation, (mental) de-pillarisation and increasing religious diversity.

## A new conflict over neutrality

The success of the degree programme in Moral Sciences was initially a thorn in the side of the CVP (Christian People's Party). It was only a question of time before a new ideological conflict flared up, with Ghent University once again at the focal point. It started with the interpretation of the concept of 'neutrality'. The Catholics believed that faith was a superior form of knowledge, inviolable and immune to modern science. Free research rejected the supernatural and was therefore not neutral in religious matters. In the slipstream of the conflicts with the Church in the nineteenth century, neutrality ended up being at odds with academic freedom and the possibility of studying religion scientifically.

For Apostel and Kruithof, neutrality meant something quite different. With a number of religious progressives, they strove for a pluralistic form of education in which professors and students would get to know each other's ideology in a spirit of tolerance, particularly in ideologically sensitive subjects. The state university of Ghent was the ideal place to put that neutrality into practice. They set a good example by inviting guest lecturers from other faiths or with opposing points of view.

This was not the sort of education that Catholic Flanders wanted. Adjunct minister of national education and culture Renaat Van Elslande spoke of an 'offensive' on the part of non-Christian milieus that was meant to separate Flemish intellectuals from the faith. The pluralistic ideal of Apostel and Kruithof threatened 'Christian morality's true message of salvation'. That Ghent University had become rationalist and positivist was echoed in CVP circles. There no longer seemed to be a place for devout students. Catholic schools warned of godless professors who coupled societal engagement with a scientific world view. Crises of faith were indeed frequent among students at Ghent beginning in the years 1960-1970. The freethinking professors only reinforced this mental emancipation process. Historian Marc Reynebeau formulates it thus: 'Looking back on those student years, I always have the feeling that, on Monday mornings with Jaap, faith (in the broad sense) was evaporating from me, of its own accord, like a pool of water drying up in bright sunlight after a time. How could I keep "believing" (and not just in the religious sense) in that den of rationalism and positivism that is traditionally Ghent University?'

The Bruges bishop Emile De Smedt took the lead in the Catholic attacks on the Ghent faculty of Arts and Philosophy as a breeding ground for free thought. The demands of the bishops and the CVP were clear: the concept of neutrality as outlined in the School Pact of 1958 had to be applied at the state universities just as it was at primary and secondary schools. Professors were to be strictly neutral with respect to the tensions between faith and science. Catholic students were not to be alienated from their religion and their social environment.

For Ghent University, however, this negative interpretation of the concept of neutrality was incompatible with academic freedom, which was at the heart of education and research. Rector Bouckaert and the Ghent Academic Council responded adamantly. Pluralism was put forward as an asset: 'At a time when all intellectual movements and philosophical convictions, in a spirit of cooperation, are seeking points of contact for dialogue, the only pluralistic university institution in the country is being pushed backwards for the benefit of free institutions with a primarily one-sided philosophical orientation.'

At the state universities, all opinions were represented among the professors as well as the students. The professors who taught the philosophical courses represented different ideologies. Pluralism promoted tolerance. Students with different backgrounds were brought into contact with one another and learned to respect other opinions. The board of governors declared that the faculty of Arts and Philosophy 'has in no way fallen short of the objectivity required of a university' and implored the public to see that the CVP was acting in the spirit of past school battles and ideological segregation.

## Pluralism in practice

Kruithof and Apostel were in favour of a pluralism that would abolish such segregation. Apostel was by no means a rabid anti-Catholic. He was a Freemason and wrote a book about atheist spirituality and religiosity. It was his great aim to build bridges between ideologies, between believers and non-believers, between world views. Apostel wanted to create an interfaith training in which all religions of the world were taught. For his part, the bishop was even welcome to appoint the professor of Roman Catholic religion. The bishop of Ghent, Leonce Van Peteghem, was favourable to the

**Leo Apostel in his office in Ghent, 1986**
(Brussels, CAVA, photo Francis Heylighen)

idea, according to Marcel Storme, who was involved in the rapprochement between Catholic and freethinking professors. He himself thought it was a brilliant example of pluralism: trying to understand what the other thinks with respect for each other's convictions. In the same spirit of openness and tolerance, he was one of the initiators of the 'Park Hotel conversations'. This now-demolished hotel on Ghent's south side was where intellectuals with differing views met regularly between 1959 and 1970 for an in-depth exchange of ideas. It led — not coincidentally in the period between the Second Vatican Council and the encyclical *Humanae Vitae* — to mutual understanding. However, Van Peteghem was called to order by the Belgian Bishops' Conference: everything that was Catholic belonged in Leuven, not Ghent.

Avowing pluralism is not so difficult, but putting it into practice is another matter. Leo Apostel even suffered a serious bout of depression because of it in 1965. There was the failure of the plan to establish a pluralistic university in Antwerp, averse to any form of ideological segregation. The confrontation with power and its machinations was a severe disappointment for Apostel. That same year, the dream of having an interdisciplinary, pluralistic faculty in Ghent also ran aground after five years of negotiations, not only because of the power of the bishops but also because of a veto from the faculties of Medicine and Engineering.

In 1970 he sent up another trial balloon. He wanted to reduce discord in the 'ideological sciences' by appointing two lecturers to each position. Only in this way could objectivity be achieved. More specifically, he had in mind subjects in the Philosophy section. A 'boundless proliferation' of teaching positions and chairs was not a good idea, however. In addition to liberal teachers (Apostel, Kruithof, Vermeersch), there would be new, 'religious' instructors, while the teachers who belonged to a 'definite church community' (Boehm, Janssens) would acquire two distinctly liberal lecturers. Five full-time appointments in Philosophy could be justified by the increasing number of students in that period. The fact that the logic of pluralism dictated that students would have no freedom to choose between one type of lecturer and the other was more difficult to sell. Both the freethinking and religious camps alike were concerned about the influence of the other camp on students. Apostel therefore provided for a system of rotation, a form of team-teaching that was unfortunately too far ahead of its time. Rector Daniël Vandepitte put the proposal to the advisory board at the end of January 1970. As expected, there were legal obstacles and practical objections, or at least they were advanced.

## Ethical topics on the agenda

'We have not achieved our dream', wrote Apostel wistfully on the occasion of Jaap Kruithof's imminent farewell to the university. Nevertheless, the Ghent philosophers had a great deal of influence in terms of getting ethically sensitive topics on the political agenda. Kruithof and Apostel never manned the barricades for the legalisation of abortion or euthanasia. Their assistants, however, actively engaged in public debates from the outset. Even before he took his doctorate under Kruithof with a dissertation on the early work of Karl Marx, Hugo Van den Enden published a scientific analysis of the ideological controversies surrounding abortion in 1971. *Abortus pro/contra* was the first Dutch-language contribution in book form to a debate that, at the time, was primarily conducted on the street and in the media. Van den Enden lucidly set out the arguments for and against the moral admissibility and desirability of legalisation. In this way he arrived at a personal position in favour of legalisation that he justified ethically, demonstrating in this way the method of critical thinking that he had mastered as a moral philosopher.

Long before the abortion law became reality in 1990, Van den Enden also played an important role, alongside Etienne Vermeersch, in the fight for a dignified end of life and for euthanasia. Vermeersch wrote his first text on euthanasia in 1961 as a student of Kruithof. Ten years later, he was the first to break the taboo on the then Belgian Radio and Television (Belgische Radio en Televisie, or BRT), pointing out that people did not have to suffer unnecessarily. Empowerment and self-determination should take precedence over medical obstinacy and paternalism. In 1983 the association Right to Die with Dignity (Recht op Waardig Sterven, or RWS) was founded, with Van den Enden as its inspiring vice-president. Numerous lectures, articles and books paved the way for the euthanasia legislation that was finally enacted in 2002 under the 'purple' coalition government of Guy Verhofstadt.

The legislation did not silence public debate on euthanasia — on the contrary. An important opinion maker is physician Marc Cosyns, associated with the department of Family Medicine and Primary Care (Huisartsgeneeskunde en Eerstelijnsgezondheidszorg). He looks at the problem of the end of life from the perspective of the doctor–patient relationship and lays bare — often in a highly personal way — the sore points of the euthanasia legislation. He was summoned before an investigating judge three times, but was each time exonerated. In 2006, dean Jean-Louis Pannier submitted a complaint to the Order of Physicians that was declared inadmissible, but it nevertheless put an end to Cosyns's doctoral research.

Hugo Van den Enden died in 2007 under palliative sedation at the University Hospital of Ghent (UZ Gent) after seventeen days in an irreversible coma, in circumstances he had fought against his entire life.

## The intellectual's 'Werdegang' in Flanders

Etienne Vermeersch developed his world view through intense interaction with Apostel and Kruithof and his fellow students. He gradually noticed that in discussions of ethical problems, he no longer needed to appeal to the existence of God. When he left the Jesuits in 1958, he turned his back on the Church, but his faith did not vanish overnight. During this period, doubt and uncertainty formed the basis of his existence. Until he realised that God and the religious dimension were fully and finally 'gone' from his thinking. It was not until many years later that Vermeersch analysed this process rationally.

In 2008, the weekly *Knack* proclaimed Vermeersch 'Flanders' Greatest Intellectual'. In a similar survey from 1989, he was stuck in second place, right after … Leo Apostel. Jaap Kruithof was number three.

It is interesting to note that the three icons of freethinking Flanders categorically refused to form a school. They radically adhered to the Humboldtian ideal of aca-

**Jaap Kruithof takes up the gauntlet against the Vlaams Blok**
Charta '91 was founded in response to Zwarte Zondag (Black Sunday), when the Vlaams Blok broke through electoral boundaries in Flanders. Jaap Kruithof was present at the founding meeting, next to royal commissioner for migration Paula Dhondt, VU member of parliament Nelly Maes and writers Hugo Claus and Tom Lanoye.
(Ghent, Amsab-ISG, photo Filip Claus)

demic freedom. The goal was to educate critical *Einzelgängers* who would forge their own paths.

The philosophers of 'the Ghent school' were also seldom in agreement. They often had incendiary quarrels that spilled out into the corridors of the Blandijn. In the auditorium, they gave classes *against* each other and criticised one another's philosophical ideas. Sometimes it was very personal. In a letter of 30 December 1979, Van den Enden accused Kruithof of repeatedly indulging in 'insinuating, insulting or derogatory value judgements and ideologically suggestive personal attacks on other department members', and of refusing 'an egalitarian, informal and personal basis for conversation and relationships in an autocratic-individualistic and thus authoritarian way'. Each time he had set himself up 'as judge and jury in his own and others' affairs'. 'Best wishes for 1980 — as far as I'm concerned ... to a better relationship!'

At his farewell celebration, Kruithof formulated sharp criticisms of his own department, after which he received an enraged letter from Etienne Vermeersch. 'The rudest letter I ever received in my life.'

But even more fundamental than their internal frictions was the fact that the Ghent philosophers were witness to a shift in academic culture that to a certain extent would make living anachronisms of them all. Apostel left the university early, in 1979, and as a relative outsider worried about his intellectual legacy a decade later: 'A good intellectual cannot be a good professional scholar, and a good professional cannot be

Jaap Kruithof, *De Zingever* (The giver of meaning), 1968

a good intellectual.' Freddy Mortier feared that Kruithof was the last 'solitary, book-writing yet engaged academic', who, 'without being provincial as a thinker, nevertheless emphasised the critical role of the detached scholar in his own cultural community'.

Etienne Vermeersch, not without a hint of pride, shows me his CV on his computer. In his long and extremely varied list of publications, it is striking how little the 'production' of Flanders' Greatest Intellectual measures up to today's bibliometric standards. I laugh when I tell him that with these publications he probably wouldn't get very far in today's university. He describes this development — rightly — as an impoverishment for the humanities. Researchers today specialise in extremely small niches and attain great heights with publications that almost nobody reads. Mortier already predicted it twenty years ago: 'The reference point of the scientist that survives the new competitive requirements is in all probability the good old ivory tower.' Koen Raes, another student of Kruithof's, observed that neither the university nor the students today see themselves as the 'conscience of society'.

And something has indeed been lost since Kruithof wrote *De Zingever* (The giver of meaning), his first book for a broad public, in 1968. Not that the Ghent ethicists no longer fulfil their social role. The work of Sigrid Sterckx, Heidi Mertes and the Bioethics Institute Ghent on stem-cell research, in vitro fertilisation and organ transplants usually remains under the media radar, but is no less important for all that — on the contrary. Several members of the department of Philosophy and Moral Sciences are also facilitators of De Maakbare Mens ('makeable man', though in Dutch it is gender-neutral), a non-profit humanist organisation occupied with critically informing the public about ethical and societal themes. Johan Braeckman, Ignaas Devisch and Heidi Mertes served successively as president. In 2013, moreover, Braeckman was the first to receive the Career Award of the Flemish Academy for his unwavering commitment to the field of science communication. A master storyteller, he is the ideal candidate to succeed Richard Dawkins as Professor for the Public Understanding of Science. Like Kruithof in his time, Braeckman travels the country as an 'apostle' of scientific and critical thinking. He is a welcome guest on radio and television for the way he sheds light on the theory of evolution, creationism, pseudo-science, bio-ethics, science and religion. Devisch, too, attached to the department of Family Medicine and the Artevelde College, as a regular columnist of *De Standaard* and author of *Rusteloosheid: Pleidooi voor een mateloos leven* (Restlessness: Towards a life beyond measure), among other things, is also very engaged. Both keep well clear of the academic rat race that threatens their primary activity: thinking. Braeckman even took a year of unpaid leave so that he could finally find the peace and quiet he needed to read what interested him.

The academic who continues to function in a university environment today while conducting societally relevant research tends to profile him- or herself more as an expert than as a public intellectual. An expert in a specific domain, or as a member of (bio)ethical commissions — no longer as the generally interested thinker who captures in words current societal developments and ideological tendencies, like Kruithof or Vermeersch did in their time. In this context it is probably no coincidence that the most critical views of society and ideology today no longer come from Ghent philosophers, but from clinical psychologists like Paul Verhaeghe. His bestseller *Identiteit* (Identity) contains a merciless analysis of the societal consequences of neoliberal meritocracy, which also dominates the university. Verhaeghe does not attribute these consequences to the 'loss' of norms and values, but rather to the norms and values of neoliberal society (efficiency, pursuit of profit, competition) and the lie that 'making it' is an individual responsibility. He admits, however, that the introduction of the meritocratic personnel policy in academia has (had) its positive side as well: one finally had the feeling that one had control over one's own career, independently of old boy networks, party politics, back rooms and other shady practices.

Paul Verhaeghe, *Identiteit* (Identity), 2012

## In the corridors of the Aula

Academic culture has indeed been heavily depoliticised since the 1990s. The time when deans had to run to the cabinet minister to argue in favour of appointments or promotions is over. 'My performances at the faculty council were sometimes more inspired by my conviction than by science', remembers Marcel Storme humbly. Among equally qualified candidates, the '*tjeven*' — a colloquial name for adherents of the CVP — always received preference. He had personally experienced how 'the other side' also worked in the same way.

In 1982 Storme was elected as the dean of the faculty of Law after no fewer than twenty-five voting rounds with eighteen votes against seventeen and one abstention. His opponent was the infamous Paul — 'Professor is my first name' — Ghysbrecht. It was a typical example of an ideologically coloured election of '*tjeven*' versus 'the Lodge' (effectively, Catholics versus freethinkers). Every member of the faculty council had a label. The college or the athenaeum where one had gone to secondary school was usually (but not always) a good indicator. People who knew each other supported each other. In this context 'the Lodge' (i.e. the Freemasons) constituted a powerful network, although it was (and is) in reality a highly heterogeneous and strongly divided association.

The formation of groups within the university in any case occurred largely along ideological fault lines. Historian Walter Prevenier places this in context. He is etched in the collective memory of the Blandijn as an inspired teacher of 'Introduction to Historical Criticism' in Auditorium E on Thursday mornings. Notoriously liberal and freethinking but not a member of the Lodge, he experienced the 1980-1990 transition period as an actively participating observer. The camps met on both sides to prepare for meetings and elections. It was part of the power play 'among professors' that the one camp overestimated the influence of the other and minimised its own machina-

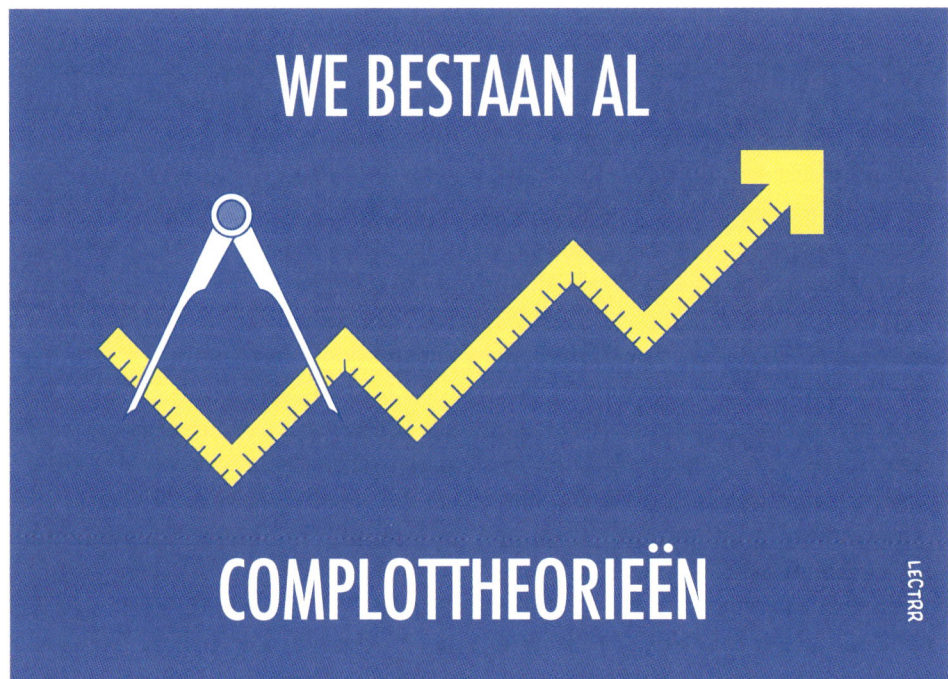

Caricature by Lectrr, 2017
Using the symbols of Freemasonry, the house cartoonist of the newspaper *De Standaard* satirises the campaign around UGent's 200th anniversary, which coincided with the unsettled rectorial elections in the spring of 2017.

tions. The blocks were always less homogeneous than they were portrayed by their opponents. For one party it was invariably the other party that set up manoeuvres and forged conspiracies. The difference between the two groups was the structure, Prevenier explains. In the case of the freethinkers, it was usually (but not necessarily) defined by membership of a Lodge and the discrete brotherhoods that facilitate the exchange of university concerns among like-minded people. The Catholics did not have such a network, but were more or less religious, church-going, Catholic by virtue of background and education, such that they found one another within the broad 'pillar' of Catholics in order to influence a dossier or win a vote. 'The *idée fixe* that "the Lodge can do everything" is of course not true', says Prevenier. There were internal tensions: liberals versus socialists, Francophones versus Dutch-speaking, conservatives versus progressives, men versus women, not to mention the personal vendettas and settling of accounts. Moreover, in elections there was always an important, almost equally large third group, the undecided, who did not belong to either of the two camps and who voted in a widely dispersed array. This was the group that needed convincing and seducing.

In the nineteenth century, the rectorship was a ceremonial function that alternated among the four faculties and was assigned to the longest-serving professor. From 1924 onwards, when the rector was given a more important role in the struggle for Dutchification, he was elected by the Academic Council, on the recommendation of the faculty whose turn it was. The Academic Council was originally the professors' corps of the university; later, the lecturers were also included. After an internal vote within this electoral college, where a two-thirds majority was required, the top three candidates were presented to the minister, who then made the final choice. The minister could therefore deviate from the order of preference recommended by the Academy

Council. The system opened the door for election campaigns and lobbying, and remained in effect until the decree of 1991 cut the umbilical cord with politics. Since then, the rector proposes himself individually as a candidate for a term of four years. Until 2013 he was appointed by a representative electoral college, in fact a merger of the representatives of ZAP (independent academic personnel), AAP (assisting academic personnel), ATP (administrative and technical personnel) and students on the faculty councils.

To ensure pluralism, the rectorate traditionally alternated between a Catholic and a freethinker. The vice-rector was then drawn 'symbolically' from the other camp. This was particularly important in order to make Ghent credible as a pluralistic university.

Notwithstanding the unwritten rules and gentlemen's agreements (ladies hardly came into play until 2013), the elections regularly spawned a host of tensions and intrigues. In 1985 the Catholic jurist Marcel Storme and the socialist historical pedagogue Karel De Clerck were candidate rectors. Neither one, however, had sufficient support to receive a two-thirds majority. And hence a third candidate was put forward: Leon De Meyer. As dean of Arts, Walter Prevenier was allowed to argue in his favour, and he did so in a particularly convincing way. He emphasised qualities De Meyer had that the other two candidates lacked, implicitly drawing a contrast between De Meyer as a moderate, reconciliation-oriented diplomat with a large network and Storme, who was painted as too obviously swayed by party politics. The tactic was a success: De Meyer became the new rector.

Eight years later, in 1993, the Liberal De Meyer was succeeded by Jacques Willems, a Catholic civil engineer. According to the unwritten rules, the vice-rector had to be freethinking and recruited from the humanities. Willems called upon voters to be guided not by ideological clichés, but by the quality of the candidate. The professor in question was the pedagogue Johan Heene, 'a serious man, moderate, highly competent as a manager, but with a Catholic stigma', says Prevenier. The murmuring in the corridors quickly made clear, however, that Willems's rational approach had to make way for classic oppositions. The three other candidate vice-rectors did not receive the necessary two-thirds majority, even after several rounds of voting. Against the background of this stalemate, Etienne Vermeersch, as a profiled freethinker, was asked by a number of colleagues from Masonic circles (of which he was not a member) to stand as candidate. The eloquent philosopher gave a resounding speech and after three rounds easily cleared the hurdle.

In any case, rectorial elections took place in a totally different setting and atmosphere than they do today. Prevenier evokes the *huis clos* of the Aula, where a limited group of professors would spend the entire day in conclave for up to twenty successive voting rounds. Equally important were the corridors, where friend and foe constantly sounded one another out as to how things were going and who was going to do what, who would 'match' as vice-rector, how convincing the speeches and interventions were, and so on. In the event of a short circuit, a new candidate had to be readied, eventually a consensus figure that nobody had anything against. If the polarisation were too great, the candidates would have to be 'dropped'. Honorary governor Herman Balthazar also recalls the old system 'in which a limited group of full professors needed many voting rounds in the Aula and backstage discussions in nearby pubs in order to reach a consensus'.

This academic culture 'among professors' finally faded into legend in 2017 once the entire university community was allowed to vote electronically, and there was not even a physical gathering in the Aula or the Pand at which candidates could present their programmes. Politically, the ideological divide has weakened since the 1990s. At the university things are no different. The autonomy of Ghent University in 1991 undid the influence of politics on professorial appointments and rectorial elections. With the extension of the right to vote to the student faculty representatives, the opaque, old-boy-network atmosphere, along with the odour of cigarettes, has gradually receded from the faculty chambers. Faculty councils are no longer divided into ideological camps. On the board of governors, the political 'colour' of professors, assistants and students is no longer so easy to determine, and has of course become more diverse. The well-coordinated duo Jacques Willems–Etienne Vermeersch, moreover, may take credit for having done a great deal to ensure that ideological oppositions ebbed away. 'Pluralism is our wealth,' says Willems, 'and that's something you only realise by working together.'

## The first female rector

The rectorial elections are about the only time when the ideological knives come out to be sharpened at Ghent University. Whoever reads *Schamper* in periods of rising election fever over the past two decades cannot escape the impression that the fight somehow lacked a subject. Major ideological differences or disputes between the '*tjeven*' and 'the Lodge' no longer seemed to exist. And yet the discord still cropped up at recent elections.

In 2013 the favourite candidate rector was Freddy Mortier, dean of Arts and Philosophy and openly Masonic. He asked Anne De Paepe, a reputed professor of Medical Genetics, to stand as candidate vice-rector and form a duo with him: a dream team in which both pluralism and gender balance was assured. A decree driven by Liberal parliamentarian and UGent alumna Fientje Moerman had determined that gender balance had to be established at the top of the university. However, the university administration made the election process needlessly complicated. For the functions of rector and vice-rector, two candidates of different gender for each position had to be proposed to the board of governors, both with a two-thirds majority of the electoral college. In a second round, the board of governors had to choose the rector and vice-rector, again by a two-thirds majority. Tiered elections, in other words. In this context, after careful consideration, Anne De Paepe joined Freddy Mortier as candidate for vice-rector.

When textile engineer Lieva Van Langenhove decided to stand for rector, Mortier and De Paepe left nothing to chance, and proposed themselves for the respective positions of vice-rector and rector as well, so that they both ran a double chance of being elected. While Anne De Paepe quickly reached the required two-thirds majority for both posts, Freddy Mortier, after his election as rector, was not as smoothly elected as vice-rector. Was this a signal that voters did not agree with their double tactics?

The dramatic turn of events took place during the meeting of the board of governors, which had the last word. The creators of the tiered system clearly had not predicted that it could work differently than the way the long-standing unwritten rules of pluralism dictated. Gender became a disruptive element. After an indicative vote, De Paepe received more votes than Mortier, after which he withdrew as candidate rector and she effortlessly achieved a two-thirds majority. In this way, De Paepe became the first female rector of UGent, and Mortier vice-rector. At the same time, her gender broke through the unwritten rules of rectorial succession: the highest office once again went to a Christian Democrat, and again to someone from the life sciences. Mortier was deeply disappointed. Not only 'the Lodge', but also certain Catholics in the upper echelons of the university felt that the gentlemen's agreement concerning rectorial succession was inviolable.

'Every way of seeing is also a way of not seeing.' Anne De Paepe, although she would have been perfectly happy with the post of vice-rector, had actually anticipated the 'unlikely hypothesis' that she might be chosen as rector. For her, it was simple: in the course of events her ambition grew, and she made it clear that she would go for the position if she got the chance. De Paepe decided that her freethinking queen-makers had never paused to consider the possibility that she might actually be chosen as rector. In their eyes she was a sidekick, not a fully fledged candidate. In any case, the election of Anne De Paepe revealed that times had changed and that the internal pluralism of Ghent University was in need of a thorough update.

## Rectorial soap opera in a festive atmosphere

To avoid a repeat of the 2013 imbroglio, the decree was rewritten again before the rectorial elections of 2017. Candidate rectors and vice-rectors had to run as gender-balanced duos and endorse the pluralistic character of the university. Dean of engineering sciences Rik Van de Walle and linguist Mieke Van Herreweghe were the first to volunteer. Bioengineer Guido Van Huylenbroeck and professor of bioanalysis Sarah De Saeger ran against them.

**Transfer of the rectorial ermine, 2013**
Vice-Rector Freddy Mortier is congratulated by his predecessor Luc Moens (pictured on the left). On 1 October 2013, Anne De Paepe (photo right) would be the first woman in the history of Ghent University to have the white ermine pinned to her right shoulder, a sartorial tradition that goes back to 1838. Since 2008, the vice-rector also wears ermine, albeit in a slightly smaller version.
(Ghent, image bank UGent, photo Hilde Christiaens)

The election battle began acridly in the media and — for the first time — on social media as well. The crucial function of the corridors of the Aula was taken over by Twitter. Instead of fostering consensus, it drove polarisation. Tweets of 140 characters were magnified and anonymous testimonies in the newspapers completed the image of a highly divided university subject to scheming and power intrigues. The old opposition between 'the Lodge' and the '*tjeven*' promptly resurfaced, harder and more ruthless than ever before.

After five digital rounds of voting in four weeks, the war of attrition was still deadlocked. In the run-up to the second voting cycle, the candidate duos struck a deal, which among other things included an increase in the number of vice-rectors. The challengers would be included along with two other professors in the rectorial team if Rik Van de Walle and Mieke Van Herreweghe finally received a two-thirds majority in the second round. The board of governors and the university community, however, were not entirely favourable to the compromise, which smacked of blatant haggling. In the sixth and seventh ballot, at least 40% of the electorate voted blank.

The voting regulations were readjusted yet again. The two-thirds majority that, according to some board members, was a crucial prerequisite for the pluralism of the university was diluted. At the end of September 2017, Rik Van de Walle and Mieke Van Herreweghe were finally elected rector and vice-rector of UGent with 71.74% of the votes after the ninth round — paradoxically, the first ballot in which a two-thirds majority was no longer required. After the gruelling election battle, the new rectorial duo will hopefully succeed in lifting the historical encumbrance once and for all and in giving a new, contemporary interpretation to the internal pluralism of UGent. So that it once again becomes a strength rather than a weakness.

## Multiperspectivism and ideological diversity in the twenty-first century

Leo Apostel noted at the beginning of the 1990s that intellectual freedom was no longer threatened by the Catholic Church, but by commercialisation and the VTM (Vlaamse Televisie Maatschappij) as a media model. Only in the neoliberal camp were people still thinking, in terms of Margaret Thatcher's credo, 'There is no such thing as society, only individuals and families'. An ideological vacuum threatened to emerge. At the university, moreover, the flattening of ideological oppositions was coupled with a rapid shift towards a technocratic policy, which excluded alternatives and opposition under that other motto, 'There is no alternative' (TINA). This had great consequences for the relationship between university and society.

Apostel looked on sorrowfully as academics increasingly shut themselves up in their ivory towers. He called for the reinvention and continuation of Enlightenment thought, and for academics to invest more in engaging with a wide public audience, even if this would not yield as much in the way of quantifiable scholarly output.

Today, this call to action has gained in topical value, not least because within that ideological vacuum, a new ideological fault line has arisen with respect to Islam. The critical, scientific approach of the Ghent philosophical school is still useful for reinventing pluralism in that context and engaging in dialogue with people and groups who think differently. The philosophy of multiperspectivism is not just about interdisciplinary cooperation in the scholarly field. In accordance with the pluralism of those days, it is also about norms and values, about how people treat one another, and how students and professors position themselves in a broader societal environment. There is, by definition, no place for the absolute rightness of a single party or opinion. Those who think they hold a monopoly on the truth are invited to think critically. 'Change of perspective' is a powerful moral learning tool. The fundamental question of how 'the other' sees the world can in this way lead to a commitment to mutual understanding and new forms of respect and tolerance in a world that is increasingly diverse. Here the laicity of organised freethinking opposes pluralism. No one promotes equality between men and women by banning the headscarf. While the aim of UGent is to reduce inequality between men and women, between 'indigenous' and 'immigrant' as much as possible, the diversity of perspectives and ideologies is an enrichment that brings the university closer to contemporary societal problems.

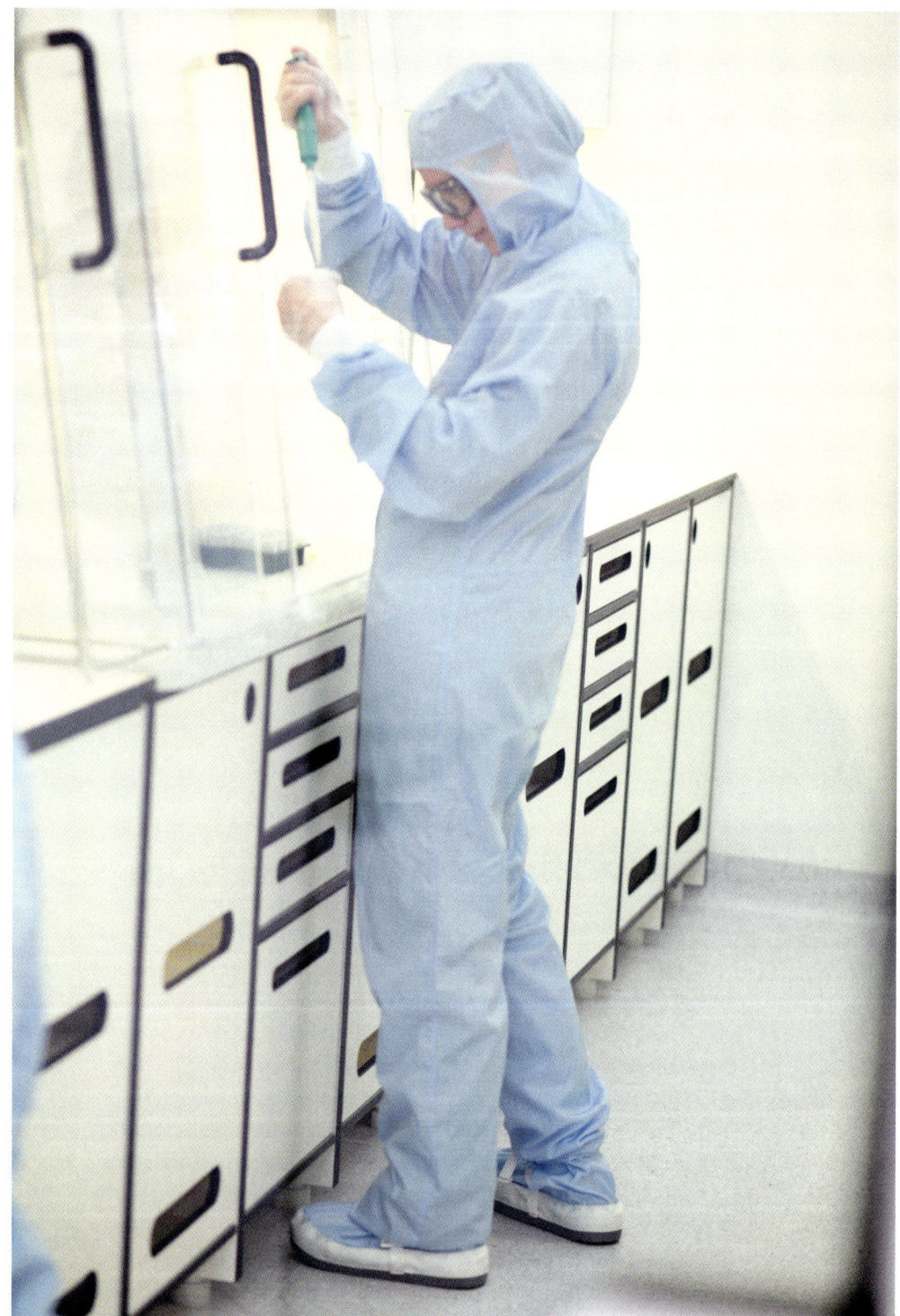

**Demonstration of multicollector ICPMS, 2008**
ICPMS or Inductively Coupled Plasma Mass Spectrometry is a sensitive technique for the chemical analysis of materials and trace analysis. Analytical chemistry has traditionally been a field in which the boundary between basic and applied research is wafer-thin. In the 1980s the department of former rector Julien Hoste was heavily involved in the Third Industrial Revolution Flanders (Derde Industriële Revolutie Vlaanderen, or DIRV), the cradle of Flanders Technology.
(Ghent, image bank UGent, photo Nele Van Canneyt)

Chapter 3

# INDUSTRY AND VALORISATION

Ghent University strives to be an 'enterprising university' with regard 'for the social and economic applications of its research results'. This mission is not new. From the very beginning, the industrial city of Ghent showed an interest in the 'technical' sciences that would foster industrialisation and technological innovation. As was the case elsewhere in Europe, this kind of 'applied' education was developed outside of the university. Special Schools were created to offer instruction on the points of contact between science and art, knowledge and action, theory and practice. The prestigious French Ecole Polytechnique (1794) served as the model for these technical education programmes. In Ghent, the faculty of Sciences fulfilled an academic bridge function with respect to the Special Schools. The city financed the buildings, with intense exchange between the university, city and industry as a result. The engineering sciences gradually became the best-regarded disciplines of higher education in Belgium. The number of foreign students was high. During the interwar period, Agricultural Sciences and Veterinary Medicine were also formed 'outside' the university. Notwithstanding the latent hostility of the four founding faculties towards the 'utilitarian' character of the educational programmes, the Technical Schools finally became the faculty of Applied Sciences in 1957.

**The Ghent Muinkmeersen, 1837**
The Muinkmeersen behind St Peter's Abbey were undeveloped and rural until the construction of the railway between Ghent and Mechelen in 1837. The city was industrialising rapidly. The university played an important role in this process.
(Ghent, Stadsarchief, Atlas Goetghebuer)

Logically, it was in the applied sciences that the first public-private partnerships on behalf of the government or business arose. Commissioned research is less recent than we imagine. From the end of the nineteenth century onwards, the government encouraged relationships between the university and industry by creating new financial channels. In 1929 the Special Bureau for Science-Industry Relations was formed, a cooperation between the NFWO (National Research Foundation) and the Central Industrial Committee (Comité Central Industriel, or CCI), the forerunner of the Union of Belgian Companies (Verbond van Belgische Ondernemingen, or VBO). In fact, it would form the core of the Agency for Innovation through Science and Technology (Agentschap voor Innovatie door Wetenschap en Technologie, or IWT). During the German occupation (December 1944), the Institute for the Advancement of Scientific Research in Industry and Agriculture (Instituut tot Aanmoediging van het Wetenschappelijk Onderzoek in Nijverheid en Landbouw, or IWONL) was quietly established and would form the immediate forerunner of the IWT, which recently joined forces with the Agency for Enterprise and was rechristened the Flemish Agency for Innovation and Enterprise (Vlaams Agentschap Innoveren en Ondernemen, or VLAIO).

At the beginning of the 1970s, the structures for public-private cooperation received new impetus from the government. The so-called third and fourth streams of money from the private sector gained in importance with respect to the first and second streams of money from the government, first in theory and then in practice. Some authors even speak of the second academic revolution since Wilhelm von Humboldt. The cooperation between university and industry assumed new forms thanks to the increased marketing of inventions made by scientists within a university context. Technological innovation and economic valorisation of research go hand in hand with the creation of spin-offs and 'technology transfer' from the university to the business world via patents and licences.

## The School of Arts and Crafts

During the first half of the nineteenth century, Ghent grew indisputably into the most important industrial city on the European continent. A second Manchester, as Lieven Bauwens had predicted when he smuggled the spinning jenny over the Channel. The economic stimuli of William I, the new overseas markets of the Dutch colonies, and the Ghent–Terneuzen Canal ensured increasing industrial expansion and affluence from the 1820s onwards.

The Dutch government had made industry and trade a spearhead, and hence was quite positively disposed towards the increasing demand for technical education and applied research. Professors of mathematics and physics were eminently suited to teaching the new applications. The goal was the education of citizens who would unlock 'new sources of prosperity' or make better use of existing sources.

The students were preferably children of parents who were active in the industrial (artisanal) classes of society. Not only the sons of artisans, but also the industrial classes in the broader sense, including children of labourers, were welcome. The emphasis on specific target groups was entirely consistent with the philosophy of the schools for Arts et Métiers or Arts and Crafts in France and England in this period. C.A. Le Normant,

**Laboratory of Applied Chemistry**
The city recognised the importance of scientific innovation for industrial development, and at the end of the 1850s financed an applied chemistry laboratory for the training of engineers. It was housed in the former Jesuit monastery in Voldersstraat. The Braun School would be located in this building later on. Today it is the headquarters of the faculty of Law and Criminology. François Donny, autodidact in chemistry and amateur photographer, was given responsibility for the laboratory in 1858.
(Ghent, Universiteitsarchief)

overseer of education in the Ghent prison, published his *Plan ter vestiging van eene school voor handwerkslieden in welke 400 jongelingen aanhoudend in de kunsten en ambachten zullen onderwezen worden, zonder iets aan den staat te kosten* (Plan to establish a school for artisans in which 400 youth will be continually instructed in arts and crafts with no cost to the state) in 1825. On 13 May 1825 the Dutch government answered this need with a royal decree that introduced applied chemistry and mechanics at the six universities in the United Kingdom of the Netherlands. The goal was to familiarise manufacturers, artists and craftsmen with the science on which their professions were based and to perfect their mastery in practice. The introduction of applied chemistry and mechanics aroused great interest primarily in the industrialised cities. The government was thus optimistic that this branch of science would flourish in both Leiden and Ghent. Mining and forestry, however, went to Liège.

Philippe De Lens, who in 1825 was not only chairman of the College of Curators of Ghent University but also governor of the Province of East Flanders, saw the royal decree as an opportunity to establish a School of Arts and Crafts in addition to the university. The city council saw only advantages for the 'numerous factories based here' and worked 'decisively' on the 'expansion and perfection of the industriousness of the Dutch people'. The factories of Ghent had at their disposal large numbers of 'industrious, diligent and inquisitive yet not inexperienced artisans' who were ready to receive theoretical instruction profitably and put it into practice. The quarters of the former cloister of St Agnes (in Lindenlei) were placed at the government's disposal for the establishment of the new school. The university had receivership, some classes were taught in university buildings, and the school could make use of the university's collections. William I was prepared to appoint two extra professors for 'Chemistry and Mechanics, adapted to the applied arts'. Cornelis A. Bergsma, a young doctor from Hoorn, and Jean-François Lemaire, a mathematics teacher from the athenaeum of Tournai, were to have the honour.

Both Bergsma and Lemaire gave public lessons – free of charge, and in Dutch. These took place every day of the week, including Saturday, beginning at 7 p.m. The Maatschappij voor 't Nut van 't Algemeen (Society for the General Good) also organised an adult education programme at the School of Arts and Crafts from 1827 onwards. Moreover, it was highly successful: there were sometimes more than two hundred in attendance. Ordinary workmen also took an interest in the public lessons. Lemaire wrote a small handbook especially for them, *De meetkunst op de kunsten en ambachten toegepast* (Geometry applied to arts and crafts). According to the *Messager des Sciences et des Arts*, numerous labourers, who hardly knew in which kingdom they lived, came to school every day with incredible diligence. Thanks to these lessons, they saw how the principles of geometry and mechanics were of practical use in their professions. The School of Arts and Crafts had thus a 'moralising' influence on youth who otherwise spent their free time in idleness or, worse yet, in debauchery.

Apart from its attraction for free students, the school had 195 registered students as of 1 November 1828. In only two years and with only two professors, the School of Arts and Crafts had grown into a sturdy pillar of higher education in Ghent.

## The success of the Special Schools

The Belgian Revolution of 1830 nipped the success of the School of Arts and Crafts in the bud. Like so many other North Netherlanders, Bergsma wisely packed his bags and would continue his career at the University of Utrecht. Even though the faculty of Sciences was abolished, the Provisory Government decided to keep the School of Arts and Crafts and the public lessons in Ghent, knowing how important this was for the industrialisation of East and West Flanders. Lemaire was appointed in Liège, where he would become rector in 1838. The two were succeeded by Charles Morren and Edouard Jaequemyns.

Jaequemyns had a doctorate in the sciences, pharmacy and medicine (Liège) and in chemistry (Berlin), and taught at the athenaeum in Ghent. As secretary of the faculty, he fulfilled a pivotal function at the School of Arts and Crafts. In 1843 he would leave the school for the private sector. Because of his great success in education, he had attracted the attention of the most important industrialists in the city. Jaequemyns became owner of a large brick factory in Minderhout, in the Campine near Antwerp, after helping found and expand the flax factory La Linière Gantoise in Ghent. He also rendered useful services in the area of agronomy and the improvement of agriculture in Belgium. Jaequemyns, who died unexpectedly in 1874, was a good example of an enlightened nineteenth-century bourgeois citizen who, thanks to the close ties between science and industrialisation, was able to amass a considerable fortune.

The definitive reorganisation of Belgian higher education in 1835 brought with it the independence (and also the Frenchification) of the School of Arts and Crafts. The two state universities divided the tasks between them. In Ghent, there was education in Arts and Crafts, Civil Engineering, and Bridges and Roads; in Liège, Arts and Crafts and Mining. In 1838, Ghent acquired the monopoly in educating civil engineers with the acquisition of the Ecole Spéciale du Génie Civil. This ensured close ties to the ministry of Public Works. The Ecole des Arts et Manufactures was more practically oriented and had greater status. For both schools, there was an Ecole Préparatoire. Students were required to pass an entrance exam and rigorous discipline was the order of the day, just as in the French polytechnics.

The education system in the Special Schools was characterised by a form of permanent evaluation *avant la lettre*, with rehearsals and assignments that counted in the final marks. Each absence or irregularity was registered, each task evaluated. The various subjects were assigned coefficients that indicated their value within the overall course of study. The Special Schools were annexes of the reinstated faculty of Sciences. In this way, the professors continued to be attached to the university, which ensured the theoretical basis of instruction and offered an ideal combination of academic and polytechnic education. Moreover, those appointed in 1835 were not unknowns: Joseph Plateau was appointed for *Physique appliquée aux arts*; city architect Louis Roelandt for *Architecture civile*.

A good example of a self-made man who, thanks to his university education, was able to build a large company was Désiré Van Monckhoven, who graduated in 1862 as doctor in the natural sciences. He grew up fatherless in the impoverished neighbourhood around Sint-Pieternieuwstraat. As a sixteen-year-old, he wrote two handbooks: *Handboek der Scheikunde* (Handbook of Chemistry) and *Elementen der Fysica* (Elements of Physics). Doing so gave him a lasting interest in photography. When he was twenty-two, in 1856, Van Monckhoven published his *Traité général de photographie* (General treatise on photography), a standard work with which he acquired international fame. After completing high school, he apprenticed with the professional photographer Charles D'Hoy in Ghent. At that time, photography was just beginning to conquer the world. The work enabled the young Désiré to pursue higher education and gain additional mastery of the wonders of the photographic process. In 1863 he took out a patent on the dialytic enlarger, an apparatus that he himself would use in his photo studio Rabending und Monckhoven in Vienna, where he lived from 1866 to 1872.

Upon returning to Ghent, he set up a small factory for the production of photographic paper behind his home in Krijgsgasthuisstraat. In 1879 he developed silver bromide gelatine plates, which formed the basis for the democratisation (and commercialisation) of photography. His company grew into a large factory at Einde Were, which after his premature death at the age of forty-eight flourished under the direction of his widow, Hortense Tackels. Van Monckhoven was also the proud owner of a small observatory, where he made astronomical and meteorological observations in his free time. After his death, his widow offered the university her husband's telescope. It took the university six years to finish paying for the device. Nevertheless, this 'inheritance' would grow into the observatory on the roof of the Plateau Building, where the Armand Pien Public Observatory would later be located.

## The second industrial revolution

In 1854, the Ecole des Arts et Manufactures was reorganised to better align theory with practice and to make the school more accessible without sacrificing quality. The 'industrial class' was still under-represented in higher education. The importance of the school in a city and country where so much capital was poured into industrialisation had to be better positioned on the market. The length of the study programme was limited to three years and emphasis was shifted to knowledge that could lead to innovation. Practical experience was essential to the education of industrial engineers, and from then on four factory visits per month were organised, among other things. The Special Schools also took advantage of technological and societal changes: in 1867 a new course in railway development was introduced, and the course *Technologie des matières textiles* (Materials technology for textiles) in 1869.

Engineers from Ghent could start leading major works in Belgium or abroad immediately after their studies. They received outstanding jobs in Italy, France, Spain, Russia and the Americas. The strict work ethic and difficult exams ensured a good selection process, so that the job market did not become saturated as it was in the liberal professions. The only thing lacking was engineers who could write well. Therefore the *exercises pratiques de rédaction* were set up in 1869 '*chose importante dans toutes les carrières et malheureusement trop negligée*'. The Special Schools were also the first to introduce courses in English and German from 1872 onwards. Given the advanced state of engineering science in Germany and England, this was indispensable.

Two academic inspectors from the Ecole Préparatoire, Charles Andries and Emmanuel Boudin, imposed their 'iron' vision on education. The curriculums were regularly revised and oriented towards specific professional knowledge. As high-level officials, moreover, both were attached to the department of Public Works. They were constantly preoccupied with the future and wanted to recruit only the best professors. Under the influence of Charles Andries, later alderman of Public Works and Education, more emphasis was placed on drawing: '*Le dessin est le véritable language écrit de l'ingénieur*'. Emmanuel Boudin taught the students to keep a *Journal de Mission* during their professional internships. By way of experiment, he introduced project exercises for civil engineers and had them make scale models of bridges, canals and buildings. The university was very proud of this, as is evident from its submissions to the World Exhibitions. Students from the Special Schools were the only students allowed to exhibit their projects there.

The engineering programme was ultimately a victim of its own success. After heated political discussions, Ghent lost its monopoly on the training of civil engineers, which it had had since 1838. Not coincidentally, this took place in 1890, under a homogeneous Catholic administration. That same year, the engineers moved into the splendid building in Plateaustraat and the Special Schools were rechristened Technical Schools, more oriented towards the needs of industry, rather than the education of civil engineers. Just ten years later, in 1900, the Laboratory of Applied Mechanics in Petroolstraat (near Wolterslaan) was opened. The main protagonists involved were the executive director Gustave Wolters, who was also chief engineer of Ghent-Eeklo, and Jules Boulvin, a visionary mind who had a great influence on mechanical engineering in Belgium.

Busts of Emmanuel Boudin and Charles Andries
(Ghent, Universiteitsarchief, photos Hilde Christiaens)

**Mechanics Laboratory**
In 1890, when the Institute for the Sciences on Plateaustraat was inaugurated, it was already too small to cope with the rapid expansion of the sciences. In 1900, at the initiative of executive director Gustave Wolters, it was possible to expand into a building on Petroolstraat. This is where Jules Boulvin did his groundbreaking research on the power of steam engines, which had a major influence on Belgian mechanical engineering.
(Ghent, Universiteitsarchief)

In the 1860s, Ghent's Special Schools counted more students than all four of the 'regular' faculties together. They also attracted an increasing number of foreign students. From the 1870s to the 1930s, their number increased to one third of the total student population. They came mainly from Central and Eastern Europe, but also from Brazil, China and Japan. In São Paulo, there is a monument to the Ghent architect Francisco de Paula Ramos de Azevedo, who designed several public buildings there after he graduated in 1878. He helped give shape to the *belle époque* in the Brazilian city, which thanks in part to his building programmes began to have the look of a modern cosmopolitan metropolis. Ramos de Azevedo also founded a Polytechnical School — along Ghent lines — at the University of São Paulo, and was director of its Liceu de Artes e Ofícios (School of Arts and Crafts).

During the first industrial revolution, which started at the end of the eighteenth century, the steam engine was the driving force behind the mechanisation of the textile and metal industries, among others. Pit coal extracted from the mines in Wallonia was the most important raw material needed in the process. During the second industrial revolution at the end of the nineteenth century, new forms of energy made their entrée: electricity, gas and petroleum for the powering of combustion engines. Mechanics, applied chemistry and electrical construction took off. The need for specialisation increased apace. Academic inspectors Emmanuel Boudin and Félix Dauge wanted to answer this demand by replacing the generic degree in industrial engineering with new, specialised courses of study: mechanical, chemical and electrical engineering. After some political tug of war with the Catholic minister Jules de Burlet, the electro-technical course was eliminated from the new programme. It would only be reinstated in 1900 on the advice of the faculty of Sciences and after protest from Liège,

**Engineering students with Frédéric Swarts, 1905**
In 1903, Frédéric Swarts succeeded his father Théodore as professor of General Chemistry in the faculty of Sciences. He was also attached to the Ecole Spéciale du Génie Civil. Unlike his brother-in-law Leo Baekeland, Swarts was mainly interested in basic research. Nevertheless, his groundbreaking scientific work in the field of organic fluorine compounds was of great importance to the chemical industry.
(Ghent, Universiteitsarchief)

and only as a supplementary course of study. The growing importance of electricity in all branches of industry, however, made it urgent. In 1904 a degree in naval architecture was also added on account of Belgium's rapidly developing financial and commercial maritime relations abroad. Nevertheless, the number of programme reforms was fairly limited during the *belle époque*, which was characterised by unprecedented technological acceleration. The innovative potential of the Technical Schools was reduced and the conservatism of the professors in Ghent increased.

The expansionism of Leopold II and the imperialism of Europe in the rest of the world also ensured other innovations in education besides the introduction of technical specialisations. The important role of Belgian industry in Russia and China forced the government to find means to send engineers to these far-flung locations to set up industries and build railways. Unfamiliarity with the languages spoken there formed an obstacle in building relations with these major powers. Therefore, in 1898, optional language courses were offered at the Technical Schools. The renowned Indologist Louis de la Vallée-Poussin was assigned to teach an optional course in Tibetan Sanskrit. The rationale was that students who overcame the initial difficulties of learning Sanskrit would thereby acquire a key to the syntax of the languages of the Far East. Sanskrit was in other words a steppingstone to Chinese, which was considered to be much more difficult. In 1906 and 1909, Ghent University received official Chinese delegations with much pomp and circumstance. These were glorious moments in which the intellectual and economic interests of little Belgium and the Chinese Empire were celebrated and intertwined.

New courses were also introduced in other faculties as well. At the faculty of Law, it was possible to follow a course in industrial and economic accounting from 1886 onwards. This single subject evolved into an additional degree in economic and consular sciences (1896) and the Bijzondere Handelsschool (Special Business School) (1906). The expansion of the latter was linked to education in the modern languages. English and German were required subjects, which were not, however, entrusted to the professors of German Philology. Their instruction was considered entirely inappropriate for students in the commercial sciences. The utilitarian use of modern languages was given priority, just as an internship in a commercial agency was also a must. The university collections were enlarged with new objects, such as a typewriter with a Belgian keyboard and a decimal tabulator. Modern times were here to stay.

## Academic entrepreneurship: Bakelite®

On 8 August 1889, Céline Swarts, the daughter of chemistry professor Théodore Swarts, married her father's promising young assistant Leo Baekeland. Two days later they embarked from Antwerp on the SS *Westernland* of the Red Star Line, destination New York. Between Théodore Swarts, who succeeded August Kekulé in 1867, and his brilliant pupil Leo Baekeland, there had for years existed a fundamental difference of opinion as to the 'use' of science. For Swarts, chemistry was a theoretical science; Baekeland was primarily interested in concrete applications. As a young university assistant in Ghent, he had already developed a technology with economic potential: photographic plates that could be developed in water. He decided to market his invention and had the process patented. At the end of 1887, together with his laboratory assistant Jules Guequier and the latter's affluent wife Valérie Gleesener, he founded Dr Baekelandt et Compagnie, a photochemical company based in Palinghuizen. Gleesener made available the capital and the infrastructure needed to commercialise the photographic product, which was mainly aimed at amateur photographers. Although there were still a number of technological shortcomings, the glass plates won a bronze medal at the world exhibition in Paris in 1889. According to a law from 1849, professors attached to the state university needed permission from the minister in order to exercise ancillary activities for remuneration, but Dr Baekeland was given the freedom he needed to conduct his industrial enterprises. Moreover, executive director August Wagener smelled talent — '*il a en lui — ce qui est rare — l'étoffe des inventeurs*'. Wagener was his main mentor in Ghent.

At Columbia University in New York, Baekeland met chemists such as Charles Chandler, who, like him, reached out to local industry, albeit in much more favourable circumstances. Baekeland's adolescent fascination with 'heroic' inventors such as Thomas Edison, Alexander Bell and Benjamin Franklin was now reinforced by personal contact with American colleagues in gentlemen's clubs and other intellectual networks. He grew increasingly alienated from his Ghent roots and expressed condescending opinions in his letters and diaries about the foolish Belgians and the corruption and decadence of *fin de siècle* European culture. Baekeland also approved of the fact that in America, the 'sickly parts' of the 'morbid, demoralising novels' of a writer like Emile Zola were left out by the translator. After five months in America, he decided to liquidate his company in Ghent, put his university career on hold and try his luck in the New World. Things did not go smoothly in the beginning, in part because Céline Swarts was far less adventurous than he was, which put pressure on their relationship. In 1893, Baekeland launched a new start-up in New York, the Nepara Chemical Co., which was a commercial success with VELOX photographic paper, his initial invention.

The sale of this company to the Eastman Kodak Company in 1898 subsequently made Baekeland so rich that he could have retired for the rest of his life. But instead, he decided to transform the barn of his immense country house on the Hudson into a private laboratory. He conducted groundbreaking research for the Hooker Electrochemical Company, which would eventually lead to Bakelite in 1905. The invention was the result of experiments with phenol and formaldehyde, which he had started more than twenty years earlier at Ghent University. The trademark was registered in Germany in 1909 and was first produced commercially by the German firm Bakelite GmbH. From the 1920s to the end of the 1950s, Bakelite was present all over the world in the living rooms, kitchens, bathrooms and offices of the average man and woman: from attractive art deco objects to everyday appliances such as

**Leo Baekeland at the Berlin zoo, 1932**
Baekeland was not only an entrepreneur, but also a family man, and in 1932 he wrote a postcard to his grandson from the Berlin zoo with this photo and the message: 'This is for little Peter to show him how Grandpa got two little live lions on his knees instead of his little Peter, who was not there.'
(Baekeland family collection)

radios, telephones, light switches, power sockets, ashtrays, cameras, light meters, coffee grinders, thermos flasks …

Baekeland donated part of his fortune to the advancement of science: in 1928 he contributed to the foundation of the NFWO. He also played a role in the exchange of European students and academics with the US. In 1939 his Bakelite Corporation was taken over by Union Carbide and Carbon Corporation. Baekeland withdrew from business life and received an honorary doctorate from his alma mater that same year. Poor health, gruelling negotiations with Union Carbide and the threat of war in Europe meant that he was never able to collect his medal, however, which today is still in Ghent in the collections of the Ghent University Museums (GUM). Céline Swarts, who survived Baekeland by thirteen years, remained in the US and was buried next to him in Sleepy Hollow Cemetery in New York in 1957.

## Gustave Magnel and reinforced concrete

During the First World War, Leo Baekeland prided himself on the fact that as a 'little' Belgian he was able to serve his second fatherland as a member of the Naval Consulting Board, an advisory body led by Thomas Edison to which many eminent scientists belonged. In that same wartime period, that other lion of Ghent, Gustave Magnel, moved to Great Britain. Graduating with flying colours in civil engineering construction in 1912, Magnel conducted research into building unsinkable ships in concrete.

After his return to Ghent, he became a supervisor in the Materials Resistance Laboratory led by his mentor Ferdinand Keelhoff, who, like him, argued in favour of the Technical Schools being of greater use to society. He immediately introduced regulations organising the performance of tests for government administrations and private concerns as a form of external service. It became a point of reference for the government and ensured that, in 1924, the laboratory conducted more than a hundred tests per year to the tune of several million Belgian francs. The university transferred the profits to the Belgian treasury and the government took care of its redistribution. It was a completely new form of public-private partnership.

**Gustave Magnel**
The black Bakelite phone accords well with the elegant, dandyish looks of Gustave Magnel, who smokes a cigarette at his desk with apparent nonchalance. Clad in the garb of a modern businessman, he gave a whole new meaning to the post of professor.
(Ghent, Universiteitsarchief)

In 1922, Magnel took on the task of teaching the first — free — course on reinforced concrete in Belgium: *Pratique du calcul du beton armé*. It was a highly specialised course that was also strongly oriented towards professional practice. Opponents on the faculty council lost out, because the subject was a raging success with considerable impact. From 1927 onwards, it was integrated into the required programme of several courses of study.

Typical of Magnel's commitment to fostering exchange between the university and industry were his motivational excursions with his students to various construction sites. He also advocated a special laboratory where theoretical education and experimental research could cross-pollinate each other in the service of government

**The Technicum**
The university buildings of the interwar period had a neutral design, typical of early modernism. Behind the brick façade of the Technicum lay an ingenious concept by steel specialist Jean-Norbert Cloquet and concrete specialist Gustave Magnel. The Technicum was spread out over a number of blocks and accommodated various laboratories of the Technical Schools.
(Ghent, Universiteitsarchief)

and industry. When minister of finance Emile Francqui christened the National Railway Company of Belgium (Nationale Maatschappij der Belgische Spoorwegen, or NMBS) in 1926, Magnel was the first to create a Reinforced Concrete Laboratory within the department of Railways. This enterprise was supported by the minister of railways, the Ghent socialist Edward Anseele, who saw an opportunity here in the context of his rationalisation policy. His son Edward Anseele Jr. was moreover one of Magnel's students. This explains why Magnel's famous Reinforced Concrete Laboratory was first accommodated in the Flandria Palace Hotel near Sint-Pietersstation and not in the buildings of the university. It became a university laboratory in 1930. The new laboratory was authorised to conduct tests on the quality of cement, concrete and reinforced concrete, and quickly grew into a renowned centre of expertise that was operated entirely with its own means and cost the university nothing at all.

In 1927, Magnel was appointed professor in the faculty of Sciences, but the external service assignments he continued to accept did not exactly advance his academic career — on the contrary. Once again Magnel was at this point a pioneer who had to force a change of mentality. At the Technische Hochschulen in Germany and the Engineering Schools in the US, the status and remuneration of professors as industrial consultants was already legally organised. But it seems quite likely that Magnel's promotion to full professor was hindered precisely because of his (supposed) income

from outside the university. He would have to wait until he was fifty to receive it. In 1932, Magnel made it a point of principle when he received a ridiculously low sum of 2,500 Belgian francs for studies he had carried out in connection with the renovation of the Aula. For him the logic was simple: either a professor had an assignment that he carried out exclusively within the context of the university, but then his salary would have to be reviewed; or he was permitted to accept lucrative assignments from outside the university, but then additional assignments for the university would have to be paid for appropriately.

In 1948 the university administration conducted a 'thorough investigation' of Magnel's outside activities. The conclusion was that he did not carry out any other lucrative activities that demanded the better part of his time. We know of course that the Ghent concrete expert was involved in a number of spectacular projects outside his duties at the university: the Basilica of Koekelberg (1930), the enormous factory hall of the Union Cotonnière in Ghent (1948), the spiral staircase of the showroom of General Motors in Antwerp (1951). Since 1937 he had moreover applied himself to pre-stressed concrete, which was brought to market by the firm Blaton. As inventor of the Blaton-Magnel system, Magnel was responsible for a number of firsts: the railway bridge over Spiegelstraat in Brussels (1943-1944) and the bridge over the river Maas at Sclayn near Dinant (1948-1949). Magnel's expertise was also in demand for the Walnut Lane Memorial Bridge in Philadelphia, the first pre-stressed concrete bridge in the US (1949-1951). As was the case with the university's building programme in the 1930s, without Magnel's reusable, one-storey, climbing formwork panels, it would have never been possible to build the 64-metre-high Book Tower.

The Technicum, a complex of technical laboratories at the university, was also built thanks to Magnel. In 1890, the Institute of Sciences at Plateau and Rozier had the ambition to unite all the exact and applied sciences under one roof, but this quickly turned out to be an illusion. In the 1920s the building was literally bursting at the seams. An extension was sought on the old Feyerick factory grounds on the Muinkschelde. The designs for the new building were, in conformity with established practice, entrusted to an in-house engineer-architect: in addition to Magnel, his colleague, the steel expert Jean-Norbert Cloquet, son of city architect Louis Cloquet. The Technicum, a sleek, functional building which used more steel than concrete, was built between 1934 and 1937. The enormous load-bearing capacity of the floors, including those above ground level, is striking: 3 tons per square metre. They had to be able to withstand extreme tests and experiments. Magnel's Reinforced Concrete Laboratory, the showpiece of the Technicum, would be housed on the ground floor, until it was moved to Ardoyen in 1975.

## The Boerenkot and the Veterinary School

In the same period as the Technicum, the eighteenth-century Rasphuis (formerly a prison), on the left bank of the Coupure canal, was demolished to make way for the construction of the State Agricultural College, a U-shaped building in yellow brick designed by August Poppe and Georges Collin. The Flemish 'Agriculture College of the State' was not part of the university when it was established in 1920; the architects of the 'Boerenkot' — literally the 'Farmers' Shack' — were not associated with the university. On the opposite side of the Coupure, August Desmet, who was an in-house architect, built a modernistic complex for veterinarians, starting in 1933. For a long time it was considered a standard for veterinary clinics in Europe, but unfortunately was allowed to languish for years.

The State Agricultural College and the Flemish Veterinary School were the direct result of the Dutchification of the university in the 1920s and 30s. In Kuregem an Ecole de Médecine Vétérinaire et d'Agriculture de l'Etat had existed since 1836. In 1860 the introduction of the scientific method to agriculture led to the establishment of the Institut Supérieur d'Agronomie de l'Etat in Gembloux as an annex of the University of Liège. The State Agricultural College, which opened its doors in Sint-Amandsstraat in 1920 (with a test farm in Melle), met the demand of the Flemish movement, which for years had lobbied for Dutch-language higher education in agriculture as an economic motor for rural Flanders.

The first pleas for higher agricultural education in Ghent, however, originated within the French-speaking university of the nineteenth century. The location of Ghent University in the eminently agrarian Flemish provinces created conditions favourable to the establishment of higher education without incurring a great deal of expense, capitalising on the specific local conditions and soil varieties. Rector Floribert Soupart, son of a gentleman farmer-burgomaster in Feluy (Hainault), launched several proposals in accordance with the German model, but the faculty of Sciences and the Academic Council would not hear of it. Soupart continued to hammer on the same point until he stepped down as rector in 1879. He referred by analogy to the combination of science and practice that was so successful at the Ecole des Arts et Manufactures. The most important agrarian problem in the transition from the nine-

**Machine room of the State Agricultural College**
In 1920 the State Agricultural College opened on Sint-Amandsstraat on the Sint-Kwintensberg. The agricultural machinery was housed in St Peter's Chapel.
(Ghent, Universiteitsarchief)

teenth century to the twentieth was the fragmentation of agricultural exploitation. Because of this fragmentation, and the application of traditional farming techniques, productivity was very low. The small farmers and tenants could not compete with the agricultural invasion from across the ocean. Countless marginal producers were obliged to seek a living elsewhere and the number of farm workers decreased dramatically. Thus, the modernisation of agricultural methods through scientific education was not a superfluous luxury when the State Agricultural College was founded in 1920. Until 1933 the college was under the jurisdiction of the ministry of Agriculture. After a great deal of political tug of war, a Veterinary School was added in 1934, attached to the faculty of Medicine, with a test farm of 21 hectares in Merelbeke built with Marshall Plan funds in 1950. Only in 1968 were the schools reformed and the faculties of Agricultural Science and Veterinary Medicine added to the university.

## From hard cheese to breast milk factory

Like the Reinforced Concrete Laboratory during the interwar period, which grew to be a showpiece of the Ghent technical schools, the State Dairy Station and its small test factory in Melle became the flagship of the State Agricultural College in the 1930s. In the meantime, these test stations have evolved into the Institute for Agricultural and Fisheries Research (Instituut voor Landbouw- en Visserijonderzoek, or ILVO), which carries out research in support of policy for the Flemish government, and is both partner and competitor of the university.

One of the driving forces behind the new dairy station was Albert De Vleeschauwer. He hoped to introduce the production of hard cheese in Belgium in order to minimise wastage of milk. He was assisted by his former student Camille Van Waeyenberge, who became director of the station in 1939. After the Second World War, however, he was suspended for collaboration and later forgotten. In 1936, De Vleeschauwer sent Van Waeyenberge to the Netherlands for six months to gain practical experience. Van Waeyenberge designed a small cheese factory along Dutch lines for the dairy station. In the spring of 1939 the first Belgian hard cheese was ready. That same year, the Farmers Union offered the first pieces for tasting at a dairy seminar in Leuven. Van Waeyenberge became a professor at the State Agricultural College in 1941. From 1941 to 1944, however, he was also chairman of the Dairy, Fat and Egg Group (Hoofdgroepering Zuivel,

**The Boerenkot and the Veterinary School**
In the 1930s two modernist buildings were erected on the Coupure. The Rasphuis on the left bank of the Coupure and the Casino on the right were demolished. A greater contrast than that between the correctional institute for beggars and vagrants and the place of civilised entertainment that hosted the annual Floraliën would be hard to imagine. The buildings were harbingers of a new era in which class differences were shrinking. It was only at the end of the 1960s that the State Agricultural College (photo left) and the Veterinary School (photo right) would become part of the university.
(Ghent, Universiteitsarchief)

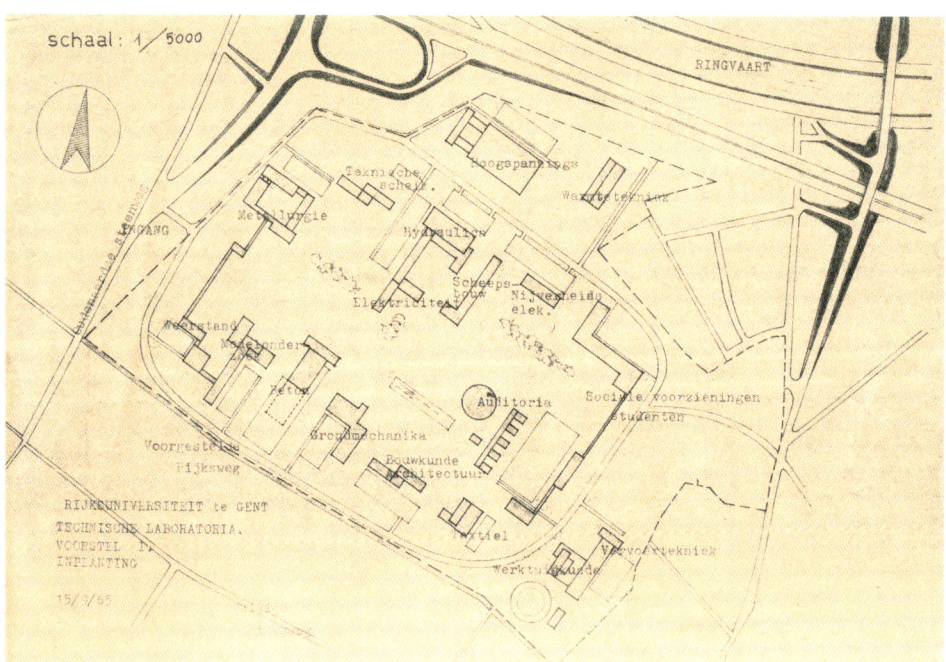

**Initial plans for a technology campus, 1965**
The first plan for the Ardoyen site in Zwijnaarde only provides for the expansion of the faculty of Applied Sciences with a number of technical laboratories. There are now ten university laboratories, eight research institutes, eleven international corporate R&D centres and sixty high-tech growth companies operating in three areas of innovation: life sciences, materials, ICT and chip technology.
(Ghent, Universiteitsarchief)

Vetten en Eieren, or ZVE) of the National Agriculture and Nutrition Corporation (Nationale Landbouw- en Voedingscorporatie, or NVLC), which reorganised the agricultural sector from the top down on the orders of the German occupiers. The closure of the dairy with an eye towards more efficient milk production was a highly unpopular measure. Although Van Waeyenberge was acquitted of collaboration in 1948, his academic career was already over in 1944.

De Vleeschauwer had already been struggling with health problems for some time when he was found dead in his office on the Coupure in 1960. The Ghent tradition in the field of food technology was continued and diversified by Hendrik Hendrickx, André Huyghebaert and Johan Debevere. Nowadays, that tradition has offshoots in the consortium Food2Know, a contact point and centre of excellence for nutrition, health and animal nutrition. In this way, companies, consumer organisations and government institutions have access to knowledge 'from pitchfork to table' and the advanced machinery of more than thirty-five research groups at UGent, HoGent (Ghent College), the VUB (Free University of Brussels), the UA (University of Antwerp) and the ILVO (Research Institute for Agriculture, Fisheries and Food).

The Flemish cluster policy concerning cooperation between universities and industry also extends further than the food and agriculture industry, which is united by the Flemish umbrella organisation Flanders' FOOD. Several Ghent spin-offs are active in this domain. There is Inbiose, for example, collaborating with Wim Soetaert, professor of Industrial Biology, in 2016 to develop a revolutionary ingredient for infant formula with nutrients from mothers' milk. It attracted large investments from the American multinational DuPont Nutrition & Health.

A long road was travelled from the State Dairy Station of the 1930s to the 'mothers' milk factory' of today. The chairman of the Industrial Research Fund (IOF) and honorary dean of Bioengineering Sciences at the University of Ghent, Herman Van Langenhove, nevertheless bemoans the fact that bioengineers were not granted a place in the Flemish Institute for Biotechnology (VIB). Emeritus Willy Verstraete, who launched several spin-offs in the area of waste processing, explains that it is not a good idea to patent 'processes' because they change constantly. The bioengineers were not able to acquire patent rights in the same way as their colleagues in the area of genetic modification, where enormous profits are to be gained with 'products'. In any case, the bioengineers collaborate with the private sector in all domains, with the exception of forestry.

## Ardoyen Campus, TechLane Science Park and Green Bridge

The structures for that collaboration, however, grew 'organically' in Flanders. In the spring of 1971, minister of science policy Theo Lefèvre and André Vlerick of Regional Economy organised a mission to the US to see how it worked there.

André Vlerick came from a family of entrepreneurs from Kortrijk, had studied law in Leuven and was briefly the assistant of Gaston Eyskens during the Second World War. When he was in his thirties, the ambitious young jurist was involved in the implementation of the Marshall Plan in Belgium. He established important international contacts and in 1949 went to the US for the first time. A whole new world opened up for him. In 1953, Vlerick was appointed professor at the faculty of Law in Ghent. That same year, Henry Kissinger invited him to take part in the prestigious Harvard International Seminar. Inspired by the management schools of the US, the young professor wasted no time in launching the 'managerial revolution' in Flanders as well. In the academic year 1953-1954, he started the Seminar for Productivity Studies and Research at the Special Schools. The seminar organised specialisation courses with a strong practical orientation for managers, business leaders and managerial staff, not only for functions at the top and in middle management, but later also for civil servants. The initiative received the support of the Belgian Productivity Department, an institution that grew out of the Marshall Plan. In Leuven and Brussels, similar educational programmes were established, and from 1961 onwards they were joined under the Industry and University Foundation. Ten years after its foundation, Vlerick could already call it a fully fledged business school, and thirty years later the 'Vlerick boys' had become a household name. All programmes were united in 1983 under the Professor Vlerick Management Institute, which split from the university in 1999 as the Vlerick Leuven Ghent Management School. In the meantime, Vlerick's political career had also

**André Vlerick**
In addition to being a professor, André Vlerick was also a politician. He was involved in the Christian People's Party (CVP) and, as director of the Flemish Economic Association (Vlaams Economisch Verbond, or VEV, now VOKA) and secretary of state for Regional Economy, he was one of the pioneers of the economic regionalisation of Belgium in the late 1960s.
(Ghent, Universiteitsarchief, photo Vlerick Business School)

**Magnel Laboratory**
In 1975 the Laboratory for Reinforced Concrete moved to Ardoyen. Since the death of Gustave Magnel in 1955, it was named after him. This 1992 photo presents a somewhat desolate sight. A vibrant campus feeling has yet to arise, in part due to the lack of social facilities.
(Ghent, Universiteitsarchief, Fotoklas UGent)

taken off. His indefatigable pursuit of synergy between university and business life took on a highly concrete form.

In 1971, shortly after Lefèvre and Vlerick's trip to America, the Ministerial Committee for Economic and Social Coordination established a policy framework for setting up 'scientific industrial zones' in the vicinity of the 'fully fledged' universities: Leuven, Ottignies, Ghent, Brussels (VUB and ULB together) and Liège. The establishments would benefit from 'government help' in the framework of the expansion legislation. The costs of equipping them would be wholly borne by the Belgian treasury. In Leuven, this policy resulted in the foundation of Leuven Research & Development (LRD, 1972) and the expansion of the science park in Haasrode. In Ghent, the new policy was initially implemented in a more traditional way. The government gave Ghent University 52 hectares of ground on the Ardoyen Campus in Zwijnaarde in 1972. According to a plan dating from 1965, the entire site was meant for the expansion of the faculty of Applied Sciences. Modern laboratories were created, such as the State Institute for Soil Mechanics and the Model Research Laboratory. The Magnel Laboratory for Reinforced Concrete also moved to Zwijnaarde. The expansion of the university site on Ardoyen went slower than planned, however, due to the economic crisis.

In 1980 the University of Ghent set up an Interface department to further stimulate contacts with industry. The partial re-purposing of Ardoyen as a science park for businesses soon followed. The first company to settle at Ardoyen was the textile expertise centre Centexbel in 1989. Two years later, the Incubation and Innovation Centre (IIC) was up and running, a cooperation agreement between the Community Development Association of East Flanders (Gewestelijke Ontwikkelingsmaatschappij Oost-Vlaanderen), the university and a number of businesses.

Twenty-five years on, the site has become a productive ecosystem for cross-pollination between the university and industry. Today, TechLane Science Park hosts ten university laboratories, eight research institutes, eleven international corporate R&D centres and sixty high-tech growth companies. Every year, ten new start-ups are welcomed. TechLane has thus become the natural habitat for spin-offs of VIB, imec, VITO and the University of Ghent itself, good for more than 3,500 high-tech jobs.

In 2006, Ghent University opened a second science park in Ostend, the Green Bridge Incubator, oriented towards blue growth, or blue energy (offshore wind and tidal energy), aquaculture, marine biotechnology and coastal engineering.

Applied research in science parks is today an obvious choice and indeed a must. The government gradually relaxed regulations so that universities could participate in the market with greater ease. By means of patents and spin-offs, universities try better to 'valorise' or reap the profits from the 'products' of scientific research.

## Flanders Technology and the Strategic Research Centres

That development coincided with the devolution of powers from the central to the regional governments in Belgium. On the occasion of 'Flemish Day' at Expo 58, the rector of Ghent, Pieter Lambrechts, still lamented that, in comparison to francophone Belgium, Flanders still had to make up for considerable cultural and scientific arrears. Under Gaston Geens, chairman of the Flemish Executive Council from 1981 to 1992,

**Ghent University at Flanders Technology International, 1993**
The cradle of the Flemish knowledge economy lies in the biennial Flanders Technology (International) fair. It was first organised in 1983 at the instigation of the chairman of the Flemish Executive Committee, Gaston Geens. The first years of the technology fair were so successful that Flanders Expo had to be built in haste to accommodate the rapidly growing number of companies and visitors. The event died a quiet death in 1999.
(Ghent, Universiteitsarchief, photo Hilde Christiaens)

that lament was answered by a combative Flemish science policy directed by the Flemish Economic Union (Vlaams Economisch Verbond, or VEV). Under the motto 'What we do ourselves, we do better', Geens launched the DIRV programme, an acronym for: Third Industrial Revolution in Flanders (Derde Industriële Revolutie in Vlaanderen). He defined three spearheads in which Flanders would invest: microelectronics, new materials and biotechnology. In 1983, Flanders Technology took place in Ghent. The logo with the handshake between human and robot is etched in collective memory and formed an important step in the formation of Flemish identity. The results are still tangible today.

The Interuniversity Micro-Electronics Centre (imec), which grew into one of the top international players in microchip technology and R&D, first saw the light of day in 1984. Although expressly created as an interuniversity effort to put Flanders on the map, imec grew with Tower and Campus in Leuven into a 'Leuven' institution and one of the world's leading innovation and R&D hubs. In 1991 the Flemish Institute for Technological Research (Vlaams Instituut voor Technologisch Onderzoek, or VITO) was set up as the successor to the National Centre for Nuclear Energy (Nationaal Centrum voor Kernenergie) in Mol. The Flemish Institute for Biotechnology (Vlaams Instituut voor Biotechnologie, or VIB) followed in 1996. Here the role and influence of Ghent University were far greater from the beginning. This was also the case for the Institute for Broadband Technology (IBBT), which dates from 2004; in 2011 it was rechristened iMinds and in 2016 merged with imec. The integration of hardware (imec) and software (iMinds) was the only logical step for Ghent University in the negotiations surrounding this bipolar hub. Moreover, imec's worldwide connections strengthened iMinds, the smaller player in the story. The condition for the fusion was that iMinds' identity as important antennae in Ghent would be preserved. With the opening of the new library of the future on the Krook in March 2017, however, it appeared that the iMinds brand had been 'taken over' by imec — it never truly became a bipolar hub.

Nevertheless, the intensive collaboration between Ghent University and imec in the area of photonics had already resulted in major breakthroughs. Roel Baets, head of the highly successful Ghent Photonics Research Group, tells how this was entirely in line with technological evolution at the end of the 1990s. Initially, it was thought that silicon was not suited to photonics. After all, you cannot use it to produce light. The gigantic investments worldwide in advanced silicon-CMOS factories with clean rooms and machines worth tens of millions of euros drove imec and the Photonics Research Group into each other's arms. 'Before, each photonics research group had its own clean rooms and machinery, but this was no longer sufficient', says Baets. It had simply become too expensive. The fact that imec not only had the most advanced CMOS technology in house, but was also close by, was a great advantage in forming a unique combination of expertise. Classic silicon as a raw material for microelectronics turned out to be usable in the development of optical chips, with a number of innovative applications as a result. In this way, the Ghent group made the international papers in 2007 with a micro-laser mounted on a silicon wafer with a layer of adhesive that was only 100 nanometres. 'The holy grail of photonics', as Baets himself expresses it. The development of bio-censors was the next step. Smart chips with all the functionalities needed to monitor complex systems using wireless technology are in the meantime a reality. It opens up an unprecedented array of biomedical applications in which the boundaries between disciplines have vanished completely.

The Strategic Research Centres (Strategische Onderzoekscentra, or SOCs) — imec, iMinds, VIB, VITO and more recently Flanders Make — bring in a great deal of contract research and are generously financed by the Flemish government. In 2017 the Flemish budget for imec and iMinds rose from 79 to 108 million euros, and for VIB from 44 to 59 million euros. Between 2017 and 2021, VIB will receive more than 300 million euros, an increase of 34% with respect to the previous five-year period.

For the research groups involved, this means an unprecedented reinforcement of people and means. The chances of success for FWO-funded projects are much smaller than with imec and iMinds, which implies that less fundamental and more applied research is conducted in the spearhead domains of the SOCs. Science and technology are almost silently yet nevertheless implacably drawn into a demand-driven context, which has given rise to extreme dependence on external financing. According to rector Rik Van de Walle, former dean of the faculty of Engineering Sciences and Architecture, this has far-reaching consequences: 'Because of the output- and result-oriented logic of the universities, young researchers today are increasingly less inclined to do basic research which entails the risk of failure, but for this very reason can also be truly groundbreaking.'

# TechTransfer: interface with the business world

Roel Baets and his Photonics Research Group also collaborate with the business world. In 2008, Caliopa was 'spun off' to become a market leader in optical silicon components. The Chinese giant Huawei bought the spin-off in 2013 from Ghent University and other stakeholders. As an interface between the university and industry, the Photonics Innovation Center 'Plateau' was established, named after the nineteenth-century optics professor Joseph Plateau. Just as Plateau's phenakistoscope was a step on the way to the moving image and hence to cinema, the mission of the 'Plateau' centre (now NB Photonics) was the transfer of new photonics technology to industrial applications and hence to the user.

The most recent spin-off to emerge from this is Indigo Diabetes, which brought to market an optical censor that can measure the blood glucose level without drawing blood, a revolutionary invention thanks to groundbreaking photonics technology.

Ghent University is a relative newcomer to the path of economic valorisation, a story, moreover, that did not always proceed without a hitch. In 1991 it was decreed that in addition to education and research, providing scientific and social services would also belong to the core tasks of the university. 'Services to society' was defined in 1995 as 'all efforts to the benefit of third parties in exchange for remuneration for services or people in the exercise of tasks arising from knowledge present at the university, results of scientific or project-based research or technology'. This made it possible to agree upon fair compensation for the relinquishing of intellectual property. In 1998, the universities were granted the property rights. Ghent University needed this framework to expand TechTransfer, the department that manages intellectual property and provides guidance from the scientific idea, to the patent request, to the spin-off and its eventual commercialisation.

The late expansion of TechTransfer explains its lag relative to KULeuven, which as a free university already had the necessary leverage in the 1970s to apply for patents and market inventions as a university. At Ghent University, which was still a rigid state institution, a very different culture prevailed. Researchers had to apply for patents to protect their inventions, as Baekeland had done in the past. The head start of Leuven's R&D is also apparent in the enormous difference in valorisation revenues between the two universities. In 2016, KULeuven received 100 million euros in revenues from patents; Ghent, only 2 million.

A key figure in the extension of TechTransfer was Marc Zabeau, who came from the Genetics Laboratory of Marc Van Montagu as a dyed-in-the-wool cowboy entrepreneur who shepherded the Interface department, rechristened TechTransfer, into the twenty-first century. Under his successor Wim Van Camp, another PhD holder in plant biotechnology from the Montagu stall, the department finally got under way and was thoroughly professionalised.

In part thanks to cooperation with the IOF, developed under vice-rector Luc Moens, the entire valorisation cycle was now managed transparently by TechTransfer — from scientific idea, to patent application, to spin-off, to eventual commercialisation of the invention. Basic research through doctorates is still the first step; only then is possibility of valorisation considered. Not the other way around. Ghent University departments cooperate with IOF consortiums that, as complementary research groups, connect the university with the market via 'business developers'. There are twenty-two business developers active in twenty multidisciplinary valorisation consortiums in many different domains: energy, cleantech and materials; electronics, photonics and ICT; health and pharmaceuticals; agriculture; biotech and nutrition.

Intellectual property (IP) is brought in under the spin-off and the university receives a certain return on investment through licensing. As soon as a spin-off can be consolidated, financing ends. IOF chairman Herman Van Langenhove states that 85% of start-ups with IOF involvement still exist after ten years and are thus viable. In this way, the IOF incubator not only provides economically and societally valorised knowledge, but also employment. Thanks to spin-offs from Ghent University, 1,250 full-time jobs have been created in the region over the past two decades. One of the side effects, however, is that the third industrial revolution has widened the gap between rich and poor. Re-industrialisation through spin-offs provides primarily highly specialised jobs for the educated, not large factories with mass employment for those with lower education levels. Moreover, collaboration with multinationals such as Huawei, BASF, Bayer and Monsanto, which only finance profitable research in high-tech domains, also raises ethical questions.

## Basic and applied research in the twenty-first century

In September 2016, the Flemish research community launched a petition for a stronger FWO. Nearly 6,000 signatures were collected in a short time. Interestingly, the petition linked the importance of basic, un-commissioned research directly to major societal questions such as sustainable energy consumption, climate change, and ageing.

The occasion for this 'cry for help' was the significant decline in success rates for mandates and projects due to the increase in the number of professors active in research. But the problem is much deeper. It touches the foundations of the knowledge society itself. In post-industrial Flanders, the 'little grey cells are one of the most valuable raw materials'. 'Claiming that un-commissioned research that expands knowledge has no economic relevance is patently false', says the petition. 'Is it societally responsible to nip the innovations of our researchers in the bud, and undercut tomorrow's welfare?'

The nature and the acceleration of technological innovation in some domains no longer permit us to draw sharp boundaries between 'pure science' and 'applications'. The false idea that the application is always at the end of the trajectory and that basic research precedes it must be adjusted. There is a constant exchange between science and industry. In the two hundred years of research at the University of Ghent this has always been the case, for that matter. All the more reason that basic (or un-commissioned) research cannot be neglected.

Since the Flemish government picked up the gauntlet at the beginning of the 1990s and began to invest more in R&D, the tendency was to the advantage of policy or goal-oriented research with an economic outcome from the very beginning. In 1997 a programme in Policy Oriented Research was set up; in 2001 the support centres for

Policy Related Research followed. According to the tracking guide of the department of Economy, Science and Innovation (Economie, Wetenschap en Innovatie, or EWI), the share of un-commissioned research (by definition the most original and innovative) decreased from 60% of the Flemish budget in 1995 to 41% in 2010, a reversal and skewing of proportions in fifteen years. Under minister of science policy Ingrid Lieten, the 50-50-relationship of commissioned/un-commissioned research was restored. Her successor Philippe Muyters promised to respect this development, but confirmed once more the shift towards applied research with the integration of IWT and Hercules in the FWO in 2015. In other words, the growing amount of directed research with respect to un-commissioned research in the funding circuit raises more questions concerning the power of the market in academia and the 'selling out' of the university to industrial interests in the knowledge economy. If power and money determine the research agenda, the independence of the university is undermined and favourable conditions for technological innovation are at risk of being lost in favour of the latest trends, short-term thinking and the quest for immediate profit.

**Flemish Institute for Biotechnology, 2013**
The Flemish Institute for Biotechnology is an interuniversity institute founded in 1996. The FSVM Research Building, (named after Ghent's pioneers of biotechnology Fiers, Schell and Van Montagu), is located on the technology campus in Zwijnaarde.
(Ghent, VIB, photo Ine Dehandschutter)

Chapter 4

# CARING FOR BODY AND MIND

When the university was founded in 1817, the faculty of Medicine relied on the Bijloke civil hospital for the practical education of its students. As the municipal hospital for the poor, it had been the cornerstone of Ghent's medical services for centuries. For this reason alone, the training of doctors cannot be seen apart from the social questions that prevailed in the city during the nineteenth century and were directly related to the consequences of industrialisation. Professors and students at the faculty of Medicine had direct, daily contact with the dire living and working conditions of Ghent's textile workers. With their enlightened ideals as a guideline and a modern, scientific mindset, several professors would dedicate themselves to improving the lot of labourers and the poor. Medical and social reforms went hand in hand. Medicine for the benefit of public hygiene was impossible without the political engagement of the city and the state.

As head physician of the Bijloke, professor Adolphe Burggraeve was a pathfinder for social housing in Ghent. Joseph Guislain, as head physician of Ghent's insane asylum, put into practice his progressive, humanitarian vision of treating the mentally ill.

The university's use of the infrastructure and patients of the Bijloke for clinical education and scientific research, however, was marked by major tensions and conflicts with the city and the Cistercian nuns who ruled the roost in the daily operation of the civil hospital. The university would only acquire a teaching hospital of its own after the Second World War, in 1961. The outbreak of polio epidemics in the 1950s accelerated its arrival. The increasingly complex and ever more expensive medical technology, combined with dysfunctional bookkeeping, led to the Academic Hospital (Academisch Ziekenhuis, or AZ) accumulating an alarming deficit of nearly four million Belgian francs in the 1960s and 70s, so that the assets of university and hospital had to be divided in 1986. On 1 January 2018, after thirty years, the University Hospital of Ghent (Universitair Ziekenhuis Gent, or UZ Gent) was reintegrated into the university, albeit under its own management and bookkeeping.

During the 'Golden Sixties', Karel Vuylsteek established a department of Social Medicine, which revived the spirit of social engagement that motivated professors of medicine in the nineteenth century. Renewed attention to primary healthcare and general well-being produced an excellent education programme in general medicine and the development of community health centres. This progressive trend made itself felt in domains other than medicine as well.

**Entrance to the Bijloke clinic at Jozef Kluyskensstraat**
The 'new' Bijloke, a neo-Gothic complex designed by city architect and professor Adolphe Pauli, was completed in 1878.
(Ghent, Universiteitsarchief)

**The Kraakhuis in the 'old' Bijloke, 1929**
The small hall in the Bijloke has existed since the beginning of the sixteenth century, and served as a ward for wounded and post-operative patients during the interwar period. Until it could open its own academic hospital, the faculty of Medicine used the civil hospital for practical education. This ward would remain in use until 1976. Now it is a multi-functional space in the Bijloke Music Centre that can accommodate 238 people.
(Ghent, Stadsarchief)

## Public health and clinical training at the Bijloke

Education at the Bijloke dates back to Napoleon, who founded the Ecole de Médecine, de Chirurgie et de Pharmacie in Ghent in 1804. Of the four professors that William I appointed to the faculty of Medicine in 1817, three were attached to the Ecole de Médecine: rector Jan Van Rotterdam, Joseph Kluyskens and Frans Verbeeck. The only newcomer was the Orangist Jacob Kesteloot, who had played a role in William I's choosing Ghent as the university town of the Southern Netherlands.

Jan Van Rotterdam established his reputation in 1793 when he was a rural doctor in Deinze, where he treated a terrible dysentery epidemic with great success. His reputation only increased when he became chief physician of the Bijloke hospital in 1804 and demonstrated on a daily basis how the old ways of medicine could be combined with modern science.

Joseph Kluyskens was even more rooted in the Flemish soil. He was the son of a village doctor from Erpe. He did not want to become a goldsmith as his father wished, but went to work for a surgeon in Ghent as an apprentice barber. At night he devoured books on anatomy and physiology, which he borrowed from the well-stocked library of his friend Charles Van Hulthem. He also learned French and English, followed courses on surgery and obstetrics, and joined the army. In 1796 he was chief surgeon at the Bijloke and the military hospital. After the Battle of Waterloo in 1815, Kluyskens was called to Brussels to organise first aid for wounded soldiers. He carried out three hundred amputations and tended nine thousand wounded.

Jacob Kesteloot was an adept of Edward Jenner, the English doctor who made his reputation at the end of the eighteenth century with a vaccine against smallpox. In 1812, Kesteloot published a Dutch translation of the popular handbook *An Inquiry into the Causes and Effects of Variolae Vaccinae* (1798) in The Hague. He would also make an important contribution to the spread of the vaccine in Flanders.

The fact that the city had a civil hospital where 200 to 250 patients were tended daily was an important argument for keeping the university in Ghent after the Belgian Revolution of 1830. After all, the medical students found it a 'fertile source' for their medical observations. In 1839 the government questioned the situation, although this form of education *au lit du malade* was also current in Vienna, Berlin, Bonn and other German and English universities. The executive director reported to the minister that the patients in Ghent were not at all reluctant towards the students, on the contrary: the presence of the students guaranteed that the professors would pay special attention to them. Lessons held after the visit would lack the very thing that made clinical education so precious: practice.

When the state universities were reorganised from the ground up in 1835, the medical schools from the French period were abolished. Belgium was the first country in Europe to educate doctors, surgeons and obstetricians at university level. The medical profession gradually increased in prestige. Traditionally trained surgeons and charlatans fell from grace, as did 'new' forms of medicine. When citizens submitted a petition in 1860 requesting that training in homeopathy be introduced at the university, it was resolutely refused, both by the provincial medical commissions and the faculties of medicine. This 'new doctrine' was out of the question, only science counted.

**The large ward, ca. 1900**
At the heart of the Bijloke is a large, thirteenth-century infirmary with an impressive oak canopy. Today it is a 975-seat concert hall.
(Ghent, Universiteitsbibliotheek)

In the mid-nineteenth century, medical students in Ghent saw an average of 213 patients a year in the Bijloke: 127 men and 86 women. Every day they practised making diagnoses, determining causes and prescribing medication. Moreover, the students were employed in free polyclinic consultations for the working class. In this way, the rich sons of the bourgeoisie were directly confronted with a wide variety of 'social' diseases, such as typhus, cholera, peritonitis, lice and vermin, consumption, dropsy and so on. Many of the poor were afflicted by eye disorders and venereal diseases, leading to the creation of special departments. The social-liberal professor Victor Deneffe, who became director of the ophthalmic department in 1869, fought a pitched battle against the trachoma epidemic caused by poor living conditions and lack of clean water.

Whenever a patient died in the hospital's sickroom, and there was no legal objection or objection from the family, the professor of Anatomy conducted an autopsy. He and his students went to the amphitheatre to carry out the dissection of the body. If the injury had any importance for science, the anatomical part was sent to the professor of Pathological Anatomy and deposited in the cabinet with a brief historical notation on the illness. The collection grew very slowly, however. The autopsies left more and more to be desired. At the end of 1874, the faculty of Medicine requested an annual subsidy of 500 francs from the government for the tools and materials needed to better preserve the bodies and specimens. The autopsy was a performance *par excellence*, meant for the education of doctors. In this sense, macroscopic pathological anatomy remained closely linked to education in the hospital. Researching the organs came only in second place, although the university created its own museum with anatomical models and specimens in 1883. However, it functioned more as a cabinet of curiosities at the Gentse Feesten (Ghent Festival) than as a special laboratory in the dissection department.

In 1844 the university entered into an agreement with the Sisters of Charity to create a clinic for childhood diseases in the children's hospital of Sint-Jan-ten-Dullen at St James's. The professor selected the young patients to suit his teaching and gave lessons in a special room with five or six beds. This form of education was particularly progressive. Each child was assigned to the care of a student designated by the professor. That student examined the child in the presence of his fellow students, made a diagnosis that was discussed by his peers and checked by the professor. The group also discussed treatment and medication. The student to whom the child was assigned recorded the history of the illness and all phases of treatment in a diary. At every lesson, he reported on its evolution until the disease was cured or 'his' child died. In case of the latter, the student also conducted the autopsy personally and recorded the results in the diary.

In the mid-nineteenth century, the government was concerned for recently graduated doctors in medicine: there was little work and many doctors could not earn a living through the exercise of their profession. Nevertheless, the number of diplomas awarded each year was not proportional to the needs of healthcare in that period, least of all in the industrial city of Ghent. Yet the number of people 'called' to serve as doctors to the poor was great thanks to the direct confrontation with the dire conditions of reality. A whole range of alumni from the faculty left traces in the collective memory of Ghent: Eugeen Cogen, Leopold Cruyl, Judocus de Hoon, Alexis Dumont, Cesar Fredericq, Charles Hulin, Ferdinand Snellaert, Adolphe Burggraeve …

## Doctors in urban ghettos

Adolphe Burggraeve graduated in 1828 with a thesis on syphilis. After that he went to Utrecht to study with the well-known professor of anatomy and founder of Dutch psychiatry, Jacob Schröder van der Kolk. Burggraeve was primarily interested in the Dutch method of injecting veins to make anatomical specimens. Back in Ghent, he tried to improve on the forgotten recipe of Leiden's eighteenth-century 'artist of death', Frederik Ruysch. He achieved his aim. Burggraeve succeeded in preserving his specimens for decades and thus laid the basis for the university's valuable anatomical collection. He made around 1,200 specimens over the course of his career, of which the 'new-born' (1837) and 'woman's head and hand' (n.d.) still survive today.

Burggraeve's rich and varied career was by no means limited to anatomy. He established himself as a surgeon in the city and in 1834 was one of the founders of the influential Société de Médicine de Gand. In 1835 he succeeded Frans Verbeeck as professor of Anatomy and, in 1848, Surgery. He wrote the first Belgian handbook on histology (1843) and in 1850 developed innovative bandages on the basis of cotton wool. His operating method was conservative; for victims of work-related accidents in particular, he took into account the irreversible consequences of amputation. His laminated lead bandages often yielded good results with the frequent factory injuries that occurred in the industrial city because they protected the wounds from the air.

As chief surgeon of the Bijloke, Burggraeve strove for modern, hygienic clinical buildings. Antiseptic had not yet been invented and the medieval Bijloke hospital was a breeding ground for infection. In 1878 the 'new' Bijloke was inaugurated. The imposing neo-Gothic building was designed by city architect Adolphe Pauli. Construction lasted fourteen years. The new hospital had eight hundred beds in separate pavilions for men, women and children.

Burggraeve was deeply concerned with social questions. He complained ceaselessly that the workers' quarters of Ghent were '*bataillons de la maladie et de la mort*'. As a Liberal member of the city council from 1857 to 1881, he used the public forum to turn his progressive ideas into practice. His starting point was that an ounce of prevention is worth a pound of cure, and that public health needed to be protected by social legislation. He launched the idea — ahead of its time — of a health centre financed by an anonymous venture, the Société Gantoise. And he literally erected a monument to the vaccination methods of Edward Jenner and Louis Pasteur. His talent for popularisation also extended to education. Doctor Burggraeve was immensely popular with students and colleagues, but also among the common people thanks to his dedication, humanity and generosity. In 1866, when the city had to brave a terrible cholera epidemic, he wrote a *Projet d'assainissement et d'embellisement de la ville de Gand*. The insalubrious lanes turned into veritable breeding grounds of pestilence that spread disease even into the homes of the affluent. It was a scandal for the city that neighbourhoods such as Batavia still existed: it was worse than the ghettos of the Middle Ages. The situation was urgent!

In 1880, Adolphe Burggraeve retired, and afterwards devoted himself almost exclusively to dosimetry, an alternative pharmaceutical approach. Even when he was in his seventies he was still giving lectures on the subject throughout Europe. His numerous publications were translated into several languages, but Belgium remained indifferent to his international success. The dedicated doctor was not such a good businessman and ended up in financial difficulties. Burggraeve lived to be ninety-six, but died obscure and penniless.

Another 'poor doctor' was Nicholas Du Moulin. Like Burggraeve, Du Moulin was committed to improving public health. He was remembered by his faculty as '*un médecin de grand renom qui joignait à une intelligence d'élite un coeur qui vibrait à toute pensée noble et généreuse*'. At the professor's funeral in 1890 his patients took up a collection so they could lay a wreath of flowers on his coffin. A Socialist flag was carried in the funeral procession. Although Du Moulin was greatly admired by the up-and-coming Socialists in Ghent, he represented the Liberals on the city council from 1875 until his death.

The presence of a Socialist flag at Du Moulin's funeral was not appreciated by the Catholic minister of Domestic Affairs and Public Education, Ernest Mélot. He called the university to order and demanded measures to ensure that the incident would not be repeated. The majority (20–8) of the Academic Council, however, rejected the prohibition of the Socialist flag at university ceremonies. They felt special regulations were unnecessary. The government responded by formulating a royal decree, which stated that public ceremonies organised by the university were to have an exclusively academic character. Apart from the national flag, no other emblem was henceforth

**Preserved head and hand of an unknown woman, ca. 1835**
In the 1830s Adolphe Burggraeve developed a successful injection technique based on an old, secret recipe for preserving the illusion of life in death. In the nineteenth century it was mainly the bodies of people who had died in the poor hospitals that were subject to dissection for teaching and research purposes. The next of kin received payment, if they handed the body over to science. The university's anatomical collection was opened to the public during the Gentse Feesten and was a source of great admiration. According to the newspapers, Burggraeve succeeded 'in exempting the body from the decomposition that follows death'. According to the *Gazette van Gend*, this woman represents not death but 'sleep', or 'the beloved who dreams of her lover'. She rests in peace.
(Ghent, Ghent University Museum, photo Benn Deceuninck)

permitted without the express written permission of the minister, rector and executive director.

## 'Saint Guislain' and psychiatry

In 1819, Joseph Guislain was one of the first doctors in medicine to graduate from the new University of Ghent. At the time, training in psychiatry was extremely rare at European universities. In Paris, Philippe Pinel, chief physician of the Salpêtrière clinic, caused an uproar with his 'moral' treatment of the mentally ill. The condition of the 'senseless' in Belgium was downright inhuman. Guislain had seen this with his own eyes at the beginning of his career in the 'madhouse' for men in the Geeraard de Duivelsteen: 'Poorly tended patients, disgusting, covered with vermin, locked up in pens so filthy it defies the imagination.' His empathy for the 'trash' of society was immediately confirmed. In 1826 his study *'Traité sur l'aliénation mentale et sur les hospices des aliénés'* received international renown. His starting point was the idea that mental illness was influenced by 'moral pain' and that psychic problems must be traced back to mental causes. His innovative point of view led to fruitful collaboration with canon Petrus-Jozef Triest, the general superior of the congregation of the Brothers of Charity. Guislain was appointed special physician to the two insane asylums in Ghent and with the help of Triest was able to carry out a drastic modernisation and humanisation of these institutions. He was not only in charge of treating the 'so-called mentally ill', but was also permitted to conduct scientific research.

In the new kingdom of Belgium, Guislain was involved from the beginning in the institutional reform of care for the mentally ill. Together with Edouard Ducpétiaux (inspector-general of prisons and charitable institutions), he helped formulate the new legislation in 1850 that removed care for the mentally ill from the arbitrary jurisdiction of local governments. The law, which remained in force until 1991, ensured that the patient was isolated and protected from the harmful influences in his environment in order to facilitate his cure. The madman had become a patient. Great store was set by therapy, with an emphasis on gentle treatment and the avoidance of brutal restraint. Every institution, for example, was required to have a central bath in order to administer hydrotherapy. The procedure to collocate was also better managed.

In 1835, Guislain became a professor and was responsible for the courses Human and Comparative Physiology and History of Medicine as well as Hygiene. His *Traité sur les Phrénopathies ou doctrine nouvelle des maladies mentales,* published two years earlier, was a reference work on the psychic causes of mental illnesses. He also continued to study the brain in order to track down physical deviations — with the question of whether they were the cause or the result of psychic disorders.

Guislain lay at the basis of clinical psychiatry training in Ghent. He was an outstanding and extremely eloquent teacher with great intellectual authority. In his lectures, *Leçons orales sur les phrénopathies* (1852), he looked for the social factors that fostered susceptibility to mental illnesses. He further developed Pinel's 'moral' treatment by seeking out therapies that had an effect on the cognitive as well as emotional functions. Activating the patients through work, physical exercise, music and play was alternated with relaxation methods and shock therapy.

As a Liberal city council member, Guislain had argued since 1848 for the construction of a new and scientifically based institution for impoverished, mentally ill men. The design by city architect Adolphe Pauli was created in close consultation with Guislain. The patients were divided into six categories, each with their own department in well-defined, symmetrical rooms: the convalescing, the calm, the anxious/excited, the loud/tumultuous, the demented/retarded and the incontinent/passive. The Guislain Institute was opened in 1857 in a quiet setting just outside the city, north of the Brugsepoort. The internationally renowned model institution, soon known by its popular name 'Saint Guislain', exuded a pleasant air of calm, space and security. Today, a hundred and sixty years later, this harmonious atmosphere has changed very little. Guislain also argued for preserving the *modus vivendi* between religion and science, which had prevailed there since his appointment in 1828. Although the Liberal city administration thought differently, Guislain insisted that organisation and care remain in the hands of the Brothers of Charity, while he as head physician would retain his scientific and therapeutic independence. Moral as well as economic motives played a role in his preference for clerics as managers and carers. The Brothers put into practice what Guislain had in mind. In the 1850s, for example, there was an in-house brass band and the 'tumultuous' patients were given military drill exercises in uniform, complete with wooden guns. As soon as he was appointed, Guislain had ensured that the Brothers were trained in nursing.

'Saint Guislain' was not even able to work in his model institution for three years. He died in 1860, after a lingering illness, only sixty-three years old. In 2006 he was chosen as Ghent University's 'Greatest Prof'.

**Children's courtyard of the Guislain Institute, 1887**
The photo is part of an album from 1887 in which *'l'hospice Guislain'* is presented as a model institution for the treatment of the mentally ill.
(Ghent, Museum Dr. Guislain)

The close ties between the university and the Guislain Institute were only restored when the psychologist Maurice Hamelinck succeeded Jean Crocq as professor of Psychiatry after the latter's untimely death in 1925. Crocq was a brilliant teacher and regularly took the students, who literally hung on his every word, to the Guislain Institute, Caritas in Melle, or the insane asylum in Uccle, where he gave masterly clinical demonstrations. He helped found the Laboratory for Psychopathology in 1923.

As adjunct-head physician to the progressive Karel Van Acker, Hamelinck advocated the establishment of a psychiatric polyclinic attached to the Guislain Institute. In 1930 a well-planned building with an auditorium was opened. The new forms of therapy that Van Acker introduced, such as electroshock, could be immediately demonstrated in front of the students.

In fact, Hamelinck was destined to succeed Jules Van Biervliet. After graduation he became an assistant in the Laboratory for Experimental Psychology, the first laboratory of its kind in Belgium, established in 1891. Van Biervliet got his ideas in Leipzig, with the founder of the new science, Wilhelm Wundt. He was appointed to the faculty of Arts and Philosophy in 1890 to teach a course on Psychology, among other things, which had branched off from moral philosophy. It marked a new, (natural-)scientific view of the discipline, which until then had had a more speculative, spiritual character. Van Biervliet, who also had a PhD in natural sciences, gave the nascent subject a strong experimental and physiological basis, and in a short time he was able to put together a laboratory with the most advanced equipment. Privileged areas of research included perception (visual illusions), attention (reaction times) and above all memory. Depth psychology, not to mention psychoanalysis in the style of his contemporary Sigmund Freud, were not Van Biervliet's cup of tea.

Psychoanalysis was introduced at Ghent University by the erudite neuropsychiatrist Jacques De Busscher, a student of Hamelinck's. Alexander Evrard, a scientific collaborator at the time, recalls how the bachelor De Busscher, who liked cats, would make his rounds as head of the department of Neuropsychiatry in the Bijloke with the hospital cat Blackie on his arm. The cat slept in the linen closet. When his house cat died, De Busscher had her laid out on a stretcher among flowers and glowing candles.

Jacques De Busscher acted as a real patron of 'his' Bijloke. He made his rounds with a whole procession behind him: assistants, interns, nurses and students. When he was appointed as head of the department, psychiatric patients in the Bijloke did not have rooms of their own, so that this procession basically had to parade through all the rooms in the hospital. De Busscher was a liberal Freemason, socially an archconservative. Even after the Second World War had passed, he still had his head in the *belle époque*. Hence he resisted the development of the university's own Academic Hospital. As a fierce opponent of vivisection, he quarrelled with the world-renowned ophthalmologist Jules François, who led the Ophthalmology Clinic and had tested an experimental eye operation on cats, De Busscher's favourite animals. The amorous tales about '*le beau Jacques*' or 'Prince Charming', a notorious skirt-chaser who voiced denigrating opinions about women, were legion. In the US, where he specialised after his studies, he is even said to have had an affair with Joan Crawford.

Until his death in 1966, De Busscher lived with his mother. The histologist Marie De Groodt, later rector of the State University Centre of Antwerp (Rijksuniversitair Centrum Antwerpen, or RUCA), was for many years his lover. De Busscher's literary enthusiasm and passion for history, especially of the French royal house and the pomp and splendour of the aristocracy, are evident in his numerous publications in the *Cahiers de la Biloque: revue médicale gantoise*, a cultural periodical for doctors that included space for hospital anecdotes. These *Cahiers* were published from 1951 onwards by head physician Urbain Thiry, and appeared until all university departments in the Bijloke were finally moved to the Academic Hospital on De Pintelaan. The renowned department of Neuropsychiatry was, together with the polyclinic of the Guislain Institute, one of the last bastions to move to the Academic Hospital in 1975.

## Gustave Boddaert and the antiseptic method

In the 1870s the latent tensions between the university and the city surrounding the Bijloke hospital came to a head. The existing regulations no longer seemed adequate, and the endless tug of war over patients and corpses was particularly nerve-racking. The growing specialisation of hospital physicians, on the one hand, and professors on the other gave rise to new problems. The conflicts even spilled out onto the streets and into parliament.

The professors were not always the most progressive party in this story. In 1873, Gustave Boddaert, then still 'just' a surgeon in the Bijloke, operated on a patient that had been referred to his clinic as a case study by the treating physician in the university department of professor Floribert Soupart. Boddaert was reprimanded by the rector, but the affair escalated. When the surgeon called Soupart's assistant 'an idiot' in front of a full operating room, the students got involved as well. Under pressure from the minister, a compromise between the hospital and the university was reached in 1874. From then on, a distinction was made between patients who were treated free of charge and paying patients. The first category had to submit to clinical training sessions and the demonstrations of university professors; the second category was not obliged to do so. Nevertheless, new problems arose with the students, who felt that the separation between hospital and university clinic should be extended even further.

The battle between Boddaert and Soupart would last for at least another five years. Stealing each other's patients, reports and counter-reports on the objectivity of diagnoses, incidents of harassment small and large, were the order of the day. Soupart was twenty-five years older than Boddaert. That is, he embodied the old notions of surgery and fought bitterly against the

**Gustave Boddaert**
Richard Boddaert, Gustave's older brother, introduced medical students to the wonderful world of the microscope. The rise of the microscope fundamentally changed anatomical research. It became increasingly focused on pathological anatomy and histology. Anatomical preparations were no longer meant to appeal to the crowd and lost their aesthetic and moral function.
(Ghent, Universiteitsarchief)

newcomer, who fought just as hard to introduce the antiseptic method in the hospital. Burggraeve's classic lead bandages were banned, to the great irritation of the direction, nuns and colleagues. Only in 1879, when Boddaert was appointed professor — in Soupart's surgical clinic, no less — did the situation improve somewhat. Boddaert won out in the end. He had studied abroad — among other places, in London, where he became acquainted with the surgical antisepsis of Joseph Lister and with the prominent gynaecologist Thomas Spencer Wells. Wells emphasised the absolute cleanliness of hands and instruments during oophorectomies and in this way reduced the operation death rate from nearly 100% to 4%. Boddaert would likewise spread the use of the strictest antiseptic rules among midwives. He was one of the first doctors in Europe to give credence to the findings of Ignaz Semmelweis on maternal mortality and put them into practice.

## New laboratories for top science

The promotion of public health was closely tied to improving hygiene and combatting epidemics. Cholera morbus, an illness that was known only in India before the nineteenth century, began to spread into Europe through England and Russia in the early 1830s. When the epidemic first broke out in Ghent in 1832, there were 1,227 deaths. Another five epidemics would follow: in 1849, 1854-1859, 1866, 1883-1885 and 1892-1893. The most destructive wave occurred in the summer of 1866 and was also nicknamed the 'triumph of death'. In Belgium, it is estimated that 43,000 people died, of which 2,769 in Ghent. The greatest havoc was wrought in the neighbourhoods with poor living conditions. In Ghent, these were the districts of Meerthem, Sassepoort and Batavia. We know this thanks to the large-scale research of Dr Nicolas Du Moulin into the physical and social circumstances that caused cholera to flourish in Ghent.

The cholera epidemic of 1866 opened the eyes of the city's industrialists, who realised that sanitation in the city for the benefit of all took precedence over their own gains. Alderman for public works and public hygiene Charles Andries took on the task of having the insalubrious ditches and stinking canals of the city centre filled and covered.

Du Moulin's research took even meteorology into account, but not the scientific breakthroughs in the area of microbiology during the same period. His colleague Emile Van Ermengem, who was appointed to the faculty of Medicine in 1885 for the courses on Public and Private Health and Bacteriology, did take note, however. He had specialised in Paris, London, Edinburgh, Vienna and in 1883 Berlin, where he worked with Nobel Prize winner Robert Koch, the discoverer of Mycobacterium tuberculosis (1877) and Vibrio cholerae (1883). In 1886 the internationally recognised standard work *Neue Untersuchungen über die Cholera-Mikroben von dr. E. Van Ermengem* was published. That year, Van Ermengem founded the Laboratory for Hygiene and Bacteriology. At the same time, optional tuition-free courses were set up to deal with subjects such as the counterfeiting of foodstuffs, not only for the regular students but also for pharmacists and physicians who wished to sign up. Van Ermengem also gave public lectures on tuberculosis. When he wanted to introduce an elective course on microbiology, the faculty of Sciences expressed reserve. His argument was that there was a series of

**The Institute for Hygiene and Bacteriology**
The Rommelaere complex, which was built opposite the Bijloke hospital between 1899 and 1905, comprises three medical institutes with associated laboratories: Hygiene and Bacteriology on Hospitalstraat, Pharmacodynamics and Physiotherapy on the Baertsoenkaai and Physiology on Jozef Kluyskensstraat. It would also house the Laboratory for Forensic Medicine.
(Ghent, Stadsarchief, photo Edmond Sacré)

**Laboratory for Hygiene and Bacteriology**
(Ghent, Universiteitsarchief)

Corneel Heymans, 1960s
(Ghent, Universiteitsarchief)

phenomena in 'biological chemistry' that had both a chemical and a physiological component in which the same organisms were active: fermentations.

In February 1896 a preliminary report on Van Ermengem's investigation of a case of food poisoning and the cause of botulism appeared in the *Bulletin* of the Société de Médecine de Gand. A year later it was also published by the *Zeitschrift für Hygiene und Infektions Krankheiten*, edited by Dr Koch. The discovery of botulism is considered one of the 100 'Milestones in Microbiology'. Musicians in the brass band of Ellezelles, near Ronse, had eaten raw ham in the Le Rustic café after a funeral. The next day most were seriously ill, and three of them succumbed to the poisoning. Local doctors called on the help of professor Van Ermengem for additional research. After bacteriological analysis of the ham and the autopsy of the victims' spleens, he was able to isolate and identify a new anaerobic bacterium in his lab, the Bacillus botulinis. He moreover succeeded in unravelling the mechanisms of the poison responsible: the extremely toxic substance botulinum, which is already fatal at doses of 1 nanogram per kilogram of body weight. Today, Clostridium botulinum is routinely detected by laboratories that research soil, water and foodstuffs. It is feared as a weapon in biological warfare, but is also used in a highly diluted form as Botox in the medical and cosmetic sector.

The discovery made Van Ermengem famous overnight. He strengthened his position in Ghent and with it his arguments in favour of modern buildings. The pharmacology lab was then still installed in an outbuilding of the faculty of Arts and Philosophy in the city centre. The barking of the laboratory dogs so disturbed the peace and quiet of the philosophers that an on-going conflict arose. In 1898 the city of Ghent was finally convinced to build three new medical institutes that would fall under the collective name 'Rommelaere', after the Ghent physician Willem Rommelaere, former rector of the ULB. The building was financed in part with the inheritance of one of his patients, a well-to-do West Flemish businessman. Adolphe Pauli had died in the meantime, and the new city architect, Louis Cloquet, was tasked with the design. The new neo-Gothic 'palace' of science rose opposite the Bijloke hospital and was solemnly inaugurated in 1905 by King Leopold II. In 1907 the new university clinics and polyclinics on Pasteurdreef were opened.

In one of the new buildings on the Baertsoenkaai, Corneel Heymans would make his groundbreaking discovery of chemoreceptors in the carotid artery after the First World War, for which he would be awarded the Nobel Prize in 1938. In 1912 his father, Jan-Frans Heymans, had already successfully attached the head of one dog to the body of another and achieved full circulation of the blood. Corneel continued this research tradition and discovered by chance the function of chemoreceptors in the regulation of breathing and how the breath centre reacts to chemical substances.

## A sound mind in a sound body

In 1906, Dr Florent Gommaerts was appointed as assistant director of the Institute for Physiotherapy (Instituut voor Fysicotherapie) in the Rommelaere complex. As an adept of massage and therapeutic gymnastics, he had long advocated the introduction of kinesiotherapy in Ghent but was rebuffed, so he started his own Institut de Kinésithérapie et Médicomécanique Zander. Gommaerts was inspired by study trips to Stockholm, Berlin, Copenhagen and Hamburg, where the movement sciences were much more advanced. The Central Gymnastics and Orthopaedic Institute of Stockholm served as a model for the institute that was set up in Ghent. In particular, the 'medico-mechanical' gymnastics of Jonas Zander, which relied on the use of specialised machines, was a revelation for Gommaerts. Medicine met gymnastics and produced

a range of therapeutic possibilities — for example, in terms of breathing. By placing greater emphasis on gymnastics instead of athletics, Gommaerts hoped to strengthen the weak — '*les débilités, les faibles, les vieillards et les malades*'. After all, they were not benefited by the extreme exertion associated with athletics.

The growing interest in the body, sports and gymnastics should be situated in the spirit of the *fin de siècle* and the bourgeois desire for 'regeneration'. Starting in the 1870s, the gymnastics movement spread from Germany throughout the rest of Europe. Swedish gymnastics followed later, but would in any case become more popular in Ghent than the German variant.

The director-general of Higher Education, Sciences and Arts, Cyrille Van Overbergh, was completely won over by the new ideology of '*culture physique*' for the reinforcement of the race, the nation and the colonial expansion of Belgium. Gommaerts was appointed to give shape to the institutionalisation of physical education at Ghent University. But the road to its recognition as science was still long. Gommaerts encountered protectionism from the physicians when it came to sharing the title of doctor. The scientific degrees of candidate, licentiate and doctor in physical education, however, were permitted to pass. Only in the 1960s would the synergy between medicine and movement sciences become a reality in Ghent, thanks to the efforts of Maurice Mussen. The polio epidemics of 1952 and 1955 indicated at any rate that it was about time for a suitable department of kinesiotherapy and rehabilitation.

The Higher Institute for Physical Education (Hoger Instituut voor Lichamelijke Opvoeding, or HILO) dates from 1908. It was 'attached' to the faculty of Medicine, but otherwise did not have its own infrastructure. Or at least, not the kind of infrastructure Gommaerts dreamed of. He had to settle for the gym at the Emile Braun girls' primary school on the Paddenhoek. It was located in the old Jesuit monastery near the Aula, where the university had housed the laboratories of the Special Schools in the nineteenth century. The director gave permission to use the gym between 3 and 4.30 p.m., except on Tuesdays and Saturdays. Those who wanted to register but had no diploma were subjected to a rigorous admissions exam. In 1909 the first female students took the exam, which highlighted the accommodation problems: separate changing rooms and showers were not provided. On the first floor, the 'gentlemen' had not only the spacious gymnasium, but also changing rooms with a dozen lockers, three showers and three lavatories. The 'ladies' had to take a steep, narrow spiral staircase to the second floor, where the university installed primitive facilities. Lecturer Anna Lundberg, who was specially appointed for the girls' exercises, only earned a fourth of what her male colleague Georg Schmitterlöw received, and ended up quitting after a year. Stability finally arrived in 1913, when the recently graduated licentiate Irène Van der Bracht took up the post, even though the wage issue was not resolved. In 1919 she still

**Physical education students**
The Higher Institute for Physical Education (HILO), founded in 1908, did not initially have its own building or infrastructure. In the photo at the lower left, Florent Gommaerts and Irène Van der Bracht in the Institute for Physiotherapy demonstrate to their students how to do an orthopaedic examination on children.
(Ghent, Universiteitsarchief)

earned less than a third of what her male colleague was paid. After facing considerable opposition, in 1925 Van der Bracht became the first female professor in Belgium.

The government encouraged student associations that organised sports activities right from the start. In 1910 the first interuniversity sports events took place, with a rowing regatta on the inland waterways of Ghent. In 1933, the Association Sportive de l'Université de Gand was rechristened the Gentse Universitaire Sportbond (GUSB). From 1934 onwards, the minister decreed that no classes could be held on Wednesday afternoons in order to give the students a chance to do research or to participate in sports activities. Moreover, students paid an extra registration fee of 10 francs so that the university could expand its sporting activities.

Until the founding of the Institut Supérieur d'Éducation Physique in Liège in 1931, the HILO was unique in Belgium, and next to Stockholm the only university institute where physical education was taught on a scientific basis. The Dutchification of the university made a French-speaking equivalent necessary. From 1931 onwards, however, medical protectionism was also reinforced: from then on, a candidate diploma in medicine was required before students could begin a licentiate in physical education. The result was a sharp decline in the number of students, a trend that would only be reversed after the Second World War. Then it was also possible to consider an appropriate sports infrastructure.

The first foundation stone of the HILO was laid at the freshly dug Watersportbaan — a manmade rowing race course — on 2 October 1958. Two years later, the building was operational, literally and figuratively giving the programme a new lease of life.

## Modern medicine in an outdated hospital

In 1899 the Leuven neurologist Arthur Van Gehuchten visited his fellow bacteriologist Emile Van Ermengem in Ghent. They shared a passion for photography. As an avant-garde professor, Van Gehuchten used the moving image to show his students neurological disorders and postoperative healing processes. His marvellous nitrate films have been preserved and are among the oldest Belgian films. They inspired the orthopedagogue and choreographer Alain Platel, who received an honorary doctorate from Ghent University, in the creation of his dance performances.

One of Van Gehuchten's students was Fritz De Beule, who played a groundbreaking role in the area of neurosurgery and was a founder of the modern surgical school in Ghent. His treatment of trigeminal neuralgia, chronic face pain caused by a nerve disruption, brought him international renown. De Beule brought about drastic changes in surgical education. His classes were of an 'admirable didactic clarity, sober, short and good'. Alexander Evrard recalls attending a mastectomy in the rotunda of the anatomical theatre. The woman was completely anaesthetised and the auditorium was packed with students: for this spectacle, the rules of asepsis had been temporarily suspended. De Beule was the prototype of a master figure with fatherly, paternalistic traits. He also preferred to be called 'master' instead of 'professor', yet was not at all in favour of magisterial *ex cathedra* pronouncements. He chose a student from the audience to come and conduct the examination himself.

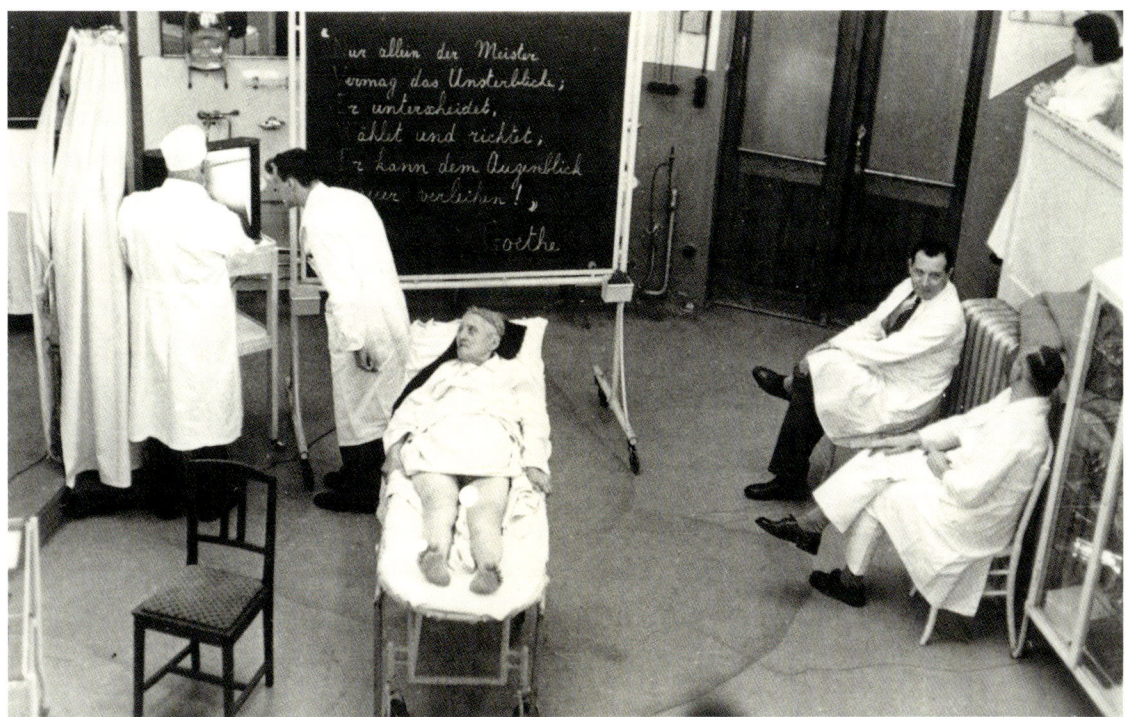

By introducing scientific research, he was able to modernise the surgical clinic in Ghent, although he had a low opinion of radiology and lab work. His successor, Emile Derom, tried to make the university surgery more attractive by introducing all the latest techniques. With the cooperation of Dr Gaby Meirsman-Roobroeck, he introduced modern anaesthetics. As a young student, Derom had often applied anaesthetics based on ether and chloroform, a method he had learned from the nurses/nuns in the Bijloke. His goal was to get ahead of the city's private hospitals, which had become fierce competition for the Bijloke after the Second World War. Since the introduction of obligatory health and invalidity insurance (Ziekte- en Invaliditeitsverzekering, or ZIV) in 1944 and the expansion of the health insurance funds, people could just as well seek treatment in private clinics such as Den Briel, Sint-Vicentius or the Refuge. The university beds in the large halls of the Bijloke — the 'poor hospital' where the needy came to stay in the winter — were increasingly less attractive to the inhabitants of Ghent. Emile Derom would also do everything in his power to give his patients more privacy. Obligatory health insurance turned out to be a real catastrophe for the university clinics.

Fritz Derom, son and successor of Emile, tells how, beginning in 1956, the polyclinic of the surgery department on Pasteurdreef 'sort of' started with heart surgery. This did not happen in optimal conditions. There were no personnel after 5 p.m., the operating room was 4 metres from the street and 300 metres from the infirmary, and the department was closed at weekends and during vacation. Nevertheless, the Bijloke was the first university clinic in Belgium where open heart surgery took place under cooling in 1957. The patient was immersed in a bath of ice water until his body temperature reached 30° before the operation began. Warming and waking the patient, however, took a great deal of time. Moreover, it was not safe for him to be left in a

**Fritz De Beule in the anatomical theatre of the Bijloke, 1938**
Fritz De Beule, left, was a gifted teacher. He did not use didactic tools such as photos or films, or even prepare for his lectures. His successor, Emile Derom, remembers: 'I still see him entering the auditorium of Anatomy, his posture erect, his cigarette on his lips, looking about with his piercing little eyes, filled with humour, at an audience on whom he imposed his stature and an air which he liked to make severe.'
(Ghent, Universiteitsarchief)

room 300 metres away without appropriate care. Derom, then assistant surgeon, describes how he, the nurses and the anaesthetist slept in the operating room to remain close to the patient until he had sufficiently recovered to be hospitalised without monitoring.

There was still tension between the city and the university over the Bijloke in the 1950s. The cat-and-mouse game with patients continued unabated. An additional difficulty was the so-called 'dichotomy': until 1965 it was an unwritten rule that surgeons remitted part of their fees to the referring general practitioner. Over time this grew into a real 'business' and amounts ran up to 30% of the fee. As soon as someone was hospitalised, the assistants could commandeer him during the first twenty-four hours and have him moved to the university rooms. However, the patient had to be concealed from the department heads of the Bijloke. Hence, students in their final year who acted as interns tried to hide the patients so that the assistants from the university couldn't find them.

Without the faculty's knowledge, rector Norbert Goormaghtigh had the Surgery department of the Bijloke hospital audited. The result was a damning report of four pages: 'a completely antiquated hospital', 'rooms are far too large', 'the hospital is

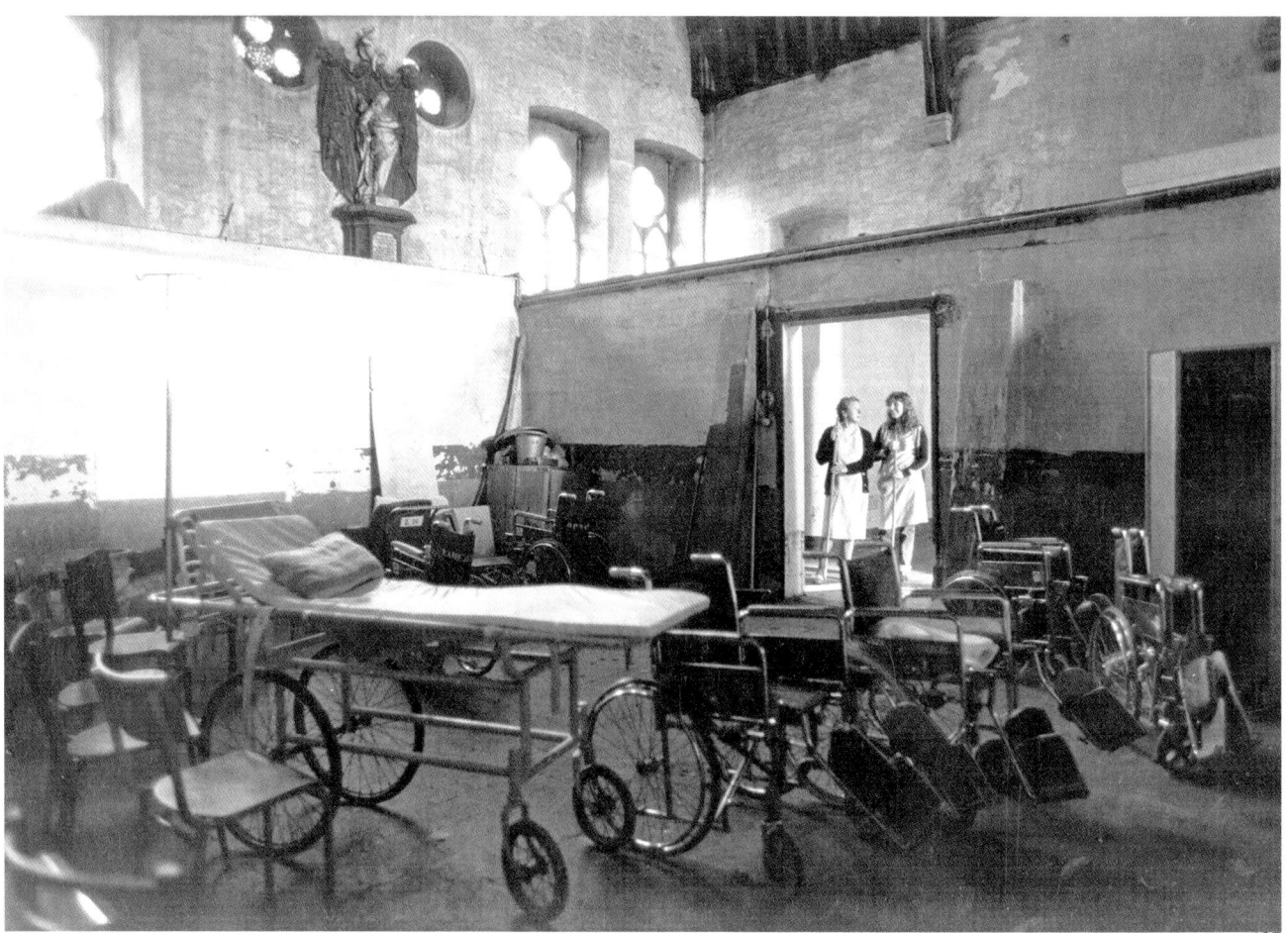

**The Bijloke just before the move to the Academic Hospital**
Until well into the twentieth century the faculty of Medicine depended on the Bijloke hospital for clinical education and internships.
(Ghent, Universiteitsarchief, photo Hendrik Eeckhout)

connected to the operating room on Pasteurdreef by a long, high-ceilinged, cold and damp corridor', 'the operating room is a small, dark pen'. The conclusion was nothing if not clear: 'Ghent's surgery clinic is more than fifty years behind the times.'

## Towards an Academic Hospital

The report was an important element in the quest for an Academic Hospital, a quest that shifted into high gear after the Second World War. Under the impulse of Frans Daels, a faculty study commission for the Academic Hospital was created in 1930. It stated that the Ghent faculty of Medicine was the only one in the world that did not have its own hospital. Yet a well-equipped, modern hospital was necessary for it to fulfil its societal and scientific tasks. In 1935, executive director Alfred Schoep took the initiative of purchasing and requisitioning property covering a large plot on the Zwijnaardsesteenweg. A College of Architects for the Academic Hospital (CAVAZ), consisting of the Ghent professors Henry Van de Velde, Armand Cerulus, Jean-Norbert Cloquet, August Desmet and Gustave Magnel, guaranteed the modern and functional character of the complex.

The works commenced in 1937. The steel armature was ready on the eve of the

Second World War. When the war was over, the works dragged on due to a manifest lack of political interest and financing. The polio epidemics of 1952 and 1955 finally brought construction up to speed. The children's pavilion — by professor Carlos Hooft — in the garden of the Bijloke was too small and unsuited to receiving polio patients. In 1953 a second wing was added to the building that was only seen as a temporary solution when it opened in 1938. In 1955 there were 150 cases of poliomyelitis in Ghent alone. Notwithstanding the inadequate infrastructure, the children's pavilion would have the first 'iron lung' in Belgium, a ventilator *avant la lettre* that ensured

Doctors and surgeons at the new Academic Hospital
(Ghent, Universiteitsarchief)

that children could breath passively. From 1956 onwards, children were admitted to the Academic Hospital.

In 1959 the first operation using an artificial heart was performed on Pasteurdreef. After Paediatrics was moved to the university hospital, it was difficult for adult heart surgery to remain there. Collaboration between Fritz Derom and children's heart surgeon Anna Blancquaert was outstanding. Blancquaert made two operating rooms in the children's clinic available for adult heart surgery. For years, however, patients were obliged to go to Pasteurdreef for aortography so that the investigation could take place under full anaesthesia. The legendary ambulance shuttle between Pasteurdreef and De Pintelaan is etched in the memory of the generation that experienced it.

Heart surgery for children and adults quickly made the new Academic Hospital in Ghent a point of reference — for people with other disorders as well. The spectacular character of heart operations ensured growing public awareness. The royal family did the rest. Alexander, the eldest son of princess Lilian and king Leopold III, had had an aorta operation in Boston in 1957. In 1962, Lilian opened two operating theatres in Ghent on the occasion of an international cardio-surgical congress. While it was nearly impossible to secure funding during the period of the Bijloke, heart surgery now received substantial investment. Jacqueline Penninck made an important step forwards by equipping a high-performance laboratory.

The department of Intensive Care grew almost organically out of heart surgery. After a heart operation, a patient needed to be monitored continuously for the first twenty-four hours. In the Bijloke, intensive care consisted of a stretcher in the corridor or the operating room. In the Academic Hospital, it was two rooms in the children's clinic next to the operating room. Word soon spread, so that after a while victims of accidents were also admitted. Operating room nurses gave blood transfusions to victims of accidents in the corridors of the children's clinic. Georges Vandeputte, director of the Academic Hospital, took the initiative of furnishing a 'real' intensive care department and emergency room. At the hospital's expense, he bought an ambulance in which the surgeons could ride along: a first! The doctor no longer had to wait for the sick or wounded to be brought to him — he could ride to the victim's location. The Surgery department of the Academic Hospital was thus responsible for the 900 emergency service for many years.

## Spectacular lung transplant

Ghent played a crucial role in developing an international system for the exchange of organs (Eurotransplant). In August 1965, Fritz Derom and nephrologist Severin Ringoir carried out the first kidney transplant from a deceased donor in Ghent, even before it was done in the Netherlands. The first-ever lung transplant with a ten-month survival took place on 14 November 1968. With earlier transplant in the US, the donor lung was rejected after only a few days. Derom received a great deal of international recognition because of it. In January 1969 he was invited to the palace at Laken. The 'lucky' patient was Aloïs Vereecken, a twenty-three-year-old metal worker from Kalken with terminal silicosis. Yet the PR service of the university was not exactly generous with information about this spectacular first. The medical performance of Derom and his team was shrouded in discretion under the guise of medical deontology. Although rector Bouckaert supported him, the university, under pressure from the publicity-shy Order of Physicians and particular colleagues, hardly gave him any notice at all. The only thing released to the world in the press was that the patient had already waved at his wife. A press conference was cancelled. 'Pathetic country', 'prophets not honoured in own country', 'sluggish and underdeveloped business', 'pioneers silenced out of envy', grumbled the Flemish papers. It was three months after the operation before the university's deontological commission decided that the time was ripe to go to the press with an earnest scientific bulletin about the operation. In May 1969 a beaming Vereecken was released. He could live and breathe again like a free, healthy person. Unfortunately he died on 10 September that year when his body rejected the transplant.

Derom received a medal of recognition from the city and the Joseph Lemaire Prize from Sociale Voorzorg, the socialist health insurance fund. The president of France awarded him the Legion of Honour. Yet his own university never paid tribute to his accomplishment. During his career, the Academic Hospital (AZ), later the University Hospital (UZ), grew to be a reference centre for three million people in East and West Flanders. But the organisation of the clinics changed drastically: the pyramidal structure, with the 'Professor' with a capital 'P' at the top, was replaced by smaller entities — departments — that functioned alongside one another and were forced to cooperate by the lightning speed of specialisation.

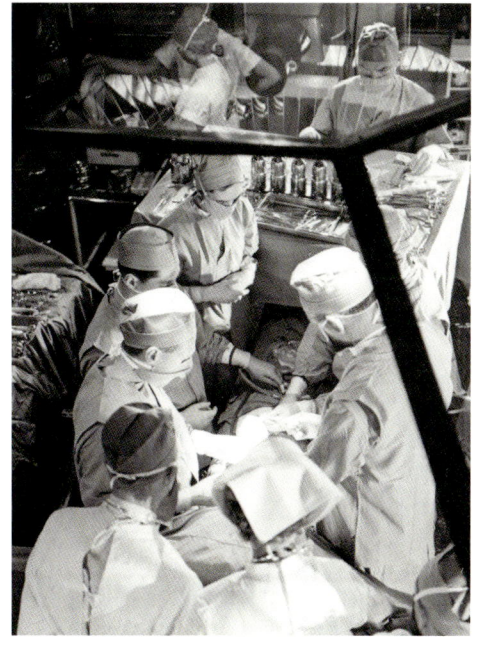

**Fritz Derom at the operating table, 1962**
When princess Lilian opened two operating theatres in the AZ in 1962, heart surgery was given an extra touch of glamour.
(Ghent, Universiteitsarchief, photo A. Van Lancker)

**Aloïs Vereecken after his lung transplant, 1969**
The twenty-three year-old metal worker from Kalken, who faced certain death, lived for another ten months thanks to a donor lung. A note from his widow is pasted in the photo album that Fritz Derom used to keep track of his great achievement, thanking the professor for his attentive care and his presence at the funeral ceremony.
(Ghent, Universiteitsarchief)

## Back to the future: social medicine

Fritz Derom's lung transplant was not remarked by 'sixty-niner' Peter Piot. The discoverer of the Ebola virus started studying in Ghent in 1966 out of a combination of will for freedom, interest in science, and engagement with humanity and society. Great was his disappointment. The scientific foundations of medicine were nothing to write home about: contact with people and patients were not part of the vocabulary of most professors, and society seemed to interest them even less. The faculty of Medicine was a largely conservative bulwark. Piot had classes with what he calls the last generation of 'really bad professors'. Some simply read their courses aloud in bad Dutch. The first candidate was the infamous Roger Moens, who taught physics. In his syllabus it stated explicitly that it was impossible for an object to be put into orbit around the earth, while Sputnik had been launched ten years before to considerable fanfare. Although he made a laconic attempt to correct this statement in his lectures, his syllabus remained unchanged. The only classes the young Piot attended were those of Frédéric Thomas on legal medicine — for the sensationalism and horrible murders, always popular among students. Apart from that, he was only interested in the microbiology course taught by Emile Nihoul, who also spoke bad Dutch, and social medicine with Karel Vuylsteek.

The 'communist' Vuylsteek was however not appreciated in the faculty of Medicine. He succeeded Numa Vlaeyen, another outsider, in 1965. He had been a driving force behind the socialist People's Clinic (Volkskliniek) that had opened in 1928 with the most up-to-date equipment, the best specialists and interdisciplinary collaboration between doctors who fully aligned their practices with the health problems of the working class. As department head of Internal Medicine at the Bijloke, Vlaeyen was in a good position to compare. A man of wide-ranging abilities, he also devoted himself to caring for Spanish children who came to Ghent as refugees from the Spanish Civil War of 1936-1939.

Vuylsteek continued the tradition of societal engagement and expanded social medicine at the Academic Hospital from nonexistence to a thriving department of sixty employees. He was particularly interested in diseases affecting the working class: cardiovascular diseases, chronic bronchitis, cancer, diabetes, alcoholism ... But he also had an eye for the new diseases of prosperity and the effects of air pollution. With national and European funding and the support of local authorities and industry, he carried out a large-scale population study that resulted in concrete projects on health education and training. In 1968, Vuylsteek established the Centre for the Evaluation and Rehabilitation of Heart Patients (Centrum voor de Evaluatie en Revalidatie van Hartlijders). The interdisciplinary approach of cardiologists, orthopaedists, physiotherapists and psychologists was highly innovative for that time. Vuylsteek's zone of activity soon expanded from the Ghent region to Europe and the World Health Organization (WHO). For him, social medicine meant innovative thinking about the

**Numa Vlaeyen in academic dress**
Numa Vlaeyen passed on his gown to his successor, Karel Vuylsteek, who in turn would pass it on to Jan De Maeseneer. A beautiful symbol of the continuity in the societal involvement of Ghent doctors and professors since 1817. In 2018 the departments of General Medicine and Public Health merged, which is only logical in light of their history.
(Ghent, Universiteitsarchief)

**Karel Vuylsteek**
(Ghent, collection of Patrick Vuylsteek)

interaction between people and the environment in a broad social framework, in which both material and immaterial factors played a role.

In line with the critical approach to health problems that classical curative medicine could not resolve, Karel Vuylsteek also introduced innovative forms of education. He found the accumulation of quickly out-dated knowledge via *ex cathedra* training and the rote memorisation of pre-processed subject matter unsuited to conveying his vision. Inspired by foreign models and the WHO, he was an early adopter of project group or workgroup education, in which students worked in groups of ten to fifteen with a supervisor on social themes: migration, factories and health, homosexuality, the Turkish community in Ghent … For microbiologist Emile Nihoul, improving the quality of education in Medicine was also a priority. In Canada he became acquainted with problem-solving education. He successfully put it into practice in Ghent.

The Socio-Medical Workgroup (Socio-Medicale Werkgroep, or SMW) was founded in 1969 as a rebellious student association that sought to offer an alternative to the traditional Flemish Medical Circle (Vlaamse Geneeskundige Kring, or VGK) as well as to reflect on the position of medicine and the physician in society. Human beings, not the stomach or the liver, had to become central again. Peter Piot was one of the founders, along with Frank Soete and Wim Van Lerberghe. He recalls how his year was a 'wonder year', with a very strong and socially engaged group of students. Women in particular excelled in their studies and on top of that organised everything else: Christine Rouneau, Eliane Collumbien, Rein Bellens. Many of his fellow male students became professors afterwards: Yves Benoit, Claude Cuvelier, Jean Marc Kaufman, Dirk Matthys.

The SMW consisted of a small, hard core of a dozen students with a lot of other people around them. They were pioneers who avidly embraced the new developments in healthcare while at the same time seeking to connect with the new social movements that emerged from May '68. Or rather: March '69 in Ghent. Maoists, Trotskyists, Christian Democrats, feminists, the politically homeless, anti-dogmatists — although not everyone was on the same political wavelength, everyone shared the same concerns about Third World problems, abortion, the mine closures, Vieille Montagne, Tessenderlo Chemie and, last but not least, the abolition of the Order of Physicians. Social engagement cast a wide net. Piot did not attend the lectures in his own degree programme, but went instead to courses taught by Etienne Vermeersch, Leo Apostel and historian Herman Balthazar in Arts and Philosophy. In that 'fantastic' time of dissent and protest, most of the people he met at his local, 't Keetje, and the cinema Studio Skoop, were either from other faculties or the broad cultural scene in Ghent.

Starting in 1971, the SMW published *De Lastige*, a magazine with analyses of social inequality in the healthcare sector and satirical cartoons by Frank Soete. The aim was

The first issue of *De Lastige*, 1971
(Ghent, Universiteitsarchief)

to educate a critical group of doctors: 'a pool of information, discussion and action that would give rise to a larger group of cooperating students and doctors that reflected critically on the various possibilities offered by their professional practice and on their place in society'. Although *De Lastige* only appeared at irregular intervals over a period of five years, the intention to develop a social movement around socio-medical themes was a success. In 1975 the workgroup merged with Mordicus, which opposed the impact of pharmaceutical companies on student life, organised 'alternative classes' and advocated free medicine. The movement produced a new generation of progressive doctors that would form group practices and get involved in neighbourhood health centres.

## Family medicine

After being turned off by the rigidity and drills of engineering, Jan De Maeseneer knew exactly what he had to do in the 1970-1971 academic year: study medicine in order to change healthcare. He immediately had the feeling that in the faculty of Medicine, everything was in a state of flux. In 1971 he became head (*praeses*) of the first year's students and immediately fired up eighty fellow students with his visionary enthusiasm. This has remained a common thread throughout De Maeseneer's forty-year career. With the SMW, for example, they conducted surveys of the living conditions of Turkish migrants and organised festive evenings for ex-prisoners and vagrants in the Prince Albert Home. Social engagement went even further. In the third year, an interdisciplinary workgroup was set up with the degree programmes in nursing and social work at the colleges. Internationally, the first texts about it only appeared ten years later. In terms of inter-professional collaboration, Ghent was at any rate far ahead of its time.

For the Hygiene and Social Medicine course taught by Karel Vuylsteek, De Maeseneer participated in a workgroup of fifteen students in 1973-1974 on the theme 'neighbourhood health centres as an alternative to a stagnant profession'. Vuylsteek secured funding to allow his students to observe how neighbourhood health centres in Amsterdam and Utrecht functioned. The examples of the Pointe-Saint-Charles in Montreal and the British health centres were also an inspiration. The 'work result', a text of sixty-eight pages, can be read as a blueprint for the neighbourhood health centres that exist today. It was a highly idealistic but at the same time highly concrete realisation of the '68 movement which went beyond mere dreaming, and in which the university played an important role. Today, there are 160 neighbourhood health centres (Wijkgezondheidscentra, or WGCs) in Belgium where 400,000 people are helped for a flat fee by an inter-professional team of health workers. They work together on the basis of equality: doctors are not higher in the hierarchy than the nurses or social workers, and are themselves employees. The pluralistic WGCs are not ideologically affiliated and are therefore 'the last in line when money is being handed out', according to De Maeseneer. Their infrastructure is subsidised by the Flemish government, but there is (still) no decree to give them a legal basis.

The new interpretation of the concept of 'general physician' was the basis for the department of Family Medicine and Primary Health Care, established in 1980. De Maeseneer's predecessor René De Smet chose resolutely in favour of innovation. It was a risky choice that turned out well. This was the first generation of general practitioners who were not doctors' sons or who did not have a 'family tree' in medicine. The era of the paternalistic doctor in his white coat on a pedestal was over. Communication between doctor and patient was central. Attention to the social determinants of health was expressed in the fact that the first WGCs in Ghent were all located in disadvantaged neighbourhoods: the Sleep, the Brugsepoort and the Botermarkt in Ledeberg. 'A university must stay in touch with society and make that connection itself', says De Maeseneer on the subject.

In what is known as COPC (Community Oriented Primary Care) week, students from several degree programmes spend a week working in a disadvantaged neighbourhood. They visit patients and discuss in interdisciplinary groups with aid workers in order to arrive at a 'community diagnosis'. This results in an 'advocacy' letter addressed to policymakers. De Maeseneer considers this form of education to be one of the central elements of the updated training programme for physicians. Many students discovered their calling as general practitioners in this way.

**De Sleep, 1993**
In August 1976 two GPs started the local health centre De Sleep, supported by volunteers (psychologists, social workers) from the neighbourhood, which was home to many immigrants. A contact person was appointed for intercultural mediation with the new citizens of Ghent. In 1993, after a long battle, De Sleep was the first in Flanders to introduce the system of flat-rate medicine, making healthcare free of charge for the patient.
(Ghent, Amsab-ISG, photo Roland Van der Sypt)

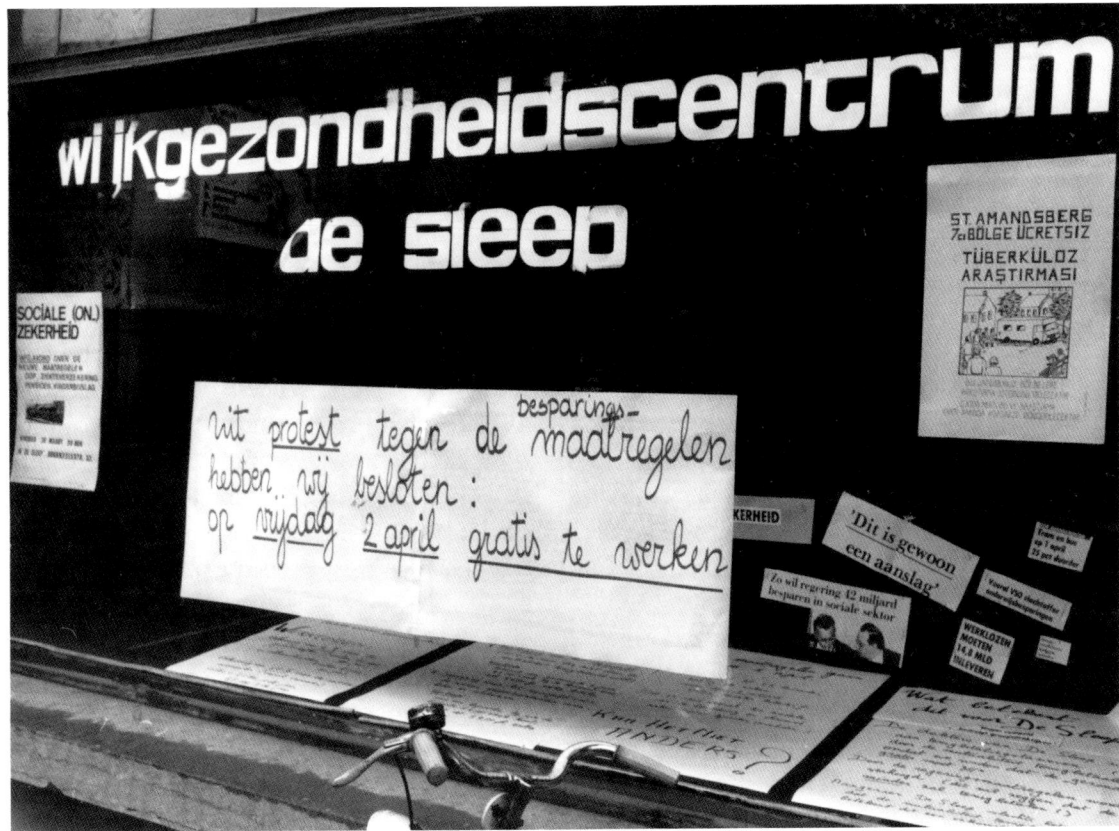

## Integration of Medicine and Health Sciences

If it had been up to Jan De Maeseneer, the faculty of Medicine would have been rechristened the faculty of Health Sciences. In 2000, dean Paul Van Cauwenberge launched the new name Medicine and Health Sciences. The story of the movement sciences clearly reveals the resistance that medical doctors put up against kinesiotherapy as a fully fledged science. Other domains such as nursing, logopaedics, ergotherapy and rehabilitation sciences also had to face considerable resistance surrounding the question of whether these programmes should be offered at university level. Pharmacy and dentistry had already been granted the status of university disciplines at a much earlier date. In 1970, Pharmaceutical Sciences even split off from Medicine to form a separate faculty, which many consider an aberration.

The Pharmacy faculty could of course point to the Nobel Prize won by Corneel Heymans and the success of his assistant Paul Janssen, founder of Janssen Pharmaceutica. Just before the division of the faculty, Romain Ruyssen also became the only Belgian to receive the Høst Madsen medal, the highest distinction of the International Pharmaceutical Federation. Ruyssen's most important contribution was the introduction of physicochemistry and biochemistry to the world of pharmacy. The education of pharmacists was in his view too limited, too focused on merely prescribing, preparing and learning how to administer medicines. His research ensured that the programme would become more scientific, and together with his collaborators Ruyssen played an important role in the international standardisation of pharmaceutical enzymes. He was also the first Belgian to use radioactive isotopes in pharmacy.

Oswald Rubbrecht, who achieved international renown with his treatment of jaw fractures among front soldiers during the First World War, was the founder of the dentistry programme in Ghent. On the eve of 1914-1918, he was appointed lecturer of an elective course on stomatology (oral medicine) for physicians. In 1933, Rubbrecht founded the Clinic for Oral Diseases (Kliniek voor Mondziekten) in a large outbuilding in his own garden in Sint-Pietersnieuwstraat. The programme in dentistry that was introduced at his urging in 1932 was expanded and professionalised by his successor, Adalbert Comhaire.

Comhaire made the move to the Academic Hospital in 1963 and succeeded — not without difficulty — in establishing a separate degree programme for dentists in 1976. But most of all, Comhaire went down in history as the designer of the dentist's chair, which ensured that dentists had better posture while working. In 1962 he demonstrated a prototype at the International Dental Show in Cologne and was met with disbelief. Today, nearly every dentist in the world sits down to work while the patient reclines.

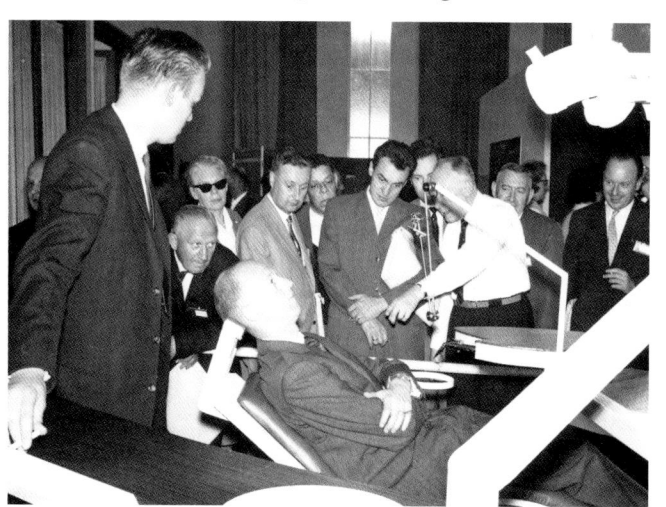

**International Dental Show in Cologne, 1962**
The revolutionary dental chair of Adalbert Comhaire (centre, wearing a white shirt) was presented here. For the first time in the history of the profession, the patient could be treated lying down.
(Ghent, Universiteitsarchief)

When Jan De Boever started as an associate professor in dentistry in 1973, however, he inherited a feeble department. He had taken his PhD in the US and advocated granting the discipline autonomy and insisting on higher scientific standards. De Boever ensured that both education and research were greatly expanded, and with his international reputation made sure that dentistry in Ghent was put on the international map.

The multidisciplinary integration of medicine and health sciences degree programmes is an answer to the shift that has become apparent in recent decades: from patient care to the research and development of increasingly refined technology for diagnosis and treatment. This shift is coupled with growing differentiation and subspecialisation, and places even greater pressure on the societal remit of the university and the hospital.

## The bridge between clinic and laboratory

Far-reaching developments in genetics and molecular biology have caused the rapid acceleration of research in a number of medical disciplines. The interaction between basic research, on the one hand, and the clinic, on the other, has at any rate brought about real progress in our knowledge of the biological and cellular mechanisms of many disorders. At the same time, high expectations of molecular genetics have been somewhat tempered. Scientific as well as public opinion have become aware that unravelling the genetic code is just the first step in understanding diseases.

The translational aspect of the bridge between clinic and laboratory has turned out to be crucial to the success of the department of Medical Genetics of former rector Anne De Paepe. Both researchers and doctors are trained to collaborate effectively and successfully. New research results are implemented in the clinic, and patients' questions and diseases feed research. This is certainly the case in the domain of orphan diseases, disorders so rare that, for policy reasons, the pharmaceutical industry has little interest in them. For De Paepe, creating solidarity and a good support framework for precisely these people is a form of social engagement. 'There are no miracle cures for hereditary diseases', she says. 'The patient mostly wants to know if and how he can be cured.' She has skilfully prevented attempts to detach her lab from the clinic for financial reasons.

As rector, De Paepe wholeheartedly supported the foundation of the Cancer Research Institute Ghent (CRIG) in 2016, a joint initiative of UGent, UZ Gent and the Flemish Institute for Biotechnology (Vlaams Instituut voor Biotechnologie, or VIB). This virtual institute unites 350 employees and 50 research groups from various disciplines spread across several campuses. Peter Vandenabeele, who as group leader of the VIB forms the bridge between molecular biology and medicine, advocates duo-research teams, in which a fundamental researcher and a clinical researcher work together right from the start, a system that already exists in the Netherlands. Cooperation with industry is also important in order to translate research results into new treatments or screening procedures that can better diagnose cancer.

## From division of assets to reintegration

The rapid expansion and differentiation of departments, on the one hand, and the increasingly complex technologies, on the other, have meant that the Academic Hospital experienced financial difficulties from the late 1970s onwards. The democratisation of higher education also caused an increase in the number of medical students — without, however, a concomitant expansion of the infrastructure for receiving them. Dependence on the ministry of Education made the management structure extremely vulnerable.

Direction and management of the Academic Hospital were under the jurisdiction of the university, which had little feeling for the increasingly complex mandate of a large hospital. A single director was responsible for a tangle of more or less autonomously functioning clinics and polyclinics where professors ruled the roost. The inefficient organisational structure, with micromanagement as its guiding principle, was completely obsolete and racked up massive debts that also jeopardised the functioning of the university. The shortage of specialised medical personnel appointed on a permanent basis was increasingly problematic. Assistants only came into consideration for temporary employment, and had to be paid from the hospital's 'own revenues'. The Academic Hospital worked with a central revenue collection department and a single 'fund': wealthy departments shared their income with poor departments. Initially, specialists did not receive compensation for losses to their own practice, while at other academic hospitals they did. In order to redress this deficiency, permanently appointed, full-time physicians and dentists who combined teaching, research and healthcare were granted compensation for clinical work at a rate of 90% of their gross wages. It did not solve the problem — far from it.

Gradually this gave rise to two separate systems with their own budgets and revenue collection departments: a ward with a hospital director, on the one hand, and medical departments managed by physicians via the university administration, on the other. The result was a disaster. The doctors built up gigantic reserves through the State Institute for Health and Disability Insurance (Rijksinstituut voor Ziekte- en Invaliditeitsverzekering, or RIZIV), while the hospital heaped deficit upon deficit. In 1985-1986, the Academic Hospital Problems (Problematiek AZ) workgroup, set up by Minister of Education Daniël Coens, determined that the Academic Hospital was bankrupt.

The incompetent management of the hospital resulted in a debt of at least 1.6 billion Belgian francs (around 40 million euros). It is said that Coens turned pale upon hearing the figures. The former dean of Medicine and chairman of the Academic Hospital Problems workgroup, André De Schaepdryver, formulated it as follows: 'A battleship sinking in abysmal depths of debts and loans, an unimaginable chaos of disorganisation and a lethal vacuum of demotivation.' Drastic reorganisation of the hospital was urgently required. Under the motto 'Make the best of everything and think the best of everybody', the then rector Leon De Meyer succeeded, during rounds of exhausting nocturnal gatherings, in getting all the members more or less in agreement and separating the hospital from the university. He helped his mission along by deliberately turning up the heat in the meeting room. The government of

Wilfried Martens did the rest. In 1986 the University Hospital (Universitair Ziekenhuis, or UZ) was granted the status of legal entity and financial autonomy. Eric Engelbrecht, the new general manager, carried out a major clean-up operation on behalf of the ministry of Education.

This led to angry protests by the nurses. 'We won't let anyone sit on our heads!' The compensation that physicians had to pay the hospital for their private practice was increased. Running a private practice with hospitalisation anywhere other than the UZ was henceforth forbidden. From then on, the system of clinic compensation was adjusted to market terms. The assistants, who previously worked far too much overtime for starvation wages, received a pay rise. Meanwhile, education had become a matter for the communities, and Coens was able to use Belgium's fabled 'waffle iron politics' — in which Ghent and Liège, as state university cities, had to receive equal benefits — to convert the university's debt to the ministry of Education into a remedial loan. After four years, the huge debts were cleared.

In 2017 a decree was approved that removed the UZ from custody of the ministry of Education and — paradoxically — granted it autonomy by integrating it into the university as a legal entity, albeit with separate bookkeeping. The decree formed part of the Flemish coalition agreement between the Christian Democrats, the Liberals and the Flemish Nationalists, and was decided independently of UGent. Through the merger, UZ has become part of the Flemish hospital network and is eligible to apply for subsidies and investment loans. UGent makes a case for rigorously maintaining this autonomy and freedom. Both institutions will have to make the best of their new relationship.

**Medical students protest, 1982**
(Ghent, Amsab-ISG, photo Roland Van der Sypt)

**François Laurent with the children of Geluk in 't Werk**
The Liberal jurist François Laurent had been a member of the municipal council since 1864 and was committed to education in Ghent. Until his old age, he visited the primary schools almost daily and made himself known and loved by generations of working-class children. Geluk in 't Werk was one of the Laurent Circles, which offered a form of secondary education for children and young adults who had to start working at an early age. Laurent is sitting on the second row on the right.
(Ghent, Universiteitsarchief)

Chapter 5

# SOCIETY AS LABORATORY

Adolphe Quételet was born in 1796 on the Korenmarkt in Ghent and graduated in 1819 with a doctorate in mathematics and astronomy. He was one of the first alumni of Ghent — and a justifiable source of pride, because in addition to the Royal Observatory in Brussels, the young Belgian nation-state had much to thank him for. Quételet is the father of applied statistics in the social sciences. His motto: to measure is to know. He showed that complex 'moral' phenomena such as crime, suicide and marital behaviour exhibit a certain degree of regularity when considered as a group. He tried to understand these recurring patterns by relating them to their possible social determinants, ranging from unchanging variables (gender, age, climate) to 'disruptive' variables such as religion and morality. His standard work *Sur l'homme et le développement de ses facultés, ou Essai de physique sociale* of 1835 introduces the concept of 'the average person'. Quételet is also the inventor of the body mass index. He entered into a dispute with Auguste Comte concerning the term 'social physics'. Comte distanced himself from the concept and invented the name 'sociology' for the discipline he claimed as founder. By using the term 'social physics', Quételet sought to imitate astronomy and the natural sciences. It indicated a positivist desire to place the social sciences on the same firm foundation as the natural sciences.

Adolphe Quételet
(Ghent, Universiteitsarchief)

Nineteenth-century society was Quételet's laboratory. His research was not purely scientific: he wanted to use statistics to investigate the causes of 'antisocial' phenomena such as begging and the criminal urge, in order to eliminate them and thereby arrive at a stable society. Many professors in Ghent — thinkers and doers — followed in his footsteps in terms of this dual longing for a scientific basis that could be used to both analyse and improve society.

## The Huet Society

In 1835 the Belgian government appointed the young French intellectual François Huet as professor of Philosophy. Huet was only twenty-one years old and a practising Catholic. His French nationality was an asset in counterbalancing the predominantly Orangist faculty. His charismatic personality and 'Christian socialism' tinted by strong positivist inclinations drew an increasing number of students and fellow professors. Huet was convinced of the necessity of integrating the latest insights from physiology into the philosophical analysis of human thought. In the late 1830s, for example, he dedicated himself to phrenology, a discipline that was then at the centre of intellectual

(opposite page)
**Beluik 't Luizengevecht**
Before the construction of the industrial belt, the working-class population of Ghent underwent a spectacular expansion into the maze of *beluiken*, interior courtyards and dead-end streets lined with small dwellings, in the inner city during the nineteenth century. This *beluik* was located between Kortrijksepoortstraat and the Leie, near the Veergrep. The photo dates from around 1900, after the major slum clearance operations that drove workers to the outskirts of the city.

interest and focused on the moral capacity rather than the anatomy of the brain. Although phrenology lent itself well to the legitimation of social and racial inequality, progressive scholars of the time embraced a 'leftist' variant in the service of social progress.

In 1846 the inspired philosopher founded the Huet Society (Société Huet), a study group that focused on contemporary philosophical, political and social problems. The gatherings took place at Huet's home and fostered the crystallisation of critical, progressive ideas about pauperism, the separation of Church and state, women's liberation, popular education, progressive taxes and universal suffrage. These ideas, which tended towards utopian socialism, were propagated in *La Flandre Libérale* and the periodical *De Broedermin*, which was published by the group. In 1850, after a smear campaign in the press, the liberal minister of domestic affairs Charles Rogier forced Huet to retire at the early age of thirty-six because of his 'inflammatory' socialist ideas and supposed role in the unrest of 1849. Together with several students, he had signed a petition for the victims of the revolution in Paris. His main work, *Le règne social du christianisme*, makes the connection between Christian doctrine and the equality of all citizens. He thus manifested himself as an important proponent of a hopeful, socially progressive movement in Catholicism.

The short time with which he was associated with Ghent University did not prevent Huet from influencing the city profoundly. A number of prominent Liberal professors — François Laurent, Gustave Callier, August Wagener, Jacob Heremans, Paul Fredericq and Emile de Laveleye — were in one way or another indebted to his inspiring progressive study group.

The genealogy of social liberalism in Ghent in all its ramifications leads us invariably back to the Huet Society and its members. In 1866, Paul Voituron, secretary of the Society, helped set up the progressive Masonic lodge, La Liberté. Some time later he founded the Cercle Progressiste, or Progressive Circle, with a programme that foregrounded social emancipation, language rights and the complete separation of Church and state.

## The research of Mareska and Heyman

The problem of workers' children in the industrialising city of Ghent was acute. The development of municipal education in the 1850s and 60s offered an answer. A state intervention in the form of legislation restricting child labour, however, was definitely not an option. At the beginning of the 1840s, under the instigation of Leopold I, the government had ordered a large-scale national investigation to map the consequences of industrialisation in Belgium. The government first wanted to make sure that working conditions really were unbearable before doing anything about it.

The research was entrusted to the local Sociétés de Médecine. In Ghent, the doctors Daniël Mareska and Jules Heyman were assigned the task. Mareska came from modest origins. His university career had followed an unusual trajectory. In any case, he was one of the many professors who embodied the close ties between the university and the city. After graduating with a doctorate in mathematics and physics, in 1826 he became an assistant in the School of Arts and Crafts under Cornelis Bergsma.

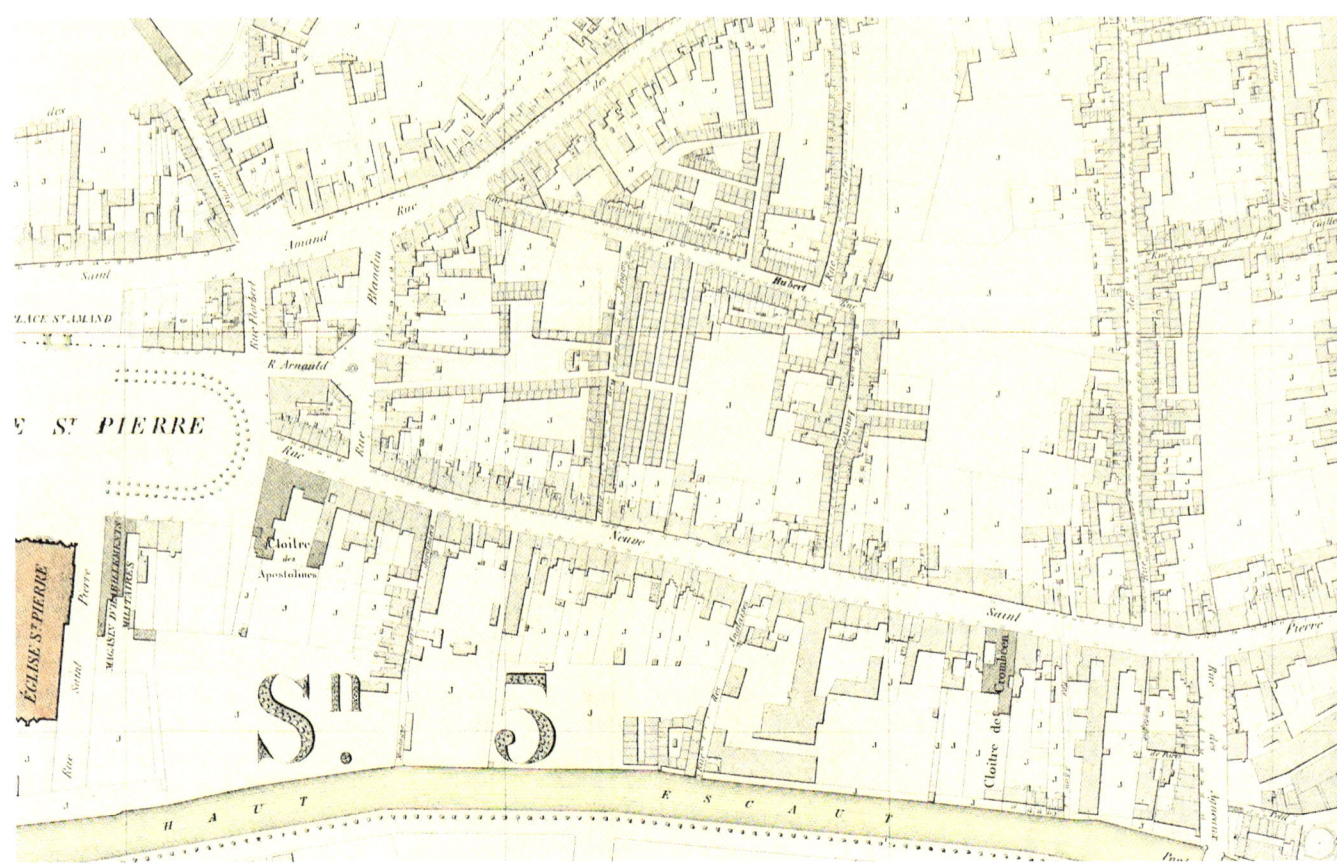

**Batavia**
On the Gerard map from 1855-1857 the Batavia district is easy to locate, in the centre of the map, above the word 'neuve' of Sint-Pietersnieuwstraat.
(Ghent, Universiteitsbibliotheek, map P. Gerard)

After that, he also graduated as a doctor in medicine and in 1836 was appointed extraordinary professor of General Chemistry. Nevertheless, he was in the first place a doctor, active as chief physician of Ghent's prison and very popular among the people.

Mareska was committed to the prevention and treatment of epidemics such as typhus, which wrought havoc in Flanders around 1840. As a founding member of the Société de Médecine de Gand, he was the ideal person to set up the first scientific investigation of the social situation in Ghent in 1843, together with his colleague Heyman. The *Enquête sur le travail et la condition physique et morale des ouvriers employés dans les manufactures de coton* was published in 1845. The focus on Ghent cotton workers was a conscious choice meant to ensure the depth of the research. Even today, the report is still one of the main sources for the social history of Ghent. However distressing their findings may have been, the doctors' opinion of industrial labour was not unduly negative. With the exception of ventilation, working conditions in the new factories were even judged favourably. For example, according to the report, every worker in Felix de Hemptinne's model mill had more than enough available space. Light entered through high windows and the use of wood had been avoided because of the large number of factory fires, against which Ghent took more measures than most European cities. Nor were labour relations a source of anxiety for the doctors. In their eyes, child labour — with working days of up to 12 hours — was simply part of the system. The children, who were older than eight years, were supervised by adult labourers rather than by the manufacturers. They were often hired and paid by their own fathers or brothers, and also punished if they neglected their work. In contrast to the shameful conditions in France and England, according to the doctors, there was hardly any question of child abuse or exploitation in Ghent. On the contrary, in their eyes, abandoned children were the spectre of modern times. It was admirable, the way those little street urchins were taken into the factories for starvation wages by workers who already had a great many mouths to feed. As soon as a woman could leave the care of her small children in the hands of their elder sisters, she also went to work in order to boost the family's income. Mareska and Heyman saw factories that opened their doors to women and children as refuges, much preferable to the beggars' workhouse or the charity office. In other words, they viewed work as a means of social integration. Social legislation that prevented families from earning income through child labour was therefore far from advisable in their eyes.

What the doctors did denounce harshly was the proliferation of shanty towns and slums that put public health at risk. The modern city consisted of sharply segregated neighbourhoods. Apparently, enormous progress had been made with the construction of broad streets and spacious residences for the bourgeoisie, but investigation into the city's abhorrent 'cloaca' had already stripped the doctors of this illusion: a modern invention known as the '*beluik*', an interior courtyard or dead-end street lined with small dwellings, had acquainted them with the existence of a 'city within the city'. On one side of the social divide was light, air and space; on the other side, families crowded into damp, dark houses crawling with infectious diseases. These shameful circumstances were to blame on the speculative drive of slumlords and factory owners, who crowded small plots with a labyrinth of dark hovels, the smell of which could hardly be tolerated. The infamous quarter of Batavia, well concealed behind the façades of Sint-Hubertusstraat and the Sint-Pietersplein, was unprecedented. Of the 14,372 houses in Ghent in 1845, 3,586 were found in *beluiken*. The largest such lanes were indeed like a small city within the city, a *cité*, with shops, pubs and everything needed for the livelihood of the residents who, after workdays of 12 to 14 hours, came there to eat, drink, make love and sleep. One third of the population lived on one three-hundredth of the built surface area. To Mareska and Heyman, it seemed impossible to pack even more people into such a confined space. Nevertheless, the inner city of Ghent had yet to reach its limits in the mid-nineteenth century. Despite the high mortality rate, the population growth continued to supply the constantly rising demand for cheap labour in the factories. Fear of undermining property rights prevented the city from taking firm action. Thirty years after the investigation of Mareska and Heyman, in 1875, the number of homes in *beluiken* had almost doubled.

## Social sciences and social progress

'Poor doctor' Adolphe Burggraeve is perhaps rightly considered a sociologist as well. His medical diagnoses of 'social' diseases were invariably aimed at healing them. In his view, society could only be built on a solid basis if the physical and moral living conditions of the factory workers were improved.

Illiteracy was part of the social problem. According to the Mareska and Heyman report, one working-class child in four was deprived of primary education. Of every thousand male workers, there were only forty-eight who could read, write and do arithmetic. Among women, the situation was even worse: ten out of every thousand had gone to school without learning much of anything. For Burggraeve, good education was the ultimate ladder to social mobility, even more important than housing.

In 1851, Burggraeve founded the Société anonyme pour l'amélioration des demeures de la classe ouvrière, the first social housing society in Ghent. The society was far ahead of its time and designed four detailed plans for modern and salubrious *cités ouvrières*. This presupposed the demolition of the crowded lanes where slumlords and industrialists earned big money, which explains why Burggraeve found little support among the Ghent elite. In his *Projet de cités d'ouvriers dans la ville de Gand* of 1851 he lists the 'insalubrious quarters' of Ghent and observes the same characteristics in each: overpopulation, pollution, lack of fresh air and natural light. He demonstrated statistically that precisely these quarters were more frequently affected by infections and that epidemics claimed more victims there than elsewhere. He also had a remedy for his diagnosis: new model neighbourhoods where simple, comfortable homes with individual gardens were combined with shops, child care, a school, a public bath house, water pumps, communal toilets and trees or parks. However, the social liberals did not have enough political clout to realise these utopian cities in Ghent, although comparable projects were given a chance elsewhere in Europe during this period. The best known is the recently restored project in the northern French city of Guise, developed by the industrialist Jean-Baptiste Godin, who also came up with the name '*familistère*': a special form of communal living for workers and their families that included a built-in panoptic element to enable social control. In Ghent, the grip of the industrialists on the city administration was too great, and Burggraeve's anonymous society died quietly. The construction of social housing would only really take shape in 1889, after Belgium was shaken by a violent workers' revolt.

Adolphe Burggraeve's local engagement did not prevent him from profiling himself in international forums. He was the very model of a rooted cosmopolitan, one who left a distinct impression locally but who was also active in a transnational and predominantly liberal intellectual network that, from the 1840s and 50s onwards, discussed social politics at all manner of congresses. Burggraeve was a member of the Association Internationale pour le Progrès des Sciences Sociales (APSS), which was established in 1862 by the Ghent lawyer Gustave Rolin-Jaequemyns. Their aim was to promote social progress internationally by organising open debates between experts.

Studying the social sciences and improving the lot of labourers were inextricably linked. In 1863, the APSS congress took place in Ghent, after which bishop Delebecque held an eight-day mass in St Anne's Church to purify the city of the blasphemy and dangerous liberal ideas spouted there.

Growing nationalism and discord between France and Germany put an end to the activities of the APSS in 1866. In socially engaged circles of liberal lawyers, it prompted thorough reflection on pacifism and the need for international rules of law.

# Education and school savings as leverage for social uplift

In 1872, François Laurent won the prestigious Jean-Baptiste Guinard Prize, named after a philanthropic Ghent physician and awarded every five years to the author of a work that 'would best improve the material and intellectual position of workers in general and without distinction, and would make the workers happier'.

Laurent won with his *Conférence sur l'épargne*. This was not an academic treatise — rather, it was a sort of handbook that teachers could use in class. The main idea was that workers could free themselves from poverty through order, thrift and foresight. The liberal idea of self-help was employed against traditional charity and care for the poor, thought to encourage dependence, lack of self-respect, laziness and promiscuity. In October 1866, the liberal jurist introduced school savings in Ghent's municipal schools: an 'ingenious idea that made his reputation throughout the civilised world', it was announced at the 1908 inauguration of his statue in the present-day Laurentplein. The joy of saving was best learned in childhood. The typical savings book of the General Savings and Annuity Fund (Algemene Spaar- en Lijfrentekas, or ASLK) was a fixture in the satchels of all Belgian schoolchildren until well into the twentieth century. The best savers (and their parents) were rewarded annually. A year after its introduction, the system was imitated in two hundred Belgian municipal schools and quickly spread abroad, even as far as New Zealand.

The professors of Ghent set great store by proper primary education as a pathway to social uplift. As the star pupil at his final year of secondary school, Gustave Callier argued in 1837 for obligatory primary education among Ghent's working class in order to save them from '*cet état d'ignorance, source de misères, de désordres et de calamités*'. For François Laurent, education offered the ideal leverage for the moral civilisation of

**ASLK report, 1867**
(Ghent, Universiteitsbibliotheek)

**School savings card**
(Ghent, Liberal Archive)

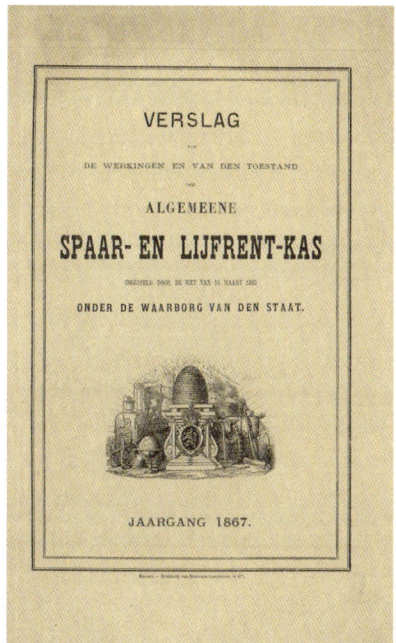

economically and socially disadvantaged groups. The Catholic Church kept people ignorant and subservient. Therefore, the schools had to be withdrawn completely from the influence of the Church. Laicised education in government hands had to be cheap, compulsory and of high quality in order to raise the children into morally conscious individuals. Child labour was out of the question; the need for obligatory schooling was obvious.

From 1858 onwards, aldermen for education Gustave Callier and August Wagener took an enormous step forwards in the development and anchoring of free municipal education, from nursery schools to adult education. Today, Ghent owes its unique position in Flanders, which is otherwise dominated by free (i.e. Catholic) education, to this initiative. During a period of five years, Callier opened no less than ten primary schools in Ghent, which caused the number of students and teachers to double. During Wagener's term of office, the number of accredited teachers increased even further, from two to three hundred. Wagener introduced medical examinations in the schools, and had cod liver oil administered and meals distributed in the city's primary schools. He also took up the gauntlet against child labour by advocating the much-needed requirement that children remain in school until they were at least fourteen. However, obligatory schooling was only introduced in 1914. Until then, the 'freedom of the head of the family' prevailed, a principle dear to the Catholics, which led to distressing situations in the households of working-class families for children who had the intelligence and talent to study. Two education-related organisations derived their name from liberal professors in Ghent: the Laurent Circles (a form of adult education in combination with cultural instruction and popular edification) and the Société Callier (a fund that supported popular education financially and 'collectivised' individual liberal philanthropy). The fact that the Laurent Circles and the Société Callier bore the names of their spiritual fathers points to the struggle of these two academicians to put their ideas effectively into practice.

The lawyer Remi De Ridder carried on the political engagement of Callier and Wagener. Together with Gustave Callier's three sons — Albert, Alexis and Hippolyte — he founded the Société Libérale pour l'Etude des Sciences et des Oeuvres Sociales in 1891, a debating society for progressive liberals. Among them were Ernest Mahaim and Emile Waxweiler, founders of the leading Institut Solvay for sociology at the ULB. After studying engineering in Ghent, Waxweiler had studied for a year in the US and reoriented himself towards the social domain of labour and industrial organisation. At the ULB he wrote his *Esquisse d'une sociologie* (1906) and argued for compulsory schooling and the abolition of child labour in Belgium.

The Ghent Société Libérale played a crucial role in the exchange of ideas about the turbulent social changes of the *belle époque*. The most diverse social, political and economic issues were raised in the pursuit of a scientifically sound policy for the expansion of liberal democracy to the working class and more social justice. The Société Libérale invited liberal as well as socialist and Christian democratic speakers from Belgium and abroad. In 1905, for example, the inspiring leader of the French socialists, Jean Jaurès, came to Ghent. Locally, the Société Libérale functioned as a study department for the city administration in the domain of social housing and employment, among other things. The wave of workers' rebellions and strikes in the spring of 1886 prompted policymakers to explore new forms of social policy on a local and national level. Now the time was indeed ripe for government intervention in the field of workers' housing. In the aftermath of the workers' revolt, De Ridder wrote a report on the approach to alcohol abuse among workers, but it was clear that the government would have to do more than just combat symptoms in order to prevent social unrest from recurring.

In fact, it was Remi De Ridder's son-in-law, Louis Varlez, who best embodied the operation of the Société Libérale as a laboratory for new social policy. As an attorney, professor of law, sociologist, and specialist in unemployment and migration, he too combined science and engagement. His *Plan Social de Gand* is an impressive four-volume study that maps the social situation of industrialised Ghent on the basis of statistics and surveys among the labour unions and factory owners. In collaboration with the city administration, he set up the Ghent Unemployment Fund (Gentse Werkloosheidsfonds) in 1900, of which he was chairman from 1900 until 1920. The Fund compensated workers who voluntarily joined in case of involuntary 'lack of work' or unemployment. It framed insurance as an individual responsibility, with the novelty that the city paid additional financial compensation to insured workers who were unemployed. In this system the labour unions functioned as a 'cashier's office' for collecting contributions, on the one hand, and paying out benefits, on the other. The Ghent system enjoyed great success and was imitated in all major Belgian cities as well as other cities abroad. Its impact can hardly be overestimated and marks the transition from the system of Christian charity to a system of social security with limited government intervention.

## The experimental schools

In 1927, the socialist minister of Fine Arts and Education, Camille Huysmans, imposed a Higher Institute for Educational Sciences (Hoger Instituut voor Opvoedkundige Wetenschappen, or HIO) on the state universities of Ghent and Liège, attached to their respective faculties of Arts and Philosophy. The HIO provided a three-year licentiate programme for teachers of primary education that aspired to a management or inspection position. The city of Ghent made a 'regular' municipal school on Molenaarsstraat available as a university experimental school. Apart from Geneva, only Ghent could boast of such a 'people's' laboratory for pedagogical research and demonstration. Because that was the idea: to demonstrate that classic education, which emphasised knowledge transfer and discipline, could be transformed into a 'new' school governed by the most progressive pedagogical principles. The goal was to demonstrate experimentally that a child was an active, creative and dynamic being, not a passive, submissive object. Working-class children were in that respect ideal 'test material'. School inspector Jozef Verheyen was appointed by Huysmans as training manager.

Louis Varlez, 1929-1930
The lawyer Louis Varlez was a good example of the rooted cosmopolitan who was active both locally and transnationally. After the First World War, his social commitment to the unemployed of Ghent received its logical follow-up when he became an international civil servant of the International Labour Organisation (ILO). In 1929 he attended a conference in Kyoto for the ILO. He stayed on and travelled the Far East. Here we see him passing through Hawaii.
(Ghent, Liberal Archive, photo Lucien Brunin)

The experimental school
in Molenaarsstraat, ca. 1930
(Ghent, Universiteitsarchief)

The Laboratory for Experimental, Differential and Genetic Psychology, ca. 1960
Students in the lab of pedagogue-psychologist William De Coster. As a student of Jozef Verheyen, one of the pioneers of the first experimental school, De Coster was concerned with the problems of deprivation and developmental disabilities in pre-school and primary education. His lab was equipped with the latest technical devices such as one-way mirrors and an internal video circuit.
(Ghent, Universiteitsarchief, photo A. Van Lancker)

That, too, was looked upon with disapproval by the University of Ghent: Verheyen did not even have a university diploma. This meant that he was one of the first students of the programme that he himself coordinated. But Verheyen did have contacts in the Institut J. J. Rousseau in Geneva, and was familiar with approaches to pedagogical reform. Ovide Decroly, the 'father' of pedagogical reform and an alumnus of the Ghent faculty of Medicine, was one of his intimates. Together with parents and local residents, the charismatic Verheyen reformed the municipal school on Molenaarsstraat. The children had a garden in the playground and each was assigned a locker with a bar of soap, a towel and a toothbrush. Physical and moral education went hand in hand under the motto 'The school is your home, you must keep it clean.' Teachers and pupils were given freedom and responsibility. Strict schedules were banned; subject matter came largely from what presented itself in the environment: a forerunner of the Freinet method, which is still popular in Ghent. For Verheyen, theoretical knowledge was only valuable if it could also be used in practice. His authority was internationally recognised in 1937 by his appointment as vice-president of the Bureau International d'Education in Geneva. Yet some colleagues still looked down on him because he did not have a doctorate and was appointed professor nonetheless.

In 1948, Richard Verbist, Verheyen's student and assistant, founded a new Experimental School in a villa in Zwijnaarde. The laboratory was connected to a new seminar on Psychological and Experimental Pedagogy. The accent shifted from education to scientific research. 'The subjects form the indispensable test material, analogous to animals in zoological laboratories, plants in botanical laboratories and patients in the university clinics', according to Verbist. Just as patients received the medical care they needed, the test children were given a full primary education. It was provided in three classes manned by unpaid teachers, Mr Marcel De Vogelaere, Mrs Nora Epsteins-Pieruccini and Miss — later professor — Marie-Louise Van Herreweghe. Without their commitment, the Experimental School would not have survived its pioneering phase. In contrast to the school on Molenaarsstraat, the 'Verbist School' was a 'special school for gifted children'. The emancipatory function was lost through the recruitment of children from elite circles. On 1 September 1960 the new building on Henri Dunantlaan opened its doors at the new campus for the rapidly growing educational and psychological sciences. However, keeping afloat the 'Pedagogical Centre Prof. Verbist', as the school was known after its founder retired, was a constant struggle. In 1991 this unusual experiment came to an end.

## The Criminology School

Although Adolphe Quételet was already searching for the social determinants of deviant behaviour in the 1830s, criminology as a discipline would establish itself only a century later. Its roots lay in criminal anthropology, which arose during the *fin de siècle* and fundamentally questioned the classic nineteenth-century view of criminal law. The liberal notion of individual responsibility and guilt was rejected. Instead, the idea was to protect society by temporarily isolating the criminal and by removing the social causes of his criminal behaviour. In other words, 'sick' society produced the pathological symptoms of the criminal. Punishing the individual who violated the rules of law made way for the 'treatment', 're-education' and reintegration of the unhealthy. The main advocate of the social defence doctrine was the liberal jurist Adolphe Prins, professor of Criminal Law at the ULB. In 1881 he proposed that the criminal should become an object of research, by analogy with the patients who helped advance medical science in the hospital. In this way, criminality as a social illness could be cured on the basis of scientifically substantiated 'remedies'. This medical view of crime opened up perspectives on biological and social factors, heredity and the environment. The doctrine of social defence lay at the basis of the Lejeune Law, which provided for the conditional release and readjustment of the delinquent from 1888 onwards. The new notions of criminal law pointed to an optimistic belief in the malleability and improvability of people and society.

Nico Gunzburg studied at the ULB at the beginning of the twentieth century and followed Adolphe Prins's teachings closely. As a toddler of three, he fled with his Jewish parents to Antwerp in order to escape the anti-Semitic pogroms in Riga, then still Russian Latvia. After his studies, he became Prins's assistant and specialised further in Rome. Thanks to Cesare Lombroso's *L'uomo delinquente* (1878), Italy was the cradle of criminology. In 1923, when Ghent University was partially Dutchified, Gunzburg, who was openly pro-Flemish, received an appointment to the faculty of Law. As a student of Prins, the connection between criminal law, sociology and criminology was essential to his thought, but the connection to education and child protection also coloured his impassioned pursuit of interdisciplinarity.

In 1938, Gunzburg was the driving force behind the foundation of the Criminology School. When it turned out that the university had no money to spare, he went to the rector and said: 'I have a house, do you want it?' He had purchased a property and offered it to the university, together with his personal library. Gunzburg was then dean and together with his colleague in Criminal Law and Criminal Procedure, Jules Simon, he wanted to create a scientifically substantiated specialisation for magistrates, lawyers, colonial officials, prison directors, internment institutions, legal doctors, police commissioners and gendarmes.

One of his successors, Willy Calewaert, who had been active as a student in anti-fascist groups, sought contact with the International Brigades that fought against Franco during the Spanish Civil War. According to legal historian Raoul Van Caenegem, the multifaceted Calewaert astonished the faculty with the large number of positions he held simultaneously. The board of governors, which monitored the extracurricular activities of the professors, 'dutifully' decided to submit his 'inadmissible accumulation of posts' to the minister of National Education with a view to having measures taken, but that minister ... was Calewaert himself! In addition to teaching assignments in Ghent, Antwerp and Brussels, Willy Calewaert was indeed politically active in the period 1968-1980 as a socialist senator and minister. He served

Nico Gunzburg
The founder of Criminology in Ghent lived to be almost 102 years old. He invariably pinned a fresh carnation on his lapel as a symbol of his social commitment.
(Ghent, Universiteitsarchief, photo W. Engelbeen)

five years in the European parliament. In addition he also ran a law firm. His colleagues wondered 'how many heads he had and whether he ever slept'. On a night out with his staff, in the euphoria of the moment, a proposal was launched for establishing a union of adulterous men. When asked if he wanted to become an honorary member, Calewaert replied, 'No — an active member!'

After the Second World War, Calewaert the criminologist continued the humanist tradition within the humanist social, rather than individual, tradition. His student Patrick Hebberecht, an adept of the critical criminology of the 1970s, was annoyed by the return of the individual, positivist doctrine of guilt and penance. He also opposed the increasing 'ethnicisation' of criminality and applied himself to the study of the social stigmatisation of deviant and undesirable behaviour. Together with Claude Cuvelier, Hein Picard and Myriam van Moffaert, Hebberecht laid the foundations for Oikonde, a shelter for homeless men (often ex-convicts) that was later absorbed by CAW Artevelde.

The social engagement of Ghent criminologists has continued right up to the present day. The late Brice De Ruyver and his colleague Tom Decorte, for example, contributed to the recent police and judicial reforms and the security and drug policy, among other things. Tom Vander Beken, for his part, is strongly committed to the fate of prisoners. He travelled through Europe following in the footsteps of John Howard, who in the eighteenth century drew up a 'state of the prisons' that detailed how many people were incarcerated in prisons and hospitals. Vander Beken explored how prisons function today, what their purpose is and what they should not (or should no longer) be.

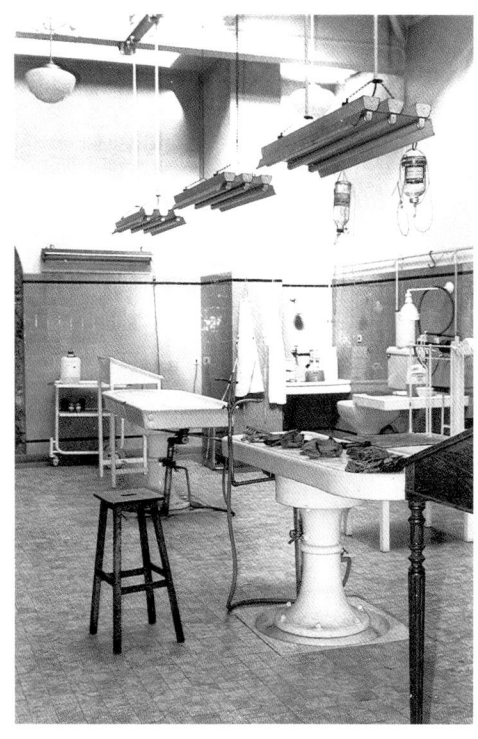

**Autopsy room in the Anatomy Institute of the Bijloke**
(Ghent, Universiteitsarchief)

For a long time the face of the Ghent Criminology School was Paul Ghysbrecht, who established his reputation as a legal doctor in forensic psychiatry. Together with internationally renowned experts such as Frédéric Thomas and Jacques Timperman, he ensured the contribution of forensic practice in education, with concrete cases that provided the students with fascinating material. Ghysbrecht saw a trial as a psychodrama that had a therapeutic, purifying effect on those who are accountable. He adopted clear social views on the problems of internment versus imprisonment and the right to re-socialisation. The controversial and extravagant Ghysbrecht is etched in the memory of tens of thousands of alumni. His eternal bow tie and stunts, but also his brutality and intimidation, setting students against one another ... 'Myths were woven around Ghysbrecht that do not always do justice to his unfathomable and highly versatile personality', says his pupil De Ruyver. For example, he was one of the first to support the radical democratisation of the university. Ghysbrecht also intervened personally when the university board wanted to expel a number of student leaders in March 1969.

## The 'wild bunch' of the Wetswinkel

In the aftermath of the March 1969 movement, the Socio-Legal Workgroup (Sociojuridische Werkgroep, known as 'sojuwé') was formed in the bosom of the Law faculty, analogous to the SMW (later Mordicus) in the faculty of Medicine. Workgroups were established at other faculties in this period, usually operating from a leftist, socially critical perspective: the Critical Action Group Psychology and Pedagogy (Kritische Actiegroep Psychologie en Pedagogie, or KRAPP), the Action Group for Critical Education (Actiegroep Kritisch Onderwijs, or AKO), the Workgroup on Engineers and Society (Werkgroep Ingenieur en Maatschappij, or WIM), the Environmentally Conscious Engineers of Ghent (Gentse milieubewuste ingenieurs, known as 'Gembir'), the Workgroup Ethics (Werkgroep Moraal), the Social Workgroup on History (Sociale Werkgroep Geschiedenis, known as 'Sowege'), the Workgroup Economy (Werkgroep Ekonomie, or WEK), the Critical Workgroup State and Society (Kritische Werkgroep Staats- en Sociale, or KRASS), the Sciences Workgroup (Werkgroep Wetenschappen), the Agriculture Workgroup (Werkgroep Landbouw, known as 'Wela'). The workgroups were a 'refuge' for progressive, often politically homeless students from 'leftist Christians to the most hard-core Marxists'; the atmosphere was one of dialogue and exchange, focused on concrete social action. In the first issues of the polemical student magazine *Schamper* (1975), law student Willem Debeuckelaere, now chairman of the Privacy Commission, explained how certain workgroups sought to connect 'outside the narrow university conservatory'. The Wetswinkel — literally the 'Law Shop' — was one of the most enduring examples.

Several progressive students met regularly in the seminar on Roman Law with professor Wilfried Roels. In the eyes of many students, Roels taught the most boring subject ever, but for the young Mil Kooyman and friends, he was one of the rare professors who supported them. Later, as external member of the executive board for the socialist labour union, Kooyman would follow the ups and downs of the University of Ghent and help shape the Transitie UGent sustainability project. In the meantime, a Wetswinkel had been established in the Netherlands as a first line of response for legal advice. Although they otherwise wanted to have little or nothing to do with the traditional Flemish Legal Society (Vlaams Rechtsgenootschap, or VRG), Johan Erauw, Eric Van Heesvelde, Rik Pylyser and Kooyman went to an exchange with colleagues from Leiden in 1971. They left the student programme of the VRG for what it was and camped out in the Wetswinkel for several days to see whether something similar could be started in Ghent. At their own expense, the students rented the first floor of a building opposite the Public Centre for Social Welfare (Openbaar Centrum voor Maatschappelijk Welzijn, or OCMW) in Onderbergen and began to offer free legal aid to the people of Ghent, beginning on 1 March 1972. There was a proper permanent service run by volunteers. Several like-minded lawyers were even prepared to check the advice for accuracy. However, they hadn't taken into account the Bar Association, which promptly forbade all members from cooperating with the 'legal assistance boutique'. For Mil Kooyman, engagement did not come without a price. His home was searched after an anarchistic journal had published instructions on how to make Molotov cocktails, mentioning the Wetswinkel as a source of legal assistance.

Another confrontation took place at the Trial Law exam, with Marcel Storme. Storme was no great admirer of the Wetswinkel, perhaps because he wished he had come up with the idea himself. Thanks to his practical experience in the Wetswinkel, Kooyman performed extremely well in his written exam (19.5/20). But during the oral exam, Storme accused him of cheating. Fortunately Kooyman could convince his professor that his good results were owed to his experience with the Wetswinkel. After a difficult oral exam, he still retained 14/20. When he graduated and started his internship at the Bar in Ghent, Kooyman was immediately summoned by the head of the Bar, who made it very clear that cooperation with the Wetswinkel was strictly forbidden. It was an order that Kooyman blithely ignored.

The Wetswinkel continued to exist and later moved to Sleepstraat. Many volunteers offered their services, among them future minister (of state) Johan Vande Lanotte. In his memorial for Koen Raes, professor of media law Dirk Voorhoof recalls how he encountered Raes for the first time, when the latter came to class with 'a motley-looking crew' to recruit volunteers for the Wetswinkel: 'The boys and girls who came to promote the Wetswinkel had long, wild hair, scruffy sweaters or baggy T-shirts. One even had a guitar; in short they looked like a wild bunch, a sharp contrast to the rest of the posh-looking law students. I wanted to join on the spot.' Raes had considerable influence on the Wetswinkel because he succeeded in placing individual legal problems in a broader social context, and was critical of the Wetswinkel's own work. He was the driving force behind *Schamper*, which became a hub for the workgroups and the New Leftist student movement in Ghent.

**De Wetswinkel**
(Ghent, Universiteitsbibliotheek, *Schamper* 31, 1977)

## Free and Happy

In June 1969 the faculty of Psychological and Pedagogical Sciences (Psychologische en Pedagogische Wetenschappen, or PPW) split off from Arts and Philosophy. The longed-awaited independence generated a new energy that was invested in laboratories aimed at improving the social and psychological well-being of society. This brought with it the necessary growing pains. In 1970 the Orthopedagogic Laboratory (Laboratorium voor Orthopedagogiek) was created under the direction of Maria Wens. She had been the assistant of '*heil*'-pedagogue René Nyssen, who in turn had succeeded Maurice Hamelinck at the HIO in 1935 for subjects concerning the psychiatry of 'abnormal children'. Nyssen was also active in the reform school Vrij en Vrolijk — literally 'Free and Happy' — a medical-pedagogical institute in Brasschaat for difficult children, the only non-Catholic institution of its kind in Flanders. Inspired by the reform pedagogy of Ovide Decroly, Edouard Claparède and Célestin Freinet, Nyssen advocated a 'remedial' pedagogical treatment for children with a mental disability. In 1942, in the midst of the war and against a background of the eugenics movement, he published the *Leerboek der kinderpsychiatrie en der heilopvoedkundige behandeling*, a handbook on remedial treatment for children. That same year, Maria Wens

**Vrij en Vrolijk**
As the head of the reform school Vrij en Vrolijk in Brasschaat, 'Miss' Maria Wens was a controversial figure – as she also was at Ghent University.
(Ghent, Amsab-ISG)

established a Medical-Pedagogical Observation and Treatment Centre within the Guislain Institute with a consultation service for parents and carers of 'handicapped children'. Nyssen was succeeded in 1946 by neuropsychiatrist Jacques De Busscher, who would help found the degree programme in Orthopedagogy, a new, post-war name for '*heil* pedagogy', which had acquired negative connotations under the Nazis.

In 1970, 'Miss' Wens was appointed as its first teacher. In this way, orthopedagogy was taken out of medicine and grouped in the newly founded PPW faculty. With her office and classroom next to the Guislain Institute, however, Wens remained an isolated and controversial figure. As a fervent adept of reform pedagogy and practice-oriented education, she organised internships in Israeli kibbutzim for her students. She was also responsible for the Vrij en Vrolijk open-air school, which she viewed as her life's work. In the 1960s, Vrij en Vrolijk grew into a white elephant of an institution with more than five hundred students. At the same time, complaints grew concerning the practices it employed. Things went from bad to worse in what had originally been a progressive, model institution. In the summer of 1971, the popular weekly magazine *Humo* wrote about mismanagement at the institution: there was a dire lack of skilled staff, the children were neglected, the pedagogical principle of heterogeneous group formation fostered the exploitation and oppression of 'retarded (or less intelligent)' pupils, the hygiene was inadequate, privacy was not respected, and so on. The bottom line was that Vrij en Vrolijk was addicted to subsidies and formed children who were addicted to care. The gap between pedagogical theory and 'pernicious reality' was also denounced. In its defence, it was repeatedly pointed out that an 'anti-humanist' attack was being perpetrated against the 'only freethinking, pluralistic institution in Belgium', which was in fact under-subsidised. 'Despot' Maria Wens found herself in the eye of the storm. Parliamentary enquiries and demonstrations ensued. The Internationale Nieuwe Scène and Vuile Mong en zijn Vieze Gasten — an alternative, socially engaged theatre troupe and a band of popular Marxist musicians, respectively — joined in the mêlée. The V&V Action Committee under the direction of Kris Coenegrachts and Laurent Bursens, which became the Workgroup on Special Youth Services (Werkgroep Bijzondere Jeugdzorg) in 1974, saw the conditions at Vrij en Vrolijk as symptomatic of what was wrong with youth services. In 1975 the Workgroup filed a civil lawsuit against V&V on behalf of ex-clients and educators. Wens was convicted of defrauding millions and violating labour laws. The university was also saddled with Wens-related problems. *Jawaade*, the periodical of KRAPP, openly denounced her tyrannical behaviour for the first time in 1977. Due to a change in pension legislation, however, university management was only able to force Wens to retire at the age of sixty-five in 1984. Even then she steadfastly resisted, responding with summary proceedings. Wens died in 1988, lonely and embittered.

Eric Broekaert, who died in 2016, was saddled with a difficult legacy when he succeeded Wens in 1987. He continued to be faithful and indebted to the ideas of the new school movement in which Maria Wens had been so closely involved. When he began his PhD, she said: 'Mister Broekaert, if you want to know what you're writing about, you must learn by acting and doing. Set up a therapeutic community and describe the communication strategies and relationships within it.' Choreographer Alain Platel states that the authoritarian Wens, 'always in a bad mood', was one of the best professors he ever had during his orthopedagogical training, despite the fact that she was an impossible person, and precisely because she insisted that students gain practical experience. An internship of at least one month during the vacation — organised and paid for by the student — was an absolute must.

Together with Geert Van Hove, Broekaert succeeded in getting the orthopedagogy programme back on the right track in the 1990s, among other things, through the creation of De Kiem, a therapeutic centre for drug-users. To his mind, it was not about the inclusion or exclusion of people, but about 'unlocking', opening and closing the floodgates in order to achieve equilibrium. While he was working on his PhD about assisted living, Van Hove experienced personally that it is really possible to accomplish something with science. In the US he learned how to let people with a mental disability participate actively in academic research projects, something he put into practice as a pioneer of Disability Studies at Ghent University too.

Gerda De Bock, from her side, contributed by integrating the practice of social work into research. She was a jurist and criminologist by training and head of the Municipal Institute for Social Studies (Stedelijk Instituut voor Sociale Studiën, or SISS) in Ghent, a school that had been training social workers since 1953. De Bock was convinced that social work could only evolve into a truly professional discipline if it had a strong scientific basis. This was the background of the Laboratory for Youth Welfare and Adult Education (Laboratorium voor Jeugdwelzijn en Volwassenenvorming), which she developed as professor of Juvenile Justice and Social Protection of Children at the new PPW faculty. The laboratory grew into the present-day department of Social Work and Social Pedagogy. The importance of prevention was central from the outset, as was the social engagement and policy-oriented character of research relating to the promotion of personal, social and cultural welfare. Willy Faché and Eugeen Verhellen followed in her footsteps. From the Laboratory arose the Youth Information Centres (Jongeren Informatie Centra, or JIC) in 1972, and the Centre for Children's Rights (Centrum voor de Rechten van het Kind) in 1977. Thanks to the research of Maria De Bie and Michel Vandenbroeck, the problem of youth care was situated within a broader social framework of poverty reduction and equal opportunity policy.

## The legacy of Quételet and Laurent

In 1977, alderman for education Piet Van Eeckhaut established the Pedagogical Centre (PC) in Ghent, a committed partnership between academics and educators. Municipal primary education

**Gerda De Bock**
Lawyer Gerda De Bock obtained a doctorate under Nico Gunzburg, with a dissertation on juvenile justice. She started her academic career in 1954 as a part-time lecturer and combined this role with the directorship of the Stedelijk Instituut voor Sociale Studiën (SISS). In the photo, she is acting in this capacity on a school trip to the mines in Limburg in the mid-1950s.
(Canon Sociaal Werk)

was in crisis and rapidly losing students. Innovative education was the answer, and it was offered by engaging three young PhDs from the PPW: director Jean Herrel and advisers Armand De Meyer and Luc Heyerick. They came from the stable of William De Coster, the pedagogue-psychologist who felt that academics had a mission with respect to society at large and put this into practice with his highly diverse psycho-pedagogical research. The campaign to eliminate 'developmental handicaps' with social origins through education was the continuous thread throughout the life and work of this shy professor. He committed himself to the cause of childcare with his model childcare centre at Ghent University (1969), Innovation in Basic Provisions for Young Children (Vernieuwing in Basisvoorzieningen voor Jonge Kinderen, or VBJK, 1986) and the Training Centre for Education and Childcare (Vormingscentrum voor Opvoeding en Kinderopvang, or VCOK, 1989). Their impact is still tangible.

Among nearly all the heirs of Adolphe Quételet and François Laurent, solid scientific research underlies the societal role that they as academics can play. Things are no different for educational sociologist Mieke Van Houtte. She finds it impossible to hide her values: social inequality reproduced in education makes her visibly angry. The fact that she forms part of the society she studies and can therefore never be neutral with respect to her object of study does not mean, however, that Van Houtte doesn't strive for the utmost objectivity — on the contrary. The status of sociology as a science depends on the distinction between value judgements and facts. This has been the case ever since the founding fathers of sociology took the natural sciences as their benchmark. The social physics of Adolphe Quételet was also inspired by this sort of positivism.

Van Houtte's teacher Herman Brutsaert — who gained his PhD in the US and, in contrast to the other professors in the (sub)faculty of State and Social Sciences published internationally — constantly hammered on about the importance of rigorous empirical research. Since her doctorate on the differences between technical and vocational education, Van Houtte and her team have examined the structural characteristics of schools, their socio-economic composition in relation to the culture of the pupils and teachers, and its effect on individual students (being held back a year, deviant behaviour, marks, sense of belonging, friendships ...). The culture among pupils and teachers is seen as a mediator. Throughout, Van Houtte and her team have tried to quantify to the greatest extent possible the indicators of that culture (engagement with studies, resistance, gender relations, patterns of expectation ...). Nevertheless, it is the combination with qualitative methods that distinguishes the Ghent sociologists from other groups, as does the integration of biological indicators in the analyses. The influence of social biologist Robert Cliquet is still tangible. And much further back in time, the philosopher François Huet also attached great importance to physiology. 'A one-sided social constructivism is not tenable', says Van Houtte. 'Sociologists cannot turn a blind eye to biology.' In cooperation with the Ghent transgender clinic, Hans Vermeersch was able to establish the interaction between social characteristics and testosterone levels after the endocrinological investigation of blood samples.

The research results of Van Houtte's group Cultural Diversity: Opportunities and Socialisation (CuDOS) are published in international peer-reviewed journals and frequently cited, which stands as a guarantee of their validity and importance. At the same time, local valorisation is ensured in different ways and the findings make their way to the department of Education of the Flemish Community. The political zeitgeist, however, is against it. As a result, the necessary reforms have not been implemented in secondary education. The social determination of school choices and performance is maintained through the the so-called waterfall system, wherein general education is largely favoured over technical, let alone vocational schools. This means that education falls short as a motor of social emancipation. Teachers' expectations of students play a large if unintended role in the process. Research has shown, for example, that schools with a high proportion of children from a working-class background or children of immigrant parents, those expectations are lower than in 'mixed' or 'white' schools. Socio-economic status also determines parents' expectations and plays a role in a student's choosing to study, say, humanities instead of industrial sciences.

The question is why this is no longer tackled in the primary schools. 'Everything is remediable these days', according to Van Houtte. 'Dyslexia, dyscalculia, ADHD … [everything] except social handicaps.' An equal opportunity policy involves compensating structural social inequalities. 'Children are not equal and hence cannot be treated equally at school.' Not everyone in sociology appreciates such outspoken views. Mieke Van Houtte is sometimes wilfully misunderstood and set aside as little more than an activist. This is another reason why she maintains a rigorous watch over the boundary between research-based knowledge and knowledge derived from opinion. In the domain of education today, everyone is an 'experience expert' and no one thinks twice about another opinion, more or less. But the voice of experience, however well intentioned, does not have the same value as a scientifically substantiated position. What gives the education expert authority and legitimacy is precisely that sound empirical basis of sociological research on which her public pronouncements are based.

'Three crowing cocks', 1911
At the beginning of the twentieth century the struggle for the Dutchification of Ghent University exerted a strong mobilising force. The ideological differences between pro-Flemish Catholics, liberals and socialists began to disappear in the common struggle for higher education in Dutch. The alliance of the 'three crowing cocks', Louis Franck, Camille Huysmans and Frans Van Cauwelaert, led to the introduction of the first bill in 1911.
(Antwerp, Letterenhuis)

# VLAMINGEN!

## 19 FEBRUARI a. zal een heugelijke dag zijn

De schitterende redenaars:

**Mr. L. Franck,** liberaal Volksvertegenwoordiger voor Antwerpen,

**Mr. C. Huysmans,** socialistisch Volksvertegenw. voor Brussel,

**Mr. Fr. Van Cauwelaert** katholiek Volksvert. voor Antwerpen.

zullen dien dag

**10 u. 's morgens in den NIEUWEN CIRKUS**

spreken over het levensbelang van ons Volk

### Een Vlaamsche Hoogeschool

Op ZONDAG, 5 FEBRUARI, bewees het schitterend gelukt Studentencongres, dat de Vlaamsche jeugd, Hooger Onderwijs wil in eigen taal, dat er studenten zijn voor een Vlaamsche Hoogeschool; dat **geen gevaar** die van Gent door hare vervlaamsching bedreigt; dat de Gentsche handelaars gerust mogen zijn.

Wie kon daar aan twijfelen toen hij die **honderden** studenten achter hun kleurrijke vaandels door de straten zag trekken, *die hoop, die toekomst van ons Vlaandrenland!*

De groote bijval van de tien meetings te Gent, tot hun beklemming bijgewoond door enkele dungezaaide franskiljons; de niet minder groote bijval van **50** volksvergaderingen op alle punten van het Vlaamsche Land; de beslissingen genomen door politieke organismen van alle partijen; de wenschen uitgebracht door een aantal Vlaamsche gemeenteraden bewijzen aan wie er aan twijfelen mocht, dat het niet eenige **heethoofden, bekrompelingen** zijn, zooals de franskiljons beweren, die het land in beroering brengen, maar dat **gansch een Volk,** zelfbewust, wilskrachtig opkomt om zijn recht te eischen.

**VLAMINGEN** van Gent en het omliggende, allen naar de meeting.

## Wij willen wat is recht en winnen wat wij willen!

De Propagandacommissie tot Vervlaamsching van de Gentsche Hoogeschool.

Gent, Drukkerij Plantyn, Korte Koestraat, 5.

# Chapter 6
# LANGUAGE

'At that time we had universal language, global, at least for higher education, and wherever he went the scholar was never a stranger.' Albéric Rolin, one of the founding fathers of international law, regretted in 1913 that Latin had fallen into disuse at universities. In his eyes, the free exchange of scholarship and knowledge through a lingua franca benefited the whole of humanity. Between the Dutch period, when Latin was the language of instruction, and complete Dutchification in 1930, Ghent University used French in research and teaching for nearly a century. In Belgium it was the language of the elite, and also marked a social divide within the city. Suzanne Verbist, later Lilar, a renowned *femme de lettres*, graduated as a doctor in law in 1925. In her memoirs, *Une enfance gantoise*, she recalls that in a city like Ghent, despite all the efforts of certain professors, only the working class used Flemish, resulting in social segregation. 'To speak Flemish classed you as surely as wearing a helmet or a workman's blue smock, while to speak French was a mark of good taste and distinction — even, with the decline of Latin, of humanism.' Everyone who wanted to move up the social ladder was obliged to use French. From this impossible starting position, the efforts of the Flemish movement towards social emancipation thanks to higher education in their own language definitely represented a heroic struggle.

For August Vermeylen, the first rector of the first Dutch-speaking university in Belgium, the language battle was inseparable from the idea of emancipation. He would continue to advocate for Dutch-speaking higher education, so that Dutch-speaking lawyers, doctors, teachers, philosophers and engineers would stream back into the society that needed them. It was his conviction that only higher education in the vernacular would elevate the people in the progress of nations. Emancipatory ideas like these have since disappeared from the current debate on language and education, while the impact of accelerating anglicisation on equal opportunities and social mobility remains unspoken.

Adolphe Quételet, *Dissertatio mathematica inauguralis. De quibusdam locis geometricis, nec non de curva focali*, 1819
In 1817 the university's language of communication was Latin: 'The language which the professors in the faculties must use, with the sole exception of professors in Dutch and French literature, law and economics, shall be Latin.' Thus, the founder of statistics, Adolphe Quételet, wrote his thesis in the language of Cicero.
(Ghent, Universiteitsbibliotheek)

## Latin as the language of instruction

Latin may well have been the lingua franca of universities and scholars for centuries, but William I's decision to use '*de Latynsche taal*' at the beginning of the nineteenth century was regarded by many as an anachronism. This was no different in the Northern Netherlands, where the three universities were likewise saddled with Latin. While primary education in the Dutch-speaking area of the Kingdom of the Netherlands was completely Dutchified between 1815 and 1830, William I did not use the language of higher education as a nation builder. On the contrary, Latin acted as a social filter: in Leiden, Utrecht and Groningen, students were also selected on the basis of their classical knowledge and the university remained inaccessible to the 'class of craftsmen and tradesmen'. Yet it soon became clear that most students did not have sufficient mastery of Latin, especially in the Southern Netherlands. Moreover, Latin was not the language in which modern science was practised. German, French and English, the vernacular languages of modern nations, had largely taken over that role. Soon a schizophrenic situation developed in which the language of the professors and students differed from the official language of the lectures, examinations, dissertations and academic ceremonies.

The committee that advised king William in 1828 about the possible reform of higher education also questioned the use Latin as the language of instruction. The idea was to introduce Dutch in mathematics and the natural sciences, certain branches of medicine and law, and to use French for diplomacy. But William did not want to give French a chance to grow as a cultural language, precisely because of the South's strong orientation towards revolutionary France, a source of deep-seated political dread.

The Belgian revolutionaries of 1830 immediately abandoned Latin as the language of instruction. It was completely at odds with modern science, which was progressive 'by nature' and hence could only be transmitted in a useful way in a modern language. It was acceptable that a course such as Roman law be taught in Latin, but that was the limit. Teaching modern sciences in a language that expressed the spirit of a two-thousand-year-old culture was another matter entirely. Students who attended small colleges or had been taught at home had great difficulty following and understanding Latin, even if they had become familiar with the pronunciation of their Dutch and German professors. Henceforth, every professor was allowed to use the language that he considered most suitable for his subject and his students.

## Language-lovers in defence of Dutch

Freedom of language vanished in 1835. The Belgian higher education law of 27 September 1835 stipulated that lectures could only be given in French. The minister could allow exceptions for certain courses — such as Dutch literature, for example. Jacob Lodewijk Kesteloot, however, was forced into early retirement at the age of fifty-seven. His literary activities in the Maatschappij voor Taal- en Letterkunde (Society for Language and Literature) in Ghent and his engagement with the emerging Flemish movement made him suspect.

At the time, Ghent University offered little opportunity for the development of Kesteloot's beloved native language, let alone scope for granting Dutch the same rights as French. In 1846 the journalist Pierre Lebrocquy was given the (unpaid) task of teaching a comparative course on Nordic Languages and Literature, including Flemish. In his opening lecture, he rejected the notion that Flemish was doomed to disappear because it was a hard, rough language unsuited to philosophy and science. He undermined his own position, however, by immediately switching to French. In 1849, the law of 1835 was tightened even further and the minister could only allow the use of languages other than French for certain courses in very exceptional circumstances.

An important milestone in the history of the Flemish movement was the establishment of the 'language-loving' student association 't Zal Wel Gaan in 1852. The oldest student association still active, it was not created at the university itself, but in the bosom of the athenaeum on Ottogracht. Three students took the lead. Their mentor was Jacob Heremans. The students, led by Julius Vuylsteke, brought their society to the university and pushed successfully for a Dutch course. The elective Cours de Littérature Flamande was the result, beginning in the academic year 1854-1855.

Heremans was only able to wear the regalia of professor ten years later. In 1871 he still had no regular students, only a handful of particularly attentive listeners whom he initiated by means of well-prepared lectures on Germanic philology. He combined his teaching assignment with political activities in the cultural organisation of the Flemisch Liberals, the Willemsfonds and the provincial and municipal councils. In the period 1879-1882, he was alderman for education in Ghent. His charisma as a teacher at the athenaeum provided the Flemish movement with important pioneers: Julius Vuylsteke, Tony Bergmann, Emile Moyson, Adolphe Dufranne, Paul Fredericq, Julius De Vigne and Julius Sabbe. Their engagement was aligned with 't Zal Wel Gaan and 'Klauwaert en Geus': both Flemish and freethinking. Many combined this engagement with an outspoken commitment to social causes and activism on behalf of the up-and-coming workers' movement in Ghent.

Jacob Heremans
The first lecturer in Dutch literature in Ghent was an active member of De Tael is Gansch het Volk, founded in 1836 by Ferdinand Snellaert, physician and alumnus of the University of Ghent.
(Ghent, Universiteitsbibliotheek, photo Edmond Sacré)

## Pro-Flemish Freemasons

After graduating in 1859, Julius Vuylsteke continued to animate 't Zal Wel Gaan and tried to push liberalism in Ghent in the direction of a broad intellectual and material emancipation movement for Flemings. Yet his struggle ran up against the unwillingness and incomprehension of the Frenchified liberal bourgeoisie. The discord within liberalism was clearly present in a number of Masonic lodges in Ghent. Liberal pro-Flemish sentiments took root in the Ghent Lodge, Le Septentrion, not least thanks to the activities of a number of professors sympathetic to the Flemish movement, such as the historian Paul Fredericq and biologist Camille De Bruyne. Vuylsteke is also an example of how socially engaged supporters of the Flemish movement penetrated the more conservative Septentrion. Conversely, the progressive Lodge, La Liberté, founded in 1866, was by no means a bastion of the Flemish emancipation struggle, despite the active role of attorney Julius De Vigne and the founder of Dutch linguistics, Jozef Vercoullie. French was spoken in both Lodges, however. The Frenchified bourgeoisie remained blind to the emancipating power of language in the Flemish movement.

't Zal Wel Gaan
The language-loving student association 't Zal Wel Gaan has been the animating force behind anticlerical Flamingantism at the University of Ghent since 1852. Here we see the board of 1928-1929.
(Ghent, Universiteitsarchief)

Historian Paul Fredericq was the son of Dr Cesar Fredericq, and through his mother Batilde Huet a nephew of exiled philosophy professor François Huet. He was directly related to Cyriel Buysse and the sisters Virginie and Rosalie Loveling. Jacob Heremans had been his teacher at the Ghent athenaeum. Fredericq began his academic career as a professor in Liège, but in 1883 was able to succeed his mentor Heremans in Ghent. He taught Dutch literature, comparative history of modern literature and modern history of Belgium. He liked to hold his seminars at his home on Winkelstraat (nowadays Notarisstraat), preferably with a good glass of wine. Fredericq was politically involved in the city council of Ghent, was chairman of the Ghent section of the Willemsfonds for thirty years, and editor-in-chief of the progressive liberal weekly *Het Volksbelang*.

Fellow traveller Jozef Vercoullie introduced scientific teaching in Germanic languages in Ghent. He was of the opinion that Flemings must orient themselves towards standardised Dutch (Algemeen Beschaafd Nederlands, or ABN) and contributed his *Nederlandsche Spraakkunst* and an *Etymologisch Woordenboek der Nederlandsche Taal* to the cause. For twenty-nine years, Vercoullie was general secretary of the Willemsfonds and became its chairman after the war. He was also politically active in the Liberal People's Union (Liberale Volksbond) and as a provincial and municipal councillor.

It took until 1935 for the first Dutch-speaking Freemasons' lodge, De Zwijger, to be established in Ghent. The Dutchification of the university was an important stimulus. Biologist Lucien De Coninck, a member of 't Zal Wel Gaan since 1922, was one of the driving forces behind it. A number of other young Ghent professors also belonged to the group of founders: the dialectologist Edgard Blancquaert, the English literature specialist Franz De Backer and the pharmacologist Romain Ruyssen. When the

**The Buysse-Loveling family**
The naturalist writer Cyriel Buysse (left rear, with moustache and cap) was the nephew of Virginie Loveling (second from the left, middle row, next to her sister Pauline). The importance of their literary work for Flemish emancipation was highly appreciated by the Ghent professors of Dutch literature, Antonin Van Elslander, Ada Deprez and Anne-Marie Musschoot. The familial network also had branches extending to the professors Paul Fredericq and Julius Mac Leod.
(Ghent, Liberal Archive)

Lodge was established in 1935, Paul De Keyser, professor of Folklore studies, was its first Master.

## Julius Mac Leod and cultural Flamingantism

The grudging introduction of Dutch in public life, with language laws on the use of Dutch in criminal cases (1873), administration (1879) and secondary state education (1883), supplied the Flemish movement with ammunition for demanding the Dutchification of higher education. The faculty of Arts and Philosophy introduced 'Flemish Normal Sections' to train teachers who would hold classes in Dutch at the athenaeums. A number of professors, including Paul Fredericq, Adolf De Ceuleneer and Peter Hoffmann, switched over to Dutch.

In 1888, Julius Mac Leod was appointed as professor of a new Dutch-language course on Botany for students of science at the normal schools. As a so-called '*cultuurflamingant*', Mac Leod was the key figure in the struggle for Dutchification of the university. His father Aimé was a gentleman wine merchant and amateur biologist, his mother a scion of the Fredericq family. A woman of literary talent, she also wrote under the pseudonym Mevrouw (Mrs) Sophia. These exceptional parents passed on to their son the ideals of the Enlightenment and belief in a better world. For Mac Leod, progress in the positivist tradition of social Darwinism was only possible through popular education and the scientific transfer of knowledge to the common man and woman. The goal was to use higher education in Dutch to form a cultural elite that would lift Flanders not only intellectually, but also economically. Hence, this cultural elite had to fulfil the task of public education and elevation — the core of '*cultuurflamingantisme*'.

**Julius Mac Leod with his students in the Botanical Garden**
Even before he began his studies, Julius Mac Leod (front row, fifth from left) had read everything by his father's good friend Adolphe Quételet and mastered his scientific methods. In 1878 he obtained his PhD in Physics. In 1887 he succeeded Jean-Jacques Kickx as professor of Botany. He was also made director of the Botanical Garden. Mac Leod's assistant, Cesar De Bruycker (to his right, with a dark beard), would become director of the Botanical Garden during the First World War. At the rear, on the right, is Marcel Minnaert, who would collaborate with the German occupier.
(Ghent, Universiteitsarchief, photo Edgard Claessens)

Mac Leod was the driving force behind Higher Education for the People (Hoger Onderwijs voor het Volk, 1892) and defended Dutch as an appropriate language for science. He used it consistently himself in his handbooks, lectures and publications. The next step was the Flemish Biological and Medical Congresses (Vlaamse Natuur- en Geneeskundige Congressen), the first of which took place in Ghent in 1897. Among his most important supporters were the biologist Camille De Bruyne and the physicist Jules Verschaffelt. In 1904, as a dissident of 't Zal Wel Gaan, Mac Leod started the left-leaning Ter Waarheid, an anti-bourgeois study group in which he was joined by Hendrik De Man, George Sarton, Paul Kenis, Leo Picard, Paul Van Oye, Peter Hoffmann and other nonconformists.

Within the university, francophone resistance was greatest in the faculty of Law. In 1884 the Flemish-Catholic organisation, the Snellaertkring launched a campaign to offer a law course in Dutch. The lawyers of the future had to familiarise themselves with the Dutch terminology of criminal law. The liberal rector Albert Callier firmly rejected their proposal, arguing that the faculty had to teach law, not language. The struggle went on for years. In the end, by ministerial decree, an elective course on Criminal Law and Criminal Procedure was offered in Dutch at both state universities from 1890-1891 onwards. A year before, the faculty of Law in Ghent had unanimously advised against it when the students demanded a practical course in Criminal Law in Dutch. Paradoxically, it was their sister faculty in Liège that had requested it. From 1885, no one in Flanders could be appointed magistrate unless he had demonstrated his knowledge of Dutch in an official exam, or unless he had taken the Criminal Law exams in Dutch at the university. Yet the exams for the Dutch-language courses in Criminal Law and Criminal Procedure were conducted in French for another twenty years or more.

## Polarisation around 'la langue flamande'

In the summer of 1896 a Hoogeschoolcommissie (Flemish Higher Education Commission) was formed at the 23rd Dutch Language and Literature Congress in Antwerp, with Julius Mac Leod as special correspondent. His report of 30 May 1897 was the first evidence-based argument stating that a Dutch-speaking university in Ghent was both possible and necessary. It was the starting point for difficult discussions concerning the modalities and tempo of Dutchification. The so-called 'Mac Leod system' provided for Dutchification in stages to be completed within twenty years. Because of their large number of foreign students, the Special Schools for engineers would remain French-speaking. Incumbent professors could teach in their language of choice, but new appointees were obliged to teach in Dutch.

Mac Leod also tried to bridge the ideological oppositions in the student movement and encouraged the Catholic group Rodenbach's Vrienden (Friends of Rodenbach) and the liberal and socialist students of 't Zal Wel Gaan to unite in the Flemish student congresses. He succeeded.

At the end of 1898 a counter-movement arose in the form of the Association Flamande pour la Vulgarisation de la Langue française en Flandre, of which leading figures from liberal, Catholic and socialist circles were members. The professors of

Ghent, in particularly those of the Law faculty, were well represented. The argument of the *vulgarisateurs* was that French-language instruction and in particular bilingualism presented the 'lower' groups of the population with opportunities for social mobility. A 'tavern referendum' spread in the pubs of Ghent moreover claimed that Dutchification would result in the depopulation of the university and lead to financial disaster for the city's merchants and middle class.

In this highly polarised context, Paul Fredericq and his pupil Henri Pirenne tried to reconcile Flemings and French-speakers with a proposal for a bilingual university. Their attempt had the opposite effect. At the end of 1899, Fredericq and his nephew Mac Leod had a falling out. Mac Leod — rightly — attributed it to pressure from the French-speaking factions in the Masonic lodges, which led Ghent's Flemish liberals to adopt a more moderate position. Pro-Flemish liberalism, which from the outset had given such a powerful impetus to the struggle for Dutchification, lost credibility and strength.

On 14 May 1899, the Academic Council deliberated on the use of *la langue flamande* in Ghent. The opponents of Dutchification won the day, but the intense discussions it occasioned showed that resistance was crumbling.

## 'Three crowing cocks'

Stubborn resistance against Dutchification led to radicalisation among the members of the Flemish Higher Education Commission. The young Brussels sociologist and economist Lodewijk De Raet wanted to strengthen the 'power of the Flemish people' and increase Flanders' economic potential by using language as leverage. This also meant that the technical schools, where engineers were trained, had to be included in the process of Dutchification. De Raet also advocated the establishment of a Dutch-speaking agricultural college as well as social and commercial sciences in Dutch. He quarrelled with Mac Leod but nevertheless managed to have his 'system' accepted by the second Higher Education Commission in 1909. This formed the basis for the campaign of the 'three crowing cocks' (*'drie kraaiende hanen'*): the Catholic Frans Van Cauwelaert, the liberal Louis Franck and the socialist Camille Huysmans. None of them were from Ghent, nor had they studied there.

(left)
**Rodenbach's Vrienden, 1910**
The pro-Flemish Catholic students united in 1887 in answer to the anticlerical 't Zal Wel Gaan, on the one hand, and the French-speaking Gé Catholique, on the other. Rodenbach's Vrienden were a precursor of the Catholic Flemish Students Association (Katholiek Vlaams Hoogstudentenverbond, or KVHV), of which they would become the Ghent branch. The photo shows the board of 1910: seated are Albert Kluyskens, Jules Storme and Adiel Debeuckelaere, pro-Flemish students in the predominantly French-language faculty of law.
(Ghent, Universiteitsarchief)

(right)
**The Fédération Wallonne des Étudiants Catholiques de l'Université de Gand**
(Ghent, Universiteitsarchief)

In the autumn of 1910 the three figureheads of the Flemish movement from each of the three major parties joined forces for the Dutchification of the University of Ghent. 'Ladies and gentlemen, we are the three crowing cocks that will awaken our people.' The three spoke of the 'vital importance' of higher education in one's own language. Three hundred and twenty meetings later, they had collected more than 100,000 signatures for a massive petition that was also supported by 500 municipal councils. But not everyone was impressed. Resistance came mainly from the Frenchified elite in Flanders, the Brussels bourgeoisie and the Belgian episcopacy. Before the war, cardinal Mercier had already shown himself to be an opponent of Dutch in higher education. In his official instructions to the directors and teachers of Catholic colleges, he made clear in no uncertain terms that Dutch was not a suitable language for the university. Francophone resistance coalesced in the Union pour la Défense de la Langue française à l'Université de Gand, an initiative undertaken by Ghent's jurists and headed by Albéric Rolin. They feared that Ghent would cut itself off from international academic culture and civilisation. French moreover formed a link between the Flemish and the Walloon 'races' that coexisted in Belgium.

When the 'three crowing cocks' presented their legislative proposal for the gradual Dutchification of the university in March 1911, they were nevertheless fairly optimistic about their chances of success. The First World War and the creation of a Flemish University (Vlaamsche Hoogeschool) by the German occupier in 1916, however, threw a spanner in the works.

## Jong Vlaanderen and activism

Ideological discord within the Flemish movement ensured that even before the First World War, many pro-Flemish liberal and freethinking students turned away from party politics and radicalised. In May 1914 the first issue of *De Bestuurlijke Scheiding* (literally 'administrative separation') appeared, conceived within the turbulent student circle gathered around Mac Leod, who had already turned his back on the Flemish movement several years earlier because of its connection to party politics. However, he maintained contact with the radical young Flamingants who saw him as their spiritual leader. According to Virginie Loveling, he had 'a miraculous ability to make the young dream'.

Mac Leod's pupil Marcel Minnaert was one of the most active editors of *De Bestuurlijke Scheiding*, which argued for administrative separation between Flanders and Wallonia and exhibited strong anti-Walloon, anti-Belgian and anti-French sympathies. Minnaert grew up in a pro-Flemish family of progressive pedagogues who avidly supported standard Dutch (ABN). At the Ghent athenaeum, one of his teachers was Hippoliet Meert, who founded the General Dutch Association (Algemeen Nederlands Verbond, or ANV) in 1895 and advocated cooperation with the Netherlands and the interests of the Dutch 'tribe'. Minnaert became president of the language-loving student association, Heremans' Zonen (Sons of Heremans) in 1907. As a biology student at the university, he joined 't Zal Wel Gaan and acted as front man of the Ghent ANV and the Greater Netherlands Student Congresses. Just before the war, he graduated with flying colours with Mac Leod as his supervisor.

When war broke out, Minnaert was convinced that cooperation with the German occupier was inevitable for securing the Dutchification of the university. This made him into one of the protagonists of Jong Vlaanderen (Young Flandres), the activist pan-Germanic organisation established in 1914. Leo Picard, the eternal history student of Henri Pirenne, and medical student Eugeen Van Oye, the poetically gifted muse of Guido Gezelle, also chose to rush ahead. At the time, Mac Leod had already fled to England to devote himself to science. Two years later, Minnaert, who was scarcely twenty-three at the time, accepted an appointment as a lecturer in physics at the new Vlaamsche Hoogeschool, opened on 24 October 1916 as part of the Germans' Flemish policy.

The rector was philosopher Peter Hoffmann, attached to the faculty of Arts and Philosophy since 1882. Only six professors from the 'old' university joined him in switching to the new Flemish Hoogeschool. Among them was head librarian Willem De Vreese, founder of Heremans' Zonen and an eminent specialist of Middle Dutch manuscripts. The activist adventure mainly attracted freethinkers. Among the newly appointed professors we find a number of old boys from 't Zal Wel Gaan, such as the classical philologist Josué De Decker and Dr Adriaan Martens. Cesar De Bruycker, Mac Leod's right-hand man, was made director of the Botanical Garden. Attorney Lodewijk Dosfel and the ophthalmologist Reimond Speleers, by contrast, came from the Catholic Flemish student movement. Altogether, forty-three professors accepted appointments, among them twenty-five Belgians. But because they collaborated with the German occupation authorities, the activists ended up isolating themselves from the Flemish people they sought to edify. Their privileged existence as professors contrasted starkly with the poverty of large segments of the populace in Ghent during the war.

Things did not turn out well for them. Minnaert's house was plundered in autumn 1918 by a violent mob. He fled to the Netherlands and was sentenced in absentia to fifteen years of forced labour. He nevertheless succeeded in building a brilliant career as an astronomer in Utrecht. But his engagement with the Communist Party cost him the rectorship during the Cold War. On the other side of the political spectrum, Reimond Speleers' house went up in flames with the liberation. He, too, fled to the Netherlands. At the outbreak of the Second World War, he returned to Ghent and was 'reinstated' as professor of Ophthalmology with the support of the Germans. After returning to Ghent, Julius Mac Leod died of the Spanish flu in 1919. As Virginie Loveling had predicted in 1917, activism resulted in a huge step backwards for the Flemish cause.

(left)
**The Vlaamsche Hoogeschool, 1916**
On 24 October 1916, rector Peter Hoffmann gave a speech at the opening ceremony of the Vlaamsche Hoogeschool, better known as the 'von Bissing university' because it was supported by the German occupying forces in the context of their *Flamenpolitik*.
(Ghent, Universiteitsbibliotheek)

(right)
**Student residence Hou ende Trou 1918**
At the inauguration of the student residence Hou en Trou of the Gentsch Student Corps (GSC) in Sint-Pietersnieuwstraat on 3 June 1918, the distinctive German helmets are a striking presence. A few months later, the curtain would fall over the Vlaamsche Hoogeschool.
(Ghent, Universiteitsbibliotheek)

## The 'horseshit parade'

The First World War did not help the Dutchification of the University of Ghent at all. Collaboration with the German occupier only exacerbated polarisation around the university during the interwar period. In his throne speech of 22 November 1918, king Albert recognised the right of Flemish people to a Dutch-speaking university. It was a concession to the pre-war Flemish struggle, just as universal suffrage crowned the struggle for social equality. The democratisation of society was accelerated by the common man's participation in the war and his sacrifices for king and country. This definitely increased sensitivity to linguistic injustice. But the recognition of Dutch as a language of instruction was not well received in the elite milieu of '*Gand français*', not least at Ghent University itself, where positions became even further entrenched.

On 28 December 1918 the Academic Council almost unanimously adopted a draft outlining the university's possible transformation into a Flemish university. According to the throne speech, it was the new legislature's responsibility to make changes in the language regime. For the university administration, it was simply out of the question. The 'healthy' part of the Flemish population was well aware of the usefulness of a French-speaking university: it put Flemings in possession of a universal language that was also the natural idiom of their Walloon compatriots. Moreover, French helped to recruit foreign students who would learn to appreciate the country, and in this way contribute directly or indirectly to useful trade relations. Contact with comrades of various nationalities and civilisations could only be advantageous to Flemish students. Dutchification would isolate the Belgian economy.

'*Française de langue, l'université est belge de coeur*'. The summits attained by artists and writers since the *fin de siècle* formed splendid proof that the university had in no way hindered the development of Flemish genius. Ghent native Maurice Maeterlinck, who graduated in law in 1885, was even awarded the Nobel Prize for Literature in 1911. Language and literature courses in Flemish now enjoyed equal footing with their counterparts in French. A Dutchified university would mean less exchange and fewer foreign students. Instead, it would be a regional university that promoted separatism and the intellectual division of Belgium. Dutchification was at odds with the interests of Belgium as a nation.

**Activist demonstration, 1918**
On 27 January 1918 student activists demonstrated at the Vrijdagmarkt. At the statue of Jacob van Artevelde, they swore their loyalty to Flanders.
(Ghent, Universiteitsbibliotheek)

The language battle only really got underway in 1922, when the parliamentary debate on the Dutchification of Ghent University was held again. It was coupled with violent agitation in the streets, in which the mostly French-speaking opponents participated actively. On 19 October 1922 parliament approved new measures for the gradual introduction of Dutch by a slim majority. Hopeful of a negative vote in the conservative Senate, opponents created the Ligue nationale pour la Défense de l'Université de Gand et la Liberté des Langues.

(left)
**Poster design, Greater Netherlands Student Congress, 1922**
From 1911 onwards, the General Dutch Association (Algemeen Nederlands Verbond, or ANV) organised Greater Netherlands Student Congresses. Graphic designer Jozef Peeters, one of the first abstract artists in Belgium, created the poster for the eighth edition in 1922.
(Antwerp, Letterenhuis, poster Jozef Peeters)

(right)
**The General Flemish University Students Association (Algemeen Vlaams Hoogstudenten Verbond, or AVHV), 1923**
The umbrella organisation for Flemish students from the various universities was founded in Leuven in 1919 by students from Leuven and Ghent. Former students of the Vlaamsche Hoogeschool were welcome. The AVHV lobbied for the complete Dutchification of Ghent University and reacted fiercely against the French-speaking counter-movements.
(Antwerp, Letterenhuis)

A month after the vote in the House, '*le tout Gand*' marched against the threat of Dutchification of the university. Mayor Emile Braun and a broad assortment of Ghent aldermen and council members, francophone notables, industrialists and merchants, legal officials, bourgeois societies, professors and students were mobilised for the demonstration. At the head of the procession were rector Eugène Eeman and a large part of the faculty corps. The French-language press counted 20,000 demonstrators; the socialist paper *Vooruit* limited its estimate to 5,000 'aspiring bourgeois of all stripes'.

There was indeed an unmistakably different public on the streets in comparison to the workers' strikes from before the war. The demonstration against Dutchification has gone down in history as the 'horseshit parade' in reference to the malodorous projectiles that were thrown. Pro-Flemish demonstrators burned tricolour flags and spat upon the '*belles dames*' of the Coupure and Bagattenstraat. Windows were broken and the excrement of the horses of the mounted police flew through the air. The 'horseshit parade' represented the peak of a decade of continuous political agitation around the university. In the end, the Senate voted down the proposal. But the triumph of '*Gand français*' was short-lived. In July 1923, the political parties in the government coalition reached a compromise.

## A half-hearted compromise

With the passage of the Nolf Law, named after the minister of arts and sciences Pierre Nolf, the university was split into Dutch-speaking and French-speaking divisions. In the Dutch-speaking division, students were required to take two-thirds of their courses in Dutch and one-third in French; in the French-speaking division, vice versa. However, the '*hoalf- en hoalfuniversiteit*' (half-and-half university) was to no one's liking.

The pro-French faction of Ghent set up a counter-university on the Korenlei, the Ecole des Hautes Etudes, led by Jacques Pirenne. For every course in Dutch, a parallel alternative was offered in French. The Ecole could count on the support and cooperation of the majority of professors. Its opening resulted once again in a violent tumult, while the opening of the 'Nolf barrack' in the Aula came off poorly. The city administration of Ghent and the francophone students did not attend. Nor did the students of the General Flemish University Students Association (Algemeen Vlaamsch Hoogstudenten Verbond, or AVHV) and the Catholic Flemish University Students Association (Katholiek Vlaams Hoogstudentenverbond, or KVHV). They had successfully called for a boycott of the half-hearted system. An electrical failure in the city, moreover, meant that the ceremony in the Aula had to take place in the dark, by candlelight.

The introduction of bilingualism also meant that professors whose Dutch was poor had to be replaced for their courses in the Dutch-speaking division. In October 1923 no less than sixteen new professors were appointed. One of them was the art historian August Vermeylen. One of his first students was crown prince Leopold, later king Leopold III, who had enrolled in Ghent. It was a strategic manoeuvre on the part of the government to overcome the boycott of the Nolf university. Entirely in line with the logic of the Belgian compromise, Leopold naturally attended Henri Pirenne's lectures too.

In his speech at the opening of the academic year in 1924, the new rector, Georges Van den Bossche, exhorted students to demonstrate friendship and tolerance. He hoped that another war would not be necessary for the rediscovery of Belgian unity. His sentiments represent a continuous thread that runs through rectorial speeches right up to the time of complete Dutchification in 1930.

## August Vermeylen between Scylla and Charybdis

In 1929 the same longing for pacification motivated the Henri Jaspar administration to Dutchify the university completely. It was imperative that the Belgian centenary of 1930 not be disturbed by the ongoing language battle. In 1928, 83,000 Flamingants had voted for the ineligible August Borms — the only activist still in prison — in Antwerp. It was a clear signal to the government that the Flemish wanted change. When the Flemish nationalists also won the parliamentary elections in 1929, the traditional political parties could no longer ignore the language demands of their Flemish members.

On 21 October 1930, the rectorate of the State University of Ghent was transferred to August Vermeylen. This was not an obvious choice. The Academic Council had another pecking order in mind, but the French-speaking liberal minister of Arts and Sciences, Maurice Vauthier, chose a Flemish socialist, a clear political concession to the Flemish movement. Vermeylen enjoyed a level of respect that transcended party lines and even the language divide. Through his friend Herman Teirlinck, he had a direct connection to king Albert and the court. A Brussels native through and through, Vermeylen was well connected before the war in the thriving cultural life of the capital. As a student, moreover, he had immersed himself in the cosmopolitan atmosphere of *fin de siècle* Vienna and Berlin. In 1893, together with a number of anarchistic kindred spirits, he founded the Dutch-language avant-garde periodical *Van Nu en Straks*. Vermeylen's ideas gave the Flemish movement an important cosmopolitan thrust.

In his opening speech, Vermeylen addressed himself specifically to the students with a call for tolerance: 'The Flemish University has nothing else to fear, except perhaps that you might bring your own house into discredit because of mindless gestures. Remember this: as you grow stronger, you provide the best proof of your strength by showing tolerance to those who think differently. Your new rector urges you expressly not to cause him any useless difficulties and to give no one a pretext for attacking the Flemish University.'

The arrival of August Vermeylen, 1930
August Vermeylen and his wife Gaby Brouhon entering the auditorium before the historic opening session of the Dutch-language university on 21 October 1930. In a letter of thanks to King Albert, the first rector writes that he is aware of the objections to his appointment. Yet he feels 'fortunate enough' to be able to use all his powers to work for the university 'which, far above all divisions of opinion and ideology, must be the most effective focal point of science and higher intellectual civilisation for the whole of Flanders and for the greater benefit of Belgium'.
(Antwerp, Letterenhuis)

The echoes of his words had scarcely faded when a hard core of radical Flemish nationalist students did exactly the opposite. At the opening of the Brabançonne, they succeeded in drowning out the national anthem with the Lion of Flanders and the Wilhelmus. The incident reverberated as far as the council of ministers.

As rector, it was up to Vermeylen to put an end to the polarisation. On one side were the Flemish nationalist students, who considered him a traitor to the Flemish cause and the embodiment of Belgium. On the other side were the Frenchified faculty of the Ecole des Hautes Etudes, who offered a competing educational programme a stone's throw away from the Aula. Minister Vauthier had forbidden the accumulation of posts. Vermeylen's assignment was to pressure the resistant '*cumulards*' one by one until they relinquished their positions at the Ecole. The only one who stubbornly refused was the eminent art historian Georges Hulin de Loo. On 17 December 1930 a group of pro-Flemish students stormed his lecture, pelted him with laundry blue, and chased him from the university buildings in a storm of jeers. The action precipitated a political crisis. The Liberals in the government turned away from their fellow party member Vauthier and his ban on accumulating posts. With the support of Jaspar and Vauthier, Vermeylen succeeded in getting a compromise approved during his first Academic Council meeting, albeit by a narrow majority. The rioters were condemned but remained largely out of harm's way because Hulin de Loo had provoked them with his 'wilful and undisciplined attitude'. The recalcitrant professor was suspended and retired quietly in December 1931.

In 1931 and 1932, in order to prevent fresh incidents, the university administration wisely decided not to organise an opening ceremony. The AVHV dominated student life in the 1930s and tended towards increasingly extreme Flemish nationalism. In March 1933, in response to the radicalisation, the Gentsch Studentencorps (GSC) was created. As an umbrella organisation, the GSC wanted to put an end to the riots and dissension at the university and to be open to every student regardless of their political convictions. The purely Dutch-language character of Ghent came before all else. A subsidiary organisation, Sociale Hulp, was set up to allow students to take action in a positive way. With the support of the Catholic professor of obstetrics Frans Daels, the GSC acquired its own student house in Sint-Pietersnieuwstraat, which was christened 'Huize Mac Leod'. However, the GSC would not simply follow the tradition of pre-war cultural Flamingantism. With the name of the periodical *Aula*, it made a more-than-symbolic link to the activist Gentsch Studenten Corps, which had been active in the Vlaamsche Hoogeschool. The memory of Mac Leod continued to form a connection between the left and right wings of the Flemish student movement during the interwar period.

## The 'general civilisation of the people' as mission

August Vermeylen was able to conclude his turbulent rectorship peacefully in 1933. The commotion around the language regime had subsided. The bad tidings concerning the depopulation of the university had not been fulfilled, even though enrolment figures stagnated during the interwar period. The Technical Schools for engineers, which were only Dutchified in 1935, recorded a considerable decrease. The decrease in the number of francophone Belgian and foreign students was compensated by new cohorts of Flemish students — largely from Leuven, which would only be fully Dutchified in 1968. In academic year 1930-1931 alone, it is estimated that two hundred students came from Leuven to continue their studies in Dutch. Ghent was becoming more and more Catholic and Flemish nationalist.

Among the professors, the old division between liberals and Catholics was replaced by a generation gap, a schism around language and a difference in mentality that was expressed in significant details such as the disappearance of the open carriage that came to deposit '*Monsieur le Professeur*' before the Aula for the opening ceremony. Frenchified professors and those whose Dutch was otherwise deficient retired early, an exodus that had already begun in 1923. New Dutch-speaking lecturers were hired to replace them. Among them was the bacteriologist Albert Bessemans, who had studied in Leuven. In October 1933, Vermeylen handed over the symbolic ermine on his shoulder in a charged atmosphere. Frans Daels was considered the most likely candidate to succeed him, but the minister considered him too radical for the office of rector. The Flemish nationalist students were outraged that their favourite had not been appointed. Yet Bessemans did his best to emphasise his roots in the Flemish student movement during his rectorial speech, appealing to the audience to 'prove to the world that in Ghent, at the new State University, we are united in working hard: in an orderly, disciplined fashion, filled with warm affection for our compatriots and our fatherland.'

Unity in Flemish nationhood, however, was more difficult to achieve than rhetoric suggested. Once Dutchification was finally a fact, other loyalties cropped up that led to growing ideological polarisation as the economic crisis of the 1930s progressed. The 'Truce of God' between the left and right in the Flemish student movement was placed under heavy pressure. The rise of fascism and National Socialism in Italy, Germany and Spain led to radicalisation in left-wing circles. In 't Zal Wel Gaan, solidarity with republican Spain played a major role. Board member Piet De Moor even died in the ranks of the International Brigades that fought against the Franco regime. An antifascist front was formed between liberal, socialist and communist students from 1933 onwards, after Hitler came to power in Germany. The proto-fascist mentality at the university was initially visible in the Dietsch Studentenverbond, a Greater Netherlands student association founded in 1922. A year later, the AVHV joined them. The breakthrough came in 1930 with Joris Van Severen's Verbond van Dietsche Nationaal-Solidaristen (Verdinaso). The new divide between right and left would be decisive for the attitude of professors and students towards the German occupier.

In 1935, Frans Daels established the Vereniging voor Wetenschap (Association for Science) at the urging of Jozef Goossenaerts. Goossenaerts had studied Germanic philology in Ghent and written his dissertation on the jargon of agriculture (1909). He had been active as a student leader in Rodenbach's Vrienden and in the Flemish Scientific Student Congresses of Mac Leod. The Vereniging voor Wetenschap fitted within the development of a whole series of Flanders' 'own' scientific organisations and institutions, the highlight of which was the Royal Flemish Academy for Arts and Sciences of Belgium (Koninklijke Vlaamse Academie voor Wetenschappen en Kunsten van België, or KVAB) in 1938, and the Flemish Academy of Medicine (Vlaamse Academie voor Geneeskunde) in 1939. The internationally renowned physicist Jules Verschaffelt had been an active member of the French-speaking Academy since 1919. Despite his active support of Mac Leod's cultural Flamingantism, he opposed the formation of a Flemish Academy and refused to join. He feared that the division would provincialise the Belgian academic community and tarnish its international aura. In the francophone Academy, he consistently gave lectures in Dutch to his largely French-speaking colleagues. The Nobel Prize awarded to Corneel Heymans in 1938 gave, on the other hand, a significant boost to the Flemish academic world.

According to emeritus Nobel Prize candidate Marc Van Montagu, who was a student in the 1950s, Dutchification has had negative consequences for the university. The permanent need for Dutch-speaking professors, for example, meant that teachers from secondary education were called upon who did not necessarily have the ambition to be a professor. Nor did the drastic dip in the number of foreign students, primarily in the engineering schools, do the university any good, according to Van Montagu. On the other hand, the Dutchification of the engineering course should also be seen in light of the increasing demand for Dutch-speaking engineers on the labour market in the 1950s and 60s. Business and technology in Flanders at that time were booming, which greatly influenced the democratisation of higher education.

However, Dutchification was not simply an answer to an economic need. In 1956, king

**The Gentsch Studentencorps, 1933**
The students of the Ghent Student Corps (Gentsch Studentencorps, or GSC) oppose the new rector, Bessemans, and in 1933 hold an alternative dies natalis in the Minard-schouwburg.
(Ghent, Universiteitsbibliotheek)

**Demonstration for the Dutchification of the Technical Schools, 1932**
Due to the large number of foreign students, the engineering courses were not yet fully Dutchified in 1930.
(Ghent, Universiteitsarchief)

Baudouin and the two surviving 'crowing cocks' — Frans Van Cauwelaert and Camille Huysmans — received an honorary doctorate from Ghent University on the occasion of the twenty-fifth anniversary of Dutchification. In his encomium, former rector Louis Fredericq praised the new doctor *honoris causa* Van Cauwelaert, who had always recognised the 'true destiny' of the university in the 'general civilisation of the people'.

## Dutch: a dead scholarly language?

While the generation of August Vermeylen, Herman Teirlinck and Karel Van de Woestijne had to fight for the right to education in their own language and culture at the end of the nineteenth century, now, more than one hundred years later, the pendulum has swung in the opposite direction.

'This is where we have come from', says Anne-Marie Musschoot, referring to the avant-garde *Van Nu en Straks*, which she has studied in depth. The eighth and last volume of the *Geschiedenis van de Nederlandse Literatuur*, a broad and comprehensive overview of the history of the literature of the Netherlands and Flanders since the Middle Ages, was published in 2017. A history of literature in eight volumes that took eleven prominent authors twenty years to complete has now become irrelevant, however. 'In those two decades something was lost', says Musschoot. 'Literature as such has lost relevance because it has been absorbed into the broader idea of culture, in which the distinction between high and low culture has become blurred.' Democratisation has led to popularisation and finally to populism. There is no longer talk of elevating the people to a higher level through culture. Postmodernism, commercialisation and the internet have not only dismantled the grand authoritative narratives, but have also eroded the roots of Dutch culture.

A child of democratisation in higher education, Musschoot retired ten years ago. 'Once you have acquired your independence as a culture, you cannot just give it away to another language or culture', she argues. As much as she likes to speak English, teaching Dutch literature in Philadelphia to a class of only five students strikes her as an exaggerated investment of time, knowing that in Ghent one hundred and fifty students are signed up for your subject in Dutch. The prestige attached to it, however, is inversely proportional. In the second half of the 1990s, Musschoot herself helped introduce anglicisation by establishing a number of Erasmus opportunities: courses in English designed to attract foreign students. She still finds it unacceptable that a discussion should take place in abominable English just because there is one non-Dutch-speaking student in the class. 'I really have a problem with that,' she says, 'with the idea that culture has to succumb to *money money money*.' A faculty of Arts and Philosophy owes it to itself to safeguard Dutch as a language of culture and science. If the university itself no longer cultivates Dutch, who will?

First issue of *Van Nu en Straks*, 1893
The magazine *Van Nu en Straks* is the Flemish exponent of cosmopolitan avant-garde *fin de siècle* currents in Europe. August Vermeylen, Henry Van de Velde and Karel Van de Woestijne belonged to the editorial staff.
(Brussels, Royal Library of Belgium, design Henry Van de Velde)

Professor of Dutch linguistics Jacques Van Keymeulen tries to attach a symbolic date to the decline of Dutch as a scholarly language in his field. Was it 2007, when a doctorate on the dialect of Maldegem — of which he was supervisor — was written entirely in English? Or was it in 2012, when the annual Taal en Tongval (Language and Accents) conference decided that its main language would be English? It is likewise symbolic that these conferences are held annually in the Royal Academy for Dutch Language and Literature (Koninklijke Academie voor Nederlandse Taal en Letterkunde, or KANTL) in Ghent, the *lieu de mémoire par excellence* of Belgium's language battle. Painted on the wall in graceful letters is Prudens Van Duyse's motto, '*De Taal is Gansch het Volk*' (Language is all of the people). Yet the vast majority of lectures are in English, even though everyone in the room, speakers and listeners alike, are Dutch-speaking. Since even Dutch linguistics no longer uses Dutch, Van Keymeulen thinks Dutch as an academic language is finished.

His younger colleague Yves T'Sjoen, who teaches Dutch literature, has a less pessimistic view. To keep their field viable internationally, scholars of Dutch studies have to publish and lecture in English, according to T'Sjoen. But even for him, teaching Dutch literature in English for Flemish, Dutch and foreign students is a bridge too far.

## Anglicisation, or survival of the fittest

The language law concerning higher education is one of the most important legacies of the Flemish movement. Yet the anglicisation of higher education still carries on at breakneck speed at Flemish universities. No one even raises an eyebrow. In 2012 the legal language regime was reformed in order to attract more students as well as to

**Tom Lanoye, late 1970s**
The 'butcher's son with glasses' was an active member of 't Zal Wel Gaan during his student days in Ghent. He studied Germanic philology and sociology. Lanoye is internationally known for *To War*, a twelve-hour adaptation in verse of eight plays by Shakespeare, originally written in inimitable Dutch (1997). But in his second homeland, South Africa, the anglicisation of higher education is also progressing rapidly.
(Ghent, Universiteitsarchief)

better prepare Belgian students for an international career. For a bachelor's degree, students can take up to 30 out of 180 credits in a language other than Dutch. At the master's level, the degree programme may be entirely in a different language, provided that the same programme is mainly taught in Dutch at another Flemish university. Soon it appeared that the new law was subject to particularly creative interpretations, such as 'zombie programmes' in Dutch, and students who are in practice forced into independent study when they would not register for an English-language equivalent.

Yet it is the Flemish universities themselves that seek to loosen the reins of language even further, according to the official memorandum on language policy of the Flemish Education Council (Vlaamse Onderwijsraad, or VLOR) dated February 2017. Ghent emeritus professor of American literature Kries Versluys, who was chairman of the advisory commission and for many years director of education in Ghent, thinks the existing language law is of an 'unimaginable technocratic absurdity' and in urgent need of revision. Courses of study at the master's level must be completely free in their choice of language. That being said, Versluys also emphasises that it makes no sense to train professionals who will enter a Dutch-speaking work environment, such as doctors, dentists, lawyers, etc., in English. Scholars of Dutch studies and historians, active in the domain of Dutch-language 'heritage', should be educated in Dutch. In research-oriented disciplines, however, it is another matter entirely. In large laboratories, there are sometimes as many as twenty nationalities that resort to English among themselves. 'Do all those students who are just passing through need to learn Dutch?' asks Versluys. It creates a double standard, with low-skilled workers who are obliged to learn Dutch in order to integrate into society, while highly educated migrant university professors, who have the skills and brains to do so, are apparently exempt from the obligation — to the extent that the Dutch language exam for non-Dutch-speaking professors who do decide to settle in Flanders is considered too strict and inhospitable.

The language of education is not a technocratic matter; it deserves wider sociopolitical debate. Pleas for multilingualism in our extremely diverse society sound good, but in the context of higher education in Flanders, it is almost exclusively about anglicisation after the example of the Netherlands, where approximately 60% of the degree programmes are now offered in English. Since the relaxation of the language law in 2012, Flemish universities and colleges are anglicising at breakneck speed despite all language barriers. Sometimes, of course, there are very good reasons for this. Still, it is worrying that in nearly all degree programmes, the number of Dutch subjects is rapidly decreasing. This trend is not so much due to the increasing presence of foreign professors and students, but to Dutch-speaking lecturers who increasingly teach their largely Dutch-speaking students in English.

Anglicisation unmistakably increases the gap between the educated and the uneducated at a time when higher education is faltering as an engine of social emancipation. A university that does not cultivate Dutch in a Dutch-speaking country or region alienates itself from the taxpayers who finance it in the interest of the common good.

If the policy of internationalisation at universities and colleges is exclusively a matter of utilitarian anglicisation, it yields a social and cultural deficit. The expansion of English as the lingua franca can promote mobility and exchange among students and teachers, but at the same time, the dominance of a single language results in the virtual exclusion of other languages and cultures — French, German or Arabic — which have less chance of contributing to the cultural exchange. The Erasmus Programme (1987) was originally set up in view of immersion in the language and culture of the host university. Unity in diversity, as August Vermeylen imagined Europe. The Bologna reforms, however, have abandoned the cosmopolitanism of Erasmus and the formation of a European polity in favour of a utilitarian logic. Higher education is made instrumental to the European education market, in which competition is the guiding principle. The element of 'social uplift' in this context can be translated into making Flanders the top region in the knowledge-based economy.

A general relaxation of the language regime and the surrender of language to the free market lead not to multilingualism, but to the victory of the strongest and most prestigious language, English. Those who wish to keep Dutch as the language of instruction must legally anchor its position (or keep it legally anchored) at colleges and universities. 'Glocalisation', or the insight that globalisation always has a local dimension at its core, can revive the connection between international scholarship and local societal domains, allowing local languages (in plural) to gain in relevance and importance. In this way, the university can once again become a place of formation and civilisation, where the connection between scholarship and society is literally *cultivated* in and through language.

Poster for a debate about anglicisation, 2010
Contrary to the sometimes very fierce battle for Dutchification, there is hardly any public debate about the rapidly advancing anglicisation of higher education in Flanders. During the August Vermeylen Year (2010-2011), UGentMemorie opened up the subject to discussion.
(Ghent, UGentMemorie, poster Randoald Sabbe and Jan Hespeel)

E. Sacré, rue de la Calandre, 1, Gand.

# Chapter 7
# WAR AND PEACE

In 1904, ten years before the outbreak of the First World War, an institute from Ghent received a Nobel Prize in Oslo for its contribution to world peace. The Institut de Droit International, founded in 1873, is still active today. It is based in Geneva and can boast of an illustrious history. Yet this story rings fewer bells in the collective memory of Ghent University than the Nobel Prize awarded to Corneel Heymans.

In 1873 Europe had changed drastically in comparison to the period in which the university was founded. Increasing nationalism was steadily undermining the delicate balance of powers hammered out at the Congress of Vienna. In France the ascendancy of emperor Napoleon III marked the rise of a new sort of leader. 'Napoléon le Petit' was elected in 1848 by universal suffrage. On the basis of a referendum, he had himself crowned emperor in 1852 after the example of his illustrious uncle. The Second Empire was an anti-parliamentarian, autocratic regime until it collapsed after the Franco-Prussian War of 1870-1871.

Germany, up to then a patchwork of small principalities, had become a unified nation-state to be reckoned with under the leadership of Prussia. Like Napoleon III, chancellor Otto von Bismarck held national interest in higher esteem than European peace. The growing rivalry between France and Germany in the run-up to the First World War was coupled with an upsurge of chauvinism and patriotism that engulfed professors and students as well as the general population. In 1900 the first volume of Henri Pirenne's *magnum opus* '*Histoire de Belgique*' was published, tracing the history of Belgium back to the early Middle Ages and positing the development of a specifically 'Belgian' identity at the crossroads of Romance and Germanic cultures. The centuries of peaceful coexistence between Flemings and Walloons in the crucible of European history was a powerful historical legitimation for Belgium as a nation-state in a period when patriotism was trickling down to broad sections of the population.

Competition among nations was also reflected in education. Other countries were jealous of the prestige that the German Humboldt model had enjoyed since the beginning of the nineteenth century. The internationalisation of scholarship and the transcending of national rivalries through intellectual cooperation was thus also a form of pacifism, though it did not prevent the outbreak of the First World War. When Henri Pirenne became rector in 1919, he broke all ties with the German academic world so dear to him before the war.

Since the catastrophes of two world wars left deep scars in the microcosm of Ghent University, successive generations have upheld the tradition of the Institut de Droit International, and Ghent's professors and scientists have handed down their commitment to world peace, international law and human rights.

**Pierre Pirenne, 1914**
The third son of historian Henri Pirenne saw it as his moral duty to serve his homeland and enlisted voluntarily in August 1914. He received preferential treatment and was initially kept away from the Yser Front. When he was nevertheless deployed to the front line at his explicit request, he was killed almost immediately, on 3 November 1914. He was then nineteen years old, had studied physics and mathematics, and was one of the eighty-two Ghent students who did not survive the First World War.
(Ghent, Universiteitsarchief)

# The Institut de Droit International

**Gustave Rolin-Jaequemyns, 1883**
The family networks of Ghent professors feature interesting twists and turns. Jean-Baptiste Hellebaut, Gustave's maternal grandfather, died unexpectedly in October 1819 after a brief illness, barely forty-four years old, after having just become rector. On his deathbed, he asked his nearest colleague, Jacques-Joseph Haus, to become the guardian of his children. The famous criminal justice specialist Haus married his widow, thus becoming the step-grandfather of Gustave and Albéric Rolin. Strangely enough, Albéric would succeed his step-grandfather as professor after the latter's death in 1881. Gustave also studied law and was active for a while as an attorney.
(Ghent, Amsab-ISG)

In Ghent city hall a modest plaque recalls the first session of the Institut de Droit International at the beginning of September 1873. Founder Gustave Rolin-Jaequemyns, a visionary with a sense of reality, passed away in 1902 — two years before the institute was awarded the Nobel Prize. His brother Albéric took over the presidency in 1906 and even after his retirement in 1913 would continue to be active in the world of international law for more than twenty years.

Gustave Rolin was the eldest of the eighteen children of the liberal Ghent lawyer Hippolyte Rolin and Angélique Hellebaut. Her father, Jean-Baptiste Hellebaut, belonged to the first generation of professors appointed in 1817. Rolin senior was president of the Bar and preferred his son to work there rather than at the university, so Gustave turned down a teaching appointment in political history. In 1859 he married Emilie Jaequemyns. She was the only daughter of Edouard Jaequemyns, who had been attached to the Special Schools in Ghent and made a fortune in industry. After his marriage, Gustave went by the name Rolin-Jaequemyns. '*Gustave et Emilie n'avaient à deux qu'un seul coeur*', recalled a friend. Thanks to her family fortune, Gustave was able to devote himself almost exclusively to the study of international law and the cultivation of numerous international contacts. We know a great deal about his foreign travels thanks to his long, passionate letters to 'Milou'. Gustave Rolin-Jaequemyns became a key figure in an international network of socially engaged jurists involved in international law, social progress and peace. Oscar Schachter later called this network 'the invisible college of international lawyers'. Through his involvement, Gustave helped establish the Association Internationale pour le Progrès des Sciences Sociales (APSS), founded in 1862. When the APSS project ran into difficulties because of the Austro-Prussian war in 1866 and growing tensions between France and Germany, Rolin-Jaequemyns revealed his pragmatic side. He rejected utopian pacifism and decided that rules of play, conventions and international laws were needed. In 1869, together with Tobias Asser (Amsterdam) and John Westlake (Cambridge), he started the *Revue de droit international et de législation compare*, the world's first and leading international law journal.

The Institut de Droit International was the next step. In 1870-1871, rising national rivalries in Europe culminated in the horrors of the Franco-Prussian War. While the armies were more or less organised the same way as at the beginning of the nineteenth century, the modern 'scientific' arms race had provided increasingly devastating military technology. The war had no laws — or at any rate, even the most elementary rules of engagement were ignored. Both camps trampled the Geneva Convention shamelessly underfoot. The first Geneva Convention was a tentative effort to improve the lot of the sick and the wounded on the battlefield. Moreover, to the considerable indignation of humanitarian activists, the Red Cross insignia were abused. Shocked by the atrocities of the battlefield, one of its founders, Gustave Moynier, felt that only Gustave Rolin-Jaequemyns had the qualities needed to set up an international organisation that could prevent such horrors of war in the future.

This was indeed the goal. To unite and join forces intellectually, to form a permanent centre and to conduct research without government support: an NGO *avant la lettre*. The Institut de Droit International was formed several months after Jules Verne published his *Around the World in Eighty Days* (1873). Rolin-Jaequemyns referred to this book in his invitation to renowned experts from nine countries and four continents. The new means of communication and transport made internationalisation that much simpler. From Belgium, François Laurent and Emile de Laveleye joined the group. De Laveleye, former member of the Société Huet in Ghent, was appointed professor of Political Economy in Liège in 1864 and was embarking on an impressive international career when the Institut was founded.

Mayor Charles de Kerchove received the illustrious company in the Arsenal Room of the city hall, where the Pacification of Ghent was signed in 1576. The Institut's mission was scholarly and humanitarian. In order to reduce the cruelty of war and the uncertainty of peace, rules of law needed to be codified. Their motto was — and still is — '*Justitia et Pace*'. The Institut de Droit International worked independently and in the shadow of the institutions for international law that were being developed in The Hague during the *fin de siècle*. In August 1914, Albéric Rolin wrote a letter to all members stating that the session planned in Munich that autumn was cancelled. With his blunt assertion that war was 'godless', he shocked his German colleagues. Several German scholars defended the war as a divine and justified mission that would spread superior German *Kultur* throughout Europe.

## Sleepwalkers

Little Belgium, which according to its constitution had to remain neutral in international conflicts, did not escape the military race that accompanied growing nationalism in Europe. Under pressure from king Leopold II — on his deathbed — the draft was introduced in 1909, applicable to one son per family. This had repercussions for Ghent students who were called up for military service. They were conscripted in the Compagnie Universitaire and quartered at the Leopold barracks, where they were drilled in marching and marksmanship from 5 to 7 a.m. before classes. The student-soldiers attracted attention because they continued to wear their uniforms in class and at pubs.

It was the kind of thing that suggested that war was in the air. The rectorial speeches were interspersed with nationalist, patriotic and even militaristic rhetoric. In 1903, rector Paul Thomas addressed the students with the message that, regardless of the diversity of opinions, they were all fellow soldiers, brothers in arms in archaic student terms.

Though the dark clouds had been gathering for some time, the German invasion of neutral Belgium on 4 August 1914 nevertheless struck like a bolt from the blue. 'No one saw it coming', wrote former student and Ter Waarheid (To the Truth) supporter Paul Kenis in *De wonderbare avonturen van Cies Slameur, Gentsch koerier en soldaat* (1919).

The *étudiants-soldats*, 1913
(Ghent, Universiteitsarchief)

'The Gentse Feesten had just ended; there was something in the papers about the big countries, about Russia and England and Germany, and others, but that had nothing to do with our little country, did it? And then, it had almost come to blows between all those countries so many times that I thought: it'll blow over again this time too.'

Together with Cies Slameur, Kenis's fictional lad who is mobilised in the summer of 1914 and manages to survive the horrors of war through all sort of tomfoolery, the students of the Compagnie Universitaire were called up to the front. The exact number of students from Ghent in the trenches is unknown. We know that eighty-two of them died over the next four years. On 21 January 1921, the bronze memorial plaques in memory of their '*mâle courage et de leurs grands exemples*' were solemnly inaugurated in the presence of king Albert in the peristyle of the Aula. More than three decades later, in 1958, rector Pieter Lambrechts unveiled a plaque in memory of Daniel Varoujean on the loan desk of the Boekentoren (the University Library's Tower, commonly called the Book Tower). From 1906 to 1909 the Armenian poet was a brilliant student of sociology and literature at Ghent University. At the end of the nineteenth century his family had fled from the Turkish genocide in western Armenia. After his studies, he returned to his country and became director of an Armenian school in Istanbul in 1914. In a short time he established his reputation as the greatest Armenian poet since the mystics of the eleventh century. In his *Pagan Songs* of 1912 he tried to invigorate the Armenian people with Symbolist poetry evoking a grand past. In the spring of 1915, Varoujean and two hundred and fifty other Armenian intellectuals were arrested by the Ottoman police in Istanbul. He was bound naked to a tree and tortured to death with knives. The 'Ghent' martyr of the Armenian genocide was thirty-one years old.

Rector Henri Schoentjes did not seem up to the difficult task of guiding the university intact and unharmed through the international conflagration. 'He lost his head', noted Paul Fredericq in his diary. The first Academic Council after the declaration of war was held on 30 September 1914. Everyone was concerned for the *étudiants-soldats*. They were not to be discriminated against in comparison to students who had not been called to arms. Courses would not be resumed as long as they were still mobilised. The rector set the opening of the academic year for 20 October. The Academic Council was clearly convinced that the war would not last long. The second session took place. Sixteen students were registered for the new academic year and their tuition had already been distributed among the professors, as was customary.

**Commemorative plaque for Daniel Varoujean**
(Ghent, Universiteitsbibliotheek, photo Benn Deceuninck)

On 12 October 1914, German troops marched into Ghent. The German flag was raised at the city hall. In contrast to Leuven, where the library went up in flames, Ghent encountered no such violence during occupation. The city was placed under military authority as a transit city in Etappengebiet IV. The opening of the academic year was cancelled in anticipation of further instructions from the Belgian government, which had fled to Le Havre. In accordance with The Hague Convention, approximately two hundred members of the teaching and academic personnel signed a declaration of loyalty stating that they would continue to occupy their posts for the duration of the war and would not hinder the German administration. In Liège, the professors refused. In Ghent, opinions were sharply divided over the question of whether courses should be resumed. In the end, the university would remain closed until 2 December 1918.

## At war

In addition to the *étudiants-soldats*, volunteers also went to the front. Among them was the lecturer Frans Daels, who would spend the four years of the war as an army doctor on the Yser Front. After fighting at Houtem, he and a number of soldiers cut across German lines to re-join the Belgian army. He would enlist the help of Marie Curie concerning the use of radium on the front. Daels was also the great animator of Christian and sociocultural actions for Flemish soldiers and students in the armed forces. He founded the Secretariat of Catholic Flemish University Students (Secretariaat der Katholieke Vlaamsche Hoogstudenten, or SKHV) and was closely involved with the Front movement, in which former Ghent student Adiel — '*ruwaard*' (the governor) — Debeuckelaere played a leading role. Their spiritual leader was the Flemish nationalist priest-poet Cyriel Verschaeve. The Front movement gave rise to the myth of Flemish soldiers who did not understand the orders of their French-speaking officers.

**The leadership of the Front movement during the First World War**
From left to right: Filip de Pillecyn, Adiel Debeuckelaere, Frans Daels, Hendrik Borginon and Victor Vangramberen.
(Antwerp, Letterenhuis)

Stomatologist Oswald Rubbrecht went to the Yser Front and worked in the Antoine Depage military hospital housed in Hotel L'Océan in De Panne. He tended the wounded with serious jaw fractures. His surgical techniques brought him international renown and played an important role in the development of modern dentistry.

The government in Le Havre made an effort to help students in the armed forces to continue their studies. They did so by setting up libraries and organising classes to disseminate university courses. But it was only a drop in the ocean.

From November 1914 onwards, the '*cours universitaires belges*' were organised in London, where Gustave Magnel and Louis de la Vallée–Poussin took part in the effort. These courses were not meant to replace regular instruction; rather, they were a form of intellectual training for professors and students who had fled the war. With more than two hundred students enrolled, the initiative was a success. Several Ghent professors were invited to give lectures at the London School of Economics (LSE) or the recently established School of Oriental Studies (SOAS). British colleagues from Oxford, Cambridge and London extended their hospitality to Belgian intellectuals and their families. A similar movement arose in the Netherlands. One million Belgians fled to the Netherlands in the summer of 1914. Deserting soldiers were housed in internment camps, citizens and families of soldiers in 'refuges'. Living conditions were poor; boredom reigned.

A university was established for student refugees in Utrecht. And in Amersfoort, under the impulse of the Utrecht Catholic professor Joseph Schrijnen and his Leuven colleague François Collard, a temporary Belgian university was created for interned student soldiers. Some thirty professors from Utrecht and Belgium (among them teachers and officers) gave instruction. Ninety-one students were enrolled, both Flemings and Walloons, who received instruction in Dutch and French.

## The 'von Bissing university'

Three sons of historian Henri Pirenne left for the front in August 1914 to defend the fatherland. The youngest of the three, Pierre, only nineteen, was killed in November at the Yser Front. During this period, chancellor Theobald von Bethmann-Hollweg sent historian Karl Lamprecht on an intelligence mission to Belgium. Its purpose was to reorganise higher education in Belgium along German lines and, within this framework, also to Dutchify Ghent University. This was the core of the so-called Flemish policy or '*Flamenpolitik*' of the Germans. Lamprecht was convinced that Henri Pirenne would be a good adviser for Berlin, but, unsurprisingly, his request was turned down. From the beginning of the war, Pirenne kept a diary that is still largely unpublished, and in which he is particularly critical of the national fanaticism of the Great War and the mediocrity of the men supposed to lead it. 'From an intellectual point of view, it's even worse. No one dreams of Europe, except for a few utopians with no voice and no power. Everyone screams for himself.' Lamprecht not least. Why were heroic soldiers, such as Pirenne's son Pierre, sacrificed in the end? 'One struggles and one fights in the purest materialism [...] After all this, I hardly see any solution except in a spiritualised socialism.'

Henri Pirenne and Paul Fredericq in exile
(Ghent, Universiteitsarchief)

On 20 September 1915 the Academic Council voted unanimously against allowing the university to reopen in October. Rector Schoentjes presented the head of the East Flemish Zivilverwaltung, Friedrich Ecker, with the collective refusal, argued in seven points and supplied with fifty-two signatures. Leaders of the opposition were the Hellenist Joseph Bidez and the historians Fredericq and Pirenne. 'I do not want to appear before my students, my face reddened with shame. I do not want to remount the lectern until our student-soldiers have returned', Fredericq declared, thereby reaping what he called an 'irresistible wind of gritty patriotism'. Individual responses to Ecker were less gritty. Twenty of the professors contacted had no moral or practical objections to reopening. After all, they had already signed a collective declaration of loyalty. Governor-general Moritz von Bissing announced at the end of 1915 that the Dutchified university would open in the foreseeable future. Immediately there arose protest from pro-Flemish quarters that the German occupier had no right to interfere with the language of the university. In February 1916, the professors were surveyed to determine who could teach in Dutch: only eight out of eighty responded in the affirmative; others referred to the language law that did not permit it. On 15 March 1916, von Bissing issued an ordinance that altered the Royal Decree of 1849 and made Dutch the official language of the university.

On 18 March 1916, Henri Pirenne and Paul Fredericq, the two leaders of the protest, were arrested and deported to Germany. The deportation of two prominent professors, intended to break resistance, had the opposite effect. Joseph Bidez, supported by sixty colleagues, sent an urgent petition to von Bissing, asking that the two historians, who were in no way a threat to public order, be allowed to return. The national archivist in Brussels immediately informed his colleague in Utrecht of the deportation with a message in Latin, disguised as a question about a medieval text. The hidden message slipped through the net of German censorship and made the fate of Pirenne and Fredericq known to the world. A wave of international protest against the 'barbarian' act of the Germans followed. Woodrow Wilson and pope Benedict XV lobbied the Kaiser to release them. But their efforts were in vain. Professors who registered resistance and continued to refuse to 'serve the Flemish people' would be suspended without fail and no longer allowed to enter the university.

The Vlaamsche Hoogeschool opened its doors on 24 October 1916. In the end, only seven professors were willing to teach there. The majority of the administrative and technical personnel resigned. They continued to receive their salaries thanks to the Comité Saroléa, of which Joseph Bidez was secretary and treasurer. The funds came from Charles Saroléa, the Belgian consul in Edinburgh, who had written a bestseller on Joan of Arc before the war and used the profits for all kinds of philanthropic projects organised by the Le Septentrion Lodge of which Bidez was a member. In his *Rapport sur l'histoire d'une société secrète sous l'occupation allemande à Gand: tracts divers répandus clandestinement à Gand sous le Régime de l'Etape* (1919), Bidez reported on the clandestine activities he undertook during the war with L'Action Patriotique and the underground journal *L'Autre Cloche*. Undermining the activist university and supporting the resigning staff and suspended professors were essential to their activities.

The Vlaamsche Hoogeschool started off with an enrolment of just sixty. Between October 1916 and October 1918 a total of 477 students registered, a sharp decrease compared to the 1,315 students that were registered in 1913-1914. The new Gentsch Studenten Corp 'Hou ende Trou' (GSC) wanted to break with the political fragmentation of the student movement and promote unity in order to shape the Flemish elite of the future. The Uylenspiegel student house in Sint-Pietersnieuwstraat, which was obtained from the Germans in 1918, was given to the university by the Belgian government after the war, as was Hotel Van Crombrugghe on Voldersstraat, near the Aula.

The centenary of the University of Ghent was celebrated on 3 November 1917 in the presence of the new governor-general Ludwig von Falkenhausen with 'great festivities', as Virginie Loveling noted in her wartime diary. The next day 150 to 200 students went singing through the streets with fluttering banners. The activist newspapers cheered. A huge popular banquet with 600 singers followed by a banquet in the elegant salons of the opera at the Kouter might give the impression that the people of Ghent were just as excited as the activists themselves.

Nothing could be further from the truth. Bystanders could only muster hatred and contempt for the students and professors, who they cursed as 'traitors attached to the enemy'. 'Almost no one greets them anymore, those who collude with the enemy', wrote Loveling. On the contrary, people secretly 'shook their fists at them in powerless rage, muttering death threats under their breath'.

In February 1918, fifty-two Ghent professors lodged a protest with German chancellor Georg Michaelis against the Council of Flanders, which in the meantime had declared unilaterally the independence of Flanders without the support of the people. The professors argued that their continual contact with successive generations of students had shown that the country's intellectual elite considered the union of the Flemish and Walloon provinces perfectly natural. The Pirenne thesis on the origins of Belgium came in handy. 'This union is the result of traditions and common interests; it has been submitted to the test of centuries of peaceful collaboration or battles endured side by side; it has even been necessary for us to play a useful role as intermediary between the great civilisations that surround us. It is an element of culture and progress.' The patriotic élan of the professors garnered admiration from around the world.

At the opening of the third academic year of the Vlaamsche Hoogeschool, on 15 October 1918, the Germans were already evacuating Ghent: they had lost the war. The activists did likewise. When Pirenne and Fredericq returned at the beginning of December, vice-rector De Brabandere spoke with pride of the patriotism of the faculty that had resisted the 'criminal Flamandisation or, to be more precise, the Germanisation of our university'.

The seven traitors — Peter Hoffmann, Ernest Haerens, Willem De Vreese, Julius Obrie, Emile Lahousse, Franz Stöber and Cesar De Bruycker — were dismissed from the university. All the universities in the world were apprised of the decision. Academic excommunication was their lot. When the 'real' university reopened on 21 January 1919, the new rector, Paul Fredericq, spoke in the name of the students who had died for their country and who issued a message for the future from beyond the grave: 'We have given our youth for our country and for justice. Do as we have, if need be.'

**Student residence Hou ende Trou, 1918**
A staged scene from student life at the time of the Vlaamsche Hoogeschool under German occupation during the last year of the war, 1918.
(Ghent, Universiteitsarchief)

## Ghent pacifists in Versailles, Geneva and The Hague

During its first session after the liberation of the city, the Academic Council decided to award honorary doctorates to cardinal Mercier, Woodrow Wilson, Georges Clémenceau, David Lloyd George, Ferdinand Foch, Gérard Leman, David Beatty, John Jellicoe and Joseph Joffre. It was the first time such a powerful political statement was made via the tradition of the honorary doctorate.

In spring 1919, Fredericq, who was suffering from health problems, transferred the rectorial ermine to his pupil, Henri Pirenne. Every year, the latter's rectorial speech was a scathing intellectual critique of Germany. Admiration for German scholarship had taken a severe beating. His address *Ce que nous devons désapprendre de l'Allemagne* (1921) was about the ideological misuse of the sciences and the importance of cosmopolitanism as a guard against nationalism. After the First World War, academics all over the world shared the feeling that scholarship, now more than ever, could stimulate international cooperation for peace and rapprochement between nations. The history of science thus became the basis for a new international humanism.

George Sarton, who had fled to America during the war, was an important exponent of this trend in Ghent. And of course the Institut de Droit International fitted within this framework. The successor of Albéric Rolin, Charles De Visscher, had fled to Oxford in 1914 and represented Belgium at the Versailles Peace Conference in 1919. Under the influence of the war, he shifted the focus of his research to international law and the newly developing concept of human rights. De Visscher was secretary-general of the Institut in the period 1927-1937, as well as dean of the faculty of Law, and between 1937 and 1952 judge in the Permanent Court of International Justice and the International Court, which was established in The Hague in 1946.

Louis Varlez, De Visscher's colleague at the Law faculty and chairman of the Ghent Unemployment Fund, had undertaken secret missions to London and Le Havre during the war to report to the Belgian government and international institutions on the predicament in the Etappengebiet. He hoped to secure emergency funding and subsidies for the Unemployment Fund and lay the foundations for the development of unemployment benefits throughout Belgium. Hence it was no coincidence that Varlez travelled to Versailles with the Belgian delegation in January 1919 as a legal adviser. In June of that year he was asked via minister of foreign affairs Paul Hymans to take up a permanent post in the Labour division of the recently established League of Nations. But before he took up his post, Varlez was offered another important position at the International Labour Organisation (ILO), also recently established. This was an offer he couldn't refuse, given his expertise. As director of the department of Unemployment and Migration, he would work on a blueprint for an international migration policy, from 1920 until his pension in 1929.

The important positions of professors from Ghent in Versailles, The Hague and Geneva reveal not only their international ambitions and connections, but also, above all, their enduring commitment to world peace and the social progress of humanity.

**Louis Varlez in Peking, 1929-1930**
In 1929-1930 the social liberal and international official Louis Varlez made a trip around the world that took him to Japan, Korea, China, Indochina, Indonesia, Burma and India, among other places. After the First World War, intellectual cooperation beyond the borders of nations and cultures was a form of pacifism even more than it had been before.
(Ghent, Liberal Archive)

The international network that Jules Verschaffelt was able to build thanks to the Solvay congresses at the ULB was very active in assisting Jewish scientists who had fled Germany after the Nazi coup. Like his colleagues in Brussels and Liège, Verschaffelt saw opportunities to attract German-Jewish physicists to Ghent. Rector Vermeylen supported the idea. In September 1933 he received a letter of recommendation from Albert Einstein, who he considered 'a model for humanity', asking assistance for two colleagues. In the end, only Erwin Schrödinger (Nobel Prize, 1933)

**Albert Einstein in Belgium, 1933**
Albert and Elsa Einstein arrived in Antwerp from New York on 28 March 1933. Alarmed by the takeover of Adolf Hitler and the events in Berlin, the Jewish, anti-Nazi physicist renounced his German citizenship via the German embassy in Brussels, surrendered his German passport and declared that he would no longer set foot on German soil as long as civil rights and freedoms were not guaranteed there. Since the first Solvay congress in 1911, he had good contacts with Belgian scientists, including Jules Verschaffelt, on the right behind Elsa in the photo. The Einsteins stayed with the Ghent histology professor Arthur De Groodt, far left, at his Castle Cantecroy in Mortsel, which was a meeting point for Flemish cultural life and Flemish-Dutch scientific exchange. Albert and Elsa Einstein spent the summer of 1933 in De Haan. In September 1933 they left definitively for the US.
(Brussels, KIK-IRPA, photo Acta)

would spend time working at the Physics Laboratory in Ghent. Since the first Solvay congress in 1911, Einstein travelled regularly to Belgium, but after his final flight to Princeton in September 1933, he would never return to Europe.

Within Catholic Flemish nationalism, another professor from Ghent, Frans Daels, would demonstrate a significant commitment to pacifism after the First World War. From the Front movement, the Yser Pilgrimage Committee was born. The Yser Tower was originally an international, pacifist anti-war monument. The verse by Verschaeve inscribed on the tower, '*Hier liggen hun lijken als zaden in het zand, hoop op de oogst O Vlaanderland*' (Here lie their bodies like seeds in the sand, hope for the harvest, O Flandersland), however, revealed the inherent ambiguity of that pacifism. The authority Daels acquired as chairman of the Yser Pilgrimage Committee, making him akin to the 'conscience of Flanders' in the 1920s, transcended party politics. But in the second half of the 1930s the Yser Tower evolved from a symbol of Christian faith, Flamingantism and pacifism into a symbol of the Flemish nationalist New Order. The anti-democratic Flemish National Alliance (Vlaams-Nationaal Verbond, or VNV, 1933) acquired greater and greater influence in the Yser Pilgrimage Committee, and would help determine its course. Daels radicalised in the process. Daels's pacifism was still evident from his membership of the Association of Ghent Professors for Disarmament and the Promotion of the Principles of International Law (Vereniging van Gentsche Hoogleraars voor Ontwapening en Bevordering van het Internationaal Rechtsbeginsel, 1932) and the International Association against War and Militarism (Rassemblement International contre la Guerre et le Militarisme, 1937), and from the fact that he advocated a recognised statute for conscientious objectors (1938). On the other hand, Daels was driven in the direction of the extreme-right VNV, which agitated against parliamentary democracy and would collaborate with Nazi Germany during the Second World War.

**The Yser Pilgrimage under German occupation, 1941**
Frans Daels addressing German soldiers during the 22nd Yser Pilgrimage in Diksmuide, 24 August 1941, in a private meeting that could be listened to by radio. (Ghent, Amsab-ISG, photo Paul De Clercq)

**Frans Daels and August Borms, 1941**
Daels and Borms giving the Hitler salute during the performance of The Lion of Flanders at the 22nd Yser Pilgrimage.
(The Hague, Nationaal Archief)

## War again

On 16 January 1940 the Nobel Prize for Physiology or Medicine was awarded to Corneel Heymans in the Aula. The award was presented by the Swedish ambassador in the presence of Queen Elisabeth. Leopold III was not present because of the threat of war. The so-called '*drôle de guerre*' was also the reason why the presentation of the Nobel Prize did not take place in Stockholm in 1939.

In the early hours of 10 May 1940 German glider planes landed in Belgium, in Eben-Emael. The next day the Second World War began in earnest in Ghent with German bombs dropped on the area around the Snepbrug. The senior alderman, Jules Storme, father of Marcel, was acting mayor of the city after the flight of Alfons Vanderstegen. As an expert in Germanic studies — and therefore familiar with the German language — Storme was sent to the Keizerpoort to negotiate with the German army. In a German Volkswagen convertible, he brought the enemy — the armed Wehrmacht sat in the back seat — to the city hall in order to symbolically hand over the keys of the city. He wanted to prevent the city being shelled.

Chaos reigned; classes at the university were cancelled forthwith. Since there were no clear guidelines being issued from Brussels, rector René Goubau, professor of Chemistry, gave the teaching and scientific staff the choice of what to do 'with an eye towards their own safety or the greater service they could render their country'. He and a number of colleagues left for Toulouse to safeguard the finances of the university. Frank Baur, the 'German-unfriendly' dean of Arts and Philosophy, acted as temporary rector. The Academic Council of 22 May 1940 paid tribute to the professors and assistants who remained at their posts: 'staying in the midst of the people' was what professors had to do. This was also the position of Leopold III, who capitulated on 28 May and broke with the Pierlot government, which fled to London in order to continue the war with alongside Allies. The king remained in the country, with his people.

A similar division arose at the University of Ghent, between the professors who remained at their posts and the exodus of the 'Toulouse professors'. Seventy of the one hundred and sixty-seven professors eventually fled to France; of the scientific personnel, thirty-nine of the eighty-five staff members then employed at the university fled.

Nora Pieruccini and Falk Epsteins
(Ghent, collection of Marc Verschooris)

Falk Epsteins and his wife Nora Pieruccini were among those who fled to France. The couple had met in Paul Van Oye's Biogeographic Laboratory. As the only son of poet-activist Eugeen Van Oye, Paul had been initiated in the freethinking leftist student milieu of 't Zal Wel Gaan and Ter Waarheid before the First World War. He had studied zoology and was a fervent adherent of Julius Mac Leod, closely involved in the development of Flemish scientific culture. In 1926 he was appointed to the Nolf university. Falk Epsteins was a Latvian Jew who had come to Ghent from Riga in 1936-1937 to continue his studies in zoology. Nora Pieruccini was enrolled in the Higher Institute for Education (Hoger Instituut voor Opvoedkunde, or HIO), which attached great importance to biology. It was love at first sight, but the Jewish student was not exactly an ideal son-in-law in times of growing anti-Semitism. Falk was moreover a convinced communist. Against the will of Nora's family, they married on 15 May 1939. The university's resistance was also considerable. Van Oye had immediately taken notice of the foreign student with a thorough knowledge of experimental zoology. When Epsteins applied for a position as an unpaid volunteer assistant in 1939 after brilliant studies, his adviser, who supported him completely, had to face considerable suspicion from not only within his own faculty, but also on the part of rector Goubau and executive director Alfred Schoep. Hiring a foreigner, whose stay in Belgium 'probably had a political background', was something the university had to approach with extreme caution. Falk's involvement in the socialist youth movement The Red Falcons (De Rode Valken), together with Nora, closed the door in his face: Falk Epsteins was not officially appointed and worked as Van Oye's personal assistant while he completed his doctoral thesis, which he hoped to defend on 14 June 1940. Adolph Hitler decided otherwise.

Leopold's capitulation sparked a protest motion on 30 May 1940 from the '*indignes fils*' in Toulouse, primarily professors from Brussels and Liège led by ULB professor Henri Grégoire. It was clear that the ULB resisted collaboration with the Nazis from the outset. The only one from Ghent to sign was Valère Billiet, a resistance fighter of the first hour. The day after, there was another meeting in Toulouse chaired by Goubau that resulted in a show of sympathy for the Pierlot government and support for the war at the side of the Allies '*jusqu'au bout*', to the bitter end. This motion was signed by most of the Ghent contingent in Toulouse. Nevertheless, the attitude of someone like Paul Van Oye was less unequivocally anti-Leopold III than might appear. This is clear from his letters to his wife Helene, which read like an 'honest confession' in diary form. 'I hope that Leopold III will be able to spare Belgium a great deal of suffering, and I still hope that he will be able to build a new Belgium from the rubble that remains', he wrote, just after the capitulation. The longer he stayed in Toulouse the more disgusted he grew with the chaos and indecision of the Pierlot government, which pushed him perceptibly in the direction of the New Order. His pro-Flemish admiration for Germany had suffered little during the First World War. Not a single critical word about the Nazi regime was to be found in his letters to Helene: 'Whatever may happen, our country and Europe can only be saved by means of a strong dictatorship', he opined on 29 July 1940. Once back in Ghent, however, he experienced a rude awakening from those who collaborated with Nazi dictatorship.

## A 'Zentrum volksverbundener flämischer Wissenschaft'

After the truce with Germany and Italy, most professors returned to Belgium between June and November 1940, among them rector Goubau and Paul Van Oye. Falk and Nora Epsteins also gave up their plans to flee further, in spite of an eloquent letter of recommendation from Van Oye intended to open doors for his pupil in the French academic world.

Meanwhile, the occupier controlled all aspects of life in Ghent. Supervision of the university was in the hands of historian Franz Petri, who was referent for *Volkstum, Kultur und Wissenschaften* with the Militärverwaltung in Belgium and northern France. Petri wanted to avoid stirring up intellectual resistance at Ghent University, as had been the case during the First World War. This time the university had to keep operating as smoothly as possible. In contrast to the ULB, which chose open resistance and was shut down as a result, Ghent opted for a 'noiseless' policy of adapting to the Nazi regime.

René Goubau was suspended along with the other 'post deserters' on 9 September 1940 and replaced by a 'German-friendly' rector. Petri's first choice was Herman De Vleeschauwer, a doctor in philosophy appointed as a lecturer in the faculty of Arts and Philosophy in 1925. De Vleeschauwer's philosophy of history was imbued with '*völkische*' ideas. A '*Volk*', in his view, was a group of people who shared a 'blood-soil', language and history. The cultivation of the '*volkswil*' through education was an important motor of history. He had already formulated his ideas about education and youth in *Volk en Staat*, the newspaper of the VNV. However, De Vleeschauwer would become secretary-general of higher education instead, a *de facto* minister in the service of the occupying authorities. He continued to teach and began his lectures with the Nazi salute — or was it the Roman salute? At any rate his students were hardly enthusiastic. In the end, the chemist Guillaume De Smet became the new rector. The Nazis had pragmatically opted for an accommodating figure who was supported by the Academic Council. Frans Daels was not in the running: according to Petri, he was too controversial and too strongly 'too exposed in terms of party affiliation and exclusively Greater Netherlands oriented'.

The goal of the occupation was to make Ghent University a 'Zentrum volksverbundener flämischer Wissenschaft'. This was accomplished in the first place by appointing pro-German professors. The internist Adriaan Martens and the ophthalmologist Reimond Speleers, dismissed and excommunicated in 1918, were 'recalled'. Leon Elaut had been a student at the von Bissing university. He was therefore punished 'socially' and only allowed to re-enrol in 1922. As a 'good Fleming', the urologist was elected dean of the faculty of Medicine by secret ballot in 1941. In April 1941, the Dietsch Student Congress paid homage to the von Bissing university and the professors who taught at the Vlaamsche Hoogeschool during the First World War. The ceremony included the Nazi salute in the Aula. Henceforth, an exchange of lecturers was organised with Germany and German guest professors were called in to give subjects such as *Volksforschung* and Germanic studies. Racial studies were also part of the programme. In June and November 1942 the most eminent professors of eugenics, heredity and racial policy were invited to Ghent.

History was explicitly seen as a '*völkische*' discipline, aimed at helping cultivate '*ein junges, völkisch verwurzeltes Geschlächt*' (a young race rooted in nationalist/populist values). The students of Ghent needed an antidote against the cosmopolitan school of Henri Pirenne, who had died in 1935 but whose students continued to spread his ideas. François-Louis Ganshof was an exception. According to historian Marc Boone, Ganshof was the 'consummate medievalist' and positivist who demolished all of Pirenne's interesting lines of research one by one. These coincided with the renowned French periodical founded in 1929 by Marc Bloch and Lucien Fèbvre, the *Annales d'histoire économique et sociale* (today *Annales: Histoire, sciences sociales*), the main guidelines of which were the perspective of the '*longue durée*', interdisciplinary research and the quest for a single, all-encompassing human science. Fortunately, the Ghent school was

**Dietsch Student Congress, 1941**
The participants of the Dietsch Student Congress on 3 April 1941 stand in formation in front of the Opera on the Kouter in Ghent and present the Hitler salute.
(Ghent, Amsab-ISG, photo Paul De Clercq)

already so well developed that others were able to continue the tradition established by Pirenne: Hans Van Werveke, Adriaan Verhulst, Jan Dhondt. Ganshof had roots in the Rhineland and maintained his contacts in Germany during the interwar period. In the summer of 1940 he received a visit from Bonn from his fellow historian Franz Petri, now in the uniform of the Wehrmacht, who tried to convince him to collaborate. Like Pirenne in 1914, Ganshof thanked him politely for the honour but nonetheless refused. Collaboration with a regime that had invaded his fatherland and kept it under military occupation was not an option. Moreover, from September 1944 onwards, his brother, auditor-general Walter Ganshof-Van der Meersch, would charge him with inspecting the internment camps for collaborators.

## Collaboration and purge

The new professors in Ghent were all extreme-right adherents of the New Order. In 1941 the impassioned history teacher and Flemish SS member Rob Van Roosbroeck was appointed — first at the law faculty, later also in Arts and Philosophy. Roger Soenen, another adherent of the VNV and dedicated advocate of racist eugenics, also re-entered through the front door after having been dismissed from his post for making derogatory statements about the Belgian fatherland during a protest meeting in the Minardschouwburg (Minard Theatre).

A number of other pre-war professors maintained cordial relations with the occupying regime, among them Frans Daels. Alfred De Waele was particularly visible, if only because he paraded about the university in a black uniform. De Waele, one of the founders of the Veterinary school, was one of the first to sign the VNV manifesto that called for a Flemish People's Movement (Vlaamse Volksbeweging). He joined the Black Brigade, the militia of the VNV. In 1943 he left the university to devote himself entirely to his new job as district leader of the VNV.

For Daels, the war was the moment of truth: he made the definitive step to the VNV. For Staf De Clercq's party, it was a special honour to be able to count this icon of the Flemish movement and the Yser Pilgrimage among its ranks. In October 1940, Daels joined the VNV Leadership Council. From the beginning, he showed himself to be an opponent of cooperation with the SS and an advocate of an offensive Greater Netherlands or '*Dietse*' attitude towards the occupier. At the beginning of July 1940, in his capacity as chairman of the Yser Pilgrimage Committee, he contacted the Germans with the message that, in his opinion, the student body would support a 'Flemish Dutch state' under Leopold III and allied with Germany. In the summer of 1941, however, Daels made propaganda for the battle against the Russians on the Eastern Front, for which the VNV rounded up volunteers. He announced that he would lead the field hospital of the Flemish Legion. Daels never left for the Eastern Front, however, because he disagreed with the absorption of the Flemish Legion by the Waffen SS. At any rate his position was not unequivocal. While he still sang the praises of the Eastern Front soldier in 1943, in April of that year he would resign from the VNV Leadership Council. Yet he never distanced himself from National Socialism. On the contrary: he felt threatened in Ghent and lamented the fact that one 'had not sufficiently evolved in the National-Socialist spirit'.

**Opening session, Dietsch Student Congress in the Aula, 1941**
Many professors were present at the commemoration of the Vlaamsche Hoogeschool. They, too, did not conceal their Nazi sympathies.
(Ghent, Amsab-ISG, photo Paul De Clercq)

**The arrival of Reichsgesundheitsführer Leonardo Conti, 1943**
SS member Leonardo Conti addressing the Aula on 23 June 1943, flanked by rector Guillaume De Smet (right) and executive director Alfred Schoep (left). Other noted participants were Corneel Heymans, Adriaan Martens, Roger Soenen, Leon Elaut, Alfred De Waele, secretary-general Gerard Romsée and Militärverwaltungschef Eggert Reeder.
(Ghent, Amsab-ISG, photo Paul De Clercq)

Jules Storme, in theory still alderman of the city, did not attend a reception at city hall on 14 June 1943 for the returning 'heroes of the Eastern Front'. At any rate, he was not willing to speak on the occasion and wish them *Gut Heil*, recalls his son Marcel. In the afternoon there followed a big celebration at the Opera that would end in an act of revenge against Storme, his fellow alderman Hector Goossens and ousted prosecutor Frans De Heem. The contents of the Storme family townhouse on the Coupure were smashed to bits by some sixty members of the Dietsche Militia's Black Brigade and the Waffen SS. Marcel, who was thirteen at the time, still 'hears' his mother's cries and the sound of boots crushing a splendid Chinese vase from the Ming period.

When Leonardo Conti visited Ghent in June 1943, Frans Daels was prominently present in the Aula, where he gave a speech on social medicine. Conti was Reichsgesundheitsführer of the SS and secretary of state for Domestic Affairs of the Third Reich. Since 1923 he had been a member of the Sturmabteilung (SA) and since 1930 of the Schutzstaffel (SS). He also led the Hauptamt Volksgesundheit of the NSDAP. His mother Nanna was chair of the National-Socialist midwives' organisation, which is how she was linked to Daels. She was closely involved with the Mütterheim or Lebensbornkliniek in Wolvertem. In 1935, Heinrich Himmler founded the Lebensborn programme in order to cultivate a race of Arian *Übermenschen*. The Mütterheim in Wolvertem dated from 1942 and was a racial procreation centre for women of Germanic origin, whether German or Flemish. In Wégimont near Liège there was a Walloon equivalent. The Flemish midwives who worked in Wolvertem were there on Daels's recommendation.

Although he was not a coroner, because of his Nazi sympathies Reimond Speleers was appointed as expert in a case involving the murder of Polish officers in Katyn, where a mass grave was discovered in 1943. Roger Soenen was involved in exposing the mass graves of Winniza in Ukraine in July 1943. Daels, for his part, used the arrival of the Reichsgesundheitsführer to transfer the Bijloke hospital to the university with the approval of the faculty and the city.

In 1944 and 1945 a purging commission led by Frédéric Thomas and René Goubau would handle more than sixty files on collaborating professors who 'remained at fault on a national level'. Around twenty professors were prosecuted and permanently

**View of the public in the Aula, 1943**
During his stay in Ghent, Conti visited the university hospital at the Bijloke. The notable presence of nurses and midwives in the Aula points to the importance that Frans Daels attached to cooperation with Conti in a local context. He had been striving for an independent Academic Hospital for years.
(Ghent, Amsab-ISG, photo Paul De Clercq)

dismissed from the university. A separate purging commission handled the files of the student collaborators. All together, punishments were meted out to 111 students, ranging from a de-merit to permanent expulsion. Corneel Heymans also received a de-merit, mainly because he went to Berlin as an 'exchange professor'. Paediatrician Carlos Hooft was suspended for a year because of his membership of the collaborating Order of Physicians. Frans Daels was condemned to death in absentia. He fled to Switzerland and would return to Belgium in 1959.

The purging process stirred up bad blood, both among its 'victims', who considered it '*une justice de rois nègres*', and among those who felt that the purification did not go far enough. The role of wartime rector Guillaume De Smet was a source of dispute. He remained free and clear, and in 1951 would even receive an award. The director of the Botanical Garden, George Funke, complained to vice-rector Goubau in 1946 about the way he and his Jewish assistants Paul Fröschel and Jacob Rappaport had been treated by De Smet: 'In 1940, Guillaume De Smet participated in an appalling way to have me and my assistants removed from the university. I can no longer consider that man a decent person.' In his memoirs of the Second World War, published four years before his death in 2014, resistance fighter and wartime student Karel Poma laments that the 'weeds' of collaboration were not more thoroughly eradicated at the university.

# 'Judenrein'

Franz Petri ordained that the 'post deserters' or Toulouse professors could not simply take up their positions when they returned to Ghent in the summer months of 1940. They were temporarily suspended. Permission from the ministry in Brussels to restart classes in October was a long time coming, however. In this grey zone, a slander campaign was launched by the collaborating colleagues. When Paul Van Oye returned from Toulouse at the end of July 1940, he was its first target. Thirty students from the Alliance of Flemish Students (Verbond van Vlaamsche Studenten, or VVS), the Ghent Student Corps (Gentsch Studenten Corps, or GSC) and the Catholic Flemish Alliance of University Students (Katholiek Vlaams Hoogstudentenverbond, or KVHV) declared themselves personally prepared to remove him from the university. Van Oye lodged a complaint against them. Frans Daels and Alfred De Waele also attacked him. The latter had quarrelled with Van Oye for years. In 1937, De Waele had denied Van Oye's protégé Falk Epsteins access to his Laboratory for General Zoology and Animal Physiology (Laboratorium voor Algemene Zoölogie en Dierfysiologie). He even filed a complaint with the rector with a letter in which he denounced Epsteins's 'provocative attitude', 'sarcastic laugh' and 'attempts to sabotage my authority' in the presence of other students. De Waele would 'never tolerate from a Belgian student what he, a foreigner, allows himself'. Rector Louis Fredericq called Epsteins on the carpet. The latter amicably offered a written apology for the incident, which according to him 'was not deliberate'. Because he had not always attended De Waele's lectures regularly, however, he was barred from taking exams that term. This inevitably meant that he would have to repeat the entire year: an example of how a brilliant student was hindered against a background of growing anti-Semitism. As mentioned earlier, Epsteins did not receive an official appointment as a volunteer assistant in 1939. When he returned to Ghent in the summer of 1940 he tensely awaited news of whether he would be able to defend his doctorate. His adviser was by then *persona non grata* and Alfred De Waele had control of the faculty of Sciences. But on 1 October 1940, Falk Epsteins defended his dissertation with flying colours and received his diploma of doctor in sciences — Zoology group. The jury, of which De Waele was a member, granted him a grudging 'distinction'.

In *Volk en Staat* on 25 August 1940, Daels had advocated a general cleansing of the university by 'the discipline of the people' and stated that 'Catholics, Freemasons and other "alien" elements had tried to save professors threatened with suspension'. A written explanation was demanded of the 'post deserters'. A committee of inquiry was called upon to investigate their activities since the German invasion. Rector De Smet submitted meekly to the Militärverwaltung and moreover requested the teaching staff to sign a declaration that they were 'not Jewish'. In October 1940, at the orders of the occupying authorities, the population register of Ghent opened a special register for Jews, in which every Jew was required to enrol. At the beginning of December, De Smet sent out a circular among the academic personnel in which he requested 'all persons of Jewish origin' to leave the university. In March 1941 he hung a message on the notice board that Jewish students were to report to the authorities and were no longer allowed to attend classes. Their registration was deleted from the rolls. The university was henceforth *Judenrein*.

Hans Handovsky had been employed as an assistant at the Heymans Institute since 1934, when the Nazis dismissed him from the University of Göttingen because he was Jewish. His great scientific merits were indisputable. He published a great deal, often as Heymans's co-author, moreover. In July 1940, however, he was not re-appointed by his 'patron' under the pretext that 'since his appointment he had had sufficient time to find another situation'. Frans Daels told him to consider himself lucky, 'because if I were still in charge, I would deny you access to the laboratory'. In January 1941, Handovsky was permanently suspended by the Wehrmacht.

Falk and Nora Epsteins-Pieruccini had wisely decided to start a new life in Riga. At the beginning of February 1941 they packed up their possessions and left the Nazi regime and Belgium behind them and headed for … the Eastern Front. Latvia had been occupied by the Soviet Union since June 1940. In July 1941, Riga would fall into the hands of Hitler's troops as part of Operation Barbarossa. Falk and Nora's mixed marriage was dissolved by the German government. This was the regulation in the occupied East. Jewish men were sent to the ghetto, while their non-Jewish wives were forced to thank the Führer for 'liberating' them from their Jewish husbands. In February 1942, Nora was arrested and sent to a concentration camp. Falk was probably executed several months later, after he and several comrades were caught stealing small portions of food for the barracks in the ghetto. After the war, Nora Pieruccini, who had survived the hell of Latvia, had a 'certificate of probable death', dated 1 July 1942, drawn up for her beloved husband.

Of the 'unwanted professors' in Ghent, 'only' nine were suspended by the ministry of Education. Paul Van Oye was spared. He defended himself as a 'good Fleming' who had remained 'true to the king' and had 'not fled from the Germans'. August Vermeylen (History of Literature), Maurice Orban (Civil Law), George Funke (Botany), Nico Gunzburg (Criminology), Fabrice Polderman (German Philology), Arthur Claeys (Geometry) and Felix De Mûelenaere (Public Law) were forbidden to resume their courses or enter the premises. The majority of the Toulouse professors would eventually be given permission to take up their posts again. This 'mildness' was aimed at smooth collaboration and 'tranquil objective work'.

## The resistance at the university

As for the student movement, in the autumn of 1941 the faculty associations broke with the Ghent Student Alliance (GSV), a New Order organisation that wanted to act as an umbrella organisation for all students. The Flemish Historians Association (Vlaamsche Geschiedkundige Kring, or VGK), with Heli Roosens and Herman Corijn, drove the schism. It created an opening for a wider resistance movement among the students. Laurent Vandendriessche's Natural Sciences Association (Natuurwetenschappelijke Kring), among others, followed the example of the historians.

At the beginning of December 1942 the eight 'German-unfriendly' faculty associations that had split from the programme were prohibited by the Militärverwaltung. Yet the fifth anniversary of the VGK in 1942 was attended by a surprising number of assistants and professors: not only the young doctores Frans Blockmans and Jan Dhondt, but also professors Gaston Dept, François-Louis Ganshof and Hans Van Werveke openly supported their students. At the beginning of 1942, under the impulse of Karel Poma, a chemistry student, a Ghent division of the National Student Group (Nationale Studentegroepering, or NSG) was created, a subdivision of the Independence Front (Onafhankelijkheidsfront, or OF). Poma was responsible for drafting, printing and disseminating the underground student paper *Klokke Roeland*. Albert Maertens's Liberal Flemish Student Alliance (Liberale Vlaams Studentenverbond, or LVSV) joined the NSG, followed soon after by the communist and non-party-aligned leftist students. There was hardly any socialist resistance to speak of — the Catholics were completely absent — with the result that approximately 5% of the student body actively or passively resisted the Nazi regime. This was a good deal more than among the Ghent population as a whole.

Anti-German sentiments escalated when first-year students had to sign up to the Arbeitsamt before 20 March 1943 for six months' compulsory 'employment'. The anti-Jewish measures at the university and the persecution of Jews in general reinforced anti-German sentiments in Ghent. The solidarity of the people of Ghent when it came to helping Jews go underground was considerable.

In the SS-Sicherheitsdienst-Aussendienststelle Gent's first Nachweisung über führende Freimaurer, Lucien De Coninck of De Zwijger was on the list of the thirteen people to keep under close observation. All Lodge activities had ceased with the outbreak of war, but De Coninck continued to be a pivotal figure in clandestine contact

**Voluntary employment, 1941**
While compulsory employment from 1943 onwards stimulated resistance among the students, the members of the Ghent Student Association (Gentsch Studentenverbond, or GSV) committed themselves voluntarily. On the back of this photo from February 1941: 'Enthusiastic return trip after completed task!'
(Ghent, Amsab-ISG, photo Paul De Clercq)

between Masons and joined the armed resistance. His research on nematodes was just a cover; his laboratory served as a hiding place for his political activities. De Coninck's adviser Paul Van Oye is often counted among the ranks of organised resistance within Ghent University as well. With his self-proclaimed New Order sympathies, however, this appears in a different light.

Nevertheless, Van Oye was held by the Germans in 1943 together with the concrete specialist Gustave Magnel and physicist Jules Verschaffelt. Van Oye was kept for a while in strict solitary confinement because anti-German flyers and a Jewish family had been found in his house. Afterwards, it turned out that he had been turned in by his colleagues Alfred De Waele and Alfred De Clercq, secretary of the Mac Leod Fund. Gustave Magnel was suspected of espionage and made no secret of his hostility towards the occupiers. Both were given a *Betätigungsverbot*, a teaching ban. Magnel had been ordered to make concrete beams in his laboratory for the defensive works. He slyly sabotaged this task by postponing delivery on some pretence or other. Jules Verschaffelt, who had retired in 1940, was held for two months on account of his anti-German attitude. He had dared to refuse honorary membership in the collaborating GSV (Ghent Student Alliance).

In total, twenty-five students and staff from the University of Ghent died during the Second World War. Two professors who were active in the resistance died in German custody. The mineralogist Valère Billiet was denounced and shipped off to Germany just before the liberation, in August 1944. He was one of approximately 17,000 prisoners that were loaded into four large ships in Lübeck at the end of April. An Allied bombardment badly damaged the ships. When Billiet was attempting to hand out life jackets among his fellow prisoners, he was shot by a member of the SS. Commercial scientist Karel Verlat died in prison on 15 April 1944. He was arrested because he defended anti-fascist and anti-German positions, even in his seminars.

In May 1996 a commemorative plaque was inaugurated in the Aula with the names of the victims of the Holocaust. The mournful list begins with 'EPSTEINS Falk Fedor — assistant'. A posthumous tribute from Ghent University to a member of the academic community who was never granted the title of assistant during his lifetime …

Notwithstanding his submissive attitude towards the occupation authorities, Paul Van Oye did in fact hide Jews. His daughter, attorney Mieke Van Oye, who was a good friend of Nora Pieruccini, was suspected of espionage from the outset of the war. She worked for the Jewish Association in Brussels, which regularly asked her to defend Jewish prisoners. The ambiguous chameleon Van Oye was the very opposite of his right-minded medical colleague Jean-Jacques Van de Velde. Van de Velde, a professor of physiology, was attached to the Bijloke hospital. Secretary of the faculty of Medicine at the outbreak of the war, he was removed from his post in 1941. He was active in the resistance as a doctor in the Secret Army and from 1944 as an agent in the intelligence network Marc. Once the deportation of the Jewish community in Ghent began in September 1942, Van de Velde and his wife Henriette De Waele helped two girls from the Podgaetzki family, Nora and Suzanne, go underground. Their father came from Bessarabia (now part of the Republic of Moldova) in 1926 to gain an engi-

**Valère Billiet**
As a young assistant in the faculty of Sciences, Valère Billiet introduced X-ray analysis to examine crystals. In 1941 he was one of the driving forces behind the Independence Front and an employee of an intelligence network. He was shot dead by the SS a few days before the end of the Second World War.
(Kortrijk, collection of Paul De Paepe)

neering degree in Ghent and worked for the metal firm Carels. The children grew up together with the Van de Velde's four daughters in their house on the Coupure without being betrayed, not even by the neighbours, who nonetheless had a reputation for being collaborators. Nora Podgaetzki went to school at the Institut de Kerchove under the name Marguerite Van de Velde. In October 1954, at the age of seventeen, she enrolled in the faculty of Medicine and became a member of the Humanist Student Association (Humanistisch Studenten Verbond, or HSV), which had just been founded that year at the university. There she met Marc Van Montagu, who was working on his second licentiate in Chemistry and to whom she is still happily married. Her 'wartime parents' Jean-Jacques and Henriette Van de Velde were honoured as Righteous in Yad Vashem.

Memorial plaque for the victims of the Holocaust, 1996 Rector Jacques Willems and the Jewish professor of mathematics Frederik Kuliasko laying a floral wreath at the newly unveiled memorial plaque in the Aula, 14 May 1996. Kuliasko had to flee as a child during the Second World War.
(Ghent, Universiteitsarchief, photo Hilde Christiaens)

## Rebuilding human rights on the ruins of war

Just as the devastation of the First World War hastened the establishment of the League of Nations and the International Labour Organisation (ILO), the United Nations rose up from the rubble of the Second World War in 1945. Three years later, in 1948, the Universal Declaration of Human Rights was proclaimed in Paris. The most important actors were NGOs of mainly Jewish intellectuals in the US. Nevertheless, a wide array of peoples, cultures, religions and ideologies contributed to the declaration. Establishing the basic rights of human beings everywhere was in this sense not a proclamation of the superiority of Western civilisation, but an attempt to save what was left of humanity from the barbarous war that had just ended.

In Ghent, the tradition of international law was continued by the multifaceted socialist Elie Van Bogaert, who received his doctorate in law in 1943 and subsequently applied himself to international law. Van Bogaert was particularly demanding with his students and in this way succeeded in educating top internationalists who would make their careers in diplomacy and major European institutions. Future European Commissioner Karel Van Miert was once one of these 'Van Bogaert boys and girls'. He spoke at the retirement of his teacher about the latter's strict but humane approach: 'It was definitely not easy and points were not handed out freely.' Another successful pupil of Van Bogaert was Marc Bossuyt, who in addition to an academic career at the University of Antwerp also worked for the UN in a host of different capacities, from UN Human Rights Officer to Belgian delegate in the UN commissions for human rights and for the elimination of racial discrimination. He was also the first commissioner-general for refugees and stateless persons in Belgium. Both Van Bogaert and Bossuyt served as judges in the Permanent Court of Arbitration in The Hague.

In the meantime, Tom Ruys and Inge Govaere have continued on the path of international public law and European law. In 2015, Ruys founded the Rolin-Jaequemyns

International Law Institute in Ghent, which covers the entire domain of international public law. Johan Erauw, for his part, as a specialist in international private law, has a seat at the Institut de Droit International in Geneva.

A professor of human rights was added in 2001, with the arrival of Leuven jurist Eva Brems. Initially it was only a part-time job: the Human Rights discipline still had to be invented in Belgium. Michel Tison, dean of the faculty of Law, explains how new domains within the law — such as human rights, foreigners' rights and environmental law — have led to a disruption of the classic domains within his faculty. The classic domains are not however less societally relevant. Whether family law, civil law, constitutional law, financial law or international law, there is always a connection with the society in which that law is in force. It explains the strong politico-institutional involvement of Ghent jurists with a number of societal reforms of their age. Fundamental research is not an obvious choice in law; the study of the norms and rules of law is usually aimed at changing and improving them.

From 2006 to 2010, Eva Brems was chair of Amnesty International in Flanders. Until she ran in the parliamentary elections of 2010 for Groen (Flanders' Green party) and was elected, she thought she would be able to continue her engagement with the NGO while sitting in parliament. The combination did not suit her. It turned out to be particularly difficult, as an academic, to adapt to an environment where there seemed to be little room for evidence-based reasoning. In politics, electoral considerations often prevail over principles. 'Yes, even with Groen', according to Brems. Yet she still believes in the value of academics in parliament. She was the only one to vote against the prohibition of the facial veil, for example, in line with the logic of the human rights activism that drives her. Academic freedom (and financial independence) ensures that you can afford to take a different position and rise above party pressure.

The group dynamics that Brems creates among her team at the university suits her better than the group pressure encountered in politics. Moreover, she finds that her work is not finished once she sends a publication out into the world; she is deeply concerned with its social impact. The Human Rights Centre at UGent meets every two weeks to discuss the rulings of the European Court of Human Rights. The results are made public in the widely read blog *Strasbourg Observers*. In addition, the group is involved with what are known as 'third party interventions', which defend clear positions and provide arguments in pending cases. In education, Brems introduced the Legal Clinic, where students learn to work with 'real' cases that come from NGOs or directly from individuals concerning refugees or the prohibition of the burkini in municipalities and public swimming pools. This form of education does not detract from the international reputation of the Human Rights Centre, since it is in the vanguard of a network of European Legal Clinic Education that is just being started. Brems formulates it thus: 'It comes down to thinking up strategies for being societally engaged in such a way that the price you pay in terms of what is academically valorised is as small as possible.' With her master's degree from Harvard, she published internationally after she returned from the US to take a doctorate in law, something that was then highly unusual in the field of Law. But internationalisation, however necessary it may be for her discipline, also creates distance with respect to the societally relevant work in one's immediate environment: work concerning racism and local multicultural conflicts, for example.

Human rights have long been the fiefdom of lawyers, for whom the domain is obviously linked to engagement and activism. The rapid rise of human rights research in recent years in other disciplines besides law, especially in a multidisciplinary context, has forced lawyers/activists to look at themselves more critically. 'Are we too naive in our desire to make the world a better place?' Brems asks herself out loud. 'Are human rights really something "good", something the world needs?' At the same time, she knows that the postmodern, relativistic view of human rights as a Western instrument of imperialism is being joined today by another critical chorus that is growing more powerful as the political climate shifts further to the right, even the extreme right. A discourse from the 'dark side' that wants to limit the basic rights of refugees, foreigners, women … and that openly questions the Geneva Convention has also raised its voice at UGent.

This only strengthens Brems in her activism. In this connection, she also thinks that the societal engagement of UGent could be greater. It currently appears in the mission statement and profiling of the university. The Amnesty International Chair, which is given to a prominent thinker or activist in the domain of human rights — from Irene Khan in 2008 to Peter Piot in 2017 — is a good example of how the university also puts itself in the picture and ensures a societally engaged aura. UGent needs to internalise its image further, however, and also make good in practice what it communicates in public. On the occasion of an actual controversy about cooperation agreements with the Israeli university Technion, a human rights policy for international relations was recently introduced. Eva Brems argues that this can provide UGent with the impetus it needs to stand in the vanguard of universities that actually mean something in the battle for human rights. The Nobel Prize for the Institut de Droit International, established in the heart of the university, can only add strength to her plea.

**Department of Study Counselling**
The establishment of the National Study Fund in 1954 marks the start of the democratisation of higher education. The Department of Study Counselling was established that same year. The service was intended to manage the new influx of students, avoid failures due to the wrong choice of study or bad study methods, and supervise young people from families without a university tradition. On the eve of the massification of higher education, the importance of public relations increased. Under rector Bouckaert, the service published colourful brochures for new students in the 1960s.
(Ghent, Universiteitsbibliotheek)

Chapter 8
# DEMOCRATISATION

When Ghent University opened its doors in October 1817 there were 190 students enrolled. All of them were men, mainly from East and West Flanders, who had studied at elite grammar schools, or athenaeums. The rites of passage of student life enabled them to redeem this status later as doctors or lawyers, or with high positions in civil service, education, magistrature or industry. Nearly a hundred years later, on the eve of the First World War, the number of students at Ghent University had increased sevenfold to 1,300, nearly 30% of which were foreigners. The greatest increase, however, occurred after the Second World War. Between 1953 and 1973, the number of full-time students quadrupled from 3,000 to more than 12,000. With scholarships for gifted and less affluent students and the development of social services, government and university both invested heavily in the democratisation of higher education. The student protests that took place in the wake of May 1968 accelerated this process, with major consequences for the functioning of the university and the relationship between professors and students.

In the 1990s the university experienced a second massive growth spurt, from around 14,000 students in 1990 to 21,000 at the turn of the millennium. The large increase in the twenty-first century is largely attributable to the Bologna Reform of 1999, the extended duration of study that resulted, and the integration of college degree programmes. The 37,328 enrolments registered by UGent in 2017-2018 is thus difficult to compare with the situation before Bologna.

But does the massification of higher education really correspond to profound democratisation? It is an interesting paradox that 'Higher education for the people', a nineteenth-century project of public edification, began to fade right when democratisation had finally become a reality in the 1970s. That Flemish universities have nevertheless remained extremely 'white' after more than a half-century of migration says a great deal about the degree to which access to higher education is still linked to one's available social and cultural capital. Our education system, which could function as an engine of emancipation, continues to reproduce socio-economic relationships from generation to generation. Children from families who are already familiar with university culture still have an advantage over those who do not.

## The dissemination of taste and enlightenment

When the Dutch minister of education Ocker Repelaer van Driel advocated the foundation of a university in Ghent in June 1816, he remarked in passing that it 'would also be useful to determine that one or more professors in each faculty would give a public lecture in the local language on the popular aspects of their science from time to time'. These lectures would be accessible not only to students, but also to other interested parties. 'That this could have an advantageous effect on the enlargement of knowledge and the taste for science need not be demonstrated.' The idea was incorporated into the Regulations of 25 September 1816.

The spread of knowledge among the populace was an important element in the education policies of William I. It amounted to bridging the gap between the 'enlightened' and 'unenlightened' segments of the population by making knowledge more accessible to more people. Whether this mission was actually fulfilled by Ghent's first professors is less clear.

In February 1860, members of parliament from the Liberal majority proposed making certain courses at the two state universities accessible to the public. This was considered progress in imitation of Paris, where brilliant things were being done at the Collège de France and the Sorbonne. But of course, Ghent and Liège were not like Paris. Interest in philosophy, history, literature and political economy in the two industrial cities could not be compared to the general level of culture among Parisians. It was therefore an illusion to think that public lectures in Belgium would attract as many people.

The proposal encountered the greatest resistance within the universities themselves. The faculties were united in the belief that the public character of education could not under any circumstances be allowed to affect its scholarly quality. The discussion dragged on for years. Eventually a compromise was reached: professors with rhetorical talent were encouraged to give public lessons in the university classrooms, outside the usual programming, for a fee. But not to excess: they were allowed to lecture a maximum of three times per week. This was very different to Paris, where *maîtres* with European reputations attracted hordes of listeners from across the nation and even from abroad.

In Belgium, 'people's education' required another approach: to address the public, the discourse had to be watered down. Rhetoric risked prevailing at the expense of depth. Moreover, a public course was not the same as a university course, which would have been incomprehensible to an unprepared public. Yet public lectures did increase the prestige and authority of the university. Another consequence was that scholarship could be disseminated among broader sections of the population.

Public lectures took place in the Aula before an ever-changing but sympathetic audience. However, their limited success was short-lived. Ten years later, in 1870, the initiative had faded from memory. The reason: the general indifference of the public.

## 'No subsidies for mediocrity'

It is often argued that the democratisation of the university has a levelling effect. The social widening of access supposedly impacts the overall intellectual level of the students. Remarkably, this pessimistic discourse has been around from the outset. Even in the days when instruction was still given in Latin, the government and the university complained that the students were too young and ill prepared and had too little prior knowledge. In 1828 the highest official of the Dutch department of education admonished the College of Curators in Ghent: 'I have been informed recently that some young people admitted to your College who were so extraordinarily weak that they could not adequately follow academic lectures.'

Pleas for raising admission standards echoed throughout the whole of the nineteenth century. Between 1817 and 1890 the admissions procedures were changed no less than seven times before a compromise was found that satisfied nobody. When the city of Ghent created a new scholarship system for less affluent students in 1837, the university immediately had a clear message for them. It came down to giving 'no subsidies for mediocrity', which would be a disservice to the families, the university and society. Parents should not cherish too many illusions concerning the intelligence of their children: 'Our university is interested not in having the most possible students, but in having the best possible students, just as society is interested not in having the most possible doctors and lawyers, but the best possible doctors and lawyers'. Students were therefore to understand that scholarships were reserved for those with distinction and talent. A scholarship was an honorary title. It was not a handout, but a reward.

It was not the number but the quality of the students that mattered. Notwithstanding this meritocratic 'openness', the University of Ghent would remain one of Belgium's smallest universities until the 1960s. During the nineteenth century this numerical minority position was due to the fact that in East and West Flanders the population was much less inclined to pursue higher studies than elsewhere in Belgium. This is also evident from the statistics of the other universities, which also attracted far fewer students from East and West Flanders than from Antwerp, Brabant, Hainaut, Liège and Namur. In addition, the majority of students from the colleges and Catholic education system were pushed in the direction of Leuven.

The Delcour Law of 20 May 1876 abolished the central examination system. The admission test for the title of *gradué en lettres* was also abolished, and even a diploma of secondary education was no longer required, which effectively meant that girls were also able to enrol. In Ghent, however, the first grammar school for girls would only open in 1907. Throwing open the doors resulted in a substantial increase in the number of registrations. In 1879, Ghent surpassed 600 enrolments.

Rector Albert Callier was unhappy with the abolition of the entrance exam. Because some students had not had the benefit of adequate secondary education, the professors were forced to reduce the intellectual level of their courses. Five years after the introduction of the Delcour Law, executive director August Wagener found that the influence of professors on their students had increased. They had become stricter, and the students more punctual and industrious. At the same time, their sense of initiative had decreased. Since their professors were now also their examiners, some students only studied slavishly and submissively what was read out to them. Because the examinations took place right after classes had ended, there was no time to assimilate and digest the lesson material. Studying amounted to learning by rote and recitation without taking much notice of the content. This type of education — *magister dixit* — was obviously not in keeping with the interest in scholarship and research that the university administration hoped to stimulate at the time.

The organisational laws of 1890 and 1891 once again made admission conditions stricter. Although an entrance exam was not reintroduced, an approved certificate of Greco-Latin education was required. As a result, it was once again more difficult for women to gain access to university training.

## Higher education for the people

The gateway to the university was in any case well-guarded. Additional efforts on the part of the government or the university to tap a social stratum other than the — largely French-speaking — bourgeoisie were negligible. The tentative attempts to Dutchify the university were therefore also attempts at democratisation. In 1888, Julius Mac Leod and his assistant Gustave Staes returned to the concept of public lectures, which had died quietly some twenty years before. Their public courses in botany were deliberately given in Dutch. Mac Leod and Staes were inspired by the English model of the University Extension, or 'college expansion', that cropped up across Europe at the end of the nineteenth century as an open university or people's college. The goal was to improve the connection between higher education and society in order to achieve a broader democratic mandate.

In 1892, Mac Leod secured the cooperation of historian Paul Fredericq and the Dutch studies experts Jozef Vercoullie and Maurits Basse. They were the founders of 'Higher Education for the People in the mother tongue at Ghent University'. The first lecture on the history of Dutch literature took place on 7 November 1892 in the large auditorium of the faculty of Arts and Philosophy. Fredericq wrote in his diary: 'At least 150 participants, including many ladies (teachers) and a few workmen.' The university prided itself on no longer working exclusively for an intellectual aristocracy. In addition to the series of literary lectures, there was also a programme in natural science at the Institute of the Sciences from 1896 onwards, with experiments and demonstrations: proof that modern science could also be taught in Dutch. In total, 96 lecture series — or 530 evening lectures — were offered between 1892 and 1914.

'Points of contention of a religious or political nature' were not allowed to be introduced in university buildings via this type of education. Nevertheless, it was clear from the outset that the initiative came from freethinking Flemish liberals with roots in the Willemsfonds and Freemasonry. Catholic and francophone alternatives were therefore not far behind. The Catholic Flemish University Extension (Katholieke Vlaamsche Hoogeschooluitbreiding), founded in Antwerp (1898), likewise aimed at the 'intellectual development of the people' with Ghent professors such as the lawyer Oscar Pyfferoen and the art historian Adolf De Ceuleneer. The ideological divisions of society were clearly reflected in the microcosm of the university, where one evening was taken up by the open lectures of the liberals and/or socialists and the other by the Catholics. Notwithstanding the ideological competition and on-going difficulties of bridging the gap between elite and populace, 'Higher education for the people' would continue to exist until 1972. After the Second World War it grew into a well-oiled machine for the popularisation of science that would reach tens of thousands of people in Ghent. When the democratisation of the university became a reality in the 1970s, the public gradually drifted away and the initiative was replaced by a scientific training programme aimed at senior citizens that still exists today.

# Democratisation in the twentieth century

The First World War resulted in a modest widening of access to the university thanks to the University Foundation, which used American money to grant scholarships and loans to less affluent students. The discourse was once again more meritocratic. After the international conflagration, humanity needed an upper intellectual and moral echelon more than ever. Higher education could no longer be reserved for a small social elite. 'Aristocracy, as it is understood by modern democracies, is no longer an aristocracy based on fortune, but an aristocracy based on merit', proclaimed Eugène Eeman in his rectorial speech of 1921. In 1937, rector Louis Fredericq warned students against what he called an 'inferiority complex': the fear of being underestimated or the suspicion, perhaps typically 'Flemish', of being misunderstood. This imaginary mental condition was understandable 'at a time when differences of class or origin determine a person's fate', but it was no longer appropriate 'now that there are equal opportunities for all'.

In 1939, Leo Coetsier, himself a perfect example of social elevation through education, devoted his dissertation in Educational Sciences to *Beroepsoriëntiering in België* and together with his adviser Jan Frans Fransen established the department of Professional Counselling that same year. During the Second World War they drew up a blueprint for the training of professional advisers and corporate psychologists. The degree programme in Academic and Vocational Counselling was established in 1947. In 1948, Coetsier founded the Laboratory of Applied Psychology (Laboratorium voor Toegepaste Psychologie) and devoted the remainder of his career to the problems of advising students and helping them choose a profession. He launched a network of Psycho-Medical Social Centres for orientation in secondary education, the so-called PMS centres, now the Centres for Student Counselling (Centra voor Leerlingenbegeleiding, or CLBs).

During the war, Fransen and Coetsier had already anticipated the massive influx of the post-war generation in secondary and higher education. In 1954, with the National Study Fund (Nationaal Studiefonds), the government extended the scholarship system for gifted and less affluent students considerably, which really accelerated the democratisation of higher education. 'Excellence' was no longer the primary criterion for receiving a scholarship. The social effect was immediately evident in the enrolment figures: from 3,000 in 1954 to 4,000 in 1958. The Department of Academic Advising at Ghent University was directly connected to the Laboratory of Applied Psychology through Coetsier. The link with the faculty guaranteed the scientifically substantiated character of the orientation programme and the expertise of student counselling. There were data on the chances of success and professional opportunities, a 'suitability test' for the transition from primary to secondary education, and flow reports on education and the labour market. In addition, students received psychological assistance in the event of uncertainty, fear of failure, family conflicts, concen-

**Higher Education for the People, 1922**
Since its foundation in 1892, the programme had been highly varied, ranging from 'Chemistry in Domestic Life' to 'The Life and Works of Schiller' and 'History of Economic Thought' to 'Hysteria, Epilepsy and other Women's Diseases'. The number of participants in the weekly evening classes was closely monitored. On average, it hovered around sixty. The initiative attracted teachers, the self-employed, white-collar workers, craftsmen, merchants and skilled workers. The 'real' factory proletariat was hardly reached at all.
(Ghent, Universiteitsbibliotheek)

**Charting intellectual talent, ca. 1960**
The personality and intellectual capacities of students are important factors in their professional opportunities and choices. Founded in 1939, the university department of Professional Counselling was 'fed' by the Laboratory of Applied Psychology from 1948 onwards. Under the leadership of Leo Coetsier, tests were developed to measure intelligence, technical capacity and working capacity. The results were literally mapped out. The study of Business Psychology would emerge from Coetsier's lab.
(Ghent, Universiteitsarchief, photo A. Van Lancker)

tration disorders and so on. Mental health could have an impact on academic performance, as could the lack of a university 'tradition' in working-class families.

Coetsier's tireless and versatile efforts to foster social mobility in Flanders was motivated by his Christian sense of social engagement, which was inspired by Jozef Cardijn's Catholic Workers Youth (Katholieke Arbeidersjeugd, or KAJ). Leo Coetsier died suddenly in 1968, a year that is considered a watershed in the democratisation of the university.

## Not predestined for university

Marc Van Montagu was born in a working-class family in Ghent in 1933, in the midst of the economic crisis. His mother, Irène Van Beveren, died in childbirth. He lived the first three years of his life as an only child, raised with much love by his grandmother and aunts. His great-grandfather on his mother's side was Edmond Van Beveren, founder of the first socialist labour party in Ghent in 1877. The living and working conditions in the *beluiken* (or tenements) of the Rabotwijk, where Marc Van Montagu lived with his grandmother, were still 'nineteenth century': no running water or electricity in most of the houses, a central pump and shared toilets outside on the street. The factories in his neighbourhood were so terrifyingly dark and noisy that as a small child, Marc hoped and prayed that he would never have to work there. At school, the spectre of the factory was used to threaten pupils who did not try hard enough to do their best.

Van Montagu, one of the pioneers of molecular plant genetics, says he was good for little else than reading books. Socialist consciousness was the air he lived and breathed, and for his family the First of May was the most important holiday of the year. His father had received his early secondary education at the 'cadet school' and was mobilised for the army when he was sixteen. The family assumed that he had died in action at the beginning of the First World War until he returned from a German prisoner-of-war camp in 1919. In Ghent he first worked as an administrator in a textile factory, and then later at a small factory on the Visserij that made packaging and paper bags. The only promotion Marc recalls his father ever receiving was being made secretary of the Ghent Socialist Union marching band. A brother-in-law of Van Montagu's grandmother, the only one in the family who had been able to continue his studies, had become a schoolteacher. It was he who insisted that Marc go to the best primary school in the neighbourhood, the Dr Decroly Institute on the Begijnhofdries. These were the war years, 1939-1945. School was compulsory up to the age of fourteen, but as the best student in his class, Van Montagu was given another opportunity by his sixth-grade teacher, who pushed him to study classics at the gymnasium on the Ottogracht. The St Barbara College, where the *crème de la crème* studied, was not an option for a working-class youth with not a farthing to his name. The Jesuits cultivated excellence more than the 'egalitarian' athenaeums, as he would later discover as a professor as well. In his third year of grammar school, Van Montagu had the good fortune that a new option was added: Latin-Sciences. Completely under the spell of chemistry, he and a friend installed a small laboratory in the attic, where they did the experiments in advance of their being introduced in class. Van Montagu was once again at the top of his class, and his great-uncle advised him to apply to the university. Because he did not have to live in rented lodgings, was able to reach the university by foot or by bicycle, and could eat midday meals at home, it was financially feasible for his parents. The enrolment fee was 5,000 Belgian francs, the equivalent of his father's monthly wage. In those days the National Study Fund had not yet been established. But his father and stepmother were so proud that their son was the first in the family to cross the threshold of the university that they gave him leave to try for a year. It was October 1951 and the arrangements were clear. Breakfast was at seven and at a quarter to eight it was off to class. From the outset, Van Montagu was actively involved in the student movement. To his parents' consternation, he did not come home until after 2 a.m. several nights a week. In his second year he was already chairman of the Socialist Flemish Students Movement (Socialistische Vlaamse Studenten Beweging, or SVSB). That year, his father lost his job. Fortunately, Van Montagu was already in the second year of the first cycle, otherwise he 'probably wouldn't have started at university'.

Marc Van Montagu as a child
(Ghent, collection of Marc Van Montagu)

Bioengineer Willy Verstraete, born in 1946 as the oldest of six children, grew up as a farmer's son in Beernem 'on a small farm where everything was possible', at one with nature. In kindergarten the teacher noticed that 'he was good with his head but not with his hands'. But even for a clever student, going from a small farm to a college, let alone to university, was far from evident. In the 1950s and 60s, people in the countryside still thought in terms of class much more than in the city. Verstraete Senior heard it as many as three times: 'Victor, mind your place; my son can go to college, your son should go to vocational school.' In any case, it gave him extra drive to succeed and to break open the fragmented class society that sought to hold him back. It was October 1963, the National Study Fund existed, and Willy's father wanted to give his children opportunities. They only got one chance: halfway was not good enough, it was all or nothing. Verstraete Junior chose a course of study that even pleased his father: agricultural engineering. As practice-oriented as his education might have been, as a first-year student he experienced the professors in the halls of the 'Boerenkot' as alien beings. The proclamation of the first candidature was the moment of truth: of eighty students, there were only thirteen who succeeded. Verstraete still remembers the tension to this day. Either he had succeeded, or it was 'over and out'. He could not afford to fail — at the time, the results were published in the newspaper. Finding his name on the list of 'Not successful' candidates would have been a disgrace for the entire village. The students huddled together outside the faculty meeting room where their professors smoked fat cigars as they decided on their future. Finally, the 'magical figure' of the dean appeared in the doorway and called out the name at the top of the list: Willy Verstraete. When he came home to tell his father and mother the happy news that he was 'the first', his father reacted coolly: 'Come on, let's go muck out the cow shed.' Another memory that still stands out in Verstraete's mind is the image of his parents 'hoeing weeds in the spring field'. It was time to study for exams and he was having a horrendous time with his soil science class, taught with military discipline by Louis De Leenheer — nicknamed 'Stone Balls'. For the first-year students, he was the 'flunker'. The students' most important task was to memorise tables by heart — up to three commas after the decimal point. It gave Verstraete a headache and he tried to make his parents party to his irritation about the mind-numbing course. Again, he was met by the simple wisdom of his father, who without batting an eyelid said: 'Go get a hoe and you can come work with us'. For Willy Verstraete, hoeing the spring field wasn't all that after all.

In *De eeuw van onze kinderen* (The century of our children) Rik Pinxten, born in 1947, also tells the 'atypical' story of how he grew up in a rough working-class neighbourhood in Antwerp and how, thanks to the post-war economic upswing in Flanders and the right encouragement from the right people at the right time, he ended up studying philosophy and moral sciences at the university. He connects his personal story to the social shifts of the last half-century and the call to reinvent democracy.

Marc Van Montagu, Willy Verstraete and Rik Pinxten may be eminent examples, but they are not representative of the post-war democratisation of higher education. Children of factory workers, low-level clerks and farmers are still less well represented at university than the children of the middle class, which was better able to take advantage of the available opportunities for social mobility. The Matthew effect (accumulated advantage) of scholarships was therefore a recurring point of concern for the social sector of the university, particularly for Rudy De Potter's Department of Student Counselling.

# Social provisions for students

During the Second World War, three professors set up the charitable organisation The Benefactors of the State University of Ghent (De Begunstigers van de Rijksuniversiteit Gent, or BRUG, which in Dutch means 'bridge') to help students in need. In 1949, rector Norbert Goormaghtigh developed this into the department of Social Services for students. In the post-war wave of democratisation, Social Services aided students with financial difficulties via scholarships and student loans and mediation in the search for student jobs and lodgings. For students who commuted, affordable warm meals were provided. The name of the student restaurant De Brug in Sint-Pietersnieuwstraat refers to the history of its creation and the original 'emergency restaurant' in the Technicum. In 1957, De Brug became an official 'bridge' between university and society, with a magazine and all kinds of crowd-funding activities *avant la lettre*.

Mrs Mussche, who ruled over the restaurant from 1954 until 1972, often gave her 'beloved students' food coupons on the sly because she knew they were in financial straits. She transformed the cold laboratory on the first floor of the Technicum into a cosy dining hall with tablecloths, plants, good food and plenty of atmosphere. The rapidly increasing number of students quickly led to long queues, suggesting the need for expansion. Together with architect and professor Gaston De Leye, Mussche visited all the student restaurants in Belgium to find the best design. The new De Brug opened in 1960 as a self-service restaurant with a modern interior and beautiful chandeliers. The university was proud of its 'first major accomplishment in the domain of social services'. With a capacity of 1,200 cheap meals per day, De Brug was known for its delicious coffee and ice cream.

Student cafeteria De Brug, 1985
(Ghent, Universiteitsarchief, photo Christian Kirschen)

Since then, seven student restaurants and five cafeterias have been added throughout the city. When the Overpoort opened in 1972 — its capacity of 15,000 meals per day made it one of the largest such facilities in Europe — the job of 'Ma Mussche, mother of students' was taken over by 'a Vlerick disciple trained in management'. That person was Walter Van Espen, who chose to return to his alma mater while he was still young rather than take a plum management job at Bell Telephone. Social engagement motivated his modernisation of the university's 'social sector'. He kept the reins of his department tightly in hand, although his staff always came first. For example, he was the first to organise team-building activities: every year the staff was dragged off to Eddy Wally's banqueting hall in Ertvelde.

In 1987 Van Espen was succeeded by Marc Bracke. He had worked at the university for ten years, and rector Leon De Meyer had given him the chance to study management at Vlerick. It was his job to reform the

**From the Technicum to De Brug**
The photo above shows the first student restaurant on the first floor of the Technicum. On 4 October 1960, De Brug was opened in Sint-Pietersnieuwstraat. The number of students rose exponentially in the 1960s. De Brug increased the number of meals to 6,000 each midday, but the waiting times kept getting longer and longer. In 1972 a new restaurant was added between the Blandijn and the Ledeganck at the Overpoort.
(Ghent, Universiteitsarchief and Liberal Archive)

social sector from top to bottom. A decree of minister of education Daniël Coens made reorganisation necessary.

A year earlier, in 1986, the Student Advisory Centre was founded to provide a number of services: academic advice, psychological consultation, doctors for students and job placement for graduates. After the reform of the central administration in 2002, the organisation became the department of Academic and Career Advice under Educational Affairs (DOWA). The department of Social Services was transformed into the management of Student Services, with four divisions: meal facilities, housing, personal social services and sports facilities. The reorganisation was not without significance: the original post-war mission of Social Services, aimed at democratisation, shifted to a more market-oriented approach in which the student was increasingly seen as a client of the university. That shift was confirmed in the new decree of 2012 on student facilities. The decree came with the integration of the colleges and universities. Until then, the colleges did not actually have their own social services, which put the funding model under pressure in times of budget cuts.

'It comes down to keeping a close eye on the social factor', says logistics manager Jeroen Vanden Berghe. He thinks it is important for the university to continue managing its own student services right through from A to Z. The full participation of the students in the Social Council is crucial in this respect. They can give shape to the policy. Both Marc Bracke and Jeroen Vanden Berghe see it as their job to ensure that this policy stays up to date, with an eye towards a sustainable and diverse university, considering the changing needs of staff and 'customers'. This includes introducing vegetarian and halal meals, for example, and giving thought to the renovation of student houses as co-housing or other new forms of living arrangements.

In 1960 the first home for female students, Home Fabiola, opened on the Overpoort. The explosion of student numbers made it necessary: there was an acute shortage of student lodgings in Ghent. The department of Social Services for Students therefore ensured the provision of affordable student lodgings that, compared to what was available on the market and according to the standards of the time, were veritable palaces: with a kitchen and spacious bathroom on every floor, recreational spaces, study areas and even a terrace or solarium on the roof. In 1966 and 1971, Home Boudewijn for boys followed, along with Home Astrid and Home Vermeylen for girls. Scholarship students were given priority and the rent was dependent on the income of the parents. Home Heymans, which opened on the Isabellakaai in 1973, allowed married couples to rent an apartment at a reasonable rate.

## The 'studentariat' occupation

The protest movement of March 1969 was not so much about democratic access to the university as about the internal power relations. The university administration had forbidden the showing of a series of slides during a panel discussion, 'Pornography: sense or nonsense', on 12 March 1969. Etienne Vermeersch was one of the invited speakers on the panel, along with musicologist Jan Broeckx, attorney John Bultinck

**Home Fabiola for female students, 1960s**
In a 1971-1972 survey of social services and housing, 50% of the dormitory students favoured co-ed homes.
(Ghent, Universiteitsarchief)

and writer Daniël Robberechts. As a philosopher, Vermeersch was deeply concerned with the subject of sexual liberation, which was entirely in line with the spirit of the times, and opposed to the rector's ban. He has kept the risqué slide show of that evening in a Styrofoam box at home for nearly half a century. Only the ancient Greek nudes could be shown, because they could be considered art. The Academic Council Chamber was packed to the gills: more than five hundred people attended, and they were disinclined to accept the 'censorship and coercive measures' of the rector's office. An incendiary speech against rector Bouckaert was fired off. Student leader Ludo Martens also preached rebellion. In 1966 the future Maoist and leader of the PVDA (Partij van de Arbeid) had founded the progressive Student Union Movement (Studentenvakbeweging, or SVB) in the heart of the Catholic Flemish Student Association (Katholic Vlaams Hoogstudenten Verbond, or KVHV). In the run-up to the protests around Leuven-Vlaams (Leuven Flemish) in 1968, he had been banned from continuing his studies there. Vermeersch recalls that the hullabaloo generated by Martens and others unleashed a huge reaction. He himself was very sceptical about the agitation and bet a crate of beer that the announced plan to march on the rector's office would end in an anti-climax. Great was his surprise the next day when the third floor of the rector's office was packed with students. It was one of those 'moments of madness' that are extremely difficult to describe objectively afterwards. Rector Bouckaert committed an 'unbelievable act of stupidity' — according to Vermeersch — by mobilising the police to bludgeon the students outside. As a result, the entire Blandijn was full by nightfall. The occupation by what quickly became known as the 'studentariat' continued until 20 March. Revolutionary slogans were everywhere: 'Not a repressive but a creative university' was written above the blackboard in Auditorium E,

Sit-in, Sint-Pietersnieuwstraat, March 1969
(Ghent, Universiteitsarchief, photo Renaat Willockx)

where no classes were held but where protest singers performed, and turbulent public gatherings were held by night. Dean of arts Antonin Van Elslander tried to mediate, while philosophy professor Rudolf Boehm fanned the flames by giving the protestors the key to his mimeograph room so that the students could print their pamphlets. Afterwards Boehm had to explain himself to the management board. A *consilium abeundi* was pronounced against student leader Renaat Willockx: he was not allowed to continue his studies in Ghent and would spend ten years in the shipyards of Temse putting the '68 adage 'Workers and students unite' into practice. There was even a special session of the Academic Council with the sole purpose of removing militant students from the university. A group of left-wing and freethinking professors — Jaap Kruithof, Rudolf Boehm, Hein Picard, Willy Calewaert, Paul Ghysbrecht, Wilfried Roels and Lucien De Coninck — took up their cause and ended up clashing with the university establishment. They defended the principle of academic freedom and the right to dissent, even when it jeopardised the 'honour of the university'. The flamboyant attorney Piet Van Eeckhaut would provide the arrested students with legal representation. However, the arguments in favour of the rebellious students were laughed out of court by the more conservative professors.

'Official decisions are not immutable', pronounced the new rector, Daniël Vandepitte, at the opening of academic year 1969-1970. Although he condemned the disturbances, it was clear that the protest movement had placed the reform of university structures on the agenda. The Vermeylen–Dubois Law of 1971, which governed the representation of students, assistants and administrative staff in the governing bodies of the university, was indeed a direct result of the protest. But there were also other, subtler signs that the authority of the professors was affected by the dissent. Etienne

Vermeersch, for example, recalls how the sign on the elevator of the Blandijn reading 'professors only' was removed in the aftermath of the disturbances. The democratic check of having students on the board at any rate ensured a new form of administrative hygiene. When official cars were purchased for the university's top administrators, the student representative insinuated that they had been bought at the cost of social services. 'Not true,' replied the administration, 'they were paid for out of the university's "black" funds and the government commissioner has already been apprised.' In the Netherlands, democratic student representation was for that matter quickly rolled back, notes Vermeersch wryly.

## Actions against the 10,000

The twenty-six-year-old doctoral student Jan De Maeseneer lent his full support to the actions 'against the 10,000'. De Maeseneer came from a family with six children and could never have gone to university without a scholarship. The definitive choice was made when he was in his fourth year of primary school in Maisstraat in the Bloemekeswijk: either continue to a secondary school or stop studying at fourteen and go to work at the UCO textile factory. De Maeseneer is grateful to society for the opportunities he had to continue his studies.

The enrolment fee of 10,000 Belgian francs (250 euros) for non-scholarship students was a symbol of higher education's restricted accessibility to lower social groups. After the golden years of the 1960s the economic crisis that had been developing since 1973 also gripped the university. The anti-crisis law of July 1978 provided a legal framework for imposing budget cuts in all areas of society. In higher education, this led to a doubling of enrolment fees without consultation with any of the rectors. The left-wing student movements had become more and better organised since the events of March 1969. As noted earlier, workgroups had been set up in various faculties to stimulate critical thinking and action. The student magazine *Schamper* also played an active role in the resistance against the 10,000. There was also the pirate broadcaster Radio Aktief — a new medium in addition to the pamphlets, petitions, banners, posters and graffiti. There was certainly no lack of actions: enrolment was boycotted, an alternative opening ceremony was organised, there were demonstrations, marches by torchlight and, once again, the occupation of the rector's office on 24 November 1978. An impressive police force was deployed, and students were treated brutally according to eyewitnesses. A week later, more than 3,000 students marched peacefully through the streets of Ghent. Rector Hoste, who had spoken out against the 10,000 from the outset, joined the demonstration, along with a dozen professors.

In March and April 1979, when the second instalment of 5,000 francs was to be collected, the conflict exploded in violent skirmishes between the federal police and students in the streets of Ghent. When the student house De Brug was searched in an effort to uncover pirate broadcaster Radio Aktief, the fuse was lit. That night six police vans were destroyed. A number of agents were injured. The police responded with brutality. The public was able to stay abreast of the fighting in the streets thanks to Daska films and Ghent Film News (Gentse Filmactualiteit). According to the police,

**Student protest at the Blandijn, March 1969**
(Ghent, Universiteitsarchief, photo Renaat Willockx)

**Clash between students and police, March 1979**
(Ghent, Amsab-ISG, photo Roland Van der Sypt)

**Radio Aktief**
(Ghent, Universiteitsbibliotheek, *Schamper* 106, 1980)

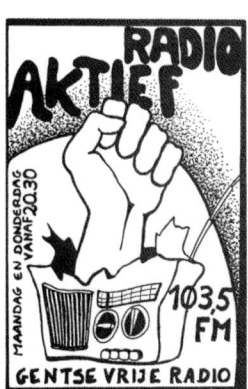

**Prof between two fires**
The left-wing professor of statistics Hein Picard mediated between the students and the police. From 3 to 11 May 1980 the Ghent Academy hosted the *Ludiek tot keihard* (From playful to rock hard) exhibition of documentary photography, with photos by Patrick Alliët, Lieve Colruyt, Titus Ramaeckers and Luc Van den Bergh. The Ghent criminal investigation team wanted to buy up the entire collection for 70,000 Belgian francs. The photos of the violence during the student actions in 1978-1979 leave little to the imagination.
(From: *Ludiek tot keihard. Studenten voor demokratizering.* Berchem)

the filming of the riots was a punishable offence. Cameramen from Daska and BRT television news were threatened and their cameras damaged. Print journalists were accused of not being objective.

On 14 March, rector Hoste was held hostage for an afternoon by demonstrating students. His resignation was demanded. There were arrests and a criminal trial. Thirty-six students were found guilty. The extra income from the increased enrolment fee was not sufficient to cover the costs of the federal police and the damage to the buildings. The Blandijn resembled a battlefield. Costs ran up to 400,000 Belgian francs. Parties were organised to pay for the costs of the students (500,000 Belgian francs). In the end, the actions were fruitless: nearly all the students meekly paid the second instalment of 5,000 francs.

## Ongoing budget cuts in higher education

In the summer of 1986 the minister of education Daniël Coens cut the university's social allowance. Social services, which were moreover exempt from indexing, had to make do with drastically reduced means. In Ghent, this meant a reduction from 132 to 91 million Belgian francs. As compensation, the universities received permission to raise enrolment fees again. The Flemisch Interuniverity Council (VLIR) decided to index the amount by 30% and to introduce a rate increase to 13,000 Belgian francs. In other words, a government deficit was being passed on to the individual student. Student actions ensued throughout Flanders. Students at the colleges were also mobilised on a massive scale. The highlight was a national demonstration in Brussels on 16 December 1986, at which thousands of students expressed their dissatisfaction with budget cuts made at their expense. It was all in vain.

In the economically prosperous 1990s and even afterwards, enrolment fees were raised again. But now the increases took place in silence, without any student protests worthy of the name. This also had to do with the altered character of the student movement: the social engagement of students for the common good had undeniably become less. The student representatives in the university's governing bodies increasingly opted for a deliberately non-political presence, focused on protecting student interests through constructive cooperation with the administration.

Since 2004, the Ghent Student Council (Gentse Studentenraad, or GSR) has functioned like a well-oiled participation machine for students. For Marc Bracke, who grew up in the turbulent 1960s, the student representatives — with a few notable exceptions — have come to resemble managers and lack the unbridled idealism of former times. 'They feel quite at home in the plush surroundings of power and enjoy having coffee with the rector', laughs Jeroen Vanden Berghe. At the same time, the logistics manager is also full of praise for the self-organisation of the 123 student associations active at UGent today, which together organise ten to twenty activities per evening. The function of the student administrator ensures that the department of Student Services does not have to bother with all those student activities, apart from facilitating self-organisation by making available a student house, the Therminal. In the meantime, it has become the bustling centre of student life in Ghent, just a stone's throw away from De Brug.

In the last few decades, the average student has come to see himself or herself less and less as part of a homogeneous social group with common interests. Instead, he or she has become a self-oriented individual: a demanding customer of the diploma factory for whom additional studies are the norm. Indeed, millennials are often the children of highly educated baby-boomers, who have been able to take advantage of the post-war wave of democratisation. In 2014, enrolment fees were as good as double in

**Student protest at Sint-Pietersnieuwstraat, April 2014**
(Ghent, image bank UGent, photo Hilde Christiaens)

**From De Brug to Therminal**
Students studying together in the turbine hall of the student home, spring 2017.
(Ghent, photo Michiel Hendryckx)

relation to 1986: from 13,000 Belgian francs to 620 euros (24,800 Belgian francs).

In July 2014 the Flemish government cut at least 163.7 million euros from the budget for higher education, while the rising number of students and their increasing flexibility require additional infrastructure and thus extra financing. Against this budget cut and its logical consequences — an increase in enrolment fees for non-scholarship students to 890 euros — students managed to demonstrate on a massive scale in Ghent, Leuven and Antwerp, with national demonstrations in Brussels. Minister of education Hilde Crevits was called upon to acknowledge her responsibilities: '*Hilde, wees wijs, investeer in onderwijs!*' (Hilde, be smart, invest in education) — a catchy slogan that rhymes in Dutch. The government once again refused to budge, even though all the Flemish universities deplored the drastic increase in enrolment fees. At UGent it was decided that the 'surplus' of 270 euros per student would be exclusively devoted to innovation in education and student facilities.

The government did not examine the possible effects of increasing tuition on open access and the democratisation of higher education. An increase in the number of scholarship students was not on the agenda either. Since the government also reduced social allowances, studying was in danger of becoming more expensive for scholarship students as well, thanks to the expected increase in the price of rents, meals and academic expenses. If the universities were moreover forced to save on counselling and supervising students, it was feared that primarily students from the so-called 'risk groups' or families with a lower socio-economic status (SES) would be the victims. That is, if they even made it to university at all. In times of 'equal opportunities', the post-war democratisation project is still far from complete — in higher education too.

### 'Bleach' and an added boost

In the campaigns for the rectorial elections of 2017, criticism fell on universities for being too 'white' in a society that has become increasingly colourful and diverse. Of the newly enrolled students in 2016 2017, there are 13.3% in Ghent with a migration background, 36% of which are of Western European origin and 20% from the Arab world. Although it is true that there is a slight increase in the number of non-Western immigrant students — from 2.6% in 2009-2010 to 6% in 2016-2017 — this has still not ensured more people of colour in the classroom. Only 10% of the newly enrolled students speak a language other than Dutch at home. There are also 13 students with recognised refugee status and 394 working students (or 1.1% of the total student population).

The problem is still the same as in the 1960s and is fundamentally socio-economic in nature. If we want to see the multicultural diversity of society better reflected at university, we need to consider the fact that a migration background usually implies a lower socio-economic status and therefore calls for an added boost. The same applies to the children of 'white' working-class and farming families.

Eighty-five per cent of newly enrolled students followed general secondary education (Algemeen Secundair Onderwijs, or ASO). The negative effects of the 'waterfall' system in secondary education are sufficiently well known. 'By that logic, we would be forced to return to the nursery to intervene drastically in the social determinism that clearly condemns us academics in our ivory tower of the university to stand by and watch helplessly as each stage in the compulsory education system inevitably fails', says education sociologist Mieke Van Houtte. Together with her Leuven colleague and pupil Orhan Agirdag, she calls for more attention to the realities of ethnic diversity in teacher training. The teacher, as a crucial actor in the student's academic career, must have required intellectual experience to work effectively in today's ethnically diverse schools, with or without the hijab.

Jan De Maeseneer makes the comparison to the University of Rotterdam, where during his guest lectures three-quarters of the auditorium is 'visibly' of a different ethnic or cultural background but speaks perfect Dutch. In Ghent, however, the language of the entrance exam for Medicine has the effect of 'bleach'. He argues in favour of positive discrimination with respect to students with a migration background. Through years of experience with the multicultural population of the neighbourhood health centres, he 'knows' that as a campus in the city, the intellectual potential is there to make more of an effort to recruit students with a migration background. As a result of the debate on the anglicisation of higher education, Koen De Bosschere, responsible for training civil engineers in computer science, says exactly the same. He would rather try to build an outstanding 'provincial' university with strong local anchoring and an unprejudiced view of the world than compete with MIT or Stanford. We can continue to hope that young people with a migration background find their way to the university, but more effort is needed from the university in order to achieve this goal. It is at least worth discussing why one is willing to move heaven and earth to attract Asian students to Ghent while talented youngsters with an immigrant background from the Muide or the Brugsepoort are not even approached. 'If we could even use half of the resources UGent has for internationalisation for this purpose,' says De Bosschere, 'I think that the composition of our student population would be much closer to that of society.'

Chapter 9

# GENDER AND SEXUALITY

Nowadays most of the students at Ghent University are women. More women enrol and graduate than men. They started catching up in the 1970s and 80s. In 1982, one hundred years after the presence of Sidonie Verhelst caused an uproar at the faculty of Sciences, there were 4,939 women enrolled out of a total of 13,042 students (37%). Twenty years later, in 2002, their number had almost tripled to 12,627. The gender ratios were reversed. In 2012, 16,892 of the 29,111 students, or around 58%, were women. In 2016, of the 5,853 students to graduate with a master's (after a bachelor's), 43% were men and 57% women. The number of female PhDs is also on the rise. Of the 696 doctorates awarded, 365, or 52%, were to male researchers and 331, or 48%, to female researchers. As regards the enrolment and graduation of students at the university, the emancipation of women during the second half of the twentieth century has clearly borne fruit.

What role has Ghent University played in this emancipation process? The sexual revolution has definitely made its way to Ghent. In the fields of contraception and sexual health as well as LGB rights and reproductive medicine, the university has played a pioneering role since the 1960s. Transgender care is the most recent example in this domain.

In 2013, Anne De Paepe was the first female rector ever elected. To this day, however, the professorial group at the University of Ghent is still something of a male bastion. The increase in the number of female students, PhD candidates and PhDs has yet to be translated into a proportionate number of female professors. In 2004 the inter-faculty Centre for Gender Studies was tasked with initiating an equal opportunities policy for women and men at UGent. It resulted in the creation of the policy unit for Diversity and Gender (2008). Under pressure from a decree amendment in 2012, the university committed itself to maintaining gender-balanced governing bodies.

## Male privilege

In the nineteenth century, studying at the university was a male privilege. Although there was no special law that denied women access, only men attended. Until 1864, there were no secondary schools for girls in Belgium. This was the main reason why Ghent University admitted its first female student relatively late, in 1882. Women were simply unable to take the step to higher education because the necessary preparation at the secondary level was not provided for them. In 1881 the anticlerical Frère-Orban–Van Humbeeck administration established fifty state secondary schools for girls, but it only offered a lower degree aimed at their tasks in the domestic sphere. In the Catholic colleges, there was no question of education for girls. The Brussels feminist Isabelle Gatti de Gamond changed all that with a municipal school for girls in the capital. Other cities soon followed her lead. Ghent did so only in 1907 with the foundation of

**Female students in Veldstraat, 1936**
Nienke Bakker was a Dutch student from Middelburg who in 1934 chose to study Germanic philology in nearby Ghent. At that time, the number of female students was only 118 out of a total student population of 1,526. A male fellow student wrote: 'Coquettish, elegant, with luxurious locks of hair under the black velvet cap, the supple waist hugged by a sporty English dress.' Ghent's student life of the 1930s is beautifully illustrated by Nienke's photo album, a unique source with more than a hundred photographs. This picture shows her on the right, with glasses. After her studies Bakker became editor of the *Woordenboek der Nederlandsche Taal* (Dictionary of the Dutch Language).
(Antwerp, Letterenhuis)

**Rhetoric class at the Ghent Lyceum, 1927**
The Athénée de Jeunes Filles, founded in 1907, was the predecessor of the Royal Lyceum and the first school in Ghent to offer a fully fledged secondary education for girls. In 1912 the first group arrived at the university. Between 1919 and 1930, 400 women enrolled, peaking at 69 in 1928-1929.
(Ghent, Universiteitsarchief, photo Koninklijk Lyceum Ghent)

the Athénée de Jeunes Filles by Rosa De Guchtenaere, a pupil of Gatti's. Several professors from the university generously lent their cooperation. Biologist Victor Willem taught science, the Luxembourgish scholar Peter Hoffmann taught German. He also served as director of the school. De Guchtenaere looked up to him immensely. They were both very pro-Flemish and would later be sentenced for activism after the First World War.

Belgium lagged far behind other countries in terms of education for girls. Elsewhere, the strict division of roles between the sexes was breached after women were allowed to pursue higher education — and they had already succeeded in the US, Switzerland, France and the Netherlands.

When Isala Van Diest wanted to enrol at the alma mater of her father, a Leuven physician, she was bluntly turned away. She returned to Bern, where she had also attended secondary school. The Van Diest affair acquired political resonance when the Delcour Law was debated in parliament in 1875. This law abolished state exams and relaxed conditions for admission to university. The initial draft by the Catholic minister of domestic affairs, Charles Delcour, did not take women's new aspirations into account. The first argument in favour of opening certain areas of medical practice to women — gynaecology and paediatrics, for example — came from liberal parliamentarian Eudore Pirmez. A lively debate followed. The minister passed the buck to the Royal Academy of Medicine and the four universities. The 'admissibility' of women gave rise to an in-depth discussion in Ghent in a special committee set up by the faculty of Medicine. Two memos with conflicting opinions were laid before the Academic Council. Dr Etienne Poirier, who served the poor as chief surgeon in the Bijloke, was in favour of the measure. According to him, women had the right to be treated in the same way as men. Morally and intellectually, women were just as capable, and they had specific physical capacities and manual dexterity that would be a great advantage in certain interventions. Hence, there was nothing to stand in the way of admitting women to the general practice of medicine. Against the objection that a woman's place was in the home, caring for her household and raising children, Poirier added that medical practice would not necessarily keep women away from the domestic sphere. Women would be even better at fulfilling their important role as mothers if they had the benefit of sound training.

Institut de Kerchove, 1927
The first municipal school for girls in Ghent, named after the liberal mayor Charles De Kerchove, was founded in 1880 in Bagattenstraat. It was the breeding ground of Ghent's of *belle époque* bourgeois feminism and revealed how education could also act as a pathway to women's emancipation. The first generation of female students at the university consisted largely of teachers.
(Ghent, Universiteitsarchief)

The author of the second memorandum, obstetrician Charles Van Cauwenberghe, head of maternity in the Bijloke, found these arguments to be too idealistic. In the daily practice of medicine, he saw a host of obstacles that were inherent in the physical and moral make-up of women. There were temporary and permanent evils they could not escape, precisely because they were women. These handicaps prevented them from the dedicated practice of a profession like medicine, which did not allow interruptions. Medical-surgical practice was highly demanding and brought with it physical and emotional fatigue. And this was the last thing to which women, with their volatile, sensitive and responsive natures, needed to be exposed. Their destiny did not lie in medical practice. Supposing a woman — by some great exception — nevertheless happened to have special capacities and neither children nor household, she would still have to pass through all the legally required stages of medical training. This was the major stumbling block. It presumed the existence of organised education for girls, and, yes, 'this is hardly possible to achieve given the current state of things and the uncertainty of success'.

With two such diametrically opposed visions, the Academic Council was not able to reach a consensus. Five members voted with Poirier, two against, and at least twelve abstained. The two memorandums were sent to the minister with the necessary reserves as to finding a short-term solution. Ghent preferred to await developments in the rest of the world before taking action. Liège, by contrast, under the influence of the progressive liberal rector Jean-Louis Trasenster, voted in favour of admitting women to the medical profession.

## 'La femme-docteur'

After Isala Van Diest, Emma Leclerq was the next woman to dare enrol, at the ULB, for the academic year 1878-1879. She had a teacher's diploma but was rejected for fear that her presence would incite moral depravity. Only after the national commission for the ratification of diplomas declared in 1880 that women could not be denied the right to a university diploma did the anticlerical ULB open its doors to female applicants. Liège followed in 1881, Ghent in 1882. In Leuven, the doors remained closed until 1920.

Sidonie Verhelst also had a teaching degree when she enrolled in the faculty of Sciences at Ghent University. Her presence in the classroom caused a great deal of consternation. Sidonie was assigned a special place in the auditorium. This became a tradition: decades later, the first row was still reserved for the female students. A Romanian student's undesired but insistent attempt to sit next to her was even placed on the agenda of the Academic Council.

After the admission requirements were tightened again in 1890, women without a secondary diploma could only continue their studies after they were examined by a central jury. In 1892, Gatti de Gamond set up a three-year course designed to prepare for it. For degree programmes at the Special Trade School (Bijzondere Handelsschool, 1906), the Higher Institute for Physical Education (Hoger Instituut voor Lichamelijke Opvoeding, or HILO, 1908), the Higher Institute for Art History and Archaeology (Hoger Instituut voor Kunstgeschiedenis en Oudheidkunde, or HIKO, 1920) and the Higher Institute for Educational Sciences (Hoger Instituut voor Opvoedkundige Wetenschappen, or HIO, 1927), a diploma was not required. This explains why so many women enrolled in these programmes. Pharmacy was also popular among the first generation of women. Before the First World War, there were ninety-nine women enrolled at the university.

In 1913 the first female lecturer arrived: Irène Van der Bracht. She taught gymnastics subjects, at the HILO that were aimed specifically at female students.

**Physical education Students with their professor, Irène Van der Bracht, 1926**
(Ghent, Universiteitsarchief)

**The 'pokers' in the auditorium**
Until the 1960s, it was customary for female students to sit in the front row of the class. This photo dates from academic year 1953-1954 and was taken in professor Julien Fautrez's anatomy class.
(Ghent, Universiteitsarchief, photo Raphael Suy)

In 1890, after fifteen years of ambiguity, the Belgian government finally approved women's right to take academic degrees and practise medicine and pharmacy. An amendment proposed by the radical liberal parliamentarian Auguste Houzeau de Lehaie enabling women to be granted a doctorate in Law was not adopted. It was the period of the Marie Popelin affair, the young graduate in law from the ULB who was denied entrance to the Bar in 1888. The Bar would remain closed to female lawyers until 1922, when Madeleine Schauvlieghe, an alumna of the Athénée de Jeunes Filles, was able to begin practising law immediately after graduation.

For women lawyers, the time was not yet ripe in 1890. Women doctors, on the other hand, were quite successful at the university. Of the first twenty-six women who obtained a doctorate in medicine, four graduated with the highest distinction, ten with high distinction, six with distinction and six as satisfactory. One of those awarded the highest distinction was Bertha De Vriese, who was able to begin her studies at the age of sixteen thanks to private instruction. She was the first female doctor to graduate from Ghent and won the interuniversity competition in 1900. When she offered a word of thanks on behalf of the five Ghent laureates, she was the first woman ever to address the packed Aula during the academic opening ceremony. The liberal mayor Emile Braun, who presented her with the gold medal from the city, was not particularly women-friendly in his speech. In the event of major operations or serious illnesses, 'la femme-docteur' was no match for her male colleagues, 'who have more endurance, more energy, more initiative and more moral authority over the patient', according to Braun. But in less critical cases, which were of course the most frequent, she threatened to become real competition for the male doctor, especially with women and children. In 1914 there were only two women doctors practising in Ghent.

For the time being, the male colleagues had nothing to fear from Bertha De Vriese. She opted for a scientific career and specialised in the blood vessels of the brainstem, at foreign universities. From 1904 to 1908 she was the first female assistant in Ghent, where she worked in the laboratory of Hector Leboucq. At that time, the modern Anatomical Institute on the Bijloke site had grown into an internationally renowned research centre. Under the direction of Charles Bambeke, the Ghent Morphological School carried out pioneering work in different domains. De Vriese went to international anatomy congresses where she was often the only woman. In 1905, with the congratulations of the jury, she was awarded a PhD in morphology with a dissertation

**The first female lawyers**
After the high-profile Marie Popelin affair, women could not register with the Bar until 1922. These are the first three female lawyers from Ghent, from left to right: Madeleine Schauvlieghe, Paule Hallet and Yvonne Deseure. Hallet was the mother of Yvette Merchiers, who, like her father Laurent Merchiers, pursued an academic career in the faculty of Law.
(Ghent, Universiteitsarchief)

**Group photo with a lady, 1904**
Bertha De Vriese was the only woman at the Anatomical Congress in Jena, April 1904. She is sitting on the first row, fourth from the right.
(Ghent, Universiteitsarchief)

on the cerebral artery. It became a standard work. But despite all her efforts and considerable merits, she did not succeed in remaining at the university. Her application for a position as work leader was given a negative evaluation by executive director Jean Vanderlinden — with a specious excuse — that was blindly followed by the minister. Just as inexorably, her mandate as assistant was not extended. De Vriese was out in the cold, albeit with the 'honorary title' of specially qualified lecturer at the faculty of Medicine. This allowed her to build a career as a department head at the children's section of the Bijloke hospital. She worked with the paediatrician-philanthropist Adolphe Miele, who gave free consultations to young mothers and advised them on the sterilisation of milk. Her position as assistant with Hector Leboucq, who was rector from 1906 to 1909, went to his son Georges in 1908, a decent anatomist but not of De Vriese's calibre. Leboucq Junior became a work leader in 1912, lecturer in 1919 and professor in 1921. The time was not yet ripe for women to enjoy such a smooth academic ascent at the faculty of Medicine.

## Obstetrics and 'women's diseases'

Until 1866, when a new maternity ward was added to the Bijloke site, education in the field of obstetrics did not (entirely) belong to the university. In 1817, William I instructed the governor of East Flanders to establish a 'maternity ward with an associated school for midwives to benefit the poor'. The provincial 'obstetric school for physicians and midwives' on what is now Jozef Kluyskensstraat was founded in 1825, the maternity ward in 1828. The 'lying-in ward' was a measure intended to prevent death in childbirth and aid single women who could not afford to pay for a midwife.

Kluyskens, one of the first professors of medicine appointed in 1817, advocated the teaching of obstetrics at the university from the outset and ensured that it was a required subject in the curriculum. For financial reasons, however, the university's practical training was conducted in the provincial maternity ward. This led to regular conflicts with the midwives, who the pregnant women incited by not allowing themselves to be examined by the professor and his male students. Alexis Lados, professor of obstetrics from 1848 onwards, also instructed the midwives. The conditions were appalling: 'I have to give instruction in an attic room where nine people have 45 cubic metres of air; it is unworthy and cruel towards the unfortunate women who come here to deliver.'

On the initiative of the university, a municipal maternity ward with a school for obstetrics that met all the requirements of academic education was established in 1852. The Mother House on the Bijloke site was opened in 1866. It was a modern building with several labour rooms, a bath installation, a laundry room and a special area for new-borns. A regulation was introduced that insisted on the strict separation of practical training for midwives from that of the students.

**The Mother House at the Bijloke**
An iconic place for many older inhabitants of Ghent. In the foreground is the statue of Jan Palfijn, inventor of the forceps in 1720. The maternity ward where thousands of Ghent residents were born from 1866 to 1977 has now been integrated into the cultural site of the Bijloke and houses the music theatre LOD.
(Ghent, Universiteitsarchief)

During the *fin de siècle*, neo-Malthusianism — as the trend was known, which advocated birth control through contraception — had not yet been introduced at Ghent University. In terms of sexuality, the nineteenth century was a very prudish period, with characteristic double standards for men and women. Only in left-wing, nonconformist student circles, such as Julius Mac Leod's Ter Waarheid, did a group of young men and women embrace the ideals of the Reiner Leven (Live More Purely) movement, which aimed at a new sexual morality, greater openness, free love outside of marriage and sex education.

Reiner Leven, which was founded in 1905 by George Sarton, was anything but libertine; rather, the intention was to lead a morally elevated life in line with the Lebensreform movement through (complete) abstention. Meetings took place in Café La Tempérance in Bagattenstraat and sought to improve student morals with the motto '*Pour être fort, sois pur*'. Vera Tordeur, the first female student in mathematics and the natural sciences, became a member, as did Melanie Lorein and Augusta De Taeye, who had studied physical education. All three of them also participated in a group of young feminists who called themselves De Flinken (The Firm), whose members were working women as well as female students.

Bertha De Vriese also joined Reiner Leven. She and her companions were pacifists,

**Reiner Leven and De Flinken in the dunes**
The network around science historian George Sarton and his British wife Mabel Elwes was interwoven with numerous innovative currents in and around Ghent University before the First World War. This photo comes from the archive of Herman Thiery, a.k.a. Johan Daisne.
(Antwerp, Letterenhuis)

vegetarian, fascinated by the Arts and Crafts movement of William Morris and John Ruskin, read Leo Tolstoy, Maurice Maeterlinck and Emile Verhaeren and tried to bridge the gap between intellectuals and workers. 'We wanted to change and improve the world so that it would be a paradise in which all people were equally happy', writes biologist Paul Van Oye many years later of his time as a student member of Reiner Leven. Mabel Elwes and George Sarton were a couple in those optimistic years, as were Augusta De Taeye and Leo-Michel Thiery. Augusta and Michel married and had three sons: Herman in 1912, and twelve years later the twins Leo and Michel Thiery, who both started studying medicine in 1942. Leo graduated in urology and dermatology, Michel in obstetrics under Firmin De Rom.

Neo-Malthusianism was a small, dissident minority movement in a country where sexuality was dominated by Catholic morals. *Les devoirs de la vie conjugale*, the pastoral letter from cardinal Mercier in 1909, was the starting shot for a Catholic campaign against abortion and contraceptives that mobilised politicians, doctors and midwives. The conservative Catholic parliamentarian Charles Woeste submitted a proposed law that was approved in 1923 and prohibited the dissemination of information and advertising relating to contraceptives.

In 1911, the Catholic government appointed Frans Daels as a lecturer in obstetrics. His arrival provoked the escalation of the latent power struggle with the midwives in the Bijloke. When he went so far as to remove equipment from the Mother House because he claimed them for his clinic, he was denied access and received a de-merit from the university. This did little to advance the reputation of his clinic. The women of Ghent still preferred the midwives to the doctors.

Daels changed tack and began to co-opt and medicalise the profession of midwife. He organised an initial consultation for mothers and babies, launched the midwives' journal *Vroedvrouwentijdschrift*, organised a bilingual congress for Belgian midwives and established a professional midwives' association. Moreover, after the First World War, he also founded a free Flemish school for nurses and midwives and as head physician of the maternity ward, he also arranged for their practical training, which once again caused quarrels with the city. In 1924, Daels 'conquered' the entire ground floor of the Mother House for his obstetrics clinic. It was the first victorious battle in his fight for an autonomous university hospital.

Under Daels, Wilhelmine Van Hove became the first female assistant at the faculty of Medicine in 1933. She was honourably dismissed at her own request in 1938 but continued to be associated with the clinic for obstetrics and 'women's diseases' on a volunteer basis. Daels would continue to modernise and professionalise the clinic during the interwar period. He was a born lecturer whose teaching was clear, humorous and, when necessary, dramatic. He was also the author of popular manuals, such as the richly illustrated *Beginselen van de praktische verloskunde* of 1920. Several generations of doctors and gynaecologists have relied on this two-volume standard work.

The Flemish nationalist priest Cyriel Verschaeve supplied the foreword to the brochure *Voor moeder en zuigeling* (1920), which Daels wrote at the front 'in the midst of death and fear of murder' for the young women of Flanders. Its claim to be scientific could not alter the fact that the sexual information provided was ideologically slanted and contained unmistakable moral lessons. 'You, as man and woman who know no discipline in love, do you not see the responsibility of sexual congress? Are you aware of the danger to which the drunkenness of love, aroused by wine or an excess of sexual intercourse, exposes a future child? Isn't purely sensual pleasure a form of cowardice towards your descendants?'

For Daels, daily sex was the equivalent of 'sexual depravity'. Among animals, fertility was limited to a few days per year, but people could 'indulge in huge excess the whole year through'. A number of practical rules for a 'clean' sex life were proffered: vaginal douching, the best time to get pregnant and the best conditions in which to form 'beautiful, well-behaved children ... in that sanctuary we call the mother's womb', all described in highly expressive terms.

Daels's Catholic-inspired ideas were directed at the harmony of the 'community'. For him, the intellectual and economic equality of men and women was simply unthinkable. Advanced studies for women could only be permitted under 'the right conditions'. The doors of medicine should not be opened too wide. In 1941, Daels gave a speech in Brussels on 'women in the new age' before the Flemish National Women's Association (Vlaams Nationaal Vrouwen Verbond, or VNNV), which collaborated with the Germans during the Second World War through the Flemish National Association (VNV). Because of his collaboration with the Nazi occupation, Daels's teaching assignment at Ghent University was ended on 25 May 1945.

Daels's successor, Firmin De Rom, had his own ideas about pregnancy and childbirth. For example, he remained in favour of breastfeeding when powdered milk began to gain ground, and insisted on home deliveries, sending his staff and students against their will to the tenements with an obstetrics kit of his own design known as the '*sacoche*'. Even Michel Thiery was unable to escape during his internship in 1948. Alone, reaching his destination by bicycle, he helped a poor woman give birth to a child in the slums. It was then that he decided: never again would he assist in a home delivery. When De Rom retired in 1963, Thiery (obstetrics) and Dirk Vandekerckhove (gynaecology) decided to integrate their areas of expertise permanently.

The new trends of the 1960s, with themes such as contraceptives, sterilisation, infertility and — to some extent — elective abortion were introduced in the Women's Clinic early on. In 1964, the year of my birth, the new polyclinic and obstetrics clinic in the new general hospital on De Pintelaan opened their doors. I was one of the first in a rising tide of babies to be delivered in this modern and attractive environment. While the number of deliveries in the former Mother House at the Bijloke had been less than 400 per year, it boomed in the second half of the 1960s at over 1,000 per year, despite the demographic trend of falling birth rates.

In the progressive 1960s, however, 'women's diseases' were still the exclusive domain of male doctors, and midwives played a subordinate role. When Marleen Temmerman wanted to specialise in gynaecology with Vandekerckhove in 1978, as a 'young miss' she was turned down. This had to do with another female assistant who had been in the programme. Her rebellious attitude had seriously worked on Vandekerckhove's nerves. Temmerman was led to understand that obstetrics was not for women: much too difficult, working day and night ... She could better spend her time studying dermatology, a speciality that was easy to combine with a family and children. Instead, she followed a peripheral, non-university course of study in Breda, which she was eventually able to finish at the VUB in the 1970s with Jean-Jacques Amy, a former collaborator of Thiery's. It was the period when the struggle for abortion was gaining ground. Amy and his team carried out abortions at a time when it was not permitted and advocated its legalisation. In Ghent the situation was much more delicate.

After a research trip to Kenya, Marleen Temmerman returned to her roots in 1992. She secured a part-time position as a gynaecologist at the University Hospital. Vandekerckhove had just been succeeded by Marc Dhont. There were still no female gynaecologists employed there, even though the patients were increasingly requesting one. The number of deliveries had fallen to 600 per year, an all-time low. Together with her staff, Temmerman built an in-house maternity ward and succeeded in raising the annual number of deliveries to 1,300. She did not, however, follow the trend of returning to home deliveries. In 1996 she was the first female professor of Gynaecology and Obstetrics in Belgium. This enabled her to develop as a teacher and researcher while at the same time pursuing a political career and continuing her tireless work in the field of development aid. The nineteenth-century male jack-of-all-trades had become a woman.

## 'Evangelists of the sexual revolution'

Michel Thiery made an important contribution to the field of contraception. In 1949, the last year of his doctorate, he wrote a working paper based on the controversial *Married Love or Love in Marriage* (1918) by the British author and campaigner Marie Stopes, the first practical guide to birth control. In Ghent, the issue was still so taboo that Thiery was allowed to defend his paper before only the professor and two work leaders. His fellow students were not permitted to be present (but they did ask for a copy of the manuscript when it was time for them to marry). Thiery was also the author of *Anticonceptie*, the first handbook on birth control written in Dutch, which was published in Leiden in 1971. Customs held it back at the Belgian–Dutch border because it was considered contrary to prevailing principles of morality. When Thiery was invited onto the women's programme *Penelope*, hosted by Paula Sémer, he explained family planning, responsible parenthood and the use of the pill in a dry, business-like tone, giving rise to a wave of indignation in Catholic Flanders.

Thiery made at least twenty-eight such television appearances in the second half of the 1960s. It was 1980 before the Belgian Order of Physicians added a paragraph to the codex of obligations stating that informing patients about contraceptives and sexuality was one of a doctor's responsibilities. In the meantime, contraception's role in the sexual revolution and the emancipation of women is well known. The internationally recognised scientific research of Michel Thiery, Harry Van der Pas and Hendrik Van Kets on the safety of the IUD was in any case pioneering in the medical field. In cooperation with the social biologist Robert Cliquet and the Centre for Population and Family Studies (Centrum voor Bevolkings- en Gezinsstudiën, or CBGS), which was established in 1962, large-scale surveys were set up to measure the use of contraceptives in Belgium. The surveys exposed the schizophrenic situation concerning sexuality that had arisen in Belgium in the meantime. In the first National Family Development Survey in 1966, 90% of the respondents said they had at some point used some form of birth control, and 10% of married women older than twenty used the pill. In 1968 the Catholic Church responded to changing sexual morality with the *Humanae Vitae* encyclical, in which the use of contraception was roundly condemned — but to no avail. In 1981, according to the same survey, which was conducted every five years, use of reliable contraception had risen to 72%.

Once again, Ghent professors and alumni were working to close the gap between law and practice. Of course, this progressive trend was not representative of the entire university, nor of all its professors. Alfons Vranckx, for example, socialist minister of Justice and professor at the Law faculty, had the entire print run of the *Rode boekje voor scholieren* confiscated. This popular booklet, which had spread to Belgium from the Netherlands, advocated liberation from prevailing laws and norms, not least in sexuality. In 1971, Vranckx's fellow professor, the senator Willy Calewaert, proposed the first legislation for the partial liberalisation of abortion. It never made it out of committee. When the socialists proposed Calewaert as minister of Justice during the formation of the next government, the CVP (Christian People's Party) took its

**Professor Thiery and the pill, 1967**
Lambert Van De Sype and his wife sit with Professor Thiery in the television programme *Kwart Eefje*, a BRT educational broadcast in the years 1966-1968. Thiery explains what the pill is and how long it has been around as well as explaining what types there are and what side effects may occur. He also talks about the pill for men.
(Brussels, VRT-Beeldarchief)

revenge because of his ethical views. In the same period, gynaecologist Willy Peers, from the francophone Free University of Brussels, was arrested for carrying out a clandestine abortion on a mentally disabled woman who had been raped. In all the commotion surrounding the case, liberal minister of justice Herman Vanderpoorten, also a jurist from Ghent, ended the ban on contraception in 1974.

A direct consequence of this was that the Centres for Birth Control and Sex Education (Centra voor Geboorteregeling en Seksuele Opvoeding, or CGSO) could emerge from secrecy. The CGSOs evolved from the Belgian Association for Sexual Education (Belgische Vereniging voor Seksuele Voorlichting, or BVSV), which was founded by several freethinkers from the Humanist Association (HV) and Freemasonry in 1955. The Ghent biologist and former resistance fighter Lucien De Coninck was its first president. At the beginning of the 1960s, medical consultation bureaus were also established in several cities. They provided assistance and advice on sexuality, relationships, contraceptives, (undesired) pregnancy, abortion and sexually transmitted diseases. The pill, which was introduced in Belgium in 1962, was also prescribed in the consultation bureaus. In Ghent, Erna Vercauteren, active as a gynaecologist in the BVSV since 1958, was the first to do so. She also used scientific research to show that the pill did not cause cancer, as its opponents claimed. Well-attended lectures were given at the request of the most diverse organisations. The 'evangelists of the sexual revolution' were armed with the Dutch-language educational film *Kringloop* and a suitcase — nicknamed the 'sexcase' — filled with sex-education books and contraceptive samples. In the early days, these were mainly diaphragms and condoms, which were sold discreetly during the break for a small profit.

## 'Sex checks', childcare and university physicians

In March 1974, students in Ghent revolted against the so-called 'sex checks' in the student dormitories. The (segregated) dormitories were governed by strict rules. Visitors had to deposit their student ID card at reception and leave the dormitory by 10 p.m. If the individual in question did not leave voluntarily, the concierge would forcibly remove them from the premises. The occupation of Home Fabiola by two hundred students was a first step in the fight for co-ed facilities, a battle that was only won in 1986.

In 1973, on the ground floor of Home Heymans, the dormitory for married students, a day-care centre — still active today — was set up for the children of students and staff. Four years earlier, on Tweekerkenstraat, the first day-care centre for staff had been established at the initiative of William De Coster. It was a response to the May '68 movement and the call for the liberation of women from the restrictions of the domestic sphere. De Coster convinced the university administration to set up a model day-care centre, a 'test garden', somewhat analogous to the experimental school of his colleague Richard Verbist. He created a pedagogically stimulating environment for children in their first years of life, with well-trained staff and a great deal of interaction —including the parents. It was worlds away from the classic crèche, where only food and hygiene mattered. The care assistants were known as the 'hippies of the crèche'. They were led by the impassioned pedagogue Paul Ryelandt. His idealism emerges from what he saw as childcare's mission: making it possible for women to

CGSO and 't Zal Wel Gaan poster, 1981
The Audio-Visual Workgroup of the Centre for Birth Control and Sex Education (CGSO) and the student association 't Zal Wel Gaan organised film screenings on sexual themes in the Academy Council room of the Aula.
(Ghent, Amsab-ISG)

participate in society through 'communal education'. The 'dream box' that my son Quinten — then under two — brought home from the day-care centre on Tweekerkenstraat has been given a place of honour in my own small museum of innocent objects.

Like the day-care centres, the department of Psychological Advice for Students (Psychologisch Advies aan Studenten, or PAS) was also spurred by the dreams of the May '68 movement. The initiative was started by behavioural therapist Jeanine Van Oppen, who observed that students had many questions about sexuality and contraceptives but did not necessarily have access to a doctor. Under the impulse of student representative Ri De Ridder and in cooperation with the department of Social Medicine, led by Karel Vuylsteek, an investigation was conducted. It resulted in the hiring of Guido De Munck and De Ridder himself (today director of the Institute of National Illness and Invalidity Insurance, RIZIV) for several consultations each week. A few years later, Koen Verhofstadt and Karen Klein joined them as university physicians. In addition to consultations paid for on a voluntary basis, they organised information and prevention campaigns aimed specifically at students. Beginning in 1976-1977, they also published their own column in *Schamper*, 'The university physician explains'. With their serene, scientific approach, they were particularly popular with the students. The student doctors also played an important role in disseminating information on contraception, sexually transmitted diseases, AIDS and condom use.

## Youth against the wall

Breaking with taboos around sexuality went hand in hand with the 'liberating' lectures of Jaap Kruithof. In his ethics course, he invited students to ask questions about sexual behaviour as part of human and moral behaviour. 'That formula was so successful that eventually I couldn't teach class any more, only answer questions', he said many years

Jaap Kruithof and *Het gelukkige gezin* (The happy family), 1967
Spurred on by Kruithof's controversial book *Jeugd voor de muur* (Youth against the wall), a panel of experts comments on the young people's statements in a television broadcast that is at least as controversial. Paula Sémer led the conversation. From left to right: Jaap Kruithof, canon De Haene, Thérèse De Geest-Materne and Guido Roscam.
(Brussels, VRT-Beeldarchief)

later in an interview. Every Friday morning, Auditorium E was filled to capacity. The course became an event, the professor a phenomenon. The only ones who weren't so enthusiastic were the parents of the students. Some mothers even asked Kruithof to help them spy on their daughters. They had a hard time understanding that their offspring had sexual desires.

Alfred C. Kinsey's reports on *Sexual behavior in the human male* (1948) and *Sexual behavior in the human female* (1953) were rather late reaching Belgian shores from the US. The research inspired Kruithof and his assistant Jos Van Ussel to launch their own survey in higher education, which was published in the controversial book *Jeugd voor de muur. Vlaamse studenten en hun seksuele problematiek* (1962). Even more controversial was the broadcast of *Het Vrije Woord*, the talk show of the Humanistisch Verbond (HV) on the BRT, which covered the book in a thematic episode. Kruithof and Van Ussel's survey showed that students wrestled with their sexuality because they weren't allowed to do anything and didn't know anything. But they didn't dare talk in public because they were ashamed, afraid of their parents and the community at large. In the TV broadcast, twelve students sat with their backs to the camera and told their sad stories. This had an enormous impact on public opinion. Kruithof was aware of the power of the television medium to open up questions of morality. In 1967 he caused another small media storm with his appearance in *Het gelukkige gezin*, a programme by Paula Sémer. The moral philosopher stated quite clearly that contraceptives were necessary for regulating the sex life of the Flemish people and that young people had to be well educated on that score, even — and especially — with an eye towards premarital 'relations'. Right before the end of the programme, Sémer convinced the three other (Catholic) panellists, including canon Piet De Haene, to agree with Kruithof. Contraceptives were still prohibited at the time.

The bishop of Bruges had a pastoral text read out from all the pulpits in his jurisdiction that parents should no longer send their children to Ghent, but rather to Leuven. The 'godless' Kruithof could not have cared less. In 2012, Paula Sémer received an honorary doctorate from UGent for her taboo-shattering programmes and her contribution to the emancipation of women.

Jos Van Ussel, Kruithof's assistant and like him a historian, never got the chance to finish his doctorate under Jan Dhondt. The otherwise progressive and freethinking Dhondt was afraid for his own reputation and position if he allowed the defence to take place. So Van Ussel had to defend his dissertation on the socio-genesis of bourgeois sexual morality, which was published as the *Geschiedenis van het seksuele probleem*, in 1968, at the University of Amsterdam. In Rotterdam, he sought cooperation from 'anti-psychiatrist' Kees Trimbos, who was renowned for his broadcasts on sexual education for Catholic Radio Broadcasting (Katholieke Radio Omroep, or KRO). Even with an interdisciplinary degree programme such as Moral Sciences, establishing an interdisciplinary, interfaculty research centre in Ghent was not among the possibilities at the time. Medicine claimed the domain of sexuality as its territory. For this reason, Sexology was taught in other faculties by Michel Thiery, not by Van Ussel.

## Reproductive rights

In 1972 the CGSO organised a well-attended national colloquium in Brussels entitled 'The contraceptive society', with contributions from Thiery and Cliquet, among others. Up until the 1970s, it was usually doctors and men who were going to liberate women from the straitjacket of the Catholic morality. The slogan 'Boss in my own belly' (*Baas in eigen buik*) — formulated by the Dutch feminist group known as the Dolle Mina's, after the Dutch feminist Wilhelmina Drucker — was an answer to this double paternalism. The second wave of feminism was indeed tangible at Ghent University, albeit more among the students than the professors.

A feminist core of female medical students had joined forces with the Dolle Minas. Among them were Christine Rouneau, Eliane Collumbien and Rein Bellens, the first Ghent abortion doctor. It was a period when feminist men were conscripted into childcare while the women went to congresses. One such man was Peter Piot, who had boundless admiration for their drive and commitment. He helped organise the first International Women's Day in 1972 and was more than happy to do the washing up.

At the faculty of Arts, it was mainly Hugo Van den Enden and Etienne Vermeersch who supported women's right to self-determination and the abortion rights movement. In 1971, Van den Enden, indignant that women had to suffer through unwanted pregnancies, wrote *Abortus, pro/contra*. That same year, Michel Thiery wrote on the medical-technical aspects of abortion, and a year later he collaborated with psychiatrist Steven De Batselier and Robert Cliquet on possible 'policy alternatives'. In a 1973 television appearance, Thiery exposed the grim reality of clandestine abortions and argued for medically responsible interventions in a legal framework. His authority as a gynaecologist helped break the taboo surrounding the topic, although he avoided offering abortion assistance at AZ Gent. A contrast with colleagues Pierre-Olivier at the ULB or Jean-Jacques Amy at the VUB, who faced prosecution for doing so.

**Abortion trial in the Ghent courthouse, late 1980s**
The trial of the fifty-two doctors and employees of Kollektief Anticonceptie (KAC) in Ghent received a great deal of media attention and fed public debate on the legalisation of abortion.
(Ghent, Amsab-ISG, photo Roland Van der Sypt)

Amy recalls how, whenever patients asked for an abortion, the 'autocrat' Thiery was in the habit of consulting the department council, which had no other freethinking members apart from them. The result was that medical abortions were carried out only rarely. Thiery relied on the 'democratic decision' of the council. One night a desperate couple appeared at Amy's door in Deinze begging for help. The gynaecologist carried out an 'at home' abortion using instruments he had been able to smuggle out of the hospital and a bicycle pump for the suction curettage.

When the first abortion centre in Flanders, Contraceptive Collective (Kollektief Anticonceptie), was founded in 1980, it was mainly supported by Ghent philosophers and the protagonists of family medicine. The Kollektief developed an alternative organisation that was averse to hierarchy and paternalism. The recently deceased Ghent historian Lucie Van Crombrugge was one of the driving forces. The 'Friends of the KAC' were a motley crew that included some of the usual suspects from Ghent University: Etienne Vermeersch, Hugo Van den Enden, Jaap Kruithof, Leo Apostel, Hein Picard and Jan De Maeseneer.

Research conducted by Temmerman, Amy, De Quint and De Poorter showed that it was usually 'normal' women who asked to have an abortion. It caused an uproar in the editorial board of the predominantly conservative *Tijdschrift voor Geneeskunde*. The article was eventually published after one of the board members resigned. Marc Cosyns was able to publish his article on the role of registration in abortion assistance in *Huisarts Nu*, but was reprimanded by dean André Kint. Doctoral research on illegal situations was impossible, despite support from professors René De Smet and Karel Vuylsteek. Head of gynaecology Michel Thiery framed the argument in the following terms: 'We are a state university, abortion is illegal; therefore, abortion cannot be investigated.' In 1985 the doctors and staff of Kollektief were shaken up by house searches, and in 1988 fifty-two of them were summoned to court. Doctors Bellens and Cosyns, coordinator Lucie Van Crombrugge and two nurses would only be acquitted in 1992.

In the meantime, the legislation proposed by the Walloon socialist Roger Lallemand and the Flemish liberal Lucienne Hermanman-Michielsens was finally approved at the end of March 1990 after years of political struggle. It was a compromise that legalised abortion under specific circumstances. Herman-Michielsens graduated from Ghent University in 1951 as a doctor in law and a licentiate in criminology. During her studies, she had seen the results of back-street abortions in autopsies. The images of horror stayed with her. She was never actually in favour of abortion, but she did support removing it from the penal code. 'A woman faced with such a heart-rending choice should not be treated as a criminal, nor should the doctor who helps her in good faith', she stated in *Humo*.

In 2003 the government requested the federation of CGSOs to unite with five aids organisations. The new organisation was named Sensoa, the Flemish centre of expertise for sexual health. That same year, *Good Lovers*, an exhibition on sexuality for young people aged twelve to sixteen, opened in the Wereld van Kina, a learning centre in Ghent. All aspects of 'knowledge' and 'ability' in the domain of sexuality were presented in a playful, positive light. Clinical psychologist Ann Buysse, who chaired Sensoa for eight years, is still wildly enthusiastic about the tone taken by the exhibition, as well as the interactive version for toddlers, *Two Bears*. The location could not have been better chosen: the former School Museum, founded by Leo-Michel Thiery, father of pioneer Michel Thiery, who together with his wife Augusta De Taeye was one of the first in Ghent to see free love as a boon.

Lucienne Herman-Michielsens in parliament, 1990
The abortion law was adopted in the Belgian parliament in 1990, despite opposition from King Baudouin, who refused to sign it.
(Ghent, Amsab-ISG, photo Filip Claus)

## Homosexuality, AIDS prevention and the welfare of gays, lesbians and bisexuals

After the departure of Jos Van Ussel in 1970, Bob Carlier was an assistant and later work leader of Jaap Kruithof's Morality and Metaphysics seminar. Carlier, who was himself homosexual, was one of the initiators of the Ghent Student Workgroup on Homosexuality in the pivotal year 1969. Carlier's scientific interests in the domain of sexuality were broad and many-sided, as was his engagement in the struggle for sexual emancipation and the fight against discrimination of sexual minorities. He was active in the Centre for Sexual Education (Centrum voor Seksuele Voorlichting, or CSV, the Ghent CGSO) and a member of the board of directors of Kollektief Anticonceptie. This enabled Carlier to act as an important bridge between the women's and gay rights movements. The 1960s had also brought about a change in attitudes towards homosexuality. Borne by successive waves of sexual emancipation movements, homosexuals and lesbians began to come out and organise openly. The Student Workgroup on Homosexuality attached great importance to scientific insights. At Carlier's initiative, they launched a well-attended teach-in in 1969, with Steven De Batselier and Jos Van Ussel as speakers. There was an interuniversity Federation of Workgroups on Homosexualit (Federatie van Werkgroepen Homoseksualiteit, or FWH, now Çavaria), which organised public kissing actions, among other things. The goal was to create an open climate for the 'normalisation' of homosexuality. In the mid-1970s, radical gay movements like De Rooie Vlinder (The Red Butterfly, 1976) and Liever Heks (Better a Witch, 1978) would turn against the mainstreaming of homosexuality. At the end of the 1980s, the Homosexuality workgroup became Verkeerd Geparkeerd (Wrongly Parked), a youth group of gay and lesbian students that is still active today.

At the beginning of academic year 1983-1984, just two years after the discovery of the AIDS virus and the global wave of panic it caused, the first 'AIDS bash' was organised in the Vooruit during Lesbian and Gay Week, and the workgroup Students Against Aids was set up. An interview with Bob Carlier in *Schamper* heightened awareness that the pandemic, or rather, the rising tide of fear it generated, contributed to the social stigmatisation of homosexuals. From the start, Ghent's university physicians played a leading role by promoting the use of condoms and supplying scientifically based information in an open way. Condoms were hung from the ceiling of the waiting room. The close ties between Bob Carlier, the CSV and the AIDS hotline facilitated the organisation of AIDS Week in December 1988, with numerous debates and contributions from the student doctors and researchers from Ghent University. Students and academic staff called on the government to take AIDS prevention more seriously and to invest more in promoting the use of condoms. Starting in March 1989, under the liberal rector Leon De Meyer, condom vending machines were

**Poster for De Rooie Vlinder, 1978**

De Rooie Vlinder came together as a socialist action group for revolutionary homosexuals in 1976. The animating force was students who opposed moderate gay groups such as the Ghent student workgroup Homofilie, and who did not find their place in the left-wing labour movements. They found an important forum in the new student magazine *Schamper* and received a lot of media attention for their provocative actions.
(Ghent, Universiteitsbibliotheek, design Krist De Munter)

installed in various locations on campus — a new phenomenon in Flanders.

John Vincke, who unfortunately died too young, was head of the AIDS team from 1992 to 1995. For this sociologist, scientific research should serve societal change. When he defended his dissertation in 1989, the question was openly voiced as to whether the university should award 'someone like him' a PhD. The same resistance accompanied his appointment as a lecturer in 2002. In this sense, Vincke was living proof that minorities were not just handed their rights on a silver platter. Not even at the university. He never wanted to be a figurehead of the gay movement, but neither did he believe in a value-free society, and as a social scientist he had a strong desire to improve social welfare and build a better society. Vincke tried to collect sound scientific information about sexual risk-taking behaviour among gay men. His stint as a guest professor in California (Pomona College) enriched his vision of AIDS research, homosexual relationships and gay communities. It led to the — controversial — use of participatory observation in gay saunas as a scientific instrument for collecting data, a method that was still quite rare in the 1990s. In this way, unsafe sexual behaviour among gay men could be sociologically visualised with an eye towards developing better prevention strategies. The book *Mannen met mannen: welzijn, relaties & seksualiteit* by John Vincke, Ruud Mak and Ralph Bolton, published by the CGSO in 1991, was a real eye-opener in Dutch-speaking regions.

Later, Vincke expanded his scope to include the domestic situations of gay men, lesbians and bisexuals (or LGBs). At the request of Equal Opportunities Policy, he launched the first extensive quantitative study of the domestic situation of LGBs in Flanders. High scores on suicidal thoughts and suicidal behaviour made it clear that despite the emancipatory struggle, there was still a lot of work to be done. At the Equal Opportunities Policy Support Centre, Vincke helped set up the so-called 'Zzzip' surveys, a versatile and a promising instrument for better mapping sexual minorities as 'hidden populations'.

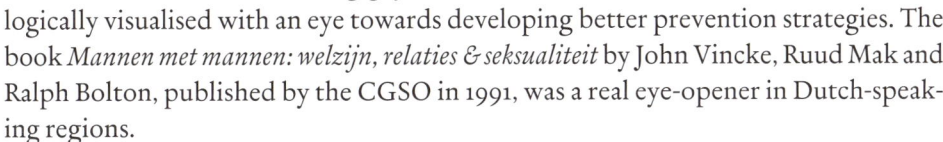

Poster for Verkeerd Geparkeerd, 1990
For many Ghent students who were 'a bit mad about their own kind', the oldest LGBT youth association in Flanders, Verkeerd Geparkeerd (Wrongly Parked), founded in 1987, represented a first step towards acceptance of being different.
(Ghent, Universiteitsbibliotheek)

## Sex under eighteen

In a very different register, the Dutroux affair in the 1990s put a definitive end to cautious attempts to make paedophilia open to discussion. Here again, the role of Bob Carlier deserves mention. In 1977 he played a leading role in the workgroup on Paedophilia, which by analogy with other workgroups at the university sought to study the theme and raise public awareness. Sex between an adult and a child was not rejected out of hand. The laws and norms of society did not leave room for the sexual desires of young people — wrongly, in Carlier's view. Etienne Vermeersch was also involved with these ideas, under the influence of taboo-breaking films such as Eric Rohmer's *Le Genou de Claire* (1970) and Louis Malle's *Le Souffle au Coeur* (1971). In 1979 the radical gay group De Rooie Vlinder brought *Snoepjes*, a Dutch musical about paedophilia, to Ghent. It was framed in the context of abolishing article 372bis of the penal code, which forbade sex to gays and lesbians under the age of eighteen, while for heterosexuals the age was sixteen. Alderman of education Piet Van Eeckhaut forbade the showing of the musical in the Zwarte Zaal of the Academy, which belonged to the municipal education system. Ghent University, however, had no problem with allowing the musical to be shown in the Blandijn on 1 December 1979. Vermeersch, then dean, wrote an opinion piece, 'Are paedophiles culprits?' (*De Morgen*, 8 December 1979). He pointed out that 'normal' paedophiles felt intense affection and tenderness for children, needed to caress them 'and be caressed [...] and to touch their genitals and, as his ultimate objective, to masturbate or allow himself to be masturbated'. According to him, it was also conceivable that children of eleven or twelve voluntarily entered into an erotic relationship 'and also experienced happiness in it'. Scientific research was still needed to show whether this was true. Nevertheless, whether the child actually had freedom of choice and the possible damage that he or she might later experience were problematic for Vermeersch. Any action that caused a fellow human being to suffer was in his view immoral, as was every action that was forced against the wishes of another. The opinion piece of 1977 resurfaced in 2011 with the widespread paedophilia scandals in the Church, generating yet another controversy.

Poster for the forbidden musical *Snoepjes* (Sweets), 1979
(Ghent, Universiteitsbibliotheek, design Krist De Munter)

## Reproductive medicine and human malleability

When Rome rejected in vitro fertilisation (IVF) in 1987 with the religious instruction *Donum Vitae*, the ethical discussion as to whether an embryo was 'human' was re-ignited, and Vermeersch jumped back into the debate. He quoted the Old and New Testaments to 'prove' that a foetus was an object, not a person. Whatever the case may be, science had made huge leaps since Frans Daels discussed fertilisation in biblical terms after the First World War. With the arrival of Thiery and Vandekerckhove at the women's clinic of the hospital, attention to fertility problems increased. In cooperation with the department of Endocrinology, led by Alex Vermeulen, the first official sperm bank of Belgium was created in 1978, enabling artificial insemination with semen from donors.

In 1985, Marc Dhont founded the Faculty Centre for Human Reproductive Biology in Ghent. A couple of years later, he was the spiritual father of Ghent's first test-tube baby. Petra (then Paul) De Sutter recalls how her professor, Dirk Vandekerckhove, said: 'De Sutter, you're still just an assistant, but I have been informed that you are familiar with laboratory work. Now go run the IVF lab!' Today, this would be unthinkable for a recent graduate who was just beginning his studies in gynaecology. De Sutter inherited his patient-oriented approach from Dhont, while colleagues from the Free University of Brussels (VUB) Paul Vroey and André Van Steirteghem made technical refinements to the fertility treatment during the same period. In the 1990s, De Sutter, together with her team, gave basic research in the Ghent laboratory a huge boost, pushing Belgium to the top in reproductive medicine. As a co-opted senator for Groen (Belgium's Green party) since 2014, she has been working on a legal framework for surrogate motherhood. 'Surrogate motherhood must continue to be an altruistic story, and the surrogate mother must not be reduced to a rental womb.' De Sutter also sees the freezing of oocytes for young women who have not found 'the one' by the age of thirty-five as another one of her tasks as a physician. Blaming women for choices they may or may not make is in any case not a part of her repertoire. De Sutter always tries to imagine herself in the patient's place. In her eyes, the human suffering that often accompanies a diagnosis of infertility deserves as much attention as the medical treatment itself. Psychosocial support is therefore of paramount importance in the patient-oriented approach of the Women's Clinic. In May 2017 the department of Reproductive Medicine received the first FertiliTIME Prize (FertiliTIJDsprijs) awarded by the expertise centre Flanders Wants Children (Kinderwens Vlaanderen).

The impact of reproductive medicine on the creation of new forms of family and the formation of children's identities is enormous. Back in the old days, a lack of openness, even in the best families, resulted in major personal dramas. But even today, in an era of greater transparency, human procreation continues to be a major source of social tension, in which secrets and lies are not so easily eliminated. Medical secrecy

**Petra De Sutter and The Malleable Human, 2016**
(Ghent, De Maakbare Mens)

and the social norm that insists on silencing male infertility have come under fire from the perspective of the donor child, who wants to know who his or her biological parents are. Although there is growing political support for the abolition of anonymity, fertility expert Petra De Sutter is not ready to answer definitively. The interdisciplinary research she is conducting with bioethicist Guido Pennings and clinical psychologist Ann Buysse on (anonymous) donor services can provide nuanced, scientific answers to such questions. In the study, donor families were not set up against 'normal' non-donor families; rather, all possible variations were examined — anonymous donation as an answer to fertility problems, transgender, lesbian and gay families, even donation of an oocyte for an infertile sister. For Buysse, the 'Not my sperm, entirely my son' campaign launched by The Malleable Human (De Maakbare Mens), is the right societal guideline for handling donors. In addition to genetic parenthood, there is also something today known as 'social parenthood', and legally speaking there is even a question of 'plural parenthood'. Reproductive medicine has greatly increased the number of choices for individuals and families, in part thanks to Belgium's progressive legislation. But there is also a flipside: society is not yet ready for all these possibilities, as Buysse knows. Assistance and medical care are lagging behind societal realities.

Research concerning donor families is just one of the large-scale projects that Buysse has set up with partners from different disciplines. Other projects tackle issues relating to adoption, new stepfamilies, foster families, divorce and abortion. In every case, the relational component is central, and Buysse adopts a scientific perspective to see through ideological prejudices and assumptions and look at the societal reality without taking the 'happy nuclear family' as the norm. No one dreams of abortion, adoption or divorce. But once they become a reality, society must deal with them humanely, making assistance and medical pathways as constructive as possible.

By listening to her patients, Petra De Sutter has become decidedly more open-minded about parenthood. For her, however, there are still boundaries when it comes to the makeable baby. Not everyone who wants to have children has the department of Reproductive Medicine at their beck and call. Anything that smacks of commercialisation of the IVF treatment or 'positive' embryo selection is excluded on principle. However, stem-cell technology has opened unprecedented opportunities for eugenics, or 'racial improvement', which was also the dream of progressive scientists like Julius Mac Leod in the 'good' tradition of social Darwinism. One hundred years later, 'magic' research into embryonic stem cells is going full steam ahead at the University of Ghent.

## Sexperts in transition

Psychology has always looked at the scientific results and status of medicine with a certain degree of envy. In the complex domain of sexuality and procreation, however, it is impossible to start from a single, all-encompassing explanatory framework. In a world in which the human being is increasingly a makeable creature, multiperspectivism is of vital importance.

This is certainly true given the current international tendency, in which every researcher is an 'expert on 1 square millimetre', laughs Buysse. For this reason, she welcomes the pendulum swing back to interdisciplinarity and cooperation in domains that only can be measured by the square metre. Interdisciplinary cooperation is firmly ingrained in strategic fundamental research (*Strategisch Basisonderzoek*, or SBO). Buysse supervised the SBO programme Sexpert — in fact, the intellectual legacy of John Vincke, whose pupil Alexis Dewaele was appointed as coordinator. The goal of this large-scale population survey was to map sexual health among Flemings. This required not only insight into the individual psyche, but also into broader societal structures, relationships, forms of domestic life and medical practice. Hence, it was conceived as a cooperative effort uniting sexologists, sociologists, endocrinologists and doctors. Sensoa served as the government partner and 'subcontractor' for the validation and valorisation of the research results.

One of the findings of Sexpert is that 17,000 people in Flanders do not feel like they are fully male or female, or at least they do not feel able to identify with one of the two possible gender roles in the classic binary division. After the relative success of the LGB movement, the emancipation of this group is now in full swing. More and more trans- or inter-sexual people are coming out, while legal voices are also arguing against the registration of gender. In April 2017 a law came into effect that allows people to change the gender on their identity card without undergoing a biological sex change. The binary categories m/f persist, however. While Anne Buysse questions this persistence, she also realises that the category 'other' can dissolve into an infinite number of sub-identities. At Sensoa, for example, there are currently three toilets: for men, women, and both/neither. Even that is not really gender-neutral.

With her transition from heterosexual man to lesbian woman, Petra De Sutter is an important figurehead in the emancipation of transgenders. At the same time, she has come to know the medical system through the patient's point of view. It has enhanced her own empathy and made the importance of psychosocial support even clearer. With its Centre for Sexuality and Gender Issues (Centrum voor Seksuologie en Genderproblematiek), directed by Guy T'Sjoen, Ghent's University Hospital has been an undeniable international leader in transgender care for more than twenty-five years. Since 2013, the Flemish government has subsidised the Transgender Infopunt within the University Hospital.

## The university as a male bastion

Paul De Sutter was still 'just' a gynaecologist in training when in 1987, at the tender age of twenty-five, he was given the chance to run the University Hospital's IVF lab. That same year, Anne De Paepe, then thirty-two, received a doctorate in biomedical sciences based on her research on hereditary connective tissue diseases. Three months before the defence, her daughter was born, leaving her physically weakened after the difficult delivery. 'Pregnancy is a biological reality which one should consider', says De Paepe, 'gender equality is impossible'. Although her doctorate more than met the requirements, she was considered too young to acquire special qualification in higher education, which was necessary to be eligible for the position of professor. Five years later, in 1992, she was specially qualified for higher education after completing a second thesis.

At the time, De Paepe already had quite a trajectory behind her, with specialised training in internal diseases, four years as an FWO (Research Foundation-Flanders) postdoc, and a sojourn abroad at a laboratory in London, where medical genetics was already much more advanced than in Belgium. Her fascination with hereditary diseases dated from the time of her initial medical training. Back then, she was asked to be a student assistant by a female work leader, Dr Maria Matton-Van Leuven, who was head of the department of embryonic genetics at the University Hospital. This allowed De Paepe to work on several projects and to follow up patients — more specifically, a large family with an unknown hereditary disease. 'Mrs Matton' was the wife of renowned plastic surgeon Guido Matton. 'She was a fantastic mentor', says Anne De Paepe. 'Very demanding but supportive, and a real pioneer in the field of genetics.'

Although Maria Van Leuven had studied in the US for five years, like Bertha De Vriese before the First World War, she was denied a professorship. She did not even get a chance to get a doctorate and remained a work leader until her (early) retirement in 1992. Being promoted to professor was a given for men, but not always for women. According to Yvonne Desirant, who became the first female work leader in the chemistry lab of Frédéric Swarts in 1931 despite resistance, this was never expressed openly: 'No one told you, but you felt it.' She too remained a work leader until her retirement in 1964. In his correspondence with the minister, executive director Schoep did not even bother to hide his negative attitude towards the 'young ladies' that the university was 'saddled with'.

Medical genetics was not yet recognised as a course of study, nor were there recognised experts in the education programme for doctors when De Paepe became an assistant at the Faculty Centre for Medical Genetics after her special qualification. There was literally no 'subject' for familiarising students with the material. When a few hours came free in the third year of medical school, there was finally an opportunity to integrate a new subject into the curriculum. De Paepe describes how she was suddenly asked to become department head in 1992. She realised she would never get this opportunity again. She did not get time to think it over, but she did get a committee of five men to which she had to report every six months. 'This committee never met', she laughs. As a result, De Paepe was free to do her own thing and expand the small laboratory with fifteen people into an internationally renowned Centre for Medical Genetics with more than 150 collaborators. In 2003 she was promoted to full professor, the highest rang on the academic ladder. In 2002 she was also the first woman to become a member of the Royal Academy of Medicine of Belgium.

The first woman appointed as a part-time lecturer in Ghent was Gerda Bock. In 1954 she received — not without a struggle — a thirty-hour teaching assignment at the School of Criminology and the HIO. De Bock would only be promoted to full professor in 1970. Marthe Versichelen-Terryn preceded her in 1965 as the first woman to break through the ultimate glass ceiling. That was forty years after Irène Van der Bracht succeeded against considerable odds in becoming the first female professor of physical education, then considered a 'lesser' domain. Since Marthe Versichelen-Terryn, there have been only forty-five female full professors at Ghent University, twenty-one of

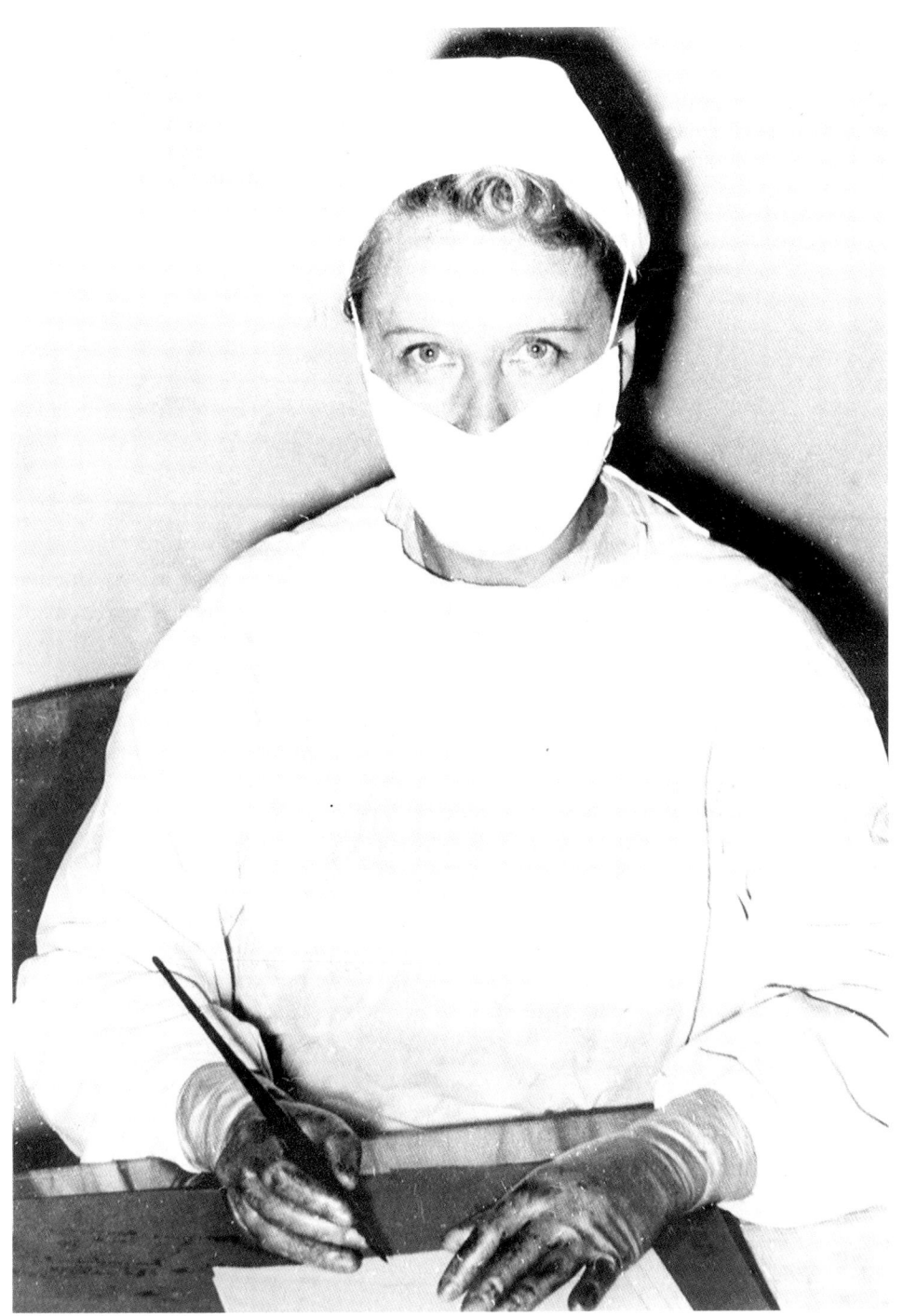

**Yvonne Hynderyckx as surgeon in the Institut Moderne**
The first generations of female students found it difficult to break through the glass ceiling of the university, where they were often not even allowed to start a PhD project.
(Ghent, Universiteitsarchief)

**After 200 years of Ghent University: five female deans**
The board of UGent has a lamentable gender balance. The list of deans is almost exclusively male. From left to right: Gerda De Bock, Yvette Merchiers, Dominique Willems, Anne-Marie Musschoot and Els De Bens.
(Ghent, Universiteitsarchief, photos Michiel Hendryckx, Yvette Merchiers, Christian Kirschen and Hilde Christiaens)

which are still actively employed. This is but a fraction of the 154 male full professors currently serving at the university.

The passage of the ravishing Marthe Versichelen-Terryn did not go unnoticed at the faculty of Law. In *Het scheermes van Ockham* (Occam's razor), his *roman-à-clef*, insider Willy Van Poucke denounces her influence on the promotion of Guido Van Parys at the expense of Herman Brutsaert. When I had just given birth to my eldest son Casper, Versichelen, already emeritus for ten years, phoned me while I was still lying in and convinced me to prepare an article from my dissertation for publication in the *Tijdschrift voor Sociale Wetenschappen*, of which she was editorial secretary until 1997. A decisive woman, as I was able to attest between breast-feeding sessions.

One near-forgotten contemporary of Versichelen, Anna Blancquaert, was daughter of the linguist and former rector Edgard Blancquaert. She graduated in medicine under paediatrician Carlos Hooft in 1951, specialised in paediatric cardiology in Leiden, and played an important role in building a European network of child cardiologists and surgeons. She was the first Belgian cardiologist (male or female) to be elected a fellow of the American College of Cardiology. In 1982 she succeeded in becoming an associate professor at the age of sixty. Twenty years later, the university hospitals of Ghent, Antwerp and Brussels christened the Centre for Congenital Heart Defects with her name, a fine tribute to a doctor who cared for her young patients above all.

The first generations of female professors did not consider themselves feminists, pioneers or role models for other women. Gerda De Bock was in this respect the exception that proves the rule. In her wake, Elisabeth De Cooman and Cecilia Vereecken succeeded in completing an entire academic career at the Higher Institution for Education (HIO), which like the Higher Institution for Physical Education (HILO) offered more prospects for women than the 'classic' faculties. The flamboyant jurist Yvette Merchiers was of the opinion that if women wanted to do the same things as men, then they should. And ask no favours. 'I'm proud of what I've achieved, but not of what I've achieved as a woman', she says. Merchiers nonetheless had a difficult time as an assistant when she had to replace Willy Calewaert during his term as minister. In the large auditorium of the Blandijn she distinctly felt that, as a woman, she was not really welcome. She had to work harder than she felt possible and was judged for her clothing. Merchiers liked to wear close-cut suits and trouser suits, which the students were quick to ridicule in the law revues.

Of the 422 deans who have taken office since 1817, only five have been women. The first was Gerda De Bock, who was dean of the faculty of Psychology and Educational Sciences from 1978 to 1980. In 1992 she was followed by Yvette Merchiers and Dominique Willems at the faculties of Law, and Arts and Philosophy, respectively. In 1995, Anne-Marie Musschoot was elected by the Arts faculty. The fifth was Els De Bens, dean of Political and Social Sciences from 1996 to 2000, which is now more than eighteen years ago. Dominique Willems was called 'Mr Dean' by the faculty and a few colleagues, just as female professors are still often addressed as 'Mrs' instead of 'Professor'. The dean of the faculty of Law literally did not see Yvette Merchiers as part of the faculty council and consistently opened the meeting by saying 'gentlemen'.

Many female academics from previous generations consciously decided to remain childless so they could give their all to their careers. Clinical psychologist Paulette Van Oost was one of them. Her successor, Anne Buysse, recalls how difficult it was to tell her that she was pregnant. This was likewise the case for women who had to report this happy news to a male 'boss'. The right to maternity leave, let alone for extended periods, simply did not exist at the university for a long time, precisely because pregnant professors were such a rarity. Only recently have female professors been able to secure a substitute from a flex pool during maternity leave. Combining work and family continues to be a difficult balance to strike for many female academics. 'We don't have a wife, you know', laughs Buysse.

## UGender policy

The Centre for Gender Studies (then the RUG-Centrum voor Vrouwenstudies) promoted awareness around gender issues from 1991 onwards under the direction of the English studies scholar Marysa De Moor. Thanks to conferences and lunch-time lectures, gender awareness at the university gradually expanded and an interdisciplinary forum for the exchange of scientific research on gender-related themes emerged.

The unacceptable level of representation of women in the professorial corpus, supported by statistics, was brought to the attention of the university administration. A similar dynamic got underway at other universities and in 2002 the Flemish Interuniversity Council (VLIR) Equal Opportunities workgroup was created. Two years later, the Centre for Gender Studies started up the project 'UGender — Equal Opportunities for Men and Women at UGent'. It resulted in policy memos that were later approved by the board of governors, but translating them into practice was another matter entirely. In 2008 the policy unit for Diversity and Gender was established. Several projects were launched to foster women in academic careers, such as the successful Menza project. In 2012 the VLIR worked out the Gender and Higher Education Action Plan, and in 2013 a university charter for sustainable gender policy was drawn up. The policy memorandum Gender-UGent is grafted onto this document, but in the meantime the decree of 13 July 2012 has ensured a decisive breakthrough. Spearheaded by Flemish parliamentarian and UGent alumna Fientje Moerman, that decree requires the administrative bodies of the university to be gender balanced, composed of not more than two-thirds of the same sex. At the request of rector Anne De Paepe, UGent even went a step further than the decree required: 60/40. This forward leap resulted in there being more women elected than men, and ironically meant that men had to be favoured by positive discrimination.

In 2013, UGent played a pioneering role with the first independent academic personnel position for Gender Studies in Belgium. The interuniversity master's degree in Gender and Diversity, which started in 2014 with UGent as the coordinating institution, exceeded all expectations. During the academic year 2016-2017, no less than 190 students enrolled in the master's and transitional programme, clearly pointing to a growing societal need.

The university is no longer a male bastion. The increasing number of female students and researchers challenges classic patriarchal power relations and traditional male sanctuaries. Increasing gender awareness, combined with channels such as the policy unit and Transition UGent, has ensured measures that promote work-life balance and psychosocial well-being in the workplace. It has also ensured greater sensitivity to professorial abuse of power in relation to students and researchers, particularly in the sexual domain. Cases of sexual harassment and sexual abuse that would have been concealed in the past now come to light more quickly, although the number of actual complaints is still quite small. The extent of the difficulties was revealed by a case of sexual harassment on the part of a Ghent professor that was widely covered in the media in 2016. The scandal caused a great deal of commotion and opened the eyes of many people to practices that were covered up in the past. Paradoxically, the affair seems to have furthered the transition to a more woman-friendly university. At the same time, it showed that the traditional disciplinary procedures of the university are insufficient to adequately address the delicate and complex problem of sexual harassment. The new policy framework being prepared by the university under the direction of rector Anne De Paepe is therefore not a minute too soon.

Gender quotas in the councils and committees of UGent are likewise subject to controversy, even among female professors. Many believe that women in a quota system will be 'token females', and they believe that in a long-term positive trend, female talent will rise to the top of its own accord. For her part, Eva Brems notes that a lot has changed in a short time since the introduction of the quota. Not so long ago, gender was a subject for which you were derided; now university leaders openly acknowledge it. Still, Brems believes that as long as there is no quota for the recruitment of female independent academic personnel (ZAP-ers), women will sacrifice a lot of valuable time to policy work in councils and committees without fundamentally changing the structures of the university.

Ann Buysse has struggled with the fact that she was asked to serve on important scientific committees such as the Research Foundation-Flanders (FWO) 'primarily' because of her gender. Her colleague André Van Dierendonck encouraged her, however, by pointing out that she is a role model for a transitional generation. Extra efforts for gender balance in academia are desperately needed. 'See it as a counterweight that compensates for the mechanisms that keep you as a woman from serving on councils and committees.' Buysse is still not in favour of positive discrimination but sees the quota as a temporary and necessary evil needed to change the old system from within.

As rector, Anne De Paepe has become more radical on that score and simply states: 'Without — temporary — quotas in a transitional phase, nothing happens!' Women shoot themselves in the foot when they reject quotas out of a misplaced sense of pride. Specious arguments for preserving the status quo of the university as a male bastion are legion. The biological differences between men and women, however, make gender equality impossible by definition. Equal treatment of men and women therefore increases inequality. For women to have the same rights, opportunities and perspectives as men, there must be compensation. 'And there's nothing wrong with that', concludes De Paepe.

Poster for the interuniversity master's degree in Gender and Diversity, 2016
(Ghent, Gender and Diversity)

**Frans Olbrechts with Dan snake girls
during the Ivory Coast expedition, 1939**
Thanks to Frans Olbrechts, Ghent was among the top institutions for the study of anthropology and African art. The Ivory Coast expedition from November 1938 until September 1939 led to the art-focused research of Pieter Jan Vandenhoute and Albert Maesen among the Dan and Senufo. Their fieldwork formed the basis of the world's first two doctoral theses on African art. The Ghent University Museum (GUM) houses 275 objects from the Ivory Coast expedition.
(Antwerp, MAS, photo Pieter Jan Vandenhoute)

Chapter 10

# COLONIALISM AND DEVELOPMENT COOPERATION

After a chance encounter with prince Damrong of Siam (present-day Thailand), Gustave Rolin-Jaequemyns, founder of the Institut de Droit International, was sent to Bangkok by king Leopold II in 1892. It was the age of Belgian expansion. As an internationally renowned lawyer and polyglot with an extensive network, Rolin-Jaequemyns helped prevent Great Britain, France and Japan from dividing up Siam among themselves. As plenipotentiary Belgian minister and adviser to the enlightened king Rama V, he modernised the state apparatus according to Western models with respect for existing Siamese law. The line of reasoning went that Siam could only preserve its independence by raising the standard of living of its people and reforming the country. Rolin-Jaequemyns effectively launched major public works campaigns, including construction of the railway network. He was also among the initiators of the first Law faculty at Thammasat University, where his statue stands today. In 1898 he was awarded the title of Chao Phya Abhai Raja (prince), the highest privilege of nobility ever granted to a foreigner. The people of Thailand still honour him today as the 'vice king' who guarded Thailand against colonisation. In 2011, Gustave Rolin-Jaequemyns was voted the most influential European in five hundred years of Thai–European relations.

What befell Rolin-Jaequemyns is a pleasant but exceptional story if we consider Ghent University's contribution to colonisation and development cooperation over the long term. The development of colonial (later, overseas) sciences was the work of a few, albeit exceptional individuals. The Belgian colonisation of Congo after 1908 was dominated by French-speakers and Catholics. In this context, colonial education and research at the State University of Ghent never really got off the ground, certainly not when the university Dutchified during the interwar period. Ghent only appeared on the scene in the mid-1950s, at the end of the colonial period, with the creation of its own, quite modest project: Ganda-Congo in Ambaki.

After the independence of Congo in 1960, followed by Rwanda and Burundi in 1962, colonialism shifted to different forms of development cooperation in the former colonies. Development projects also sprang up in other regions in the postcolonial period, particularly in the areas of medicine, agricultural sciences and veterinary medicine. Some of them turned out to be extremely successful and sustainable. In any case, university development cooperation took place in fits and starts, without a coherent vision set out by the institution.

In September 2014, Ghent University Global Campus opened in Songdo, South Korea, financed by the Korean government and aimed at bachelor's education in several spearhead domains in biological, environmental and food technology. Cooperation with one of the Asian Tigers, however, has been dictated by a completely different logic than 'classic' development cooperation.

## Exploring the 'heart of darkness'

Jules Cornet received his doctorate in mineralogy in 1890. His adviser was Alphonse Renard, who had just reached a pinnacle in his career with the results of the *Challenger* expedition, making him one of the founders of marine geology. Cornet would succeed Renard in the domain of Physical Geography in 1903. In May 1891 he embarked from Antwerp with captain Lucien Bia and lieutenant Emile Francqui, subsequently the leading banker of the Société Générale, on the *Africa*, headed for South Katanga.

Their journey was undertaken at the order of king Leopold II. Six years after the Berlin Conference, the 'scramble for Africa' was not yet fully settled. The goal was to block British expansion in the south of Congo Free State, a free trade zone that, on paper, had been under the exclusive dominion of Leopold II since 1885. It is moreover striking how Leopold managed to convince influential but basically anti-colonial figures from the Institut de Droit International, such as Rolin-Jaequemyns and Emile Laveleye, to contribute to the intellectual labour and lobbying needed for the legal construction of his Congo Free State.

The Bia–Francqui expedition landed in Boma. After a difficult journey through Stanley Pool and Lusambo, the caravan reached Katanga. For Leopold II, who was convinced that there was gold in the soil of Katanga, exploration of the area was equal to annexation and the subjugation of the local population. Cornet's mapping of the soil resources was by no means a purely scientific undertaking. As the founder of

**Expedition to Matadi, 1895**
Geologist Jules Cornet (standing).
(Ghent, Universiteitsarchief)

Congolese geology, Jules Cornet contributed to the economic exploitation of Katanga's natural wealth.

At the beginning of 1892, the expedition reached Bunkeya, the capital of the Yeke kingdom. There may not have been any gold in the soil of Central Africa, but the rich veins of copper ore that Cornet discovered in the Kambove mine would figuratively amount to a gold mine for Leopold's Congo Free State and later also for Belgium. During a private dinner at the palace in Laken, the king impressed upon the young geologist that he must not publish his findings on Congo's soil resources without his majesty's express permission. This was only allowed in 1894, after the official signing of the Belgian–British treaty that established the southern borders of Congo Free State. Not a word could be said about the economic potential of the copper mines. In 1906, the Union Minière du Haut Katanga, financed by Emile Francqui's Société Générale, established its factories near the Kambove mine, also known as the 'pearl of Katanga'. The Union Minière confirmed the status of Lilliputian Belgium as the industrial giant of the *belle époque*.

Geological prospecting, South Katanga, 1891
At the rear, with beard and tie, captain and expedition leader Lucien Bia; standing next to him is Jules Cornet. In the foreground, with legs spread, Lieutenant Emile Francqui.
(Ghent, Universiteitsarchief)

In the summer of 1892, Bia died of liver disease. At least 80% of the indigenous bearers died of hunger and deprivation during the expedition. The caravan had covered a total of 6,212 kilometres on foot when the group arrived back in Lusambo after a journey of fourteen months. In August 1895, at the request of the Compagnie du Chemin de Fer du Congo, Cornet set off again along the 366-kilometre Matadi–Leopoldstad railway route, which was then under construction. Together with the Ghent engineer Tobie Claes, inspector-general of Roads and Bridges, he was part of a commission of inquiry tasked with examining whether the horror stories concerning the construction of the railway were justified. The commission's report painted a euphemistic picture of the actual situation.

Meanwhile, the international renown of Cornet's scientific publications on Congolese geology and mineralogy had grown great indeed. In 1897 he was involved in the Colonial Exhibition held in Tervuren as a prelude to the Royal Museum of Belgian Congo (now, Middle Africa). The main attraction was a Congolese 'Negro village' with 144 'real natives'. In addition to twelve reconstructed huts, there was also a grotto that fed the myth of the existence of African cave dwellers. Cornet likewise assumed that a very primitive and aggressive race of pygmies lived in Katanga that resembled apes and practised no agriculture. During his expeditions, however, he had found no evidence to support this assumption. At the end of the nineteenth century, the idea that black people still lived in a prehistoric age, like the cave dwellers of European prehistory, was a tenacious element in the 'civilising mission' that the white coloniser took upon himself.

The colonisation of Congo created a huge laboratory for scientific research into which the Belgian government pumped a great deal of money. In Ghent, fascination for Africa and the exotic was growing slowly. Biologist Camille De Bruyne, who was at the root of the Biogeographic Institute (Biogeografisch Instituut) and 'human geography', preferred to acquire his ethnographic objects from the Museum für Völkerkunde in Berlin.

Alfred Schoep, subsequently executive director of the university, took part in a geological expedition to Katanga in the years 1910-1913. He was still just an assistant at the time. His discovery and description of the uranium-rich minerals in the mines of Kalongwe, Kasolo and Shinkolobwe brought him reputation and fame. The Shinkolobwe mine supplied the enriched uranium used in the atomic bomb dropped on Hiroshima in 1945, and played a central role in the Manhattan Project and the Cold War.

From 1911, internationally renowned botanist Emile De Wildeman taught a course on colonial crops at the Special Trade School in Ghent, the precursor of the faculty of Economics. As curator of the Botanical Garden in Brussels, he dedicated himself to the study of the numerous Congolese plant specimens that arrived in Belgium from 1895 onwards. He became one of the undisputed specialists of Congolese flora and left behind an impressive oeuvre of precious iconographic material without ever having set foot on Congolese soil himself. In 1904, together with Louis Gentil, he published the richly illustrated *Lianes caoutchoutifères de l'Etat Indépendant du Congo*. The plunder economy based on the inhumane cultivation of wild rubber — known as 'red' rubber — brought Leopold II untold riches, but also contributed to his downfall as 'civiliser' of Congo. Emile De Wildeman advocated a more humane form of science in the service of colonial exploitation. He was concerned for the indigenous farmers and the problems caused by deforestation in Congo.

Leopold II's colonial science policy was continued almost seamlessly by his nephew Albert I, who became King of the Belgians in 1909. Congo Free State had been transferred to the Belgian government for just over a year. Only then, on 15 November 1908, to be precise, did Congo become 'Belgian' Congo, a colony in the strict sense of the word.

In 1903 a Laboratoire des Maladies des Pays Chauds was founded in Ghent with sophisticated scientific equipment for bacteriological research. It formed the basis for a new colonial medicine collection. Paul Van Durme, who had specialised in tropical medicine in Liverpool, London, Hamburg, Marseilles, Bordeaux and Paris, was appointed to the Special Trade School to teach the elective courses Diseases of Warm Countries and Colonial Medicine. He was a member of the commission that was responsible for the organisation of an institute or school for exotic medicine and hygiene. In 1906, Leopold II founded the School for Tropical Diseases in Brussels. In 1933, under the impetus of the future Leopold III, the Institute of Tropical Medicine moved to the splendid art deco building in Antwerp where it is still housed today. The special elective courses created by the government in Ghent and Liège had turned out to be insufficient for the 'fight against the scourges of the exotic pathology'. For the royal family, an independent, specialised training that served as a complement to rather than a substitute for the universities answered to the 'real needs of national interest' with an eye towards the 'reunion' of Belgium and Congo.

# Flanders sends forth its sons

From 1920, the Colonial College (Koloniale Hogeschool) in Antwerp took the lead in educating the colonial officials, magistrates and merchants that would populate the network of government institutions and organisations. After the First World War, Belgium also controlled the trust territory Rwanda-Urundi. Ghent University placed itself at the service of colonial ideology and the civilising mission. Paul Van Oye, for example, undertook a dozen or so trips to Congo at the order of the minister of Colonies, to study among other things opportunities for cultivating fish. In 1925 he had live fish shipped from Antwerp to Stanleystad. At the end of the 1920s he expanded Camille De Bruyne's Biogeographic Institute into an Ethnographic Museum.

With the creation of Albert National Park (now Virunga National Park), Belgium played a pioneering role in nature conservation in Africa. In 1932, the Ghent palaeontologist Victor Van Straelen, director of the Museum of Natural History in Brussels, accompanied king Albert on his last journey through the Congo. Several years earlier, he had been on a study trip with prince Leopold and princess Astrid to the Dutch East Indies, where he displayed his considerable organisational talent and enjoyed the full support of the court. In 1933 he was involved in the creation of the National Institute for Agricultural Studies in the Belgian Congo (Nationaal Instituut voor Landbouwstudies in Belgisch-Congo) and in 1934 became the head of and driving force behind the Institute of the National Parks of the Belgian Congo (Instituut der Nationale Parken van Belgisch-Congo). After that, Van Straelen was appointed professor in Ghent and made an impact as chairman of the Charles Darwin Foundation of the Galapagos Islands (1959).

There had been a degree programme in Trade and Colonial Sciences at the Special Trade School since 1919, which included subjects such as colonial economy, law, geography, tropical medicine, construction and transport. During the interwar period, the 'colonial' faculty was expanded with the addition of the jurist Charles De Lannoy, Armand Hacquaert for colonial geology, George Funke for colonial crops, Paul Van Oye for ethnology and Amaat Burssens for indigenous languages. Since its beginnings in 1920, the State Agricultural College (Rijkslandbouwhogeschool) on the Coupure also offered a degree programme in agronomic engineering with a specialisation in colonial agriculture. The engineers who graduated from the programme were plantation administrators who cultivated palm oil, rubber, cacao and cotton for Belgian companies in Central Africa, South East Asia and Latin America. Nevertheless, the attraction of the colonial degree programmes in Ghent was quite limited. The Dutchification of the Special Trade School in 1923 and the Dutch-Language Agricultural College (Landbouwhogeschool) were not ideal for making a smooth transition to the largely French-speaking colonial apparatus.

Victor Van Straelen and king Albert in Congo, 1932
(Ghent, Universiteitsarchief)

In 1947 the Ghent professor Frans Olbrechts was appointed director of the Museum of Belgian Congo in Tervuren. His former student Herman Burssens recalls how the casual lecturer, who smoked fragrant English cigarettes during lectures and was known to order soft drinks and beer on the terrace outside the Boekentoren on sunny spring days, began to treat his students to weekly train and tram tickets to Tervuren so he could hold lectures in his office at the museum. 'Now and then Olbrechts walked with us through the rooms of the museum, or we would visit the reserves, where he made the occasional comment while at the same time giving instructions to the staff.'

The founder of the 'cross-cultural study of art' in Belgium had studied with the world-famous anthropologist Franz Boas at Columbia University in New York in the 1920s, and through him had established contacts with numerous eminent scholars of ethnology and folklore. Boas stimulated Olbrechts to do fieldwork himself. His stay with the Cherokee in North Carolina and among the Tuscarora and Onondaga in New York yielded a unique collection of ethnographic material. After his return from the US, Olbrechts built up the department of ethnography in the Royal Museums for Art and History in Brussels. In the 1930s, Olbrecht shifted his focus from Native American to African cultures. From a prospecting trip, or rather a 'collecting trip' through French West Africa in 1933, he brought back more than 1,800 objects to Brussels. In 1932 he introduced the course 'Art of Primitive and Semi-Civilised Peoples' at the University of Ghent; seven years later it was followed by the Centre for the Study of African

**Frans Olbrechts with his students, ca. 1935**
(Antwerp, Letterenhuis)

Art (Centrum voor de Studie der Afrikaanse Kunst) after he organised a monumental exhibition on the Congo in Antwerp. The Ivory Coast expedition in 1938-1939 once again yielded a treasure trove of objects. Thanks to Olbrechts, Ghent was at the top of the field internationally in anthropology. He was a born lecturer and a very compelling, charismatic man who attached great importance to the popularisation of science. His book *Vlaanderen zendt zijn zonen uit* (Flanders sends forth its sons), published by the Davidsfonds in 1942, is a good example of this engagement.

Amaat Burssens was such a son. He was the younger brother of the expressionist poet Gaston Burssens, a close friend of Paul van Ostaijen. At the age of seventeen, Amaat went to the Yser Front as a volunteer. After the war he studied in Leuven and at the Colonial College. He was also a convinced Flamingant and would take this commitment with him to Congo. Under a pseudonym, he wrote *Een Vlaming op reis door Congo* (A Fleming's travels through the Congo, 1929), in which he not only reports on his first expedition in 1924, but also criticises the French-speaking colonial administration and calls for 'the Negroes, who are receptive to further development' to learn the language of the Flemings as well as that of the Walloons. In the meantime, he applied himself to the study of African languages, particularly Tshiluba and Kiluba. Burssens made seven trips to Congo between 1924 and 1958. In addition to diaries, linguistic notes and sound recordings on wax rolls, the University Library also preserves a beautiful and extensive collection of Burssens's photos.

**Amaat Burssens in Congo, 1937**
Amaat Burssens immersed himself in the culture of the Baluba in Katanga and Kasai, the Abashi in Kivu, the pygmies and the Babira in the Ituri forest, the Bakongo in Lower Congo and the Alur at Lake Albert. His fieldwork yielded a wealth of material. The enormous collection of photographs reflects the erotic, exoticising gaze of the Westerner on black female nudity, but also contains less stereotypical images of Congo during the interwar period. Burssens's reflections on 'Negro word art' in a collection of Congolese fairy tales also bear witness to prevailing prejudices against 'primitives' as well as to a lyrical admiration for his objects of study.
(Ghent, Universiteitsbibliotheek)

Amaat Burssens in Congo, 1937 (Ghent, Universiteitsbibliotheek)

## Ganda-Congo in times of decolonisation

Colonial research and education only really got off the ground in Ghent after the Second World War. Even then, it remained fairly limited in scope. In the meantime, the war had thoroughly redrawn the map of the world. The United States and the Soviet Union had claimed world power for themselves. During the Cold War, the two great powers played a decisive role in the process of decolonisation, not least in Belgian Congo.

The Belgian colonial government wanted to increase its legitimacy in this new context by increasing its scientific activities and reinforcing the Belgian presence in Congo and Rwanda-Urundi. It was the time of 'developmental colonialism', which sought to 'neutralise' the most flagrant forms of exploitation with modern scientific tools. Lode De Wilde, professor of tropical botany at the Ghent Agricultural College and former plantation director of the Bamboli Culture Society (Bamboli Cultuur Maatschappij), stated in 1948 that: 'In Congo, the White Man has subjected the resources "subsoil", "agricultural land" and "human beings" to empirical exploitation at a pace that left science in the dust.'

Combating diseases and food shortages caused tropical agriculture and medicine in Congo to take flight as scientific research came to be increasingly independent of the colonial state. Unilateral exploitation was gradually replaced by the insight that the 'civilisation' of the Congolese was not merely a one-way street. African traditions and their specific adaptation to Western culture had to be considered. The result of the acculturation process was a mix of (desirable) African and Western elements. Nevertheless, Belgium hardly distanced itself from the colonial paradigm. Racial segregation remained in place in the towns and villages. In addition, it was inconceivable that the colonial sciences themselves would be held up for critical examination.

In response to the suggestion of the ministry of Colonies to invest in the education of a colonial elite, De Wilde founded the Colonial University Study Group (Koloniale Universitaire Studiekring, or KUS) in 1946 in the hope of stimulating the colonial ambitions of professors and students — without much success. The ULB and especially Leuven, then still French-speaking, continued to have an advantage over the Dutch-speaking University of Ghent despite the efforts of individual professors.

In 1954, the year that the Catholic satellite university of Leuven, Lovanium, opened its doors in Leopoldstad, the state universities of Ghent and Liège received more room for manoeuvre under liberal minister of colonies Auguste Buisseret. The violent battle of the schools that raged under the socialist-liberal government of Achiel Van Acker was carried over into the colonies under the motto 'the time of the missions is over'. As long as the Catholics had control over the ministry of Colonies, there was hardly any funding for the two state universities in this area. Now the university 'scramble for Congo' could really begin. In 1955 the Université Officielle du Congo et de Ruanda-Urundi was opened in Elisabethstad as an answer to Lovanium. A number of Ghent University professors, among them Lode De Wilde and Natalis De Cleene, were involved in this bilingual university and defended the Dutch language against the largely French-speaking administration. After Congolese independence and the Katanga secession, historian Jan Dhondt and after him the jurist René Dekkers served as rector in Lubumbashi (1963-1970).

The Université Officielle du Congo in Lubumbashi, 1964
Rector Jan Dhondt during the official opening of the academic year 1964-1965.
(Ghent, Universiteitsarchief)

The Congo Commission, a Ghent think tank dating from 1947, was reinforced in 1955 with colonial heavyweights such as De Wilde, Olbrechts and Van Straelen. The geologists Armand Hacquaert and René Tavernier, the philosopher Edgar De Bruyne (briefly minister of Colonies in 1945) and the economist André Vlerick were also members.

Ganda-Congo saw the light of day in 1956 and had as its goal the establishment of a colonial campus for medicine and interdisciplinary scientific research. The University of Leuven was already present in Kisantu near Leopoldstad, and the ULB was based in Uele. Much to the chagrin of Vlerick, Liège claimed Elisabethstad and the rich region of Katanga. All that remained for Ghent was Ambaki in the densely populated Ituri region near Lake Albert and the Ugandan border. For the Belgian government, Ghent University's presence in the peripheral regions in the north-east of Congo was ideal for resisting 'the threat of Islam, Arabic imperialism and Ugandan Alur irredentism'. The Fund for Indigenous Welfare (Fonds voor Inlands Welzijn) was only too happy to finance a hospital there. The dean of the faculty of Medicine, Jean-Jacques Bouckaert, subsequently rector, called on the services of Jan Cnops, architect of the Ghent Academic Hospital (AZ). He drew up the design for a hospital complex

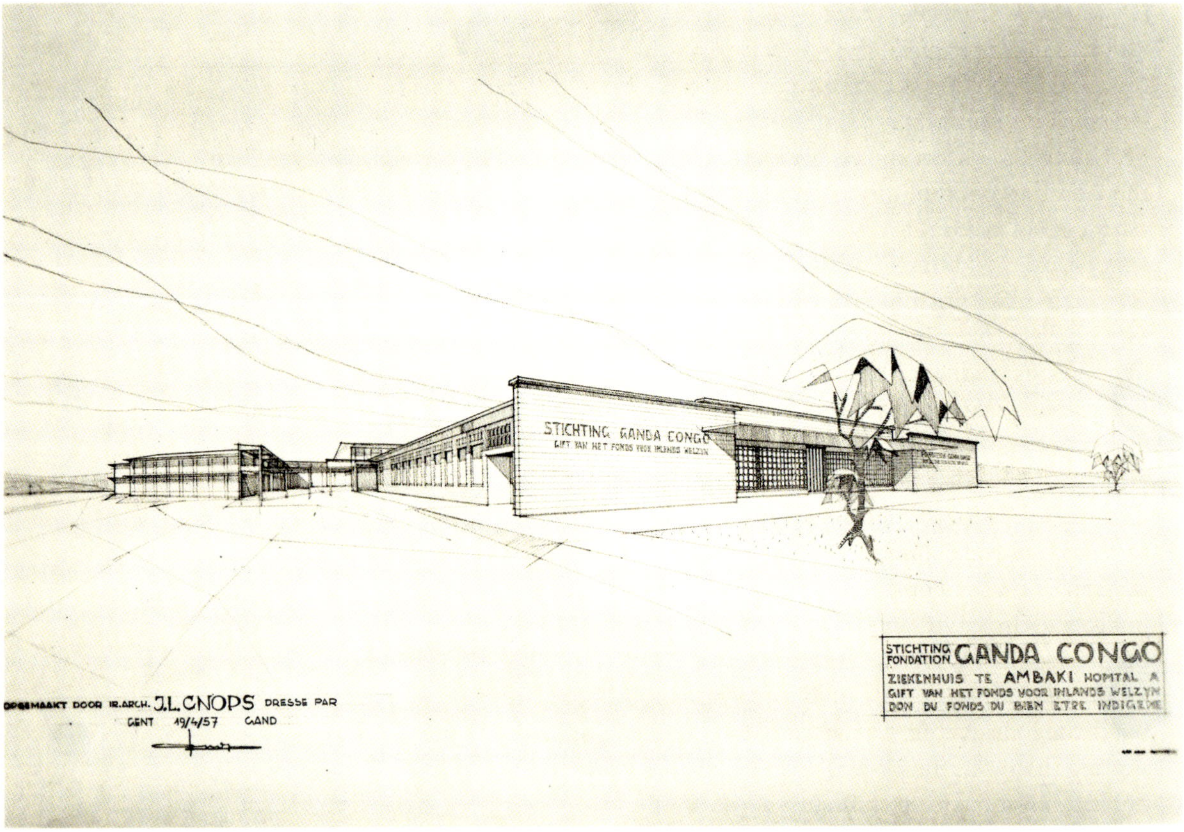

**Design for a hospital in Ambaki, 1950s**
Drawing and scale model by architect Jan Cnops for the Ganda-Congo foundation, with the support of the Fund for Indigenous Welfare. Congo's independence proved problematic, and only the foundations of the hospital complex would be built.
(Ghent, Universiteitsarchief)

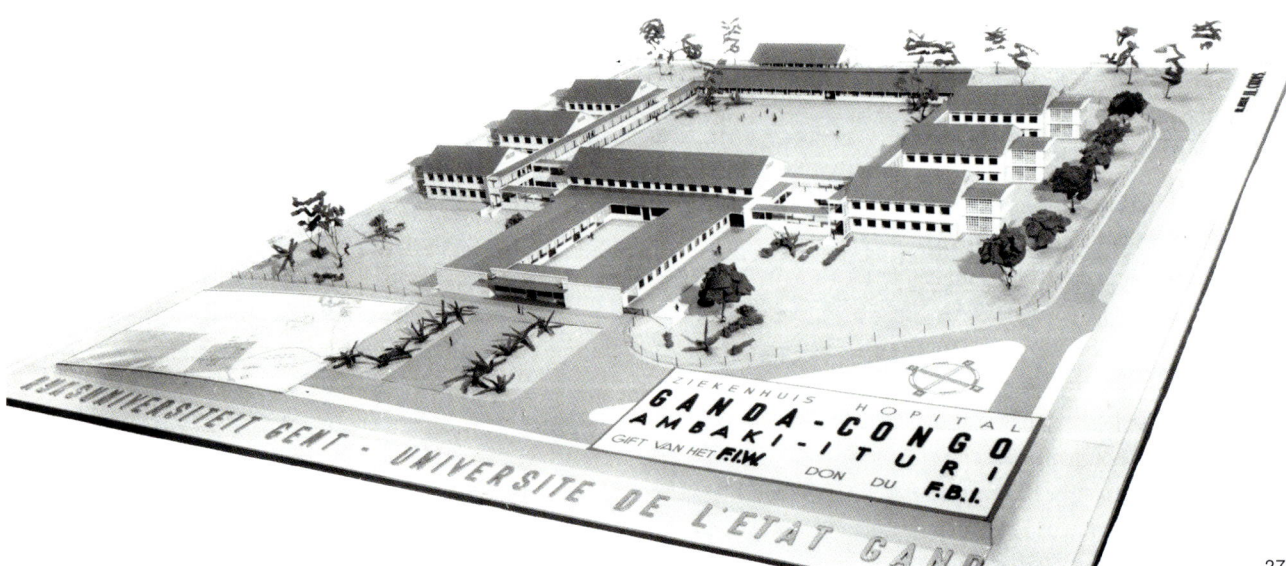

in Ambaki. Eventually, Congolese doctors were to be trained there under the supervision of the Ghent faculty of Medicine.

In the summer of 1958, several leading researchers made an exploratory trip to Ituri headed by Bouckaert and rector Pieter Lambrechts. Amaat Burssens had mapped out the whole thing. Biologist Lucien De Coninck reported very enthusiastically about the region, the flora and fauna, the hot-water springs and 'the tribes that live from the cultivation of livestock and are beginning to take an interest in agriculture and cultures'. The 'thriving mine exploitation' in the goldmine of Kilo-Moto was interesting for Ganda-Congo. 'In short, this is a region where an exceptionally rich work terrain lies open', according to De Coninck.

The mine site had a surface area the size of Flanders and employed more than 40,000 workers in conditions that were no longer possible in Belgium. There were major problems in terms of providing sufficient food, housing and health care. The Ghent parasitologist Pieter Gustaaf Janssens had been employed in the region since 1937 as a colonial company doctor in charge of two hospitals and a laboratory. In 1955, Janssens published on the extremely high infant mortality among the workers' families at the mines. It was typical of his engagement to see health problems from a broader social perspective.

In 1959 a dozen or so assistants were dispatched to put his research into practice. Among them was the psychologist Etienne Van der Straeten, who spent eleven months in Congo and — in contrast to other young colleagues — took his mission very seriously. He contacted the Alur people in the north-east and learned their language. His psychological-cultural-anthropological research fitted into the new concept of acculturation, which appraised local traditions and customs according to their value. Amaat Burssens was also aware of this and warned against a colonial policy that 'endangered the inner balance and spiritual health of the population' with all the consequences this entails.

**Etienne Van der Straeten, ca. 1960**
Psychologist Etienne Van der Straeten wanted to stay in Nyarambe in the hot summer of 1960, but his adviser William De Coster obliged him to return from Congo and leave everything behind. The result of his fieldwork is part of the heritage of Ganda-Congo.
(Ghent, Universiteitsarchief)

The change of course came too late, however. On 30 June 1960, king Baudouin proclaimed the independence of Congo in Leopoldstad. In a speech permeated by paternalistic colonialism, he called independence the ultimate 'crowning achievement of the work conceived by the genius of king Leopold II'. The first elected prime minister of independent Congo, Patrice Lumumba, saw things somewhat differently. He took the floor unexpectedly and gave the historic address that also turned out to be his death warrant. A few days later, mutiny broke out in the Congolese army. There were Belgian victims and the government sent troops to protect Belgians in Congo, a flagrant violation of the recently acquired national sovereignty. On 11 July 1960, with the support of Belgium, Moïse Tshombe declared the independence of the rich mining province of Katanga, followed several days later by the diamond province Kasai. Many Belgians fled in the hot summer of 1960, among them the researchers from

Ghent in Ituri. Many members of the Ganda-Congo foundation were convinced that, after this 'intermezzo', they would be able to resume their activities. Like many other Belgians, they misjudged the situation completely. Half-hearted plans for the construction of the hospital were never realised. In 1970 the Ganda-Congo foundation was permanently disbanded. The colony had become a developing country. All that is left of the colonial dream are the overgrown foundations of the hospital in Ituri.

## Medical development cooperation

In 1955, Jef Van Bilsen published his *Dertigjarenplan voor de ontvoogding en onafhankelijkheid van Belgisch Afrika* (Thirty-year plan for the emancipation and independence of Belgian Africa). It highlights just how suddenly the Congo crisis of 1960-1961 developed. The charismatic founder of Third World studies already had a remarkable professional journey behind him before his appointment in Ghent in 1962. As a law student in Leuven, he was part of the radical Flemish nationalist student movement and in the 1930s worked closely with Joris Van Severen, with whom he later quarrelled. During the Second World War, Van Bilsen was involved with the upper circles of the Catholic party and maintained contact with the government in London. In 1946-1947, with the support of the government in Leopoldstad, he set up an African division of the press agency Belga, which he led until 1949. In 1950 he became a lecturer at the Colonial College in Antwerp. Although he was already vilified in conservative colonial circles, even with his long-term plan, Van Bilsen proposed that Belgian and Western interests could best be preserved by creating stable administrative structures and conferring power on an African elite with a solid political education. After the Bandung Conference in 1955, the independence of Sudan that same year and that of Ghana in 1957, it became increasingly clear that the decolonisation of Congo would not wait thirty more years. In 1958, on the occasion of the World Expo, a Congolese elite of *évolués* came to Brussels. There, Van Bilsen had contact with the subsequent leaders of Congolese independence: Joseph Kasavubu, Patrice Lumumba, Moïse Tshombe and Joseph-Désiré Mobutu. Van Bilsen was adviser to the 'ethnic' Abako party and personal counsellor of Kasavubu. In 1960 he advised the round-table conference on the independence of Congo in Brussels. As to his exact role in the conflict between president Kasavubu and prime minister Lumumba and his relationship with the US, the last word has yet to be written. On 17 January 1961, with the knowledge of the Belgian government, Lumumba was murdered by the authorities of independent Katanga.

That same year, Van Bilsen went to Harvard, where he worked with Henry Kissinger. In 1962 he was one of the initiators of the Belgian Service for Development Cooperation (Belgische Dienst voor Ontwikkelingssamenwerking, or DOS, from 1971 the General Board for Development Cooperation, or Algemeen Bestuur voor Ontwikkelingssamenwerking, also known as the ABOS), of which he was the first secretary-general. In the 1960s he was also active as the royal commissioner for development cooperation (1965) and cabinet chief for Development cooperation of the Christian Democrat minister of Foreign Affairs, Pierre Harmel (1966-1968).

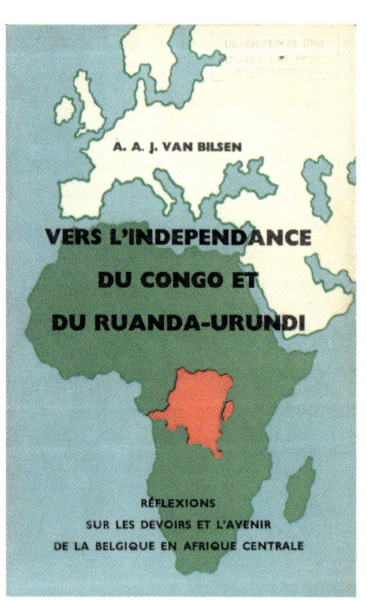

Jef Van Bilsen's thirty-year plan, 1955
(Ghent, Universiteitsbibliotheek)

University Hospital
in Butare, 1991
(Ghent, Universiteitsarchief)

Thus, Van Bilsen was a key figure in the transition from Belgian colonial administration to postcolonial development cooperation.

In this capacity, Van Bilsen commissioned another key figure, Pieter Gustaaf Janssens, in the meantime director of the Institute of Tropical Medicine and lecturer in Tropical Pathology in Ghent, to assist in the turbulent faculty of Medicine at the Université National du Ruanda (UNR) in Butare. The Belgian mandate area Rwanda-Urundi had become independent in 1962, just as abruptly as Congo. As in Congo during the colonial period, there was little in the way of higher education. Medical assistants were trained, but not doctors. In the summer of 1966, professor of social medicine Karel Vuylsteek set up a new faculty of Medicine under the supervision of Ghent; in 1967, Laurent Vandendriessche was named dean.

Remarkably, this included a centre for traditional medicine, the Centre Universitaire de Recherche sur la Pharmacopée et la Médicine Traditionelle. Research into the chemical composition of medicinal plants even led to the dissemination of plant-based medicines. Hence, it was not simply a question of medical traffic in one direction only. Nevertheless, in 1990, André De Schaepdryver, for a long time a driving force behind the Butare project, would write a critical report pointing out its structural flaws. The development model in Butare was strongly oriented towards Western models of modernisation and progress. The greater part of the budget went to curative medicine, aimed at a largely urban elite. Preventive medicine aimed at local communities had been neglected. Two hundred and fifty Rwandan doctors graduated between 1966 and 1990, most of whom were engaged in the municipal hospitals of Butare and Kigali even though the need for medical care was much greater in rural areas.

Peter Piot experienced this himself in the autumn of 1976 when he went to the village of Yambuku on the Congo River, where the outbreak of an unknown disease was causing high fever, diarrhoea and severe haemorrhaging. Two years after graduating from Ghent University, Piot was employed at the Institute of Tropical Medicine in Antwerp as a specialist in microbiology. Since his youth in Keerbergen, his only ambition had been to get out of Belgium. Father Damiaan's pilgrimage site in neighbouring Tremolo made him dream of distant lands. The Tropical Institute gave the children of May 1968 wings, enabling them to demonstrate their solidarity with what was then known as the Third World. Development work tended to exoticise societal engagement, but at the faculty of Medicine in Ghent in the 1970s, it was certainly not a central concern.

Pieter Gustaaf Janssens coordinated Ghent-Butare in the 1970s, when the collaboration with the Rwandan government, which from the outset considered Ghent's support temporary, began to show cracks. The agreement was renewed three times with the explicit aim of increasing the number of Rwandans on the faculty. Between 1966 and 1993, thirty-seven Rwandans from the UNR received a PhD in Belgium, ten of them in Ghent. The readiness and dedication of qualified professors to commit to Rwanda on a long-term basis, however, was gradually eroded. Janssens referred to the inexperienced Belgian applicants that did apply as 'freebooters', because in his view they were mainly concerned with avoiding mandatory military service. Between 1974 and 1978, twenty-one recently graduated Rwandan doctors also took up responsible posts in the faculty. They were not always the most competent candidates for the job. Hasty 'Africanisation' undermined the functioning of the faculty. In the meantime, financial management was in the hands of the ABOS, and the role of the Ghent faculty had become largely educational and administrative. In 1975, Marleen Temmerman served as an intern there at her own cost.

In September 1976 a blue thermos containing blood samples from a Flemish missionary nun was delivered from Kinshasa to the Antwerp laboratory for microbiology. Under the electron microscope the researchers saw — to their great surprise — not a 'normal' virus but a huge, worm-like structure that had never previously been observed. With a C-130 arranged by Mobutu's personal physician, the twenty-seven-year-old Peter Piot, who had never been to Africa, was flown from the Congolese capital to the rain forest to study this mysterious virus on location and stop the epidemic. After three months of observation and improvisation, he succeeded. The virus was given the name of a neighbouring river, the Ebola. Forty years later, the sociopolitical circumstances in which the Ebola virus thrives have hardly changed: political destabilisation, a dysfunctional health system, superstition, denial, poverty. The classic curative approach, with vaccines, medicines, isolation and quarantine is not enough without considering political, social and cultural factors. In addition, there is the failure of international organisations such as the World Health Organization (WHO), which are supposed to guarantee the universal

**President Kayibanda in Ghent city hall, 1966**
In 1966, Rwandan president Grégoire Kayibanda visited the AZ in Ghent. This sealed cooperation between Ghent and Butare.
(Ghent, Universiteitsarchief)

human right to health. When a new, severe Ebola epidemic broke out in West Africa in 2014, the WHO only sounded the alarm after two Americans were flown home with the disease. In the meantime, there had already been more than a thousand deaths in Africa. By then, Piot had the moral authority to denounce this distressing fact internationally. In his autobiography *No Time to Lose. A Life in Pursuit of Deadly Viruses* from 2012, he reports on his life-long commitment to placing viruses such as Ebola and AIDS in a global sociopolitical policy framework. For the most influential Belgian in the world, science cannot be seen in isolation from activism and politics.

In 1984 the Belgian government abruptly cut off financing to the Ghent-Butare project and it was officially dissolved. Cooperation was reduced to a 'sister' programme with the Université Nationale du Ruanda (UNR): an exchange of lecturers and students and limited research funding. During the Rwandan genocide of 1994, the faculty buildings were plundered and the medical equipment and library collection stolen and destroyed. Dozens of Rwandan doctors who had studied in Ghent were murdered in the civil war. The hatred between the Hutu and Tutsi — ethnic identities that were introduced by the Belgian administration after the First World War — also claimed victims among the colleagues within the walls of the hospital. From 2012 to 2016, Rwanda was no longer on the list of twenty partner countries for Belgian university development cooperation in the framework of the Flemish Interuniversity Council (VLIR-UOS). The Ghent-Butare project was a disastrous failure because of geopolitical shifts and national political decisions. It prompted Ghent emeritus professor Leo De Ridder to ask a pertinent question in *Tijdschrift voor Geneeskunde*: 'What have we been doing [there] for the last half-century? And why?'

The VLIR-UOS *'former les formateurs'* programme for the reorganisation of medical education in Cambodia after the Khmer Rouge (1975-1979) and Vietnamese occupation (1979-1989), however, did manage to succeed. The NGO Doctors Without Borders — under the chairmanship of Ghent alumnus Reginald Moreels, later Belgian state secretary for Development Cooperation — asked French-speaking universities in Belgium and France to set up a 'medical university' in Phnom Penh. The project envisaged the education of lecturers who could then start training students at the medical faculty themselves. In the end, only Ghent and Leuven participated. Under the leadership of histologist Leo De Ridder (UGent) and heart surgeon Raf Suy (KULeuven), doctors were trained as professors from 1991 to 1996 and given a chance to serve as interns in Belgium and France. The cooperation continues today: under the leadership of Ghent professor of surgery Piet Pattyn, joint PhDs are still earned in Ghent and Phnom Penh.

## 'Saint Bob' and the 'white man's burden'

In 1967 the Interfaculty Study and Training Centre for Development Cooperation (Interfacultair Studie- en Vormingscentrum voor Ontwikkelingssamenwerking, or ISVO) was set up with the aim of reinforcing development cooperation from Ghent University with an interdisciplinary (Dutch-language) postgraduate programme of one year. Its first director was paediatrician Carlos Hooft. The new postcolonial context required a thorough overhaul of the colonial education that had been offered up to then. After Congo and Rwanda-Urundi ceased to be Belgian colonies, the field of action expanded considerably to include North and West Africa, South East Asia and Latin America.

Lode De Wilde was a protagonist in the transition to a postcolonial university. He proposed transforming Ganda-Congo into UNIKO–Ganda (Universitaire Koöperatie Overzee–Ganda) and including other developing countries in its scope. The agriculture faculty, where the loss of the colonies was felt the strongest, would also contribute most to the new 'development education', which for the first time was also aimed at students from the 'overseas territories'. It indicates just how much continuity remained with colonial thought patterns. The 'white man's burden' of bearing Western civilisation as an elevated means to 'help' developing countries did not disappear immediately after decolonisation. During the Cold War, many were also motivated by anti-communist sentiments to keep Third World countries out of the hands of the Soviet Union by means of development aid.

Some projects were highly successful from the outset and remain so today. In 1963, under the impulse of René Tavernier, the International Training Centre for Postgraduate Soil Scientists (ITC) was created. Half a century later, this programme can boast of more than a thousand alumni from more than ninety countries. The ITC also cooperates with the International Centre for Eremology (ICE), founded in 1988 by the agricultural engineer Marcel De Boodt. In addition to soil erosion and soil conservation in humid, tropical regions, De Boodt's research also takes in the desert regions of North Africa, the Middle East and Latin America in order to prevent desertification. The highly mediatised African famines in the 1970s and 1980s opened the eyes of the world. In 1986, Bob Geldof received an honorary doctorate from Ghent University in recognition of his humanitarian contributions in the context of Live Aid (later the subject of controversy). Saint Bob already doubted that De Boodt's project would receive financial support from Live Aid during the heavily attended press conference in the Blandijn's Auditorium E.

**International Training Centre for Postgraduate Soil Scientists, 1988**
International students at work in Ghent.
(Ghent, Universiteitsarchief)

In 1989 the ICE started with the 'Green Wave', a reforestation project that made desert soil fertile again. In the early 1990s, De Boodt had a 12-metre-long wind and rain tunnel built for experimental research on erosion processes in the faculty of Bioengineering Sciences. Since 2008, the ICE has occupied the prestigious UNESCO Chair on Eremology, one of three Flemish UNESCO chairs.

In the meantime, the Interfaculty Student and Training Centre for Development Cooperation (ISVO) had already ceased to exist because of its limited financial strength and disagreement between the exact and social sciences. In addition, the postgraduate programme in Development Cooperation only attracted a small number of foreign students because of the language barrier. In 1986 the programme was transferred to the Law faculty, where Jef Van Bilsen had led the department for the Study of Third World Problems since 1974. Van Bilsen had gradually distanced himself from the postcolonial Catholic establishment and his progressive image resonated with many among the post-'68 generation, the Third World movement and NGOs interested in developing cooperation.

Van Bilsen could offer the students guest lectures by prominent figures such as Ivan Illich, Johan Galtung and Julius Nyerere. He thus paved the way for a new, non-paternalistic approach to the global South. In 1992 his pupil and successor Ruddy Doom helped found the faculty of Political and Social Sciences. The Third World Studies department has since been rechristened the department of Conflict and Development Studies and is presided over by Koen Vlassenroot. His research focuses on armed groups and spiralling violence in East Congo that are the result of the erosion of state power after the Cold War.

The Political and Social Sciences faculty, 1992
The founders of Pol&Soc, from left to right: Helmut Gaus, Hillary Page, Bob Van Hooland, Frida Saeys, Ruddy Doom, August Van den Brande, Els De Bens, Herman Brutsaert and Dirk Voorhoof.
(Ghent, Universiteitsarchief, photo Willy Dée)

## The Artemia Reference Centre: a unique story

Another important protagonist in the field of development cooperation is Patrick Sorgeloos. The biologist, who retired in 2013, still had one major frustration after his extraordinary career: that aquaculture in Africa develops so slowly. Only 1.8% of all aquaculture worldwide is located on that continent, where there is an immense latent potential. Although many students from Africa took (and still take) an international master's in Aquaculture, education and a lack of faith in their own ability are the major problem in his view. Vietnam's history, which is where it all began for Sorgeloos, shows that things can be different. At the beginning of the 1980s, Vietnam was a lot worse off than many African countries today. After the disastrous war between the communist North and the US-supported South, the country was left with nothing. The new socialist republic was moreover boycotted economically by the West. In this difficult context, Sorgeloos explored the 3,000 kilometre Vietnamese coast in search of brine at the request of the UN Food and Agriculture Organization in 1982. In the Mekong Delta, perhaps the poorest and most remote area of the country, he found what he was looking for: an ideal biotope for his Artemia brine shrimp.

The special feature of this small (1 centimetre) shrimp is that its embryonic development stops after about 4,000 cells. In the past it was thought that this was its dormant state, but it actually has to do with a reversible death that can last up to fifty years and perhaps even longer. In the right conditions, brine shrimp can be brought back to life by human intervention. For his thesis, Sorgeloos was assigned the task of developing a standard cultivation test for Artemia by Anatomy professor Julien Fautrez. He

Patrick Sorgeloos in Vietnam, 2006
(Ghent, Laboratory of Aquaculture & Artemia Reference Centre)

suspected that understanding the shrimp's reversible death would provide better insight into the division of cancer cells. In 2015, Chinese researchers were indeed able to identify the gene that halts the embryonic growth of Artemia.

After his studies, Sorgeloos was able to follow courses at the Marine Lab of Duke University in the US, thanks to his adviser, Guido Persoone. By chance, the professor there — a world authority on the development of crabs — used Artemia to feed the crab larvae. He had found the subject of his PhD: Artemia as a resource for aquaculture. Sorgeloos began to write letters — this was the predigital era — to universities all over the world to map out where Artemia could be found. Every now and then he received letters back: from Russia, Australia and other regions. Subsequently, while still young and relatively inexperienced, he was allowed to represent Belgium at the first world congress on aquaculture in Kyoto. As it turned out, it was the opportunity of a lifetime. At this very formal conference, held under the auspices of the UN, the future of Artemia as baby food for fish was to be decided. Modern aquaculture was at a pivotal moment in its history. Techniques for cultivating fish had spectacular results. The Japanese were the first to import Artemia from the US. They purchased the dried eggs in pots and cultivated them in seawater, so that they could use them a day later as food for baby sea bream or shrimp. However, the Indian chair of the congress rightly pointed out that in developing countries, such as India, Thailand or the Philippines, it made no sense to practise aquaculture if cold, hard cash in the form of dollars was needed to buy Artemia for the fish. Sorgeloos then had the courage to claim that although the situation was true, it was also artificial, as Artemia was available all over the world — a claim he dared to make based on the few letters he had received in response to his inquiry. An Australian was sitting to his left and a Brazilian to his right — the admiral Paolo Moreira da Silva, a national hero — once again a happy coincidence. They confirmed the hypothesis of the young researcher from Ghent. In the resolutions of the congress, Artemia was given a chance and then the ball really got rolling. Sorgeloos was invited to Brazil, where, at the greatest salt works in the world, north of Recife, there were apparently no Artemia to be found. Fortunately, he had had the presence of mind to bring along the right sort of Artemia and was able to inoculate them on site — at a time when the concept of biodiversity did not yet exist. This was in April 1977. In August the first tonne of Artemia could be harvested. The news went round the world and the FAO was quick to jump on it. Several months later, Patrick Sorgeloos found himself with his wife and children in the Philippines. Artemia was indeed the key for the exponential development of aquaculture. In the 1970s, 95% of all aquatic products in world trade still came from fishing; today, half comes from aquaculture.

Sorgeloos's cultivation projects in Brazil and the Philippines were so successful that he was advised to patent his invention. In 1983, Artemia Systems NV was set up with financing from the Regional Investment Company of Flanders (Gewestelijke Investeringsmaatschappij Vlaanderen, or GIMV), Petrofina and Tractebel, each for 10 million Belgian francs. The patents were registered under the name of the Artemia Study Bureau (Studievennootschap nv Artemia), which allowed Ghent University to participate with profit shares. For Sorgeloos, it was a very frustrating period because, as a board member, he knew nothing about business, and within the university ignorance on that score was also considerable. Between 1983 and 1986 the company emerged from the red. When it reached break-even, GIMV sold its share to Petrofina and exited for good. Petrofina was extremely interested in the research and invested heavily to promote it. The underlying reason was Sorgeloos's extensive address book. Petrofina was thus able to secure the first concession for oil exploration in Vietnam.

At the beginning of the 1980s, the country still relied exclusively on traditional fishing. In cooperation with Can Tho University, Sorgeloos laid the basis for Vietnam's booming aquaculture industry. Gigantic fish and shrimp farms have been responsible for a growing share of Vietnam's rapid economic expansion since 2000. Few know that the lucrative (and sometimes controversial) shrimp and pangasius fillets that have flooded supermarkets and restaurants since then started off in an embryonic state in Ghent ...

At the end of the 1980s, Petrofina sold Artemia Systems to INVE, a Flemish company active in animal nutrition. Ghent University did not earn a single cent out of the transaction, but the whole construction nevertheless yielded international prestige and therefore symbolic capital. The good reputation and scientific know-how of the University of Ghent is good for 1 million euros in research contracts annually. Its field of action has since expanded to include the entire world.

Up to the end of the 1990s, Sorgeloos continued to energise aquaculture through development projects in countries that are now doing quite well under their own steam. The first European-funded Science Technology Development (or STD) project

**Aquaculture in Zanzibar, 2008**
(Ghent, Universiteitsarchief, department of Marine Biology)

**Aquaculture in Vietnam, 2006**
Children of local salt farmers on their way to school passing the salt extraction fields.
(Ghent, Laboratory of Aquaculture & Artemia Reference Centre)

in China even served as a bargaining chip at the highest level of diplomacy. In June 1989 diplomatic relations with China were broken off after the events of Tiananmen Square. Nevertheless, two years later, with the outbreak of the first Gulf War, Europe was able to convince China to approve Operation Desert Storm in the Security Council on the condition that diplomatic relations be restored. Sorgeloos's project, which had been put on the back burner until then, played a role in the negotiations. When he received the China Friendship Award in Beijing in 2014, which is the highest award China grants to foreign experts, the story could finally be made public. At any rate, it set the tone for fruitful cooperation with China, which has continued for more than three decades. In November 2016, the FAO set up an Artemia Reference Centre in China modelled on that of Ghent.

The Ghent Artemia Reference Centre was created in 1978 at the request of the FAO and is still the number one internationally when it comes to baby food for fish and shellfish. The synergy between research, education and services to society appeared to be a magic formula. Interaction with development cooperation actually arose of its own accord. From 1978 onwards, this laboratory hosted one foreign student after the other. In 1985, king Baudouin visited incognito and seemed especially interested in the miraculous multiplication of the Artemia brine shrimp. Ever since then, Sorgeloos has maintained good contacts with the Belgian crown. The support of rector Leon De Meyer, who was always glad to accompany Sorgeloos and his colleagues on trips abroad, was also an important factor. He encouraged Sorgeloos to establish an English-language master's programme in aquaculture. It was launched in 1991, initially in cooperation with the university of Wageningen. In the faculty of Agricultural Sciences, however, Sorgeloos's efforts were not always appreciated as they were abroad. He literally worked in the margins: until 2016, his laboratory was located in the basement of the Rozier, where an extremely dedicated team of twenty-five to thirty researchers worked on externally funded projects. The 'Flemish' orientation of a project in a niche domain close to home was not for him. Throughout his career, Patrick Sorgeloos has supervised seventy dissertations by researchers from twenty-one different countries. Every one of them has become an international ambassador for UGent.

**Farming installations for Artemia brine shrimp, 1985**
Until 2016, the laboratory of the Artemia Reference Centre was located in the basement of the Rozier next to the departments of the Arts and Philosophy faculty.
(Ghent, Universiteitsarchief)

At the end of the 1990s the Belgian government transferred the financing of university development cooperation from the from the General Organisation for Development Cooperation (ABOS) to its university equivalent (VLIR-UOS). This implied a shift from demonstration projects to 'education and training' in partner countries. In this new context, state secretary Erik Derycke launched the idea of setting up a master's programme in aquaculture in Ecuador, which over the short term meant a loss of foreign students in Ghent, but over the long term promised to forge close ties between the partner universities. In this way, 'capacity building' became the key term in transcending the classic forms of development cooperation in spite of the very limited resources of the Belgian/Flemish government.

## Africa revisited

Ghent University can boast of the only fully fledged degree programme in African Languages and Cultures in Belgium. There is a great deal of expertise on Africa spread throughout the university. Since 2007, it has been bundled together as the Ghent Africa Platform (Gents Afrikaplatform, or GAP), which along with the China Platform, India Platform, Russia Platform, ASEANPlus and CESAM (Latin America) forms one of the six regional platforms that supports the internationalisation of UGent.

The genealogy of the Africa Platform takes us back to the colonial period. Already in the second half of the 1950s, Amaat Burssens nurtured plans for an interfaculty research institute for African sciences, with a broad range of disciplines, from languages and ethnography to psychology, public health and agricultural engineering. This proved to be too ambitious. In May 1958 the faculty of Arts officially opened its Higher Institute for Oriental, East European and African Linguistics and History (Hoger Instituut voor Oosterse, Oost-Europese en Afrikaanse Taalkunde en Geschiedenis). Rector Pieter Lambrechts stressed that the Ghent Institute was not to be limited to linguistics alone: 'I would not like to see the operation degenerate to linguistic *Kleinarbeit*.' Oriental problems were at once 'everlasting' and 'current', and he found it hard to imagine that someone who is specialised in classical Arabic would not be concerned with the penetration of Islam into Belgian Congo. 'Our Institute must learn to see Oriental problems in a broad context and must also be set up for it.'

In its first year, exactly one student signed up for the Africa programme: Marcel Van Spaandonck. He would become the driving force behind African Studies in Ghent. Together with Lode De Wilde and art historian Herman Burssens, he was one of the founders of the Africa Association of Ghent University (AVRUG), the forerunner of the Ghent Africa Platform (GAP). After decolonisation, however, African studies research in Belgium struggled with limited resources and lack of interest on the part of government. The African Studies programme in Ghent is thus a story of trial and error.

In a programme with roots in colonialism, 'decolonising the mind', a motto coined by the Kenyan writer Ngugi wa Thiong'o in 1986, was a long-term process. The history of African culture was often approached not from the perspective of Africa itself, but through a Western filter. Only one professor with African roots, Ngo Kabuta, was ever permanently employed by the African Studies department, from 1992 to 2011. Only very recently has the exchange been expanded by attracting doctoral students, assistants and visiting professors from African countries and strengthening ties to the diaspora in Belgium. The GAP plays a stimulating role in this process by educating a network of experts across disciplinary boundaries, faculties and continents.

The first chairwoman of the GAP was Marleen Temmerman. She went to Kenya in 1987 in the context of a research project on AIDS set up by Peter Piot. In October 1983, six years after the discovery of the Ebola virus, Piot encountered more than fifty AIDS

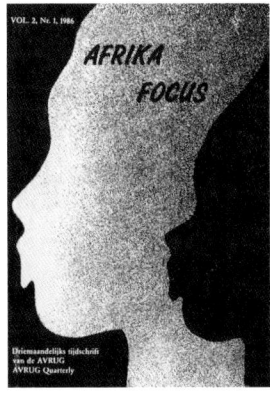

Journal of the Africa Association of the RUG (AVRUG), 1985
(Ghent, Universiteitsbibliotheek)

Marleen Temmerman, 2004
(Ghent, photo Michiel Hendryckx)

victims in Mama Yemo Hospital in Kinshasa: both men and women. This confirmed the hypothesis that contamination could also be passed on through heterosexual contact. It was a major eureka moment, also for Piot: 'Incredible. A disaster for Africa. This is what I want to work on. It will change everything', he noted in his diary.

Project SIDA in Zaire was the first international AIDS project in the world. In the 1990s, 'in order to change the world', Piot shifted his focus from medicine to international institutions, where he held leading functions in the International Aids Society and the AIDS programmes of the WHO and UNAIDS, combined with the role of assistant secretary-general of the UN.

In Nairobi, Marleen Temmerman investigated if and how women and children could be infected with HIV. In 1992, the year she returned to Ghent, she received 2.4 million European ecu from the European Commission for an HIV-AIDS project in Kenya. She wanted to tackle the problem structurally and asked UGent's permission to create a multidisciplinary research centre. 'That's good, my child, where do I sign?' said rector Leon De Meyer — 'As long as it doesn't cost us anything.' In 1994, the International Centre for Reproductive Health (ICRH) was founded. De Meyer gave the initiative his full support and the ICRH could thus be anchored in Ghent, with branches in Kenya and Mozambique. In twenty years, it grew into one of the world's largest centres of expertise in the domain of reproductive health. One of the centre's major assets is the dynamic interaction between multidisciplinary science and development cooperation and the implementation of research results in policy. Given this background, it is certainly no coincidence that Temmerman decided to go into politics. In her view, the academic world has an obligation to provide politics with the language needed to ask the right questions about public health, a subject close to her heart. The millennium goals — now called sustainable development goals — of the UN are a good guideline.

From 2012 to 2015, Temmerman was director at the WHO in Geneva. Since 2015, she has been back in Kenya, where she leads the department of gynaecology and obstetrics at the Aga Khan University and is active in women's health in the Aga Khan Development Network.

The ICRH was also an important pillar in the ambitious cooperation program Dynamics of Building a Better Society, which four Flemish universities have set up with the University of Western Cape (UWC) in Cape Town. The project ran from 2003 to 2013. What set this project apart was the significant contribution of the social sciences and humanities, at the UWC's request, and its highly interdisciplinary character, based on reciprocity and focused on ambitious but concrete societal goals, from sports and development to multilingual citizenship in the cities, digital inclusion and HIV prevention. In addition to Temmerman, Ghent contributed with sociolinguists Jan Blommaert and Stef Slembrouck, political scientist Marleen Bosmans, architect Pieter Uyttenhove and literary scholar Kries Versluys as project leaders.

In 2005, UGent awarded an honorary doctorate to Desmond Tutu for his role in the Truth and Reconciliation Commission. It was a symbolic gesture, but at the same time an expression of the commitment of Ghent's researchers in post-apartheid South Africa. However, this cannot erase the fact that, at the time, some professors in Ghent openly sympathised with the apartheid regime. The philosopher Herman de Vleeschauwer, who was sentenced to death in absentia after the Second World War because of collaboration, migrated to Pretoria in 1955, where he was employed until retirement at the University of South Africa. Professor of economy Marcel Van Meerhacghe was notorious in the Blandijn for his teaching and his arbitrariness on exams, but also for his support of the apartheid regime. Last but not least, his eminent colleague in economics, André Vlerick, was one of the founders of Protea in 1977, an organisation that fostered friendship between Flanders and South Africa and an important pro-apartheid lobby.

## The future of cooperation with the global South

The days in which people saved aluminium foil 'for the Congo' without knowing why are long gone. Yet there is still a lack of vision regarding university cooperation with the global South, notes Patrick Sorgeloos regretfully — at the European level, at the level of VLIR-UOS and at the university itself. He is convinced that more needs to be invested in partnerships with the South, even though that cooperation does not always guarantee an immediate return on investment. Unfortunately, the current academic culture of result-driven research is stacked against it in that respect. Getting a Congolese doctoral student to Belgium is no easy task. Training foreign doctoral students requires more work than advising Flemish doctoral students and could therefore be encouraged more and better.

Sorgeloos's recipe for successful internationalisation is: continue investing in foreign alumni as ambassadors, help them set up projects and education programmes, and in this way build a global network of sustainable relationships with selected partner universities based on reciprocity. He points to the long-standing partnership in Cape Town, but also to similar arrangements with Can Tho University in Vietnam and with ESPOL in Ecuador. These are examples of Institutional University Cooperation (IUC) in which several Flemish universities are (have to be) involved and which offer the best opportunities for lasting motivation and return. It is not just a matter of attracting foreign students; projects must be able to build momentum in partner countries through education, research and development that can then pave the way for industry in certain domains.

The regional platforms and international thematic networks that were recently formed at UGent are certainly a step in the right direction. Yet for Sorgeloos it is still too little, too late. Too many opportunities are still missed because of the compartmentalisation of education and research in separate directions. The 'transversal' direction of internationalisation may perhaps bring solace. Another obstacle is the minor importance of services to society in relation to research and education, even though this too is a core task of the university. A policy that prefers to allow initiatives to rise from the bottom up is not enough. A coherent, top-down vision must be elaborated on the basis of the success stories of the past. These are usually the result of interdisciplinary synergy, mutual confidence and enthusiastic, visionary personalities. It is therefore important that UGent continue to nurture and build on the good relationships it has developed in Asia, Latin America and Africa.

Over the last ten years, however, administration after administration has cut VLIR-UOS financing. Ever since the communist threat in former Third World countries diminished after the fall of the Berlin Wall and the collapse of the Soviet Union, development cooperation has come under attack. This partly explains why neoliberal policy dictates that more be invested in the 'poorest' countries. VLIR-UOS distributes scarce resources among too many fragmented projects. Interuniversity cooperation is also undermined by growing mutual competition in which each university tries to maximise its own advantage. Partners in the South are thus faced with different delegations from Flanders that want to establish joint ventures without consulting one another. Policy, on the contrary, must start from strong interuniversity development cooperation in Flanders and Belgium if it is to lead to effective dialogue with both the regional and the federal government.

In the broader context of shifting geopolitical relationships, Sorgeloos is not the only one to view the advent of Ghent University Global Campus in South Korea with Argus eyes. UGent has jumped on the bandwagon of globalisation as defined in the Lisbon 2000 objectives. It is not inconceivable that such forms of internationalisation will increasingly supplant traditional development cooperation in the future. The impetus for the campus in Songdo came from the South itself, more specifically from the South Korean government, which laid a few million won on the table to attract the expertise of foreign research institutions. UGent saw this as an interesting opportunity to valorise its biosciences — an area in which it excels — in the highly regarded Shanghai ranking. In 2011 an agreement was concluded for the creation of a bachelor's programme in biotechnology, environmental technology and food technology. Long-term prospects include exchange programmes for doctoral research in the high-tech environment that the campus provides. In the meantime, the gigantic campus in Songdo, with the most modern infrastructure, laboratories and equipment, was built at breakneck speed with the help of South Korean funds.

In 2014, Ghent University was the first European university to take up residence at the hyper-modern Incheon Global Campus along with three American universities. The permanent academic staff includes thirty-five UGent professors and researchers. In addition, there is a 'flying faculty' of lecturers, who offer separate modules over a period of four weeks. It is not the intention of the South Korean government to 'Koreanise' the university — on the contrary: only 10% of the staff may have Korean nationality. The entire project is an example of UGent's assertive internationalisation policy, but like the Ghent-Butare and Ganda-Congo colonial initiatives, its success depends on (geopolitical) factors that go beyond the university's control. Hence, it is anybody's guess whether the Global Campus has a future without Korean funding to sweeten the deal. As far as the recruitment and success of the students is concerned, the Campus has nearly reached its stated goals after a difficult start-up phase. The operation will have to be self-sustaining once Korean subsidies cease. Continuing to motivate UGent personnel to accept a teaching or management assignment there,

Rector Anne De Paepe and students of Ghent University Global Campus in Songdo, South Korea, 2014
(Ghent, Image bank UGent, photos Rudy Gevaert and Filip Martin)

however, is not an easy task. Perhaps the motto of William the Silent, forefather of UGent's founder, might be said to apply: 'There is no need to hope to undertake, nor to succeed to persevere.'

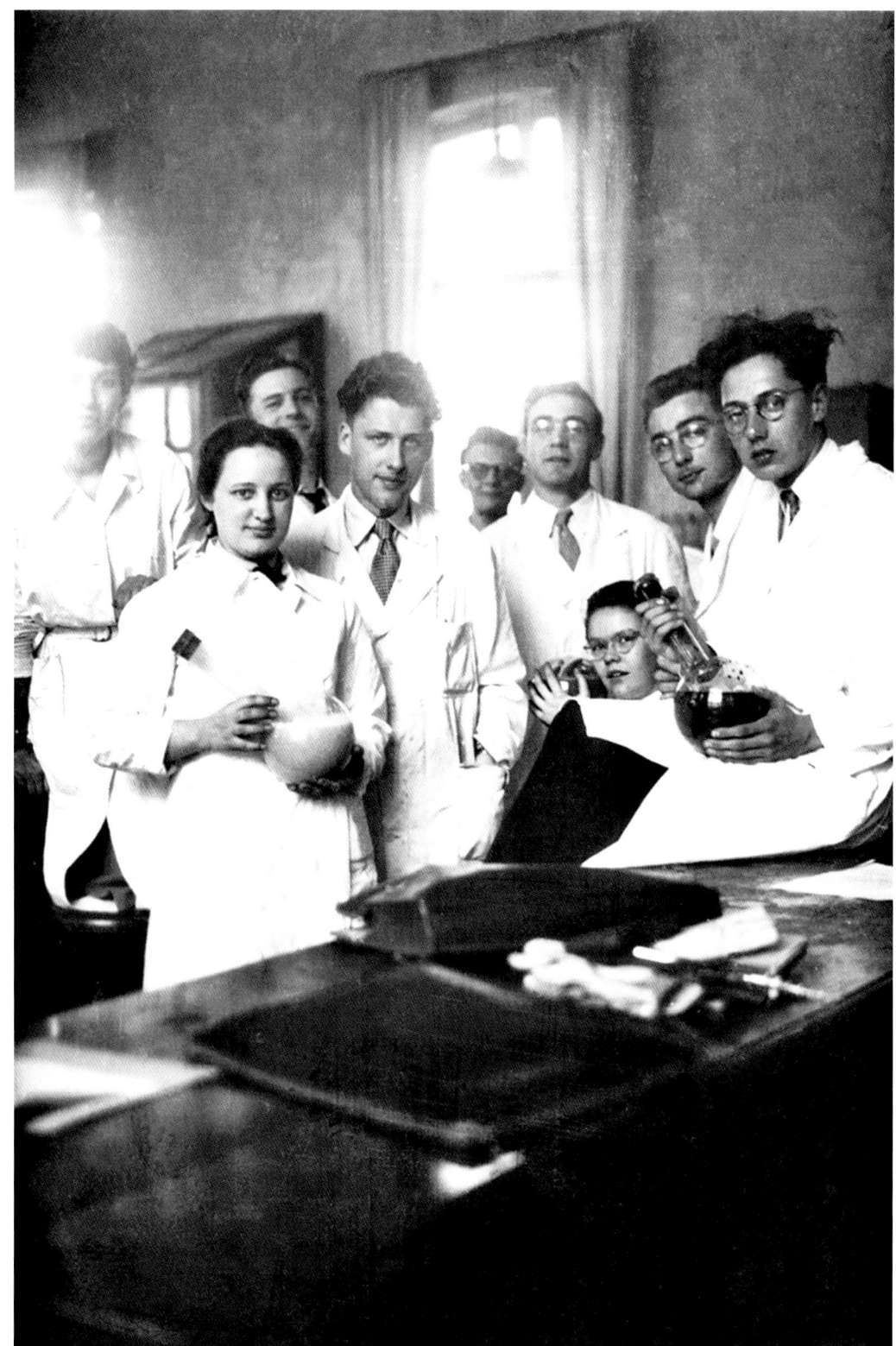

**Marc Van Montagu as a chemistry student, 1950s**
The renowned founder of plant biotechnology (right) studied chemistry, then still in Plateaustraat. His academic career shows that the nineteenth-century division into faculties had been completely overtaken by scientific developments in molecular biology and the life sciences. Moreover, in the field of biotechnology there is a strongly felt need for interdisciplinarity with the humanities.
(Ghent, collection of Marc Van Montagu)

Chapter 11

# ENVIRONMENT AND BIOTECHNOLOGY

In 1900, Ghent University's new Botanical Institute was erected on Ledeganckstraat, opposite the Citadel Park. Louis Cloquet's colourful neo-Gothic building, with its surrounding greenhouses and gardens, was ready for the scientific turn of the twentieth century. Two years previously, the Austrian botanist Erich von Tschermak-Seysenegg had planted his peas in the old Botanical Garden on the Baudelo. The results led him to rediscover the laws of heredity first set out by Gregor Mendel, whose original publication had gone unnoticed for more than thirty years. At the time, Julius Mac Leod was not only director of the Botanical Garden, but also, as a student of the Ghent morphological school of Charles Van Bambeke, was engaged with Darwin's theory of evolution and its popularisation. The 'educator' of the Flemish people developed an idiosyncratic social theory of heredity that corresponded to his belief in human makeability.

**The orangery of the Botanical Garden, 1815**
View from the greenhouses of the orangery and part of the Botanical Garden on the Baudelo.
(Ghent, Universiteitsbibliotheek, drawing Jean Baptiste De Noter)

In 1957, Tschermak-Seysenegg received an honorary doctorate from Ghent University. A half-century after its original date of publication, an English translation was published in *Genetics*. He died in 1962, the year that James Watson, Francis Crick and Maurice Wilkins were awarded the Nobel Prize for Medicine for their description of the double helix structure of DNA. Rosalind Franklin died of cancer in 1958, perhaps as a result of exposure to the X-rays with which she made her DNA photos. For this reason, she never received the recognition she deserved in the revolutionary development of molecular biology and genetics.

On 15 June 1959 the first stone in the foundation of the new faculty of Sciences building was laid next to the Botanical Garden and the Botanical Institute. Three years later, professor Laurent Vandendriessche could move his Laboratory for Physiological Chemistry into the fifth floor of the — still unfinished — low-rise building. It was there that the 'Ghent' revolution in molecular biology played out. Three brilliant, ambitious researchers, each from a different scientific background, were united by their interest in breaking genetic codes: agricultural engineer Walter Fiers, biologist Jeff Schell and chemist Marc Van Montagu. 'We felt like the alchemists of a new age', says Van Montagu, with his characteristic chuckle.

Of the world-famous trio, Van Montagu dreamt the most. As a left-leaning intellectual, he was (and is) strongly committed to society, a 'red baron' who believes in the makeability of man and nature. It was the period when the Club of Rome came out with catastrophic predictions about the relationship between population growth and the consumption of raw materials, food production, industrialisation and pollution. There were limits to growth based on the exploitation of natural resources. The capacity of the earth was not great enough for the survival of humanity if humanity did not intervene quickly and radically. One year after the publication of the first Club of Rome report in 1972, the oil crisis broke out, confirming speculations of doom. Events only intensified emerging environmental awareness at Ghent University. In 1971 the Interfaculty Research Centre for the Study of Air, Soil and Water Pollution (Interfacultair Centrum voor de Studie van Lucht-, Bodem- en Waterverontreiniging) was founded, the first in Europe to offer specialised training in environmental sanitation.

During this period, Jozef De Ley's Microbiology Laboratory served as a breeding ground for two important spearhead domains that developed independently of one another: the first around molecular plant genetics, the second around microbial waste processing. The traditional distinction between basic and applied research became blurred. The molecular relationships between organisms on a micro level and ecosystems between people, animals and plants on the macro level not only made a multidisciplinary approach necessary, it also undermined nineteenth-century disciplines and faculties. New scientific developments sought and found their way among the fragmented structures of the university. A few narrow bridges have since been established, but the structures themselves have largely been retained.

In the meantime, the environmental movement expanded in the 1990s, widening its scope from nature conservation and preservation to global sustainability, in which new (bio)technological developments have an important role to play. Science and technology are no longer the enemies of the ecologist. Marc Van Montagu, however, regrets that the immense possibilities of genetically modified organisms (GMOs) for eliminating hunger in the world have been thwarted by the 'emotional' approach of the green movement and excessively rigid European regulations. It is one of the many areas of tension in the transition to a sustainable society in the twenty-first century that must be examined through multiperspectivity.

## DNA transfer in a nature-loving network

When Julius Mac Leod became director of the Botanical Garden in 1887, when it was still on the Baudelo, he recognised its public function as a municipal park and green lung of the nineteenth-century industrial city, in contrast to his predecessors. He liked the fact that ordinary people went there after work. The once renowned garden in the inner city, however, had become dirty and increasingly fenced in by the many factories 'spewing out streams of smoke'. Upon his appointment, Mac Leod also founded the Dodonaea Botanical Association (Kruidkundig Genootschap Dodonaea) for lovers of the biological sciences.

Horticulturist Hubert Van Hulle drew up plans for the new Citadel Park in 1871. The university and the city finally reached an agreement in 1897, and the new Botanical Garden was established not in the Citadel Park, but on the opposite side of the street. This ensured physical separation between the municipal park for the citizens of Ghent and the botanical garden for research and education. In 1903, Mac Leod gave his first lesson in the auditorium of the Botanical Institute, considered well-equipped

**Julius Mac Leod and the Dodonaea Botanical Association**
(Ghent, Universiteitsarchief)

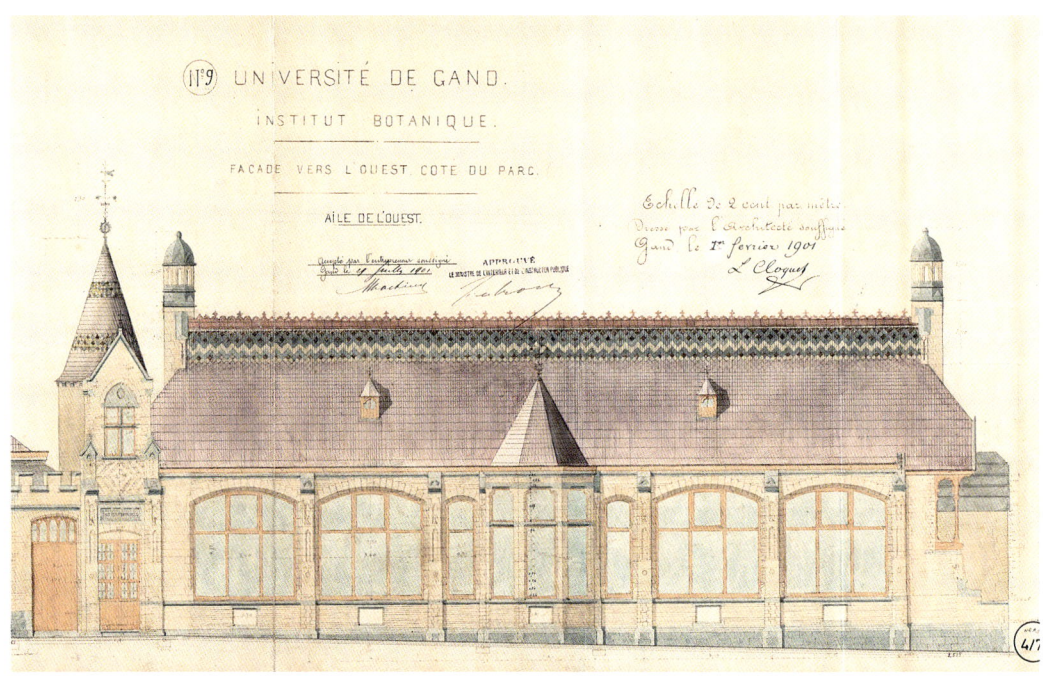

**Plans for the Botanical Institute on the Ledeganck, 1900-1901**
City architect and professor Louis Cloquet drew up the plans for the neo-Gothic Botanical Institute on the Citadel Park. Inside, the lighting and heating worked according to the latest gas technology, which was crucial for a building in which scientific research was paramount. The architect paid particular attention to the garden fence, the only part of the original complex that remains. In the 1960s the Botanical Institute had to make way for Jules Trenteseau's Ledeganck building.
(Ghent, Universiteitsarchief)

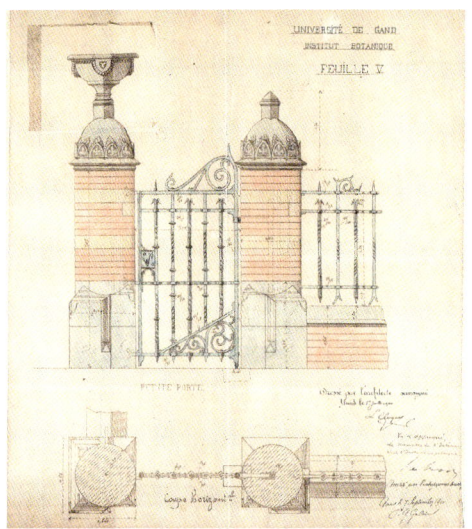

for the time, with an orangery, herbarium, museum and modern laboratories. The beautifully finished fence by city architect Louis Cloquet is all that is left of the original complex.

Julius Mac Leod and his wife Fanny Maertens joined George Sarton's Reiner Leven society. Nature and culture were not considered separate worlds. The doctrine of social evolution that was then gaining ground in left-wing circles was the unifying factor. It was the work of both men and women. Julius and Fanny were both fascinated by anarchism. He collaborated on *Van Nu en Straks* and corresponded with August Vermeylen, Jacques Mesnil and Ferdinand Domela Nieuwenhuis. She was a cousin of the artist Frans Masereel and studied Russian. Her greatest pen pals in Russia were the anarcho-communist revolutionaries Sofia and Pyotr Kropotkin. In 1904, Maertens translated Kropotkin's doctrine of social evolution into Dutch under the title *Wederkeerig dienstbetoon. Een factor der evolutie* (Mutual Aid: A Factor of Evolution), with a foreword by her husband. In addition to the utopian ideals of social progress and world peace, the members of Reiner Leven, the Flinken and Dodonaea also nurtured 'green' ideas *avant la lettre*. An enthusiastic professor, Mac Leod took them on botanical excursions in the moors of Drongen. He shared a rowing boat with Leo Baekeland before the latter's departure for the US, and kept it moored by the old Romanesque church in Afsnee. Boat trips along the river Leie in the summer with former members of 't Zal Wel Gaan, the liberal students' organisation, were a source of great fun and friendship.

Leo-Michel Thiery and Augusta De Taeye regularly participated in Mac Leod's excursions. Before their marriage, the two teachers were in the habit of hiking together in the moors around Drongen to study the plants. Their shared love of botany was an idyll. In the early days, the young couple had very little money and lived in a workers' cottage near Ekkergem. Thiery turned down a chance to become director of the municipal school in Geitstraat where he taught classes. He came from a working-class milieu and there he intended to stay, went his reasoning. As a teacher of sixth-year students, even before the First World War he focused on experience-based projects that started from actual events: the first snow, a mining disaster, a hike outdoors. Plants bloomed on the windowsills of his classroom, freshwater creatures swam about in a small aquarium, and on the playground he laid out a garden with a pond. Thiery took his working-class pupils on trips to the Botanical Garden, the Flemish Ardennes, the woods, the Institute of Natural Sciences in Brussels ... He understood that the children would not attend school beyond the age of fourteen. Thiery became a central figure in the intellectual life of Ghent, certainly where nature conservation and ecology were concerned. The degradation of natural beauty by industrialised society struck deep in his Romantic soul. He was one of the first to openly complain about 'vandalism' against nature. Posthumously, *Terugkeer tot de natuur* (Back to nature, 1952) was published with an *in memoriam* by biologist Lucien De Coninck, also a member of Dodonaea.

In 1922, Victor Willem, pupil and successor of Felix Plateau and director of the Zoology Museum (Museum voor Dierkunde), had part of the Cabinet Zoologique transferred to the former typesetting school on the Berouw. This was where Leo-Michel Thiery would establish his School Museum at Willem's insistent urging. That the university's zoological collection had lost some of its scientific value had everything to do with the widespread breakthrough of the theory of evolution. The general classification systems of the animal and plant kingdoms that botanists and zoologists had been using since the seventeenth century had become obsolete. Except for a limited

(left)
**The Botanical Garden, 1931**
The staff posing with shovels and watering cans by a flowerbed. Bending forwards is Camille De Bruyne, Mac Leod's successor as director of the Botanical Garden.
(Ghent, Universiteitsarchief)

(right)
**Leo-Michel Thiery**
The director of the Ghent School Museum was a member of Dodonaea and a faithful visitor to the Botanical Garden. In 1947 he wrote an ode to mark the 150th anniversary of the Botanical Garden.
(Ghent, Thiery family collection)

number of seminars, the animal science collection remained in the cupboard and was no longer enlarged. However, it could still be used to ignite the scientific curiosity of children. When Julius died in 1919, Fanny Mac Leod-Maertens donated her husband's private collection of shells, minerals and insects to her good friend Thiery. The School Museum that opened its doors in 1924 had nine thematic rooms, four of which were named after Ghent University professors: Victor Willem (mammals, birds and fish), Julius Mac Leod (shells), Joseph and Felix Plateau (physics and chemistry) and Henri Pirenne (history and civilisation).

Lucien De Coninck (right) and his collaborators
(Ghent, Universiteitsarchief)

Together with Mac Leod, the versatile Victor Willem was the scientific forerunner of ecology in Ghent. He also liked to take his students on excursions — for example, to the northern French coastal town of Wimereux, and he often enlisted his wife and daughter on these occasions. It made for a family atmosphere that brought teacher and students closer together. During the excursions, Willem talked about a lot more than just nature, and with his insights on literature and art history, he contributed significantly to the general education of his students.

Lucien De Coninck, who began his academic career in 1931 at the National Research Foundation (NFWO), spent three years specialising in Utrecht with the nematode specialist J.H. Schuurmans Stekhoven, before returning to Ghent. This formed the basis for his international reputation in this domain. Nevertheless, even with his fascination for the nematode — a tiny organism of 1 millimetre that is difficult to study — De Coninck was the exact opposite of the unworldly scholar who busied himself with hyper-specialised research in a niche field of zoology.

Frank Roels, retired professor of Anatomical Pathology, vividly recalls the first time he heard De Coninck speak. That was the end of 1951, at the creation of the Antwerp division of the Humanist Association (Humanistisch Verbond, or HV), in which De Coninck was a driving force. His concern for all people on the planet and for the way unbridled population growth and exploitation depleted the soil, attacked plant growth and changed the climate was far ahead of his time. Twenty years before the Club of Rome report and more than half a century before Al Gore's *An Inconvenient Truth*, De Coninck set up discussion groups with his best students on the question of how a better understanding of biology could lead to a better society. He made them aware of the vast damage caused to the planet — even then — by humanity's extreme anthropocentrism.

De Coninck organised long evenings and weekends of discussion and excursions to bring the students closer to and create a sense of connection with nature. Frans Snacken, who had just finished his PhD, was enlisted to create a Humanist Youth League (Humanistisch Jeugdverbond). In 1945, Snacken was one of the founders of the coeducational Sea Scout group De Wilde Eend (The Wild Duck) in Drongen and had an exceptional talent for organising countryside outings with the students. There were music evenings, and 'thanks to the biology students encouraged by Professor De Coninck, the famous biological outings', says Frank Roels, who was there in 1954-1955 as 'a propagandist of the first hour', enthralled by the 'immense élan of these free-thinking young people'. So was his classmate in the second cycle of medicine, Nora Podgaetzki. 'She argued violently, knew everything about art and philosophy, was of East European origin and knew Russian: who wouldn't dream of such a sweetheart?' It was Marc Van Montagu, the 'skinny assistant with buck teeth', who 'surprised everyone by managing to catch the prettiest girl of my year', writes Roels in his friend's *Liber amicorum*. 'We don't know what compelling arguments he used: he just had the knack.'

The university students wanted to have control over their own organisation and the future Free University of Brussels (VUB) professor of marine biology Philip Polk, a student of De Coninck's, founded the Humanist Students Association (Humanistisch Studenten Verbond, or HSV). The second president of the HSV was once again a biologist, Jeff Schell. In spite of being under the spell of the dedicated teaching and charismatic personality of De Coninck, he turned down an offer to become an assistant in the zoology lab. Instead, he chose an adviser in the domain of microbiology, Jozef De Ley. A choice that contributed ten years later to Schell and Van Montagu turning biology on its head by infecting plants with Agrobacterium tumefaciens, which put them on the trail of gene transfer.

## Nature conservation and environmental protection

Jan Hublé's career path was more classic. He studied biology during the Second World War and specialised in zoology. Born in an educational milieu, Ghent's freethinking spirit was in his blood, inherited from both parents. His father Arthur Hublé was a director in the municipal education system; his mother, Irma Walgraeve, was a colleague of Leo-Michel Thiery in Geitstraat. Membership of 't Zal Wel Gaan and, immediately after graduation, of the Masonic lodge De Zwijger, of which his father as well as his adviser, Lucien De Coninck, were founding members, was the natural course of family tradition and friendships for Hublé. Through that same network he met his future wife, Nadia Vankenhove. Hublé Senior and Lucien De Coninck were 'godfathers' not only to Leo-Michel Thiery, but also to his eldest son Herman Thiery (Johan Daisne) in De Zwijger. The latter's novel *De wedloop der jeugd* (The contest of youth) is about his younger twin brothers Leo and Michel, who as boys liked to go to the family's country house in Sint-Martens-Latem, where they went swimming and canoeing with Jan. In Latem, Jan's interest in nature, birds and moors grew. The educational approach of father Thiery and the enthusiastic excursions of professor De Coninck did the rest. Nature education and preservation were Jan Hublé's goals in life alongside his academic work.

Excursion to the Damvallei, 1954
The second candidacy in Chemistry on a trip to the Damvallei. Jan Hublé is second from the right.
(Ghent, Universiteitsarchief)

**The documentary *SOS Natuur*, 1969**
In this BRT documentary, professor Jan Hublé explains why requirements for hunting licences need to be tightened, and discusses the habits of wild geese, the white-fronted goose, and their migration from Siberia to Damme. He argues in favour of rational nature conservation.
(Brussels, VRT-Beeldarchief)

Hublé graduated in 1945 and began working as an assistant in the Zoological Laboratory with De Coninck. Newly married with Nadia Vankenhove, who recently graduated as a doctor in law, he went to Berkeley in 1951 to study growth hormones in rats. There, however, it became clear that his real interest lay in ornithology. In 1966, Hublé became head of the Laboratory for Animal Ecology, Zoography and Nature Conservation (Laboratorium voor de Oecologie der dieren, Zoögeografie en Natuurbehoud) that was set up in 1960. The name alone reveals the new ecological trends predominating at the time. In 1968, Hublé was the first professor in Belgium to introduce the subject of nature conservation in the curriculum. With lectures, nature guides, popular publications and programmes on radio and television, he demonstrated his considerable societal engagement in this domain. Eckhart Kuijken, scion

of the musical family, received his PhD on the 'oceanology of wintering geese in Damme in a Western European context' under Hublé. Until 2007, Kuijken taught subjects such as landscape ecology and nature conservation, nature and green management, and brought generations of students into contact with the problems of biodiversity. In the 1980s, Kuijken worked with the new Flemish government institutions for nature conservation, among them the Institute for Nature and Forest Science (Instituut voor Natuur- en Bosonderzoek, or INBO). Like his adviser Hublé, Kuijken was (and is) a nature activist, as is evident from his chairmanship of the Belgian Youth League for Nature Studies (Belgische Jeugdbond voor Natuurstudie, or BNJ) and the non-profit Natuurreservaten, now Natuurpunt.

**Plant-A-Tree, 1970**
The public was mobilised at the tree-planting action in the Aelmoeseneie forest on 21 March 1970. An information brochure from Sylva Gandavensis of the Forestry Laboratory provided the necessary explanation of how and why the action was taken.
(Ghent, collection of Labo Bos & Natuur UGent)

1970 was a key year for nature conservation. On 14 January, Hublé was called upon to kick off the European Year of Nature Protection in Brussels with a speech on the ecological crisis. Long before there was talk of global warming, he pointed out the great importance to the international community of the search for sustainable solutions for the protection of natural resources.

The European Year of Nature Protection firmly established environmental problems on the political agenda in Belgium and at the same time gave environmental research in Ghent a serious boost. In the meantime, environmental awareness was placed in the spotlight by a range of environmental action groups. Hublé was one of the initiators of an action committee that advocated the protection of the Bourgoyen-Ossemeersen in Ghent. The Hublé Plan of 1971 formed the basis of the nature reserve as we know it today.

Hublé was certainly not the only one at the university who got involved with environmental issues. In the experimental forest Aelmoeseneie in Melle, which the university acquired in 1969, agricultural engineer Marcel Van Miegroet studied the impact of air pollution on forest ecosystems. The television broadcaster BRT took the Year of Nature Protection as an opportunity to organise the highly successful Plant-A-Tree action, with the eponymous ditty by media character Nonkel Bob. Frustrated with the 'regionalisation' of environmental issues, Van Miegroet nonetheless put his effort into the Flemish Forestry Association (Vlaamse Bosbouwvereniging) and advocated a Flemish forestry decree, which would only be enacted in 1990.

In the 1970s there was also new environmental research from what might seem like an unexpected angle: the Institute for Nuclear Sciences (Instituut voor Nucleaire Wetenschappen) in Proeftuinstraat. There, the new nuclear reactor Thetis made research on air pollution possible. Using neutron activation, Richard Dams and Ronald Heindryckx analysed the presence of fine dust in the Ghent canal zone, where Texaco, Sidmar and Volvo permitted daily samples to be taken on site. The research formed the occasion for a national study on air pollution in Belgium.

Karel Vuylsteek, for his part, researched the effects of industry and pollution on the air passages of the local population from the perspective of social medicine. And at the faculty of Agricultural Sciences, Guido Persoone set up the Laboratory for the Biological Research of Water Pollution in 1974. Persoone came as a biologist from Hublé's Laboratory of Ecology when he was appointed as a lecturer in the faculty of Agricultural Sciences in 1972 and became one of the movers and shakers behind the Interfaculty Centre for the Study of Air, Soil and Water Pollution, established in April 1971 (since 1980 the Interfaculty Centre for Environmental Sanitation, and from 2011 CES&T, Centre for Environmental Science & Technology). In its first year, a record number of forty-five students enrolled from a broad range of backgrounds: engineers, pharmacists, chemists, geologists, biologists ... That first generation of environmental studies students branched out into industry and waste processing, or to new (semi-) public departments in the growing environmental sector. The societal engagement of the Centre for Environmental Sanitation was also reflected in the choice of three mediagenic honorary doctors: ocean researcher Jacques-Yves Cousteau (1983), chairman of the Environment Foundation (Stichting Leefmilieu) Paul Knapen (1988), and documentary film-maker Richard Attenborough (1989).

## The microbe of environmental technology

One of the first lecturers at the Centre for Environmental Sanitation was Willy Verstraete. He graduated with flair in 1968, but as a farmer's son from Beernem, an academic career was not an obvious choice for him. His adviser, Jules Voets, encouraged him to go further afield and apply for a scholarship to study in the US. Verstraete was highly motivated but had little means. 'This is where [the money from home] stops; I have five more children', said his father. 'Willy always cost money and never earned a cent', said his mother in a Canvas documentary many years later. To ensure that his girlfriend could go with him, he had to get married. Without consulting his parents, in-laws or even his future wife, Verstraete was determined to go for it. He wanted a wedding photo by the Minnewater in Bruges and on that symbolic spot not only

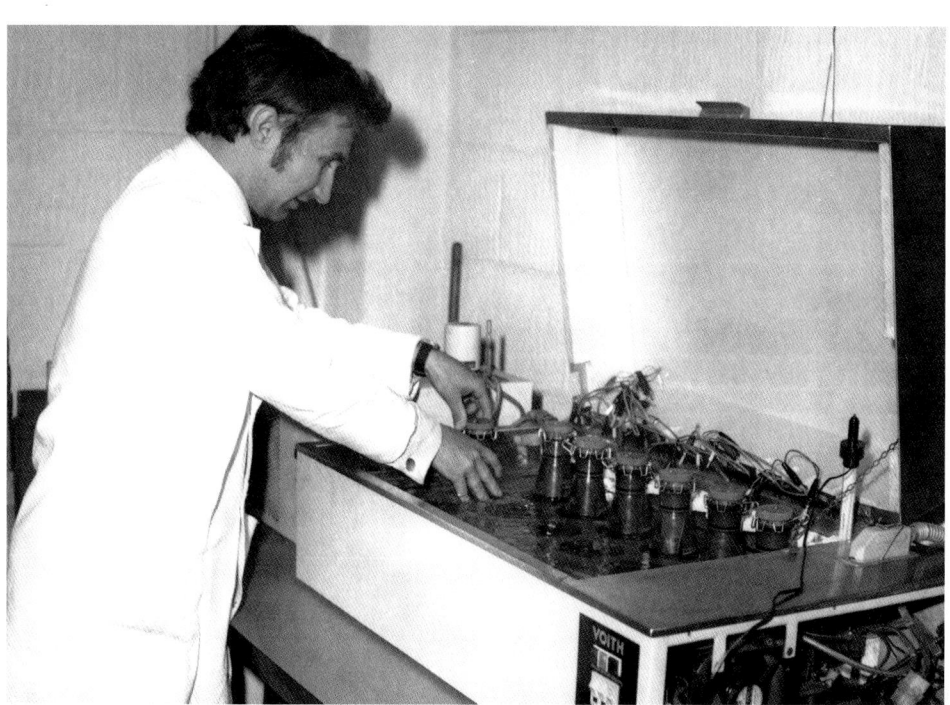

Willy Verstraete at work in his lab, ca. 1980
(Ghent, Universiteitsarchief)

swore eternal loyalty to his wife, but also pledged to do something in the future about the tainted water. The newly-weds left for New York — at that time still a boat journey. Verstraete earned his PhD at Cornell University with the broad-minded Jewish professor Martin Alexander, who was conducting groundbreaking research. 'Dutch boys' usually took five years to finish their doctorate. But this was not an option, financially speaking, and the ambitious Verstraete succeeded in graduating with flying colours in only two and a half years. In Alexander's lab, Verstraete first encountered the environment as a domain of scientific research and saw how everything in nature was connected 'holistically'. It was only then that the importance of sustainability really got through to him. How preserving what exists over the long term can be a guideline for the future. At the time, waste was still dumped into the water unthinkingly, not to mention the nuclear waste in the sea. In the US, awareness was dawning that water is hallowed goodness that belongs to everyone.

Verstraete left Ghent as an agricultural engineer and came back in 1971 as a scientist with a PhD in microbiology. However, he landed right in the middle of a major interfaculty research battle among professors. Both his adviser, Jules Voets, and Jozef De Ley, the eminent microbiologist from the faculty of Sciences, claimed ecology as their domain. Voets was scientifically 'a dwarf' compared to De Ley, but De Ley was a 'rascal' who found it difficult to keep himself in check at the university. Verstraete was drafted as Voets's general in the 'war' with De Ley, which was very difficult for him precisely because he held the man in such high esteem. On one occasion De Ley showed him the door when he requested an appointment and mentioned that he worked with Voets. When Voets died of a heart attack at the age of fifty-three in 1976, a position came free for the young lecturer Willy Verstraete — as well as an opportunity for interdisciplinary cooperation with De Ley, an interfaculty alliance that has lasted to this day.

On his return to Ghent in 1971, Verstraete was allowed to teach one course in the new postgraduate programme: environmental technology. During the summer, his wife typed out his 246-page course, '*Microbiologische aspecten van de milieuverontreiniging. Water — Bodem — Lucht*' (Microbiological aspects of environmental pollution: Water — Soil — Air). With Voets as the primary author, Verstraete was only his 'subsitute'. He had a hard time readjusting to Ghent; he found the 'oppressive inertia' of the administration particularly problematic. While the staff at Cornell literally roller-skated through the library, it sometimes took three days to secure a book from the University Library in Ghent. Even worse, the faculty of Agriculture — hardly an ivory tower — literally turned up its nose at the scientific environmental research that Verstraete enthusiastically sought to introduce. Waste water, manure, working on the rubbish belt: it was pure horror for the gentlemen academics in their white lab coats. The dean refused to tolerate people sloshing through the corridors with buckets of manure. Colleagues initially refused to believe that it was possible to combat environmental pollution with the help of bacteria. Bacteria were exclusively and negatively associated with diseases and viruses. It took Verstraete all the effort in the world to convince the university and the outside world that bacteria, if properly managed, could have very positive effects.

In his microbiology lab on Ledeganckstraat, Jozef De Ley collected all the bacteria he could in small test tubes. His famous culture collection comprised 25,000 different 'little miracles', with a single, neatly isolated germ contained in each tube. Thanks to developments in genetics and molecular biology, it was common practice at the time to isolate bacteria from nature in a 'pure culture' and study them separately with DNA hybridisation techniques. With the insights he had gained at Cornell, Verstraete did exactly the opposite. It came down to studying bacteria and their interactions in their own biotope rather than isolating them by artificial means. In nature, microorganisms work like people in coordinated teams that, depending on ambient conditions, show different systems of exchange. A microbial team, or 'microbiome', as they are known today, is capable of much more than the individual parts. This insight is still the driving force behind Verstraete's research today. Hence, it is common to speak of Microbial Resource Management (MRM), by analogy with Human Resource Management (HRM). By allowing the bacteria to cooperate in optimal conditions, certain processes — such as fermentation or composting — can be accelerated or improved.

Verstraete's revolutionary vision was initially met with great scepticism. Only by producing practical solutions for concrete problems was he able to convince the world of his insights. To this end, he travelled to the landfill site of Vlierzele, which caused heavy soil pollution and problems with wastewater. By studying how the landfill worked, Verstraete arrived at the idea of accelerating the fermentation process in an anaerobic or oxygen-free environment and capturing the biogas to generate new energy. This is how he discovered dry anaerobic composting — or the Dranco process — in 1983. The first biogas plant in Ghent was built in 1984, followed by an entire Dranco factory in Brecht in 1992. Nowadays, there are twenty-five waste processing plants with this technology worldwide.

In a similar way, solutions were devised for water purification by converting and reusing 'waste products' such as ammonia and greenhouse gases, sometimes in combi-

Guido Persoone and the Simulator of the Human Intestinal Microbial Ecosystem (SHIME)
The SHIME was the source of inspiration for Wim Delvoye's Cloaca or 'poop machine'.
(Ghent, Universiteitsarchief)

nation with algae. Hospital bacteria, for example, can be kept in check by probiotic soap. In other words, the proven MRM-process of cooperating bacteria can be deployed in the most diverse areas. It even inspired artist Wim Delvoye to build his *Cloaca* after he came to look at Verstraete's Simulator of the Human Intestinal Microbial Ecosystem (SHIME)', or 'poo machine'.

Still, things did not always go smoothly for Verstraete. In the struggle for scarce space in the Boerenkot, as a young lecturer he was at first relegated to a tiny, unsafe room full of Bunsen burners and recycled tables from Civil Engineering. He was forced to expand his territory by seeking out all kinds of 'nooks and crannies'. In 1979 was founded LabMet (now, CMET or Centre for Microbial Ecology and Technology), the number one worldwide in environmental technology. After a visit from king Baudouin in 1984, the laboratory finally received faculty recognition as well and was further expanded. At the time, cooperation with industry was far from being a given, certainly not in the environmental sector, which was largely populated by left-wing students. Verstraete, however, deliberately sought concrete connections with society on the demand side. In 1988 he founded his first spin-off, Organic Waste Systems (OWS), to market the innovative fermentation Dranco technology internationally. There would be another five spin-offs, each time driven by young people from his academic stable.

In 2005, Willy Verstraete received the 'Flemish Nobel Prize' from the FWO, crowning his pioneering work while at the same time showing how inextricably basic and applied research are connected in the field of environmental technology. His three successors, Nico Boon, Korneel Rabaey and Tom Van De Wiele, have the same bug and continue his story with the same élan.

Reminiscing on his successful career, Verstraete realises that at the beginning of the 1970s he was 'surfing' on the wave of the emerging environmental movement. He managed to get his board on the right wave at the right time, which involved a lot of luck and a lot of chance. As the son of a farmer, Verstraete was by no means an idealistic green or environmental activist. He didn't demonstrate against nuclear energy, although he did find the dire predictions of the Club of Rome sufficient arguments for putting his engineering skills to work for the improvement of the environment. A pluralistic debate on 'environment and pollution' organised by the Willemsfonds on a Sunday afternoon at the beginning of the 1970s still stands out clearly in his mind. The participants: a bishop, a mufti, a rabbi and a clergyman, and Verstraete as an engineer — for the technical explanations. The bishop denied that there was a problem and found in Christian charity a justification for exploiting the soil to the fullest. The Protestant clergyman brought up stewardship of the earth for future generations, while the rabbi, citing the Torah, said magnificent things about the beauty that nature gave to all people. It was a combination of these three elements — the visionary predictions of the Club of Rome, the Calvinist notion of stewardship and the Jewish idea of nature's sacredness — that gave Verstraete the 'higher' inspiration for his pragmatic engagement as an environmental engineer. He regrets that in his faculty at the time, only the technological dimension was taught. In the Interfaculty Centre for Environmental Sanitation, a multidisciplinary approach was and still is more present. Verstraete was moreover one of the initiators of the English-language master's in Environmental Sanitation and notes with satisfaction that he has helped raise the status of the 'sanitary engineer', at the time 'the lowest of the low' in the strictly hierarchical world of engineers. He is also the father of the title 'bioengineer'. After lengthy discussions between Ghent and Leuven within the Royal Flemish Engineers Association (Koninklijke Vlaamse Ingenieursvereniging, or KVIV) and a phone call to the cabinet of Daniël Coens, it would replace the dowdy appellation 'Agricultural Engineer' in the mega-decree of 1991, which permanently elevated the status of the 'farmers' from the Coupure in the academic hierarchy.

## From 'smear chemistry' to life sciences

Walter Fiers graduated from the Coupure in 1954 as an engineer for the chemical and agricultural industries. His parents envisioned him making a career in Congo, but the young man from Ypres was obsessed with fundamental research. With a doctoral scholarship from the Institute for Scientific Research in Industry and Agriculture (Instituut voor Wetenschappelijk Onderzoek van Nijverheid en Landbouw, or IWONL, now the IWT), he joined Laurent Vandendriessche's Laboratory for Physiological Chemistry later that year. The lab was still in the Rommelaere Institute on Apotheekstraat back then. Chemistry student Marc Van Montagu did the research for his licentiate thesis there in 1954-1955. Highly exceptionally, he was the first to be allowed to complete his thesis in the domain of biochemistry under Lucien Massart in the Veterinary School, since there was a sudden population explosion of chemistry students because of the democratisation of higher education. For the young Van Montagu, the chemistry of living beings accorded with his interest in society. At the beginning of the 1950s, however, the academic status of what was sometimes known as 'smear

chemistry' was still quite low: 'Tierchemie ist Schmierchemie', according to the German dogma. Chemists clearly had little regard for the biochemical mess.

The genealogy of biochemistry in Ghent dates all the way back to the end of the nineteenth century, when the highly versatile Albert Jacques Joseph — A.J.J. for short — Van de Velde became an assistant in the Laboratory for General Chemistry under Théodore Swarts, the successor of August Kekulé. Van de Velde was highly influenced by his 'master' Julius Mac Leod, who urged him to do scientific research at the interface of chemistry and biology. At his urging, Van de Velde wrote a dissertation on the morphology and physiology of 'the germination of seed plants' in 1896. Biochemistry *avant la lettre*, and with it he won first prize in the university competition. That year, A.J.J. married Marguerite Leboucq, daughter of Hector Leboucq, who would hinder the academic career of their contemporary Bertha De Vriese ten years later.

In 1900, Van de Velde was appointed director of Ghent Municipal Laboratory, which since 1886 had carried out checks on the chemical composition of foodstuffs in the buildings of the Ecole Industrielle on Lindenlei. In 1906, under his leadership, the Municipal Laboratory moved to the vacant residence of the horticulturist of the former Botanical Garden on the Baudelo: a remarkable redesignation, which in view of the close contacts between Mac Leod and Van de Velde was no coincidence. Van de Velde would run the Municipal Laboratory for thirty-two years. There he established a service for the bacteriological examination of food and the inspection of food products. André Vander Stricht, general manager of the Ghent Excelsior brewery, was his assistant. At the time, A.J.J. also taught at the Ecole Professionnelle de Brasserie de la Société des Brasseurs Belges, popularly known in Ghent as 'the brewery school', of which he was later director. This was also where the seeds were planted for the biochemistry programme, initially considered technical training. The structures of the brewery school were indeed less limiting to innovation than the university. In 1920, Van de Velde belonged to the first group of professors at the Agricultural College, where he introduced biochemistry in 1937.

In the meantime, Lucien Massart had started his academic career in 1934 at the newly established Veterinary School. During the war, he helped Vander Stricht set up biochemical research that could be applied in the world of breweries, malt houses and food companies. From 1943 onwards, Massart was charged with teaching the new subject of biochemistry in the faculty of Sciences, although it was only an elective. He made the definitive transition to Sciences in 1948. Compared to the head of organic chemistry, Firmin Govaert, he had little to say at the time. Nevertheless, the foreword to Massart's standard reference work *Biochimie Médicale* (1943) was written by Nobel Prize winner Corneel Heymans, who grasped the enormous importance of 'biological chemistry' for what are now known as the 'life sciences'. In Medicine, however, resistance to biochemistry was even greater than in Sciences, according to Marc Van Montagu. It was Jean-Jacques Van de Velde, the son of A.J.J., who eventually made room for it.

Jean-Jacques Van de Velde was appointed ordinary professor of Physiological Chemistry and General Physiology in 1936. In 1951 he detached Physiological Chemistry from his teaching assignment as a separate subject and entrusted it to the young

(opposite page)
**The Ghent Municipal Laboratory, 1913**
Biochemist *avant la lettre* A.J.J. Van de Velde, wearing a white coat, left, was director of the Municipal Laboratory on Lindenlei from 1900 to 1932 and developed the food inspection department. His assistant André Vander Stricht, seated in the middle, was a brewery engineer and manager of the Excelsior brewery on the Steendam. The Municipal Laboratory would close its doors for good in 2009.
(Ghent, Universiteitsarchief)

**Laurent Vandendriessche**
Laurent Vandendriessche in front of a Warburg device for measuring tissue respiration.
(Ghent, Universiteitsarchief, photos A. Claerhout)

lecturer Laurent Vandendriessche, who had just obtained his higher aggregate in biochemistry after a long study period in the Carlsberg laboratories in Copenhagen. Prior to his appointment in medicine, Vandendriessche was also employed by the Veterinary School, first as assistant to Massart and from 1945 as the replacement of Willem Libbrecht, who had been dismissed because of his role in the collaborating Order of Physicians.

As a mentor, Vandendriessche played a pivotal role in the breakthrough of biochemistry and molecular biology in Ghent. This former resistance student had a large international network and good contacts behind the Iron Curtain and in China. His communist background, however, meant that he was barred from entering the US during the McCarthy period and was therefore unable to attend important conferences. Although he never attained the same scientific heights as his students, he, like Massart, made a crucial contribution to their successes, first and foremost by 'sniffing out' their talent and by subsequently providing the right support, incentives and resources. With his fantastic gift for lobbying, Vandendriessche created the right opportunities at the right time, and, more importantly, was able to look beyond faculty structures and barriers.

At the end of 1955, Walter Fiers and Marc Van Montagu met for the first time in Vandendriessche's small laboratory on Apotheekstraat. At the time, the US had a tremendous advantage in the domain of molecular biology compared to Europe, which had been effectively cut off from scientific progress between 1939 and 1945. The ULB, which had been shut down during the war by the German occupier, was much further along than Ghent, thanks to Jean Brachet. He had gone into hiding in the Ardennes and, in a small laboratory, developed the Unna-Brachet method for staining nucleic acids. Lucien De Coninck, who had good contacts with Brachet, included this in his lectures after the war and used Brachet's method to demonstrate to his students the presence of DNA and RNA in all cells of living organisms. But that was about the extent of innovation in scientific education at the University of Ghent. By way of contrast, Van

Montagu refers to the outdated teaching methods employed in inorganic chemistry by René Goubau, purge rector after the war, who retired in 1956. The most recent references in his course dated from the years 1881-1890. Even in his laboratory, the equipment — the 'fume cupboard', gas flame and vacuum pump — chiefly recalled the nineteenth-century practice of science that had migrated with Kekulé from Germany. Fiers and Van Montagu organised lunch seminars in the Rommelaere Institute, together with their young colleagues from the Laboratory for Bacteriology and Virology, headed by Emile Nihoul. The spontaneous interactions with Nihoul and his team were very fruitful and complemented their mainly chemical education with biomedical knowledge.

In October 1960, armed with a scholarship from the Rockefeller Foundation and a letter of recommendation from the Carlsberg laboratories, Fiers left for two years in the US, where he would conduct research at the California Institute of Technology (CalTech). He had chosen his destination with care: the laboratory of biophysicist Robert Sinsheimer, a pioneer in the investigation of nucleic acids, bearers of the genetic code. It was one of the labs where the biotechnological revolution was being prepared. On the eve of the revolution, Sinsheimer wrote in an essay about the future that 'the ability to synthesise, sequence and manipulate genes' meant 'a new horizon in the history of man'. Fiers, too, caught 'a glimpse of another route' — the chance to intervene in the genetic material inscribed in DNA and rewrite human destiny. Scientific curiosity was his main motivation, as he put it. He specialised further in Madison, Wisconsin, with Har Gobind Khorana, who would receive a Nobel Prize in 1968 for cracking the genetic code that converted DNA into protein through RNA. It was a bit like deciphering the Rosetta Stone. In various labs around the world, scientists were feverishly searching for the key. It came down to finding the connection between the language of genetics (DNA and RNA) and that of biochemistry (proteins as chains of amino acids). The revolution in molecular biology started from the insight that DNA gives instructions for the construction of RNA, which ultimately brings genes to life through the production of proteins. Or, to put it another way: by executing the genetic message stored in the DNA. The letters contained in the genetic code only acquire meaning through their sequence, which in turn generates a specific sequence of amino acids in a protein. The very thorough and precise Fiers participated in these 'alchemical transcriptions' of RNA into amino acids. On his return to Ghent, he dedicated himself entirely to the study of bacteriophages. A phage is a virus that infects bacteria. In 1972 he succeeded in determining the entire first sequence of the MS2 RNA virus, a Herculean task that no one had dared to attempt before him. The genetic material of the MS2 consists of an RNA chain of 3,569 nucleotides, while for the average doctoral thesis it was sufficient to determine twenty letters of a genetic code. Fiers sent his students abroad to learn the techniques of DNA sequencing. In 1976 he could apply them to the entire genome of the cancer virus SV40, which is built from more than 5,000 nucleotides. Fiers was thus the first in the world to determine the full genetic sequence of an infectious organism. He received the prestigious Francqui Prize for his work in 1976, and — according to my sources — gave a memorable party in his garden in Destelbergen to celebrate.

It was fundamental research from which a great deal was learnt, but it was also of

Marc Van Montagu, Walter Fiers and Jeff Schell, 1974
In May 1974, Fiers, together with Schell and Van Montagu, organised a workshop on 'Restriction enzymes as tools in molecular biology' at the abbey of Drongen.
(Ghent, collection of Marc Van Montagu)

great importance for the development of medical biotechnology. 'Fiers asked simple questions in a broad context, from molecule to clinic', explains his pupil Peter Vandenabeele, who has since been celebrated repeatedly for his research on cell death. In the 1980s, Fiers focused on the influenza virus with an eye towards developing a universal vaccine. In 1985 he isolated tumour necrosis factor (TNF) in the gene of a mouse, an essential factor in the immune system that can cause some cancers to shrink. Because of its extreme toxicity, however, it can only be used on a highly limited scale in cancer treatment. It was soon clear that TNF also played a decisive role in major inflammatory diseases such as Crohn's disease, psoriasis and rheumatoid arthritis. Medications that directly inhibit TNF are now blockbusters in the pharmaceutical industry.

Walter Fiers received several offers to continue his career in the US but was unwilling to do so for family reasons. 'Then he probably would have received the Nobel Prize he deserved', says his brother-in-arms Marc Van Montagu. At the end of 1962, Fiers returned to provincial Ghent and, as an associate lecturer at the College of Agriculture, moved into the third floor of the brand new low-rise building in Ledeganckstraat. Vandendriessche's laboratory in the Rommelaere Institute was bursting at the seams after three years and had already moved to the fifth floor by summertime. My uncle Lucien Lepoutre was Walter Fiers's first doctoral assistant, and his wife, Annie Deneckere, served as Laurent Vandendriessche's dedicated secretary, starting in 1959. Together with Lucien De Coninck, Vandendriessche campaigned for a chair and a postgraduate course in molecular biology, so that Fiers could be appointed to the faculty of Sciences — which he was in 1967.

As a biochemist, Marc Van Montagu was also immensely fascinated by bacteriophages as a model system for the relationship between coding and the biological activity of genetic material. He was therefore a welcome guest at the discussion meetings and journal clubs of the growing research group that Fiers developed with a great deal of strategic insight. Both labs used each other's equipment and built up a common library. The pioneers discussed the latest articles in the *Journal of Molecular Biology* and expanded their scientific horizons with the work of the Parisian bacteriological geneticists François Jacob and Jacques Monod. Van Montagu graduated in biochemistry in 1965 and was 'finally released from organic syntheses to devote himself to research that really interested him', says Fiers. In this way, with a great deal of 'improvisation and tightrope-walking', and more despite than thanks to university structures, an entirely new line of research was created *ex nihilo* that would grow into one of the crown jewels of Ghent University.

## Alchemists of a new age

In 1966, Jeff Schell appeared on the scene. He came from a Brussels bourgeois milieu and had considerable presence. Everywhere he went, he filled the room. Ideologically, he was strongly influenced by the Jewish historian Leopold Flam, who had been his teacher at the athenaeum in Antwerp. Like him, he joined the Humanist Association (HV). His motto was: 'If you do something, do it well and be the best.' A fervent sailor, he won the Sailing Olympiad in 1974. His attitude towards life inevitably brought him into conflict with ambitious colleagues at the university. Schell had the ambition to get a PhD in microbiology, like biochemistry a young discipline. The former assistant to Massart, Jozef De Ley, was its founder. In 1959, De Ley was appointed as a lecturer in the faculty of Sciences and he introduced microbiology as an elective subject within Plant Physiology. That same year, he founded the Microbiology Laboratory, where Willy Verstraete came to get bacteria for his MRM experiments in the early 1970s. Chemist Jozef Van Beeumen did his doctorate there on the enzyme responsible for 3-Keto-lactose formation by the plant tumour-causing bacterium Agrobacterium tumefaciens. The development of the 3-Keto-lactose test was published in *Nature*. As mentioned earlier, De Ley was primarily involved with the metabolism and the taxonomy of bacteria — one germ per test tube — and acquired international renown with his work and his collection of bacteria cultures.

Jeff Schell, 1974
(Ghent, collection of Marc Van Montagu)

Van Montagu tells how chance helped Schell along in his scientific career. The subject of his dissertation, the taxonomy of acetic acid, only interested him moderately. As a substitute for compulsory military service, the young biologist accompanied the new Gerlache expedition to Antarctica in 1962. After that eighteen-month interruption, he decided to apply for a scholarship for a summer course with Bill Hayes. De Ley's lab was closed for the summer term. Hayes was a major player in bacterial genetics, confirming Schell's intuition that the investigation of bacteriophages was really hot. He gave his dissertation a different but decisive twist, which did not please De Ley at all. Thanks to Vandendriessche and De Coninck, Schell was appointed as a lecturer in 1967 and thus able to work closely with Fiers and Van Montagu to build a new Genetics Laboratory in Ledeganckstraat.

Van Montagu's career path is, if possible, filled with even more bizarre twists and decisive coincidences than Schell's. Through Vandendriessche's contacts in the Eastern Bloc, Van Montagu spent three months in Prague in 1963 after reluctantly completing his military service and working for several years at the Centre for the Study of Nuclear Energy (Studiecentrum Kernenergie) in Mol. For him, Prague marked the final step in the direction of basic research. After working as Vandendriessche's assistant, a National Research Council (NFWO) scholarship would have enabled him to get his PhD at the ULB with molecular biologist and Francqui Prize winner Hubert Chantrenne. Although the left-wing bohemian and his wife Nora had already left provincial, CVP-dominated Ghent for cosmopolitan Brussels, he did not accept the scholarship. A position as work leader with Marcel Sebruyns in the faculty of Medicine had become available. Sebruyns had been director of the Histology Laboratory since the death of Arthur De Groodt in 1952. Van Montagu tells how the entire laboratory, electron microscope and all, simply fell into his lap. Sebruyns was a very good teacher with many anecdotes about patients but would have rather become a general physician and was not really interested in research. In the golden sixties, in the faculty of Medicine, which was well off financially, he had the means to purchase advanced equipment and hire technicians. It created a situation in which Van Montagu had to navigate between two laboratories with vastly different work cultures: the young, dynamic Genetics Laboratory, with its limited budget, on the one hand, and the well-equipped but indolent Histology Laboratory on the other. Although Sebruyns gave Van Montagu *carte blanche*, the personnel showed a certain reluctance to join in the exciting adventure of plant genetics. Certainly Schell, who made a rather haughty impression, had difficulty getting things done. However, Van Montagu had a very dynamic, dedicated secretary, Yvonne Van Espen-Van Doorne, who acted as a go-between. Van Montagu served as work leader under Sebruyns until 1979.

The development of the two new laboratories — Fiers's in Molecular Biology and Schell's in Genetics — started with a minimum of resources. Initial support came from ASLK, a Belgian public institution, for Fiers's cancer research, while Van Montagu was constantly in search of funding. This was balanced by the enormous dedication of the staff in both labs. The precarious financial situation prevented them from purchasing expensive equipment. Hence, it was necessary to make use of the highly labour-intensive methods of the 1950s. The separation of amino acids, for example, was still done manually, with a piece of paper in water and a spectrometer. The future Flemish Life Sciences Research Institute (VIB) group leader Joël Vandekerckhove started off this way as a PhD student with Van Montagu. Regardless of the method, the research itself was so thorough and innovative that Van Montagu was invited to give courses and lectures on the international circuit of molecular biologists and phage geneticists. Like Fiers, he sent people to the US to learn the new techniques and transfer them back to Ghent. The telephone bill of this international network supremo was higher than that of the entire university.

**Ledeganckstraat, 1960s**
(Ghent, Universiteitsarchief and collection of Marc Van Montagu)

Marc Van Montagu, 1980s
(Ghent, collection of Marc Van Montagu)

With their limited budgets, Schell and Van Montagu decided to focus their research on plant tumours. They joined forces, not only to make better use of scarce resources, but also because working together was so much more motivating than fighting each other. 'What we did was abnormal at the university', smiles Van Montagu wistfully. Plants were cheaper and less controversial than research on live animals. Almost no one else was doing it. Moreover, De Ley's Microbiology Laboratory had a collection of more than 150 strains of Agrobacterium. Tumefaciens caused crown gall disease in a wide range of plants. By using Sebruyns's electron microscope to compare a large number of pathogenic strains — virulent and non-virulent — Schell and Van Montagu were able to gain new insights into the role of plasmids in tumour development, such as the identification of Ti-plasmid (tumour-inducing plasmid), which resulted in an international breakthrough in plant genetics.

It meant working intensely, day and night, in the lab, with an especially close-knit atmosphere among the staff, who were by no means merely links in a hierarchical system dedicated to the greater glory of the Prof with a capital 'P'. The work was highly technological but did require asking the right questions. It was not enough just to stay in your corner of the laboratory with your little part of the project. Involvement was expected, a broader vision that placed your research in a wider scientific perspective. The outcome was inconclusive, and the results were by no means known in advance. Soon there were a dozen or so people working at the lab. When he retired in 1999, Van Montagu headed three hundred collaborators.

Academic manager Koen Goethals was one of them. 'The main idea was: basic research is being carried out here that will change the world. It opened new fields of knowledge, broke through barriers that no one had ever broken through before and few people even knew existed. It was science as passion. It wasn't a job you did dutifully at best because you were paid for it, but a way of life because you were driven by it.' Goethals spent every waking moment with it. 'It may sound exaggerated, but there were times when you looked at the results of an experiment with your heart in your mouth because suddenly you saw a connection that nobody had ever seen before.'

In the lab run by the introverted Walter Fiers, a strong work ethic was also combined with agreeable social dynamics. Fiers motivated his people very differently from the passionate Van Montagu and was at least as demanding — of himself as well as his collaborators. Life went on in and around the labs, which were equipped with relaxation rooms where you could play ping-pong and where the staff concentrated on their analyses and sequencing until deep into the night. 'Nobody talked about work-life balance, individual targets or publication pressure', says Peter Vandenabeele. 'In today's meritocracy, everything is calculated and counted, and lab research is strongly individualised. Back then, social contacts were much more intense. Work and play just ran together.'

In 1975 the Genetics Laboratory in Ghent was the world leader in unravelling the molecular basis of the carcinogenic property of Ti-plasmid. Then it was discovered that non-oncogenic bacteria could become virulent as a result of a plasmid transfer. That insight opened new avenues of research. The core of Schell and Van Montagu's discovery was that gene transfer exists in nature and that Ti-plasmids could be used to introduce foreign or new DNA in plants 'just like that'. 'It's actually quite simple', says Van Montagu, with his enigmatic magician's smile. 'We observed the simple laws of nature and didn't at all have the feeling that we were making a revolutionary discovery.' It was (and is) much more difficult to get people to accept the feasibility of the genetic transformation of plants. 'Evolution is a mess,' he adds, 'and that proves that there can be no question of intelligent design.' The discovery of gene transfer opened the way for the revolutionary technique of genetic engineering, which could directly insert new, non-oncogenic traits in a plant, opening up immense possibilities for plant breeding.

Notwithstanding the scientific breakthroughs and successes, Van Montagu would only receive his first permanent appointment as an associate lecturer in 1979, just as Jeff Schell became the director of the Max Planck Institute for Plant Breeding Research in Cologne. It was the crisis period after the university expansion of the 1970s, and there was a general hiring freeze at the two state universities. According to the then cabinet chief of socialist minister of education Jef Ramaekers, Van Montagu's appointment was the result of a deal with CVP prime minister Leo Tindemans. At the University Centre of Antwerp (RUCA), where the Ghent histologist Marie De Groodt had become rector in 1977, another professorial position needed filling. Incidentally, Van Montagu had had spectacular quarrels with the flamboyant De Groodt in Sebruyns's lab in the 1960s. In a package deal that included the CVP appointment of Dietrich Scheuermann, De Groodt's son, to her chair in Antwerp, Van Montagu was appointed in Ghent with the support of the Belgian Socialist Party, BSP. In 1987 he was finally made full professor at the age of fifty-four. Ten years later, at Fiers's retirement celebration, there were no fewer than three Nobel Prize winners present: Har Gobind

Khorana (1968, Medicine), Paul Berg (1980, Chemistry) and Phillip Sharp (1993, Medicine). Molecular biologist Harvey Lodish was also there. Two of his pupils received a Nobel Prize for Medicine: Francis Crick (1962) and Sidney Brenner (2002). There had never been such a high concentration of Nobel Prize winners in Ghent.

## Innovation and valorisation

The Ghent plant geneticists understood that genetic engineering could also start a revolution in agriculture. At the beginning of the 1980s, plant biotechnology really got off the ground. But at that time, Ghent University knew very little about technology transfer — to put it mildly. Leuven Research & Development (LRD) was founded in Leuven in 1972, with the banker Fernand Collin as chairman and the general manager of the university as managing director. As a state university, however, Ghent reacted cautiously to the means offered by the Belgian government for encouraging cooperation between university and industry. There was no in-house expertise to take the appropriate legal steps to protect intellectual property in the form of patents, and the rector did not call on the services of jurists in the faculty of Law. UGent still loses out on huge valorisation revenues because of the backlog incurred at that time. After all, the position of KULeuven as the most innovative university in Europe in 2017 is largely due to the patents that 'golden goose' Désiré Collen took on his intellectual property in the 1970s thanks to adequate support from LRD. Revenues from the marketing of Ghent's inventions in plant genetics, by contrast, still flow into the Max Planck Institute.

Walter Fiers at his retirement, 1997
(Ghent, Flemish Institute for Biotechnology)

As soon as the Agrobacterium story became known, the business world showed an interest in setting up a biotech company along American lines. The San Francisco start-up Advanced Genetic Sciences (AGS) had succeeded in obtaining impressive amounts of money to invest in the best laboratories with the best researchers. Why not 'jump right in', even in Ghent? Jeff Schell received offers from Harvard and the agro-multinational Monsanto in Saint Louis but refused, keeping in mind his motto 'If you do something, do it well and be the best'. In 1978 he became director of the Max Planck Institute for Plant Breeding Research in Cologne, where they did have experience with registering patents. He remained attached to Ghent University as a visiting professor. As a 'good government official', Van Montagu contacted the minister of education and jurist Willy Calewaert in 1981; the latter, however, believed the university was 'not there to make products' and therefore not to set up spin-offs either. As with Patrick Sorgeloos's Artemia Systems NV, the Regional Investment Company for Flanders (GIMV) was called in. Innovi, an association of industrialists from Antwerp, sought capital and investors. The CEO of Innovi was the lawyer Jos Bouckaert, the very model of a broker in the grey area between science and technology on the one hand and the business world on the other. Between 1979 and 1982 he concentrated mainly on technology transfers, in his capacity as director of KULeuven Research and Development (LRD) and Haasrode Research Park. Later he was responsible for capital investments and the management of start-ups, particularly in agro-biotechnology. He was CEO of the aforementioned Advanced Genetic Sciences (AGS) and was involved with the Ghent spin-off Plant Genetic Systems (PGS) as an adviser and subsequently also as CEO. Of course, between Ghent and Silicon Valley there was a world of difference. Marc Zabeau, one of the original scientific staff members, became director of PGS's research laboratory. Many other scientists and technicians from the Genetics Laboratory also joined. First, the focus was on herbicide-tolerant plants to arm them against herbicides. PGS then began breeding crops, a world first.

Bouckaert was more familiar with the financial world than were the Ghent scientists. In 1979 he took care of the patents on the invention of Désiré Collen, an assistant in Leuven. He granted the exclusive right to the latter's anticoagulant drug to Genentech in San Francisco and negotiated royalties for LRD and Collen himself. After the drug was registered in 1987, this ensured significant financial returns for KULeuven. How different to the fate of the University of Ghent! According to Julien Hoste, rector between 1977 and 1981, the Ghent University could not apply for patents because, as a state university, it did not have legal personality. He therefore suggested that the Max Planck Institute (PGS) do it, since Schell was director in Cologne. Therefore, the lucrative patents ended up at Max Planck, not UGent. A few years later PGS was able to buy it all back, but in the meantime Max Planck had received the returns for three early herbicide-tolerant products that are still used in the agro-industry. In 1996, PGS was sold for 436 million euros to the German firm AgrEvO, which was then taken over by Bayer CropScience in 2002. It is still located in the Technology Park on Ardoyen. Many people from the pioneering phase still work there; the best technicians opted for a higher income, more security and additional benefits. In this way they brought their know-how and expertise to the business world, which in a sense meant a drain on the university.

Walter Fiers has another story to tell from the time when Ghent University did not yet have technology transfer. As an inventor, he has several patents with Biogen, started in Geneva in 1978 by visionary scientists, himself included. Biogen sought to introduce the European pharmaceutical industry to biotech without losing scientific independence. In San Francisco there was the American example Genentech, which functioned as a bridge between venture capital and scientists who needed money to get their labs up and running. Traditional sources of income were quickly becoming insufficient to cope with the rapid expansion of biotechnology in the late 1970s and early 1980s. On the other hand, publicly funded universities still served as the breeding ground for up-and-coming talent that needed to learn the 'trade' and techniques. Without Biogen, however, it would not have been possible for so many people to get their PhDs and keep up with the rapid speed of new developments. Biogen's venture capital came from Inco, a company that processed nickel and had nothing to do with biotech but had nevertheless made an agreement with the pharmaceutical sector to market the products of molecular biology. The great example was Désiré Collen's antithrombosis drug, which was brought to market by Genentech. At the time, Fiers was working on interferon beta, a drug for the treatment of multiple sclerosis. In March

1983, Biogen went to the stock market, where the big money was. Fiers emphasises that all the money from Biogen returned to his lab through the appropriate university channels. He has trained more than one hundred PhD students, who now have important positions in biotechnology all over the world, both in universities and spin-offs. Without Biogen, this would have been impossible. 'The pharmaceutical industry has a lot of money but no ideas,' emphasises Peter Vandenabeele, 'or at least, a way of working that is too rigid.' The success of companies such as Genentech lies precisely in the combination of the large-scale, efficient approach of the pharmaceutical industry, on the one hand, and elements from university research culture, characterised by fundamental questions and serendipity, on the other. Pharmaceutical companies are extremely well organised for performing millions of tests on a large scale, but 'the layers of insight are becoming deeper and deeper and specialised knowledge flourishes best in a more academic research context', concludes Vandenabeele.

In 1996 the Flemish Institute for Biotechnology (Vlaams Instituut voor Biotechnologie, or VIB) was established by Luc Van den Brande, minister-president of the Flemish government. Van den Brande realised that government subsidies to the life sciences were completely insufficient to continue to fulfil this 'Flemish' promise in the future. In November 1993 he invited Jo Bury and Rudy Dekeyser — who were responsible for the Flemish Biotechnology Action Programme (Vlaams Actieprogramma Biotechnologie, or VLAB) within the IWT — to discuss possibilities. The minister-president wanted to invest 1 billion Belgian francs (25 million euros) every year in order to put Flemish biotechnology on the map internationally. The money that Van den Brande managed to secure for his biotech showpiece was from the reconversion credits for the dismantling of the shipping industry and the Boelwerf, an important shipyard on the river Scheldt in Temse. Bury and Dekeyser were given *carte blanche* to forge a plan that would consolidate biotech's economic and social value. The result was the establishment of an interuniversity institute with four core departments consisting of the research groups of Désiré Collen and Herman Vanden Berghe in Leuven, on the one hand, and Walter Fiers and Marc Van Montagu in Ghent, on the other. These were complemented by five associated departments at the Free University of Brussels (VUB), the University of Antwerp (UA) and UGent. The four stars of the core departments were approaching retirement. Their intellectual legacy could be retained and further developed thanks to the VIB. Van Montagu is very happy with the situation. In his words, the VIB is an important structure that transcends the traditional compartmentalisation of disciplines, keeping the life sciences together as a whole and making them work together.

Over the past two decades, the VIB has grown into a successful joint venture between Flemish universities and industry. It employs no fewer than 1,500 researchers, 500 of whom work in Ghent, spread over various campuses. In the meantime, it has generated 18 spin-offs that employ nearly 700 people. Ablynx is the most visible, with a stock market value of more than 750 million euros. Walter Fiers's original Molecular Biology Laboratory has since been merged into the Department of Molecular Biomedical Research/Inflammation Research Centre, which today has more than 200 collaborators and is headed by Bart Lambrecht. Another VIB branch of the Fiers tree, Medical Biotechnology, is located in Rommelaere with Jan Tavernier as group leader. The Genetics Laboratory of Jeff Schell has grown into the Department of Plant Systems Biology under the leadership of Dirk Inzé and remains strongly interwoven with the plant biotechnology and bioinformatics departments of Anna De Picker and Yves Van de Peer. CropDesign was founded in 1998 as a spin-off of this department with venture capital from the Flemish Investment Company (GIMV). In 2006 it was bought by BASF Plant Science.

The VIB receives an annual subsidy of 59 million euros from the Flemish government, more than twice as much as it received at the start twenty years ago. According to Jo Bury, this means Ghent is playing in the sector's Champions League. Marc Van Montagu ventures to put this into perspective. He finds it fabulous that something like this is possible in a small region like Flanders, but also has his reservations. Although UGent scores better and better in the rankings, a stronger international structure needs to be built up in order to bring scientific know-how even more to the fore. Van Montagu also regrets that the rivalry between Leuven and Ghent, which no longer has any ideological basis, continues to have such a decisive influence. It detracts from the international reputation of Flemish biotechnology.

## Green biotechnology and the controversial potato field

In 2013, as the father of green biotechnology, Marc Van Montagu received the World Food Prize, the Nobel Prize for food and agriculture. The now eighty-four-year-old founder of GMOs still travels around the world with just as much fire and conviction to spread his message. In the past year, he has been more 'in orbit' than in Brussels, travelling from São Paulo to Hyderabad, Ouagadougou to Beijing and Kyoto. It is an 'obsession' that in five or ten years' time he will no longer be able to do so, as the resistance to genetically modified crops that still needs to be overcome is so strong. The applications of medical biotechnology in the pharmaceutical industry are much more easily accepted by society than GMOs. The fact that a gene could simply be transferred from one organism to another is apparently so frightening to many that it has caused an irrational panic over the irreversible harmful effects on health and the environment. 'This is not supported by any scientific evidence', says Van Montagu, who has quarrelled with Greenpeace. 'Nature is a gigantic laboratory where organisms constantly activate and shut down genes due to environmental factors. This is simply the process of adaptation as the basis of evolution. Making a transgenetic organism through human intervention is just a minor surgical procedure compared to what happens spontaneously in nature, and certainly compared with what mainstream crossing and breeding techniques do in the agriculture and the livestock industries.' Biotechnology has the advantage of refinement; something is changed minimally in an organism and has major consequences.

To Van Montagu's great frustration, the expected innovation boom in plant biotechnology has not occurred, whereas he believes that molecular farming could contribute to sustainable agriculture and a healthier environment. The green potential of biotechnology is quite large, not only in the production of human food and animal feed, but also in terms of bioenergy. A few years ago, for example, fieldwork was carried out at UGent on the genetic modification of the wood composition of poplars to make it easier to convert this source of renewable energy into bioenergy.

Social engagement is in Van Montagu's blood, because as a child he witnessed the misery of the Ghent slums. Since the 1970s, his commitment has mainly been to the most disadvantaged in developing countries. 'Ninety per cent of farmers are based there and with GMOs can realise higher and more sustainable yields', he says. This would improve the standard of living of small farmers and reduce social inequality. Van Montagu is convinced that knowledge and technology are crucial to meeting major societal challenges and achieving the UN's Sustainable Development Goals (SDGs). However, little is to be expected of large industrialists and politicians in this respect, and scientists have too little influence on world politics to push through their rational vision. Only fifteen years ago, Greenpeace spectacularly blocked container ships carrying genetically modified soya beans from the US. But in 2016, 78% of the soya, 64% of the cotton and 26% of the maize worldwide was based on genetically modified crops. In the Americas and Asia, regulation is also much less strict than in Europe, where the principle of prudence prevails. The cost of complying with the rules in terms of research and development is so high that it causes a chronic investment deficit in research and development. There is a general ban on GMO field research in Europe. An exception must therefore be requested for each test, which is granted more easily in some member states than others. However, scientists dependent on public funding cannot afford the cost of a commercial licence for cultivation and imports, which only increases the power and influence of agro-industry on research. For Van Montagu, there is no choice but to lobby internationally to make European regulations more flexible, so that the applications of plant biotechnology can lead to greater social justice globally.

Van Montagu has students from all over the world, but also — and especially — from developing countries. After his retirement, that commitment has been perpetuated in International Plant Biotechnology Outreach (IPBO), now also a VIB department. Its mission is fourfold: communication, training, networking, and project development in developing countries. As a non-profit organisation, the International Industrial Biotechnology Network (IIBN) promotes sustainable biotechnology aimed at low- and middle-income countries. Various projects are currently under way in Africa, such as the Sweet Potato Action for Security and Health in Africa (SASHA), which aims to improve the food safety and living standards of poor families in sub-Saharan Africa by exploiting the potential of the sweet potato using biotechnology. In 2015 the Ghent research team of Lieve Gheysen, together with the International Potato Centre (CIP) in Lima, discovered that sweet potatoes contain integrated hereditary material from Agrobacterium. A good example of DNA exchange across species without human intervention or an argument for the "naturalness" of GMOs', says Gheysen. She is director of the IPBO and Van Montagu's successor at the faculty of Bioengineering Sciences, where she heads the Applied Molecular Genetics Laboratory. The research focus of this lab is the analysis of the interactions between rice and parasitic nematodes — perhaps not coincidentally the chosen domain of Gheysen's spiritual grandfather, Lucien De Coninck.

Gheysen also conducted the notorious GMO potato field research in Wetteren. On 29 May 2011 some 450 Field Liberation Movement (FLM) activists stormed the field and destroyed about 15% of the experiment (including six genetically modified plants). It led to a fierce controversy in the scientific world as well as in public opinion, not least because Barbara Van Dyck was immediately fired from KULeuven. The bio-engineer in Forestry and Nature Conservation had participated in the action out of green conviction and subsequently refused to distance herself from the violence and destruction that, in her view, had also been exaggerated in the media. The criminal court of Dendermonde summoned the activists; UGent, VIB and the Flemish Research Institute for Agriculture, Fisheries and Food (ILVO) filed as injured parties in a civil action. The university community was called upon to join in condemning the destruction of the plants. There followed opinion pieces by Eva Brems, Jean Paul Van Bendegem and Dirk Voorhoof, who disagreed with the university's position and strongly criticised the criminalisation of the protest action. The court sentenced ten activists to a suspended prison term of three to six months and a fine of 550 euros per person for gang formation. An indemnity of 20,000 euros was also claimed — a disproportionate penalty that caused great indignation. In this way, the 'war on the potato field' had much greater impact than the researchers ever dared dream the experiment itself would have, precisely because the public debate was so intense. In more than a hundred television reports and press articles, freedom of expression and freedom of research in relation to genetic modification and sustainable agriculture were discussed extensively, with arguments for and against, but also with prejudices and misconceptions on both sides.

While anti-GMO activism was trapped in the fear of the precautionary principle regarding the risks and dangers of genetically modified plants, there was also pertinent criticism of the commercial interests of agro-multinationals in such research. The lack of transparency in the way the university had communicated about BASF's vested interest in the experiment was an important stumbling block for the activists. It was found that 4 of the 108 modified potatoes were BASF specimens. FLM wanted to denounce the fact that fundamental research serves a commercial agenda in Flanders, which has made biotechnology an economic spearhead. According to this line of reasoning, neither scientific interests nor societal interests are paramount at the VIB;

The storming of the potato field, 2011 (DeWereldMorgen, photo on the left by Geert Lenssens)

The storming of the potato field, 2011
(DeWereldMorgen, photo Geert Lenssens)

instead, return on investment takes pride of place. Successful spin-offs are bought up by multinationals, such as CropDesign by BASF. Private companies hide behind universities to pursue their own interests, which have nothing to do with science and everything to do with money. In the meantime, the agro-industry continues to be wilfully blind to the social inequality and environmental problems that capitalism continues to create. Van Montagu's social and green engagement is also strikingly at odds with the highly controversial practices of pesticide giant Monsanto. 'His' PGS is, after all, an integral part of it thanks to the merger of Bayer and Monsanto in April 2017. This merger not only implies that farmers will become even more dependent on the multinationals (and their prices) for the purchase of their seeds and pesticides; small local farmers are also banned from using their own seeds. In addition, Monsanto is the main producer of the herbicide glyphosate under the brand name Roundup. A global protest movement has arisen to have the poisonous weed killer banned because of its extremely harmful effects on the ecosystem. This citizens' movement has the wind in its sails after the leaking of the Monsanto Papers, which show that the chemical giant spent millions to block the prohibition of the product and hired scientists to sow doubt with respect to glyphosate's carcinogenic properties. The European Food Safety Agency (EFSA) denies the problem and for the time being has given the green light for continued production and use of Roundup. European commissioner for health and food safety Vytenis Andriukaitis stresses the importance of science in his policy and denounces the 'misleading' information disseminated by activists, while the World Health Organization states that glyphosate is 'probably' carcinogenic. It is clear that the current controversy surrounding Monsanto and glyphosate is to a large extent about the (in)dependence of science and that a naive belief in scientific progress is not enough to counter criticism.

The scientific results of the potato field experiment in Wetteren caused far less fuss than the FLM activism. The resistant genes that were added appeared to be the right combination for resistance against the potato disease that was responsible for the Great Famine in Ireland in the 1840s and is still the biggest threat to potato cultivation worldwide. The next step is to apply that insight on the *Bintje*, the popular potato variety that has made Belgium the largest exporter of processed potato products in the world.

Marc Van Montagu considers the economic exploitation of GMOs by the agro-industry to be less problematic than the research that has been blocked by multinationals for business reasons. The quality of seeds is greatly improved by industrial production, which means that small farmers are less likely to fall victim to fraudulent practices. It is much more scandalous to know that the hunger problem can be solved and that it's not happening, says Van Montagu. Unfortunately, scientific and technological progress cannot automatically be equated with social progress and environmental sustainability, just as industrialisation in the nineteenth century did not automatically lead to social redistribution through taxation and social security. That is why Van Montagu advocates adequate science communication and a university that, on the model of Paris-Saclay, also involves social scientists in biotechnological research. In any case, his own story makes it clear that only a multiperspectival approach can provide a solution to the societal controversy that persists with regard to GMOs.

## Transition UGent

Etienne Vermeersch's bestseller *De ogen van de panda — een milieufilosofisch essay* (The eyes of the panda — an essay on environmental philosophy) was published in 1988 and would be published again twenty-five years later. The essay was an attempt to place environmental issues within a coherent global and societal framework. Vermeersch was one of the founders of the Centre for Sustainable Development (Centrum voor Duurzame Ontwikkeling, or CDO), which was founded in 1995 at the faculty of Political and Social Sciences at UGent. Environmental engineer Bernard Mazijn was the driving force. As student chairman of the Social Council, he was already involved in initiatives concerning development cooperation at the university in the second half of the 1980s, including the award of an honorary doctorate to Bob Geldof. Around the time of the 1992 Rio Conference, he began to see that environmental technology alone was not up to the challenges of the future. This also prompted him to study development cooperation and to set up the CDO with his supervisor Ruddy Doom. Its aim and mission were to develop multidisciplinary research on the social and political dimensions of the environment and sustainability in order to better understand, influence and accelerate the transitions needed for ecologically sustainable and socially just societies worldwide. The CDO is now led by Thomas Block. Political scientists, pedagogues, economists, (bio)engineers, sociologists, ecologists, physicists and philosophers work together on a variety of projects that can be described as 'sustainability research'. The relationship between science and society and cooperation with non-academic actors are paramount.

Because of the failed Copenhagen climate summit in 2009, the 10:10 climate campaign was launched at schools and universities around the world with the aim of reducing $CO_2$ emissions. At UGent, the commitment was translated into the association UGent1010 and a sustainability pact, which was signed by eighty departments and commits them to specific sustainability actions, such as the use of recycled materials and sustainable caterers.

The university administration tasked the central Environment department with developing a long-term vision of sustainability. Academic manager Koen Goethals and Mil Kooyman, as external member of the executive board, formed a core group together with a few members of the CDO. Sustainability was very broadly defined as an overarching concept covering mobility, energy, waste, food, education and research. According to this vision, a university that wants to be relevant to the social challenges of its time at the beginning of the twenty-first century must not only stimulate research that contributes to a socio-ecological future, but also feed the public debate surrounding it with content and produce students who are familiar with sustainability issues. And of course, set a good example itself.

In 2013 environmental coordinator Riet Van de Velde got behind the Transition UGent initiative, 'Together for a Sustainable University', a participatory think tank that mobilised more than two hundred experts, policymakers, students and staff. It turned out to be an infectious formula that translates burgeoning ideas into concrete actions, from fair-trade jerseys in the gift shop to a Student Square on the Rozier, a vegetable garden for students and a participatory wind turbine on Proeftuinstraat. 'The next big thing will be a lot of small things', was written in large letters on the side of the University Forum (UFO) in the context of Tipping Point, an art route through the city during the 2015 climate conference in Paris. It fits in seamlessly with the principles of Transition UGent. At a time when great ideologies are a thing of the past, the transition to a more sustainable living environment will mainly come about by starting up and connecting countless small actions and initiatives from within the 'communitas'. Transition UGent is also one of UGent's comparatively rare bottom-up initiatives that really 'works' quite well. At the top, awareness grew that if UGent really wanted to be a leading knowledge institute for an ecologically, socially and economically sustainable future, it would also be necessary to take concrete and probably less popular measures, such as the 'hard' accountability of staff and departments within the framework of the university's mobility and energy policy.

The independent sustainability office, or Green Office, is central to all sustainability activities. It is run by Riet Van de Velde and her team. Flexibility and the solid basis provided by Transition UGent ensure that a great deal can be done. Ideas that were dismissed as unrealistic a few years ago are now being put back on the agenda by the university departments themselves. Although the progress generates enthusiasm, the environmental coordinator guards herself against excessive optimism: environmental problems continue to be of the utmost urgency.

Thomas Lommée,
*The Next Big Thing*, 2015
(Ghent, image bank UGent,
photo Hilde Christiaens)

Loecki Vervenne at the top of the Book Tower, 1944-1945
(Ghent, collection of Patricia Vervenne)

Epilogue

# MEASURING THE CLOUDS

Frans Vervenne — known to friends as Loecki — claimed to have held the 'highest post' in Ghent, the lookout post built by the Germans above the twenty-first floor of the Book Tower during the Second World War. In September 1944 the city was liberated and the acting mayor, Edward Anseele, authorised the installation of an air observation station there by Passive Air Protection. Captain Franciscus Joannes Vervenne, militia class of 1935, was charged with monitoring the airspace for enemy planes. The risk of the city being bombarded did not change until the armistice of 8 May 1945. Vervenne had experienced this personally when the Allies demolished his parental home in Sint-Salvatorstraat.

Loecki Vervenne was in the habit of dressing up. The man who boasted of occupying the highest post in the city must have felt like king of the world that fine day when he was immortalised in black and white. Perhaps his image was captured by the photographer who lived down the street, where all the neighbours went to hide from the bombs because it was the only place with a dry cellar. The war seems to have had little effect on Vervenne. Freshly groomed in his dark bespoke suit and starched white shirt, with a tie and obligatory pocket square, the *'maître de la tour'* poses with his binoculars, gazing at the cloudless sky.

Even before the war, Vervenne liked to order the latest jazz music and scores from America. He had a jazz band on Seeleskest and could play piano, saxophone and banjo. His three children were also brought up surrounded by music and art. His daughter Patricia recalls a black tap dancer with baggy pants who came to visit from the US, who danced with such conviction that she decided to take it up herself. Born in March 1944, she was one of the sixteen female civil engineers who graduated from Ghent University between 1945 and 1975. There were only two girls in her year. This was in 1969. Her father was very proud of his youngest daughter, who was the first in the family to graduate from university. A bookkeeper by training and foreman by trade — in the La Liè024ve flax factory on the Wiedauwkaai — he spoke of the university as a place of knowledge. You had to plough through 'thick books with thick covers', but whether you actually acquired wisdom there was another matter …

## 'A mighty bookcase vertically arranged'

In 1939 it was time to move the university's book collection from the old library on the Baudelo to the Book Tower. When Henry Van de Velde received the commission in 1933, he conceived the new library as an imposing tower with clear lines and balanced, sober forms. In his farewell lecture upon his retirement in 1936, he said: 'I have the ambition to create a structure that will testify to my belief in the future of a more rational architecture, but above all to the sense of willing devotion that unites me with all those I have learned to know and appreciate here at the university.' Even before the

Scale model of the Book Tower and the Blandijn, according to Henry Van de Velde's original design, 1934
(Ghent, Universiteitsarchief)

works were completed in September 1942, it turned out that it was a 'luminous idea' to build a vertical library. Rector Louis Fredericq spoke of 'a symbolic beacon' rising above the city, others of a 'cathedral of knowledge'. Twenty floors high, it was crowned with a glass belvedere. With its 64 metres atop the Blandijnberg, itself already at an elevation of 21 metres, the Book Tower literally towers over everything else in the urban landscape. Van de Velde wanted his tower to serve as a symbol of science alongside the symbols of religion and the city, St Bavo's Cathedral and St Nicholas's Church, on the one hand, and the Belfort, on the other. Unfortunately, the fourth tower of knowledge and culture opened its doors in a very dark period. The beacon full of 'thick books with thick covers' was not able to illuminate the city during the occupation – particularly after the Germans installed a command post with anti-aircraft artillery in the belvedere.

To build the modernist construction, Henry Van de Velde's only public building in Belgium, it was necessary to level an entire working-class neighbourhood. Just as Batavia had to make way for the Institute of Sciences in the nineteenth century, its counterpart, De Vreese on the opposite side of the Rozier, was demolished at the end of the 1930s. Progress had a price: the university expanded in height at the expense of the working class, who had little access to the wonders of science from their position at the bottom of the social ladder. The Book Tower fitted into a larger plan for the site, visualised by Van de Velde in a magnificent model from 1934. Lending architectural consistency to the tower, the Higher Institute for Art History (Hoger Instituut voor

Kunstgeschiedenis, or HIKO) would be built along with two low, elongated buildings on Blandijnstraat. These would house the Institute for Zoology and the Pharmacy department on either side of a wide passageway, a reference to the demolished entrance to De Vreese. Passers-by had a splendid view of the Book Tower from Sint-Pietersplein. Van de Velde worked on this project for twenty-one years before finally giving up in 1954.

At Ghent University, Van de Velde's designs collided with 'a miserable, drip-like subsidy policy' that was moreover hindered by the 'machinery of bureaucracy'. It was a source of real suffering for the renowned artist, who had returned in 1925 after a brilliant career in Weimar and Otterlo to head the Higher Institute of Decorative Arts (Hoger Instituut voor Sierkunst) in Ter Kameren and was appointed as a lecturer at the HIKO in Ghent. The actual construction of the Book Tower only started after his retirement in 1936 and lasted seven full years, whereas it could easily have been built in two and a half years.

The architectural fee set by the Belgian state amounted to 2.5% of the building price. Van de Velde had to share this with fellow architect Jean-Norbert Cloquet, who received a third. According to his memoirs, his own two-thirds did not even cover the costs of his office. His bookkeeper pointed out to him that the losses caused by the delays and intrigues between the various public authorities were slowly but surely bringing him to the brink of bankruptcy. In addition, the university constantly changed its plans. After the Second World War, the university administration decided to house Arts and Philosophy on the Blandijn instead of Zoology and Pharmacy. In 1954, after years of hassle and delay — the plans had already been worked out in detail

**The Book Tower, 1955**
(Ghent, photo Walter De Mulder)

— the university and the ministry again made additional demands, including an auditorium in the form of a cinema. Now the ninety-one-year-old Van de Velde had had enough. He passed the assignment on to his assistant Eugène Delatte. It was not until 1957 that the necessary funds were collected and construction could finally begin. The result is what it is, but does not correspond at all to the original design from 1934. With the Book Tower in the background, the main entrance to the Blandijn reveals at a glance a fundamental contradiction in the 200-year history of Ghent University: it is capable of achieving great things, but just as capable of hindering greatness at every turn. 'The machinery of bureaucracy', the cumbersome decision-making process, institutional compartmentalisation and petty human jealousy expertly suppressed so much creativity that the great things that were eventually realised can often be considered small miracles.

The restoration of the Book Tower is plagued by the same contradiction. Apart from a few inspiring advocates such as the cataloguer and interwar expert Norbert Poulain, the university completely neglected and mistreated its tower of knowledge and wisdom for decades. In 1992 the Book Tower was designated a protected monument, but Gustave Magnel's concrete continued to rot silently. That is, until architect André Singer discovered archives of the original drawings by Henry Van de Velde in a Brussels auction house in 2002. Because this Ghent heritage was so important, he was able to convince rector André De Leenheer to carry out a preliminary study on the poor condition of the building. The cost of restoration was estimated at 41 million euros. If something were not done quickly, the building would have reached the point of no return, according to the damning study. 'In the event of total negligence, we will have to demolish the building within thirty years.' De Leenheer realised that the university was responsible for a masterpiece. At the last meeting of the board of governors that he chaired as rector, on 16 September 2005, he convinced the university community to take on that responsibility with a passionate plea. Good connections with mayor Frank Beke, provincial governor Herman Balthazar and science policy minister Fientje Moerman meant that the university did not have to bear the heavy financial burden alone.

The green light marked the beginning of the resurrection of the Book Tower. The new head librarian Sylvia Van Peteghem, a key figure in the restoration story, succeeded in mobilising students, staff and the inhabitants of Ghent *en masse* in 2007 in the battle for the historic monument. It gave the UGent community a growing sense of pride in its fourth tower of knowledge and culture. Anyone could finance a step in the tower, one of the first successful forms of crowdfunding within the university, which increased the sense of identification.

Under Van Peteghem's leadership, the University Library was transformed from a dusty storage institution into a digital knowledge centre. In the early 1990s I conducted my own doctoral research using the grey index cards and catalogues in the central library, as well as struggling to find my way through the incomprehensible classification systems in the maze of seminar libraries in the faculties of Arts and Philosophy and Political Science. At that time, there was only one computer in the catalogue room on which to consult the incomplete digital catalogue on CD-ROM. Internet did not exist yet. Nonetheless, mathematician and computer scientist Herbert

Van de Sompel was already working on his revolutionary invention of the OpenURL link resolver in that period, sold as SFX in 2000 and marketed by the Israeli company Ex Libris, the market leader in library automation. It made UGent a global player in the domain of library technology. The agreement with Google Books to digitise copyright-free books has meanwhile served the University Library well, as has its very progressive open access policy, in which Van de Sompel also played a pioneering role. The University Library has thus responded outstandingly to the revolutionary possibilities of automation and digitisation in the world of books and scientific knowledge.

After the principle decision, it took another six years before the restoration of the Book Tower could be started according to the plans of architect duo Robbrecht and Daem. Ambitions for the project were high: not only to build an underground depot and provide the building with a new skin, but also to become a better library for people and books. The aim was to complete this massive project by 2017, but the 'machinery of bureaucracy' got in the way from time to time. In the end, the restoration will take at least as long as the construction of the Book Tower itself — in any case, a fine symbolic coincidence.

## The Centre for Interdisciplinary Synthesis

In fact, after the faculty of Arts and Philosophy moved from Universiteitsstraat in the early 1960s, 'De Blandijn' did not need a beautiful building to turn it into an icon of the university.

When George Sarton received the first George Sarton Medal from the History of Science Society in 1955, a year before his death, he said: 'Scientists of future generations studying my life will sometimes wonder if I was crazy; I wasn't crazy, but I did seem crazy because I was overwhelmed by two passions, a passion for science and a passion for the "humanities" that was equally fierce.' During his studies in Ghent, Sarton had already played both sides. Disillusioned with his studies in philosophy, he switched to mathematics in 1902 and wrote a doctoral thesis on Isaac Newton. In 1912 he applied for a vacancy as a tutor in the engineering department. He did not get it — otherwise this apostle of the history of science would have been even more connected to Ghent. But perhaps then he would not have become so famous. In 1915, Sarton left for the US, where he continued his career at Harvard from 1916 onwards. For the Ghent-American father of the journal *Isis. The International Review devoted to the History of Science and its Cultural Influence*s, founded in 1913, the history of science fits into a broader humanist ideal and the quest to bring science and culture closer together. He succeeded in doing so at Harvard after the atomic bomb in Hiroshima convincingly demonstrated that building bridges between the 'humanities' and the 'technicalities of science' was a matter of life and death.

When he was still in Ghent, Sarton shared his ideals with Julius Mac Leod, who published his *Place of Science in History* (1915), in which he developed his utopian vision, while in exile in Manchester. This history of science showed 'the spectacular of progress achieved by peaceful work' and should be offered at all levels of education as well as through various forms of popularisation. The advocate of Higher Education for the People (Hoger Onderwijs voor het Volk) in Ghent was convinced that the history of science made humanity 'better', as Sarton argued in *The History of Science and the New Humanism* (1931).

The same ideals inspired Albert — A.J.J. — Van de Velde when he founded the Museum for the History of Science in 1948, after his retirement. The godfather of biochemistry in Ghent had not only inherited Mac Leod's love of botany, but also his passion for the history of science. His museum was originally supposed to be called the Professor Julius Mac Leod Museum. It opened its doors in the premises of the Archaeological Museum of Ghent (Oudheidkundig Museum van Gent), now the STAM. In 1965 the Museum for the History of Sciences (Museum voor de Geschiedenis van de Wetenschappen) came under the management of the university and was housed on the Korte Meer.

In his speech in the Aula on the *dies natalis* in 1964, rector Jean-Jacques Bouckaert announced the establishment of a Centre for Interdisciplinary Synthesis. He started from a sense of pride in several 'sons' in the pantheon of the university who, 'although remarkable specialists in their field, have managed to preserve the humanist spirit by expressing their deep and active interest in areas of culture that a priori seemed to be

Aerial view of the Blandijn, Rozier and Plateau
(Ghent, Universiteitsarchief)

far removed from their own, and who have thus united in their mind different aspects of knowledge and culture'. Bouckaert referred among others to Henri Pirenne's synthetic vision, the many-faceted knowledge of Joseph Bidez and August Vermeylen, and the literary talent of ophthalmologist Daniël Van Duyse. He juxtaposed 'the ability to unite the most diverse areas of human knowledge in a synthetic mind' with the far-reaching specialisation that made synthesis impossible in the 'century of technology'. The university was in danger of educating more and more people who, although thoroughly trained technically, lacked a broad synthetic vision. Bouckaert's own personal experiences in the 'experimental' sciences, by contrast, had taught him that scientific progress was no longer possible without interdisciplinary collaboration. In many cases, the boundaries between the classical disciplines and even between faculties had become outdated. The question therefore arose as to how interdisciplinary cooperation could be promoted by the university. Rector Bouckaert drew inspiration from the essay by C.P. Snow, *The Two Cultures and the Scientific Revolution* (1959). Although written sixty years ago, it remains surprisingly topical: the English molecular physicist and novelist describes in crystal-clear terms how the gap between the humanities and the natural sciences, alpha and beta, between basic and applied science, between arts and sciences, had become so great that there were effectively different cultures and different languages, with 'scholars' and 'scientists' who could no longer understand one another, or no longer even wanted to. 'Much of it rests on misinterpretations which are dangerous', he wrote presciently. The polarisation was 'a sheer loss to us all'. Snow's influence was already great in his own time. He saw a way out of the conundrum in a new form of education that transcended the trend towards specialisation.

Bouckaert had noticed at MIT how engineers were not merely offered a superficial introduction to the humanities; rather, they had to study literature and culture in depth. The separation of humanistic and scientific education had an impoverishing effect, 'so that one may regret that a linguist cannot understand the wonderful elegance with which Watson and Crick established the structure of DNA, and that a physician cannot appreciate the beautiful systematics of language as explored in the works of Trubetzkoy.' The conclusion emerged that no university that hoped to be more than just a vocational school could afford not to create structures that promoted synthetic thinking. The Centre for Interdisciplinary Synthesis that Bouckaert had in mind had to search and to strive for connections 'from all sides' (multiperspectivist!). In this way, a synthesis could be achieved at the highest level, that of philosophy and science. The rector was therefore particularly pleased that the members of the Philosophy department at the University of Ghent 'enthusiastically agreed with this viewpoint'. The Centre for Interdisciplinary Synthesis was indeed the fulfilment of Leo Apostel's dream, which was already touched upon in the chapter about Pluralism and which Bouckaert gave his full support.

A workgroup was set up consisting of interested colleagues from different disciplines and 'intellectual trends'. There was support from industrial circles where it was felt that industry needed not only technically skilled personnel, but also people with a general education. The planned centre would consist of three levels: a Science department, a Cultural Synthesis department and a super-structural Religious Studies department, where education would be conceived in a pluralistic way. This would, 'through mutual contact between believers of different faiths and non-believers', lead to 'a spirit of understanding, tolerance and rapprochement'.

'Would', because if this visionary plan had not been 'talked to death in too many committees' in May 1965, according to rector De Meyer, and finally tabled by the physicians and the engineers, Ghent University would certainly have been a European forerunner in the field of interdisciplinarity. As Apostel put it in 1988: as a great dream of May '68, the interdisciplinary project in Ghent had already foundered three years earlier on the reality principle of the faculties. In line with Sarton, Mac Leod and Van de Velde, Apostel saw the popularisation of science as a necessary condition for connection and synthesis. In 1984 his pupil Marc De Mey compared his teacher's dreams and ambitions with those of Sarton in the context of the Sarton Centennial and came up with striking parallels. The hundredth anniversary celebration marked the start of the annual interfaculty George Sarton Chair for the History of Science, with emeritus professor Michel Thiery as chairman.

In 2003, the inspired Romanist Fernand Hallyn founded the interdisciplinary Sarton Centre for the History of Science in the faculty of Arts and Philosophy, now led by the philosopher and physicist Maarten Van Dyck. Sarton's continued omnipresence at Ghent University provides lasting inspiration for the strongly felt need for a new, binding project for the future of 'humanities' in relation to science and society.

A.J.J. Van de Velde's overarching ideal for a Museum for the History of Science was in the meantime fragmented in a plurality of sub-collections — medicine, science, morphology, ethnography, archaeology, anatomy, zoology, the Botanical Garden — each with a specific history and logic. Together, Ghent's university museums manage 640,000 objects, the largest collection of academic heritage in the Benelux. Since 2013, the Ghent University Museums (GUM) interfaculty partnership has been working on the design of a new, contemporary museum on three floors of the Ledeganckstraat. The opening is planned for 2019. For logistics manager Jeroen Vanden Berghe, this can become a beautiful story at the interface of science and culture. In the GUM, the university literally comes out of its ivory tower to show society what it has meant in the past — not for the sake of the past itself, but with an eye towards the future. A sense of wonder that breeds an interest in research and a dialogue with society forms the guidelines of the museum, not the diversity of its collections. The opening question 'Can science save the world?' links seamlessly to the humanist vision of science shared by Sarton and Van de Velde. The museum will be ideally located, right in the middle of the Arts Quarter, with the Museum of Fine Arts (MSK) and the S.M.A.K. (Stedelijk Museum voor Actuele Kunst) right across the street. The Botanical Garden functions as a 'natural' access point to the wonderful world of culture and science that will be opened in the GUM.

'Making the most of our university and encouraging our university to make the most of us', the motto of the Ashmolean in Oxford, the mother of all university museums, is not aiming too high for the GUM, according to Vanden Berghe. The aim is to turn it into a participatory and dynamic museum, with the active involvement of the academic community. He sees the museum as a 'powerhouse of teaching and research', in which knowledge is placed in a broader societal context. The concept would undoubtedly have charmed Julius Mac Leod. Exactly one hundred years before the planned opening of the GUM, he died of Spanish flu upon his return to Ghent. Previous chapters have shown how he planted the seeds for a thriving story of the popularisation of science at his alma mater before the First World War, right on this very spot.

## On art, science and poetry

At the opening of the academic year 2015-2016, the young art historian Koen Jonckheere gave a remarkable speech, inspired by *The Man Who Measures the Clouds*. Jan Fabre's 1998 sculpture balances on the roof of the S.M.A.K.: a man standing on a library ladder, straight as an arrow, sleeves rolled up, measuring the clouds with a yardstick. 'The sculpture is a sublime metaphor for art, science and poetry,' said Jonckheere, 'three disciplines that — as Leonardo da Vinci already knew — are inextricably linked. The man who measures the clouds exposes our dreams and the dangers that lurk around the corner.' The clouds are our dreams, which are impossible to measure, and which are in danger of being smothered by the yardstick.

'It is a fantastic visualisation of the awkward split between oppressive regulation and the power of imagination. It is precisely this tension that universities around the world are struggling with today.' Nowadays, universities measure just about everything. Teaching time and educational efficiency, scientific output and scientific communication, project applications, publications and citations, and, last but not least, impact and demonstrable valorisation! We measure literally everything. And when we are not measuring, we evaluate: research reports and educational portfolios, testing policy and tenure tracks, quality control and feedback systems, evaluations of evaluations of evaluations. This requires a great deal of meeting in committees that use not yardsticks but very accurate pharmaceutical scales to neatly calibrate publication output and weighting coefficients in objective-looking tables and formulas. For example, a colleague who was on sick leave for three months saw her personalised research targets shift to 10.2 from 10.4 for publications and to 3 from 3.1 for project applications, while the 2.1 PhDs she must have supervised remained unchanged 'because of the rounding rules'. No wonder people get sick, I thought. But of course, malaise is also measured and evaluated. In this way, the evaluation criteria as well as the ranking, review and monitoring systems can constantly be refined and optimised. So that the allocation keys can be adapted to the improvement of well-being and team spirit at work, which in the end will only increase productivity and output.

As an art historian, Jonckheere knows only too well that the future lies elsewhere. 'Academic' is a derogatory term for art that is stifled by the illusion of being able to measure quality. What the university and science need is even more poetry. 'It is time to break free from department cells and faculty prisons and start measuring clouds again in the most wonderful interdisciplinary constellations.'

The financial distribution keys that dominate publication culture in academia have mainly the humanities in a stranglehold. But if a subject like history starts to conform to the prevailing academic criteria, which focus on output, data sets, citation indices and top journals with impact factors, it will lose all meaning and significance. Loecki Vervenne's 'thick books with thick covers' have been replaced by A1 articles and h-indices. Measuring your impact in 'the cloud' via 'stats', 'reads' and 'clicks' is more important than reading itself. The question is who becomes wiser this way.

After all, over-specialisation has more harmful consequences in the human sciences than in the natural sciences, life sciences and — to a certain extent — social sciences. If the 'scientist' also replaces the 'scholar' in the human sciences, then nowhere will intellectuals be educated with a broad synthetic vision, who can transfer knowledge in context and in this way contribute to a coherent world view that improves people's lives — and humanity. American universities such as Stanford have long recognised this. Our world in transition is confronted with problems that can only be tackled if the gap between the 'humanities' and the 'technicalities of science' is bridged once again. Compared to George Sarton's time at Harvard, this challenge has become even greater, to the extent that the 'arts & philosophy', 'arts & humanities' and 'literature & philosophy' themselves have become fragmented due to the wanton proliferation of specialisation and niche formation. Distribution keys and evaluation criteria force the humanities into the straitjacket of so-called top research (i.e. in more technical fields), which does not fit them at all. Education is also increasingly tailored to a small (internationally recruitable) elite of subject specialists rather than to the broad university education that rector Leon De Meyer advocated twenty years ago. Top researchers in the humanities may well excel in their own narrow domain, but they no longer have the time or the stomach for the humanist mission of the university, or they find popularisation beneath their dignity. With their hyper-sophisticated jargon, alien to any form of poetry, they simply cannot tell an engaging story for a public broader than their own peers, whom they meet at international conferences and workshops around the world. This is related to *l'histoire en miettes*, or history in pieces. Along with the end of the age of Great Narratives, the sense of synthesis has also vanished in the mists of history. In this way, science has lost its long-term work, that which lasts and can take root. Today, the contribution of the humanities is exactly what is needed for the strongly felt need for interdisciplinarity in education, which once again raises the question of a broad general education or *studium generale* in all areas of the arts and sciences, across disciplinary and faculty boundaries.

The man measuring the clouds is the scientist-artist who reaches hopefully towards the poetry of coherence that science has lost. 'The history of science should be the leading thread in the history of civilisation', wrote George Sarton in 1917. One of the craters on the moon is named after him. He indeed aimed a little higher than just the clouds.

Jan Fabre,
*The Man Who Measures the Clouds*, 1998
(Ghent, photo Michiel Hendryckx)

# BIBLIOGRAPHICAL ESSAY

This jubilee book is the crowning glory of the work of the collective UGentMemorie. UGentMemorie has been building the virtual memory of Ghent University since 2008. The driving forces behind it are Fien Danniau, Ruben Mantels, Davy Verbeke and Frank Cotman. Christophe Verbruggen and I are promoters. Its hub is the website www.UGentMemorie.be. UGentMemorie brings together memories, stories and heritage from the university. The leitmotif is the role and impact of UGent in the city and society, and vice versa. UGentMemorie is more than just a showcase of the past. UGentMemorie encourages researchers and students to actively explore the history of a scientific discipline, to draw up the family tree of their predecessors or to recharge the university's *lieux de mémoire* with meaning. It offers a platform for translating knowledge of and about the university to a wider audience. Without the treasure trove of historical information that UGentMemorie has accumulated over ten years, I would not have been able to write this book. I therefore owe a great deal to the work of my colleagues and all those who have already contributed to UGent's burgeoning collective memory — not least the students. Among them are Adriaan Eerdekens, Lore Goovaerts, Fred Libert, Kristof Loockx, Anke Stefens, Liesbet Van Crombrugge, Ine Van Nuffel, Michiel Vantongerloo and Sofie Veramme, who wrote their master's theses in the context of celebrating the 200th anniversary of Ghent University. Their work is valorised on UGentMemorie, which they actively helped to construct.

A book is of course a different medium from that of an associative website with short informative texts. On my trip down memory lane I have travelled along two paths. In the first place, there was the classic highway of history through literature and archival sources. The chronological and thematic breadth of the book necessitated choices that are accounted for chapter by chapter below. More in-depth archival research per theme or period is certainly necessary to give more relief to the broad outlines I have tried to sketch in each chapter. The fact that *From the Ivory Tower* turned out to be anything but an abstract narrative is due to the many testimonies I have been able to collect from my second path, that of oral history.

Once the ten major themes had been defined — pluralism, industry and valorisation, care for body and mind, society as a laboratory, language, war and peace, democratisation, gender and sexuality, colonialism and development cooperation, environment and biotechnology — the first step was to identify the key witnesses of contemporary history through discussions with former rectors and deans. I had exploratory talks with André De Leenheer (rector 2001-2005) and Paul Van Cauwenberge (rector 2005-2013), and with the deans of the four founding faculties: Marc Boone (Arts and Philosophy 2012-2018), Michel Tison (Law 2014-2018), Herwig Dejonghe (Sciences 2005-2018) and Guy Vanderstraeten (Medicine 2011-2017). Subsequently, Rik Van de Walle (Engineering Sciences 2012-2018), Marc De Clercq (Economics and Business Administration 2008-2017), Geert De Soete (Psychology and Educational Sciences 1998-2018), Herman Van Langenhove (Bioengineering Sciences 2002-2008) and Herwig Reynaert (Political and Social Sciences 2009-2018) were also interviewed. In this way, the blueprint for the book could be drawn up and a long list made of key figures who could give my story texture and flavour.

The timeline with key moments on UGentMemorie was given additional depth by reading the basic works in the field of (Ghent) university history: the jubilee book published on the occasion of *175 jaar Universiteit Gent. Een verhaal in beeld* by Elienne Langendries and Anne-Marie Simon-Van der Meersch (1992), the books commemorating twenty-five years of Dutchification (1957) and the 150th anniversary of the University of Ghent (1967), the extensive series *Uit het verleden van de R.U.G.* edited by Karel De Clerck, his *Hoofdmomenten uit de ontwikkeling van de Gentse rijksuniversiteit (1817-1967)* (1967) and the recent standard work by Ruben Mantels, *Gent. Een geschiedenis van universiteit en stad, 1817-1940* (2013). Highly useful for the general context were Ginette Kurgan-Van Hentenryk, *Laboratoires et réseaux de diffusion des idées en Belgique (XIXe-XXe siècles)* (1994) and the synthesis by Robert Halleux, Geert Vanpaemel, Jan Vandersmissen and Andrée Despy-Meyer, *Geschiedenis van de wetenschappen in België 1815-2000* (2009). The parts on the modern university in the monumental series by Walter Rüegg, *A History of the University in Europe*, namely Universities in the Nineteenth and Early Twentieth Centuries 1800-1945 (2004) and *Universities since 1945* (2010), as well as the monograph by Robert David Anderson, *European Universities from the Enlightenment to 1914* (2004) were also particularly inspiring for my work. For the Flemish context after 1968, *De stad op de berg. Een geschiedenis van de Leuvense universiteit 1968-2005* by Jo Tollebeek and Liesbet Nys offered a firm handhold.

Biographical information about professors could to a large extent be drawn from the personal rubrics on UGentMemorie.be and the extremely handy, user-friendly database of professors UGentMemorialis.be, where the printed *Libri Memoriales* of the university from 1913 and 1960 are accessible in fully digitised form and linked to the *Biographie Nationale*, the *Nationaal Biografisch Woordenboek* and Bestor.be. The *Nieuwe Encyclopedie van de Vlaamse beweging* (1998) is another rich source for the engagement of professors active in the decades-long struggle for the Dutchification of the university.

## Prologue
## From Bildung to Bologna

The tone of *From the Ivory Tower* is set by critical reflections on today's university. A selection from the broad range of literature consulted: Simon Bastow et al., *The Impact of the Social Sciences. How Academics and their Research Makes a Difference* (2014), René Boomkens, *Topkitsch en slow science. Kritiek van de academische rede* (2008), Stefan Collini, *What Are Universities For?* (2012), Herman De Dijn et al., *Het professoraat anno 2016. Reflectie over een beroep in volle verandering* (2016), Frank Donoghue, *The Last Professors. The Corporate University and the Fate of the Humanities* (2008), Patrick Loobuyck et al., *Welke universiteit willen wij (niet)?* (2007), Christopher Newfield, *Unmaking the Public University* (2008), Martha Nussbaum, *Not for Profit. Why Democracy Needs the Humanities* (2010), Willem Otterspeer, *Weg met de wetenschap. Een pleidooi voor de universiteit* (2015), Helen Small, *The Value of the Humanities* (2013), Isabelle Stengers, *Une autre science est possible! Manifeste pour un ralentissement des sciences* (2013), Casper Thomas, *Competente rebellen. Hoe de universiteit in opstand kwam tegen het marktdenken* (2015), Ad Verbrugge et al., *Waartoe is de universiteit op aarde?* (2014).

## Chapter 1
## Inter utrumque: between science and society

For the wider context of the history of the University of Ghent, the PhD of Pieter Dhondt, *Un double compromis. Enjeux et débats relatifs à l'enseignement universitaire en Belgique au XIXe siècle* (2011) is the standard work. It could be supplemented by specific documents on the choice of Ghent as a university city in the Nationaal Archief in The Hague and documents on its establishment in the Stadsarchief in Ghent.

The modernisation of the university up to and including the First World War was reconstructed in brief on the basis of the university's yearbooks and the triennial reports submitted to parliament on the state of higher education in Belgium. I systematically consulted these collections in the Ghent University Archives. The following chapters also use material from this interesting serial source.

On August Kekulé in Ghent, there is the old work by Jan Gillis, *Kekulé te Gent (1858-1867): de geschiedenis van de benoeming van August Kekulé te Gent en de oprichting van het eerste onderrichtslaboratorium voor scheikunde in België* (1959), which was recently revised by Pierre De Clercq, 'In het spoor van Kekulé te Gent (1858-1867)', in *Symposium 150 jaar Benzeenstructuurformule — Ontstaan en Huidige Toepassingen* (2015). Jules De Nobele's story features in Edgard Ossieur, 'Radiografie te Gent 1896-ca. 1906', in de *Handelingen van de Maatschappij voor Geschiedenis en Oudheidkunde te Gent* (1995). The last word has yet to be said about Jules Verschaffelt and his network, but the work of Bart Van Camp and Maurice Dorikens in the series *Uit het verleden van de RUG* (1995) offers a good start.

The story of university expansion is based on Karel De Clerck, *Rector Bouckaert had toch gelijk* (1985) and several contributions to the periodical *De Brug*, which appeared from 1956 onwards and is named after the association B.R.U.G., or Begunstigers van de Rijksuniversiteit Gent (Beneficiaries of Ghent University), who wanted to build a bridge between the university and society. The successive rounds of savings, attempts at rationalisation and student protests since the 1970s have been voiced and analysed in the student magazines *RUG-nummer* (1972) and *Schamper* (1975-present), which can be consulted digitally. Luc Van den Bossche's legendary speech as president of the Faculty Convent at the opening of the 1970-1971 academic year was given to me by Lieve Bracke.

Finally, for the recent period in this opening chapter, I was able to rely on interviews with former rectors Jacques Willems (1993-2001), André De Leenheer (2001-2005) and Paul Van Cauwenberge (2005-2013), government commissioner Yannick De Clercq (1987-present), academic manager Koen Goethals (2004-2017) and logistics manager Jeroen Vanden Berghe (2012-present).

## Chapter 2
## Pluralism, religion and science

On the traces of William of Orange and the Calvinist republic of Ghent, see Johan Decavele and Herman Balthazar, *Het geheugen van Nederland in Gent* (2011); on the educational policy of William I, Coen Tamse and Els Witte, *Staats- en natievorming in Willem I's koninkrijk* (1992). The anathemas of the Belgian bishops against the Ghent University and its anticlerical professors are covered by Emiel Lamberts, *Kerk en liberalisme in het bisdom Gent (1821-1857): bijdrage tot de studie van het liberaal-katholicisme en het ultramontanisme* (1972), more specifically in 'De Heilige Stoel en de zaak-Brasseur', in: *Belgisch Tijdschrift voor Nieuwste Geschiedenis* (1970), 2. Marc Reynebeau wrote about the ideological conflicts in *De Gentse universiteit als katalysator in het politieke groeiproces (1846-1870)* (1979). Herman Balthazar studied the history of the 'language-loving student association' in *Het Taalminnend Studentengenootschap 't Zal Wel Gaan (1852-1977)* (1977). The Ghent law faculty as a liberal stronghold is discussed by Liesbeth Vandersteene, *De geschiedenis van de Rechtsfaculteit van de Universiteit Gent. Van haar ontstaan tot aan de Tweede Wereldoorlog 1817-1940* (2009). Els Witte extended this line of reasoning into the 1960s in 'Professoren aan de Gentse Rijksuniversiteit tussen academische vrijheid, pluralisme en neutraliteit (1817-1965)', in: *Docendo discimus. Liber amicorum Romain Van Eenoo* (1999).

Much has been published about François Laurent. We only mention the voluminous collection edited by Johan Erauw et al., *Liber memorialis François Laurent* (1989). Wouter Dambre wrote *August Wagener (1829-1896). Een leven voor het onderwijs* (1987). The informative biographies of Ghent liberals by Bart D'hondt on the website of the Liberal Archives can also be consulted in print form: *Van Andriesschool tot Zondernaamstraat. Gids door 150 jaar liberaal leven te Gent* (2014).

The section on Alphonse Renard is indebted to the contribution of Jan Art in the compilation by Danny Praet et al., *Religion, Politics and Science during the Modernist crisis* (2018). On his scientific merits, see Jean-Pierre Henriet, 'The face of the Ocean: Alphonse-François Renard (1842-1903) and the Rise of Marine Geology', in *Sartonia*, 23 (2010). The Cumont affair is a hobby-horse of Danny Praet. 'L'Affaire Cumont. Idéologies et Politique académique à la Université de Gand au cours de la crise moderniste' in the above mentioned collection edited by him is a small masterpiece. Praet's pupils Annelies Lannoy and Elien Scheerlinck wrote their doctorates on Cumont's scientific vision of religion.

On the significance of Edgar de Bruyne, I refer to the tribute organised by Marcel Storme and Carlos Steel in the Flemish Academy in 2003 and the essay by Umberto Eco, 'L'esthétique médiévale d'Edgar De Bruyne', in *Recherches de théologie et philosophie médiévales* (2004), 2. On his impact on Eco, see also: Jean-Pierre Rondas, 'Steeled in the School of Old Aquinas: Umberto Eco on the shoulders or Edgar De Bruyne', in Franco Musarra et al., *Eco in fabula. Umberto Eco in the Humanities* (2002). Rajesh Heyninckx devotes a chapter to De Bruyne's philosophy of art in *Meetzucht en mateloosheid. Kunst, religie en identiteit in Vlaanderen tijdens het interbellum* (2008).

The publications by and about Leo Apostel, Jaap Kruithof and Etienne Vermeersch are numerous. I will confine myself to their farewell anthologies: Diderik Batens, *Leo Apostel. Tien filosofen getuigen* (1996), Jaap Kruithof, *Een wereld zonder stuurman. Gesprekken 1962-1995* (1995), Ronald Commers et al., *Over Jaap Kruithof gesproken. Liber Amicorum* (1996), Etienne Vermeersch, *Van Antigone tot Dolly. 40 jaar kritisch denken* (1997). The diaries of Leo Apostel are kept in the University Library but cannot be consulted. I was, however, able to use Jaap Kruithof's remarkable collection, 'Personalia'. In 1996 it was distributed among intimates in an edition of twenty-five copies; one copy is held in the library as 'a gift for the inhabitants of Ghent'.

The texts of Hugo Van den Enden were collected by Johan Braeckman and Etienne Vermeersch, *Op het scherp van de rede. 40 jaar kritisch denken* (2003). Marc Cosyns wrote *Zoals ik het wil. Gesprekken over euthanasie* (2003) and spoke to Kruithof and Vermeersch, among others.

For this chapter I had detailed discussions with the philosophers Freddy Mortier (dean of Arts and Philosophy 2004-2012, vice-rector 2013-2017) and Etienne Vermeersch (dean of Arts and Philosophy 1978-1980, vice-rector 1993-2001). In addition to *Schamper*, the sections on the rectorial elections are mainly based on interviews with the two of them, and with Yannick De Clercq, André De Leenheer, Anne De Paepe (rector 2013-2017), Geert De Soete, Koen Goethals, Luc Moens (dean of Sciences 2002-2005, vice-rector 2005-2013), historian Walter Prevenier (dean of Arts and Philosophy 1984-1986), jurist Marcel Storme (dean of Law 1982-1984), Paul Van Cauwenberge, Jeroen Vanden Berghe and Jacques Willems. Hopefully this has produced a multiperspectivist vision.

## Chapter 3
## Industry and valorisation

A standard work on the historical relationship between university and industry in Belgium is Kenneth Bertrams, *Universités et entreprises: milieux académiques et industriels en Belgique, 1880-1970* (2006).

The story of the Special Schools and the history of engineering is derived from *150 jaar ingenieursopleiding aan de Rijksuniversiteit Gent (1835-1985)* (1986).

On François Donny, Désiré Van Monckhoven and Leo Baekeland as pioneers of photography, see, among others, *Focus op fotografie: fotografie te Gent van 1839-1940* (1987). Entrepreneur Leo Baekeland was the subject of Joris Mercelis's doctorate, *Leo H. Baekeland (1863-1944) as scientific entrepreneur: a transatlantic perspective on the science-industry nexus* (2013). See also his articles 'Leo Baekeland's Transatlantic Struggle for Bakelite: Patenting Inside and Outside of America', *Technology and Culture* (2012) and 'Learning from Entrepreneurial Failure. Leo Baekeland's Exit from Europe', *Belgisch Tijdschrift voor Nieuwste Geschiedenis* (2013) 4. Stephanie Van de Voorde wrote her dissertation on the work of Gustave

Magnel, *Bouwen in beton in België (1890-1975). Samenspel van kennis, experiment en innovatie* (2011).

The history of the Agricultural College and the Veterinary School is covered in the *Jubileumboek 1920-1995* (1995) by the faculty of Agricultural Sciences and Applied Biological Sciences, edited by Erick Vandamme, and *50 jaar Nederlandstalig diergeneeskundig onderwijs aan de R.U.G.* (1984), edited by Karel De Clerck.

The archive of the Advisory Board in the University Archives has interesting material about the structures for university/industry cooperation since the 1970s, as does the archive of André Vlerick in KADOC in Leuven. A broader framework for the development of degree programmes in management is found in Kenneth Bertrams, 'From exchange programmes to the legitimization of university-based management education: the case of Belgium 1920-1970,' in Matthias Kipping et al., *Americanisation in 20th Century Europe: business, culture, politics* (2002).

The recent history of the public-private partnership has been supported by my conversations with Ignace Lemahieu (research director UGent), Luc Moens, Freddy Mortier, Herman Van Langenhove (chairman Industrial Research Fund IOF), Rik Van de Walle (iMinds-imec) and Willy Verstraete (chairman FWO). The interview with Roel Baets on photonics comes from *Kennismakers. 80 jaar FWO* (2008). The annual *Speurgids Ondernemen en Innoveren* published by the department of Economy, Science and Innovation of the Flemish Government is particularly illuminating in terms of the shift in financial flows.

## Chapter 4
## Care for body and mind

For general orientation, consult *Gent: 300 jaar Geneeskunde* (1990) and André De Schaepdryver, *Faculteit der Geneeskunde. Rijksuniversiteit te Gent. Liber Memorialis 1930-1980* (1980). The history of the university buildings on the Bijloke is well documented in Elienne Langendries and Anne-Marie Van der Meersch, *Het Rommelaere Complex. Onderdeel van het gebouwenmasterplan voor de Gentse universiteit op het einde van de 19$^{de}$ eeuw* (1999). The *Jubileumboek 50 jaar UZ Gent* (2009) offers a number of thorough contributions, also about its history. On Joseph Guislain and the origins of psychiatry, see *Geen rede mee te rijmen. Geschiedenis van de psychiatrie* (2011). The magazine *Psychoanalytische perspectieven* dedicated a memorial issue to Jacques De Busscher in 1999.

The anatomical preparations of Adolphe Burggraeve were brought up again during the Ghent University Museum's exhibition *Post Mortem. Vesalius tussen kunst en wetenschap* (2015) and are the subject of an article by Veronique Deblon and Pieter Huistra, 'Het geheim van de anatoom: Adolphe Burggraeve en de ontwikkeling van de Belgische anatomie in de negentiende eeuw,' in *Studium. Tijdschrift voor Wetenschaps- en Universiteitsgeschiedenis* (2017) 4.

Emile Van Ermengem is covered by Sofie Onghena, 'Altruïstisch ambtenaar of heroïsch genie? Het gepropageerde beeld van provinciale en academische directeurs van bacteriologische laboratoria in België (ca. 1900-1940)', in *Studium* (2009) 4.

On the HILO, see Matthieu Lenoir, Jan Tolleneer and Willy Laporte, *100 jaar opleiding Lichamelijke Opvoeding en Bewegingswetenschappen aan de Universiteit Gent* (2007).

My sources for contemporary history of this theme were professors Jan De Maeseneer (Primary Care) and Anne De Paepe (Medical Genetics), Fritz Derom (emeritus, Surgery), Alexander Evrard (emeritus, Psychiatry), honorary doctor and alumnus Peter Piot (Tropical Medicine) and Bob Rubens (emeritus, Internal Medicine).

## Chapter 5
## Society as a laboratory

The intellectual trajectory of Adolphe Quételet and François Huet is addressed in the doctorate of Kaat Wils, *De omweg van de wetenschap. Het positivisme en de Belgische en Nederlandse intellectuele cultuur* (2005). There are also a number of studies on Huet's economic ideas by John Cunliffe and Guido Erreygers, among other places, in the

*European Journal of the History of Economic Thought* (1999). The archive of Paul Voituron, secretary of the Société Huet, is held in the University Library and enables a network analysis of social liberalism in Ghent, with many branches extending to the university. Carmen Van Praet partially explains this network in her dissertation *Liberale hommes-orchestres en de sociale kwestie in de negentiende eeuw. Tussen lokaal en internationaal* (2015). In this respect, Guy Schrans's oeuvre is also a gold mine, including his *Van wit naar blauw. Gent tussen 1780 en 1842* (2010), *Fredericq en Co. Een geslacht in licht en schaduw* (2014) and *Tussen burgerpak en blauwe kiel. Sociaal-liberalen te Gent, 1789-1914* (2015). For the links between the University of Ghent and Freemasonry: Jeffrey Tyssens, *Van wijsheid met vreugd gepaard. Twee eeuwen vrijmetselarij in Gent en Antwerpen* (2003) and René Vermeir and Jeffrey Tyssens, *Vrijmetselarij en vooruitgang. De Gentse progressistenloge La Liberté (1866-1966)* (2016).

Guy Vanthemsche published on liberal think tanks in Gent, 'Laboratoires d'idées et progrès social. Le cas de l'Association belge pour le progrès social et ses prédécesseurs (1890-1960)', in Ginette Kurgan-Van Hentenryck et al., *op. cit.* (1994). Jasmien Van Daele is the author of the biography *Van Gent tot Genève. Louis Varlez* (2002), Angelo Van Gorp wrote *Tussen mythe en wetenschap. Ovide Decroly (1871-1932)* (2005).

The experimental schools and other educational innovations are discussed in Karel De Clerck, *Vijfenzeventig jaar pedagogische wetenschappen aan de Gentse universiteit* (2002), in the *Liber Amicorum professor dr. J.J. Verbist: pedagogische perspectieven en vluchtlijnen* (1981) and *Ontwikkeling, persoonlijkheid en milieu: liber amicorum William De Coster* (1986). The Criminology School and its prominent figures are dealt with in *75 jaar Criminologie aan de Universiteit Gent* (2013). In addition, the website canonsociaalwerk.be was frequently consulted for this chapter and I was also grateful for the shared recollections of jurist Mil Kooyman and scientific insights of educational sociologist Mieke Van Houtte.

## Chapter 6
## Language

Of all the themes, the Dutchification of the University of Ghent is the best researched. I refer to the *Nieuwe Encyclopedie van de Vlaamse beweging* (1998), which explores the struggle in all its dimensions. In addition, there is the *Kroniek van de strijd voor de vernederlandsing van de Gentse universiteit* (1980), compiled by Karel De Clercq. Lode Wils recently published a voluminous biography of one of the 'crowing cocks', *Frans Van Cauwelaert. Politieke biografie* (2017). Activism was thoroughly studied by Daniël Vanacker, *Het activistisch avontuur* (2006). *Maar wat een wespennest! Het rectoraat van August Vermeylen en de vernederlandsing van de Gentse universiteit* (2010) by Ruben Mantels and Hans Vandevoorde was published in the Vermeylen Year, after 80 years of Dutchification, when the anglicisation of higher education in Flanders was also on the rise.

For the shifts in academia with regard to the language of teaching and research, I spoke with Dutch literature emeritus professor Anne-Marie Musschoot, professor of Dutch linguistics Jacques Van Keymeulen and Kries Versluys, emeritus professor of English literature and for many years education director of UGent.

## Chapter 7
## War and peace

The history of the Institut de Droit International is told by Marti Koskenniemi, *The Gentle Civilizer of Nations: the Rise and Fall of International Law 1870-1960* (2005).

The diary of Virginie Loveling, *In Oorlogsnood*, edited by Ludo Stynen and Sylvia Van Peteghem (1999), remains an important source for the history of the First World War, also with regard to the university. Sarah Keymeulen wrote her dissertation on *Het fenomeen Henri Pirenne. De geschiedenis van een reputatie* (2017) and is currently studying his unpublished diaries from the war years. Elienne Langendries compiled the source edition *De Vlaamsche Hoogeschool te Gent (1916-1918)* (1985). Recently, Herman Balthazar and Nico

Van Campenhout published *Twee jonge Vlamingen in den Grooten Oorlog. Oorlogsdagboeken en levensverhaal van de jonge flaminganten August Balthazar en Leo Picard* (2014).

On Ghent University in the Second World War: Dirk Martin, *De Rijksuniversiteit Gent tijdens de bezetting 1940-44. Leven met de vijand* (1993) and Bart Carnewal, *Collaboratie van professoren en assistenten aan de Rjksuniversiteit Gent tijdens de Tweede Wereldoorlog* (1992). A series of essays on the faculty of Medicine and the collaboration by Yves Louis and Marc Verschooris, 'Artsen tussen Hitler en Hippokrates', appeared in the *Artsenkrant* in 2014 and was also reworked as a dossier on UGentMemorie. Also interesting is the contribution of Wouter De Raes, 'Dr. Roger Soenen and Dr Jan De Roeck: 2 Vlaams-nationalistische artsen en rassentheoretici in het interbellum en de Tweede Wereldoorlog', in: *Docendo discimus op. cit.* (1999). The Liberal Archives published Karel Poma's *Student in het verzet. Mijn herinneringen aan de Tweede Wereldoorlog* (2010). The war diary of biologist Paul Van Oye is held in the University Library and was made available in 2015. It sheds new light on his attitude towards the New Order and the German occupying forces.

I interleaved my story with elements from Iñez Demarrez's heart-rending book *Brieven tussen hemel en hel. Het oorlogsverhaal van Falk & Nora Epsteins-Pieruccini* (2015).

In addition, for the contemporary story I spoke with Eva Brems, the first professor of Human Rights in Belgium, about her scholarly work and her activism.

## Chapter 8
## Democratisation

A thorough history of the democratisation and massification of higher education, and more specifically that of Ghent University, has yet to be written. The figures in this chapter come from the dossier 'UGent in cijfers' on UGentMemorie and, with regard to students with a migration background, from the Diversity and Gender Policy Unit.

The role of scholarships in the early period is covered by Myriam Verhas, *Studiebeurzen van overheidswege aan studenten van de Gentse Universiteit (1836-1849)* (1988). For the post-war period, I would refer to the contemporary contributions of Leo Coetsier, André Bonte, Rudy De Potter and others. See also: Barbara Tan, *Blijvende sociale ongelijkheid in het Vlaamse Onderwijs* (1998).

On higher education for the people, see Maurits De Vroede, 'Hogeschooluitbreidingen en volksuniversiteiten', in: *Belgisch Tijdschrift voor Nieuwste Geschiedenis* (1979) 1-2 and Dirk Van Damme, *Universiteit en volksontwikkeling. Het 'Hooger onderwijs voor het volk' aan de Gentse universiteit* (1983). Emeritus professors Marc Van Montagu and Willy Verstraete told their personal stories in this context. Rik Pinxten published it in book form in *De eeuw van onze kinderen* (2017).

I interviewed director of student facilities Marc Bracke and logistics manager Jeroen Vanden Berghe about the development of social services at the University of Ghent. The March Movement of 1969 was still fresh in the memory of Etienne Vermeersch. The student protests are discussed in numerous theses. An overview is provided in: Anne-Marie Van der Meersch, *20 jaar RUG-studenten in actie, 1968-1988* (1988). The digitised *Schampers* are an ideal source for this topic.

## Chapter 9
## Gender and sexuality

The figures on the number of female students and PhDs come from the dossier 'UGent in cijfers' on UGentMemorie and from the policy unit for Diversity and Gender.

On the first women at the university, see Anne-Marie Simon-Van der Meersch, *De eerste generaties meisjesstudenten aan de rug (1882-1930)* (1982), Annick Vandenbilcke, *Meisjesstudenten aan de Rijksuniversiteit Gent, (1930/31-1945/46)* (1987) and Denise Keymolen in 'Feminisme in België. De eerste vrouwelijke artsen (1873-1914)', in *Bijdragen en Mededelingen tot de Geschiedenis der Nederlanden* (1975). The dossier on this issue at the Ghent faculty of Medicine is held in the University Archives.

The history of obstetrics at the University of Ghent is handled by Alfred Van Heddeghem, *De oude Bijlokematerniteit 1828-1978. Anderhalve eeuw patiënten, vroedvrouwen, dokters* (1983). On Reiner Leven, see Christophe Verbruggen, 'Het egonetwerk van Reiner Leven en George Sarton als toegang tot transnationaal intellectueel engagement', in: *Belgisch Tijdschrift voor Nieuwste Geschiedenis* (2008) 1-2; on the Thiery family, see the article by Anthony Verbaeys et al., 'Prof. em. Dr. Michel Thiery en de familie Thiery', in: *Heelmeesters: befaamde artsen en figuren uit de geschiedenis van de geneeskunde* (2014). On the requirement for doctors to attend to the needs of students: *Onderzoek naar de behoefte aan een studentenarts aan de Rijksuniversiteit te Gent* (1977).

Jos Van Ussel received a tribute from Jaap Kruithof and Ignace Geurts, *De seksualiteit herzien* (1979), and is an important protagonist in the doctorate of Wannes Dupont, *Free-Floating Evils: A Genealogy of Homosexuality in Belgium* (2015). The life and work of Bob Carlier are the focus of *Diep en duizendvoudig leven, over seksualiteit, relaties en ethiek* (1993).

The story of Petra De Sutter and reproductive medicine in Ghent is told in her book *[Over] Leven. Mijn strijd als transvrouw, arts en politica* (2016). The other testimonies for this chapter come from conversations with Jean-Jacques Amy, Ann Buysse, Marc Cosyns, Anne De Paepe, Anne-Marie Musschoot and Marleen Temmerman.

## Chapter 10
## Colonialism and development cooperation

On the relationship between colonialism and science, see Johan Lagae, 'Het echte belang van de kolonisatie valt samen met dat van de wetenschap: over kennisproductie en de rol van wetenschap in de Belgische koloniale context', in: *Het geheugen van Congo: de koloniale tijd* (2005). An introduction to the biography of Frans Olbrechts can be found in Constantijn Petridis et al., *Frans M. Olbrechts: Op zoek naar kunst in Afrika* (2001). Maarten Couttenier also devotes considerable attention to him in *Congo tentoongesteld. Een geschiedenis van de Belgische antropologie en het museum van Tervuren (1882-1925)* (2005), as well as to Jules Cornet. On the Flemish colonialism in Congo, see Bambi Ceuppens, *Congo made in Flanders? Koloniale Vlaamse visies op 'blank' en 'zwart' in Belgisch Congo* (2003).

The transition from (de)colonisation to development cooperation is discussed by Leo De Ridder, 'Medische universitaire samenwerking tussen Gent en Rwanda', in: *Tijdschrift voor Geneeskunde* (2013) 12, Bert Govaerts, 'De universiteit van Elisabethstad (1956-1960): arena van het laatste Vlaamse gevecht in Belgisch-Congo', *Wetenschappelijke Tijdingen* (2010), 2, and Pieter Janssens, André De Schaepdryver and Herwig Onghena *Medische ontwikkelingssamenwerking aan de RUG* (1993).

For the contemporary history I was able to rely on extensive interviews with Ruddy Doom, Peter Piot, Patrick Sorgeloos and Marleen Temmerman.

## Chapter 11
## Environment and biotechnology

The (social) hereditary doctrine of Julius Mac Leod is briefly dealt with by Raf De Bont, *Darwins kleinkinderen. De evolutietheorie in België (1965-1945)* (2008), his application of statistics in biology by Geert Vanpaemel, '"Als 't ware een nieuwe wetenschap." De toepassing van de statistische methode door de Gentse botanici rond 1900', in *Gewina* 15 (1992). On the links to Hugo de Vries: Erik Zevenhuizen, 'The Hereditary Statistics of Hugo De Vries', *Acta Botanica Neerlandica* (1998) 4 and his *Vast in het spoor van Darwin. Biografie van Hugo De Vries* (2008). I intend to dedicate a biography to Mac Leod to further investigate the continuity of his ideas in (molecular) genetics.

On the intellectual environment in Ghent on the eve of the First World War: Jan Desmet, *De natuur als assepoester: leven en werken van Michel Thiery* (1988), Denise De Weerdt, 'De Sartons en België', *Brood en Rozen. Tijdschrift voor de geschiedenis van sociale bewegingen* (1999) 1 and Christophe

Verbruggen, 'Het egonetwerk van George Sarton', *op. cit.* On bridge figure Lucien De Coninck: Wilfrida Decraemer, August Coomans and Etienne Geraert, *Life and work of Prof. Dr Lucien De Coninck. Biologist, humanist and freemason* (2009) and the testimonies made on the occasion of his one hundredth birthday (fondsluciendeconinck.com).

For an introduction to the history of biotechnology in Ghent, see Walter Fiers, Jozef Van Beeumen and Marc Van Montagu, *Bio-ingenieurs: Biochemie & Biotechnologie aan de UGent* (2013). For Marc Van Montagu's personal story, I refer to his *Liber Amicorum* (1999). Both he and Willy Verstraete were featured in the six-part documentary series *Alles voor de wetenschap* on Canvas in 2010-2011. The Leuven knowledge-broker Martin Nihoul wrote *Silicon Valley. Een uniek verhaal van talent en technologie, van visie en charisma, van intriges en geld* (1999).

For this last chapter I interviewed Walter Fiers, Claude Libert, Marc Van Montagu, Peter Vandenabeele and Willy Verstraete. Fien Danniau had a conversation with Riet Van de Velde about Transition UGent.

# ACKNOWLEDGEMENTS

My thanks go to Ghent University, where I was trained as a historian and was given the privilege of writing this book, a jubilee book that wants to be something more, as part of the 1817-2017 bicentennial. The steering committee led by curators Lieve Bracke and Rik Van de Walle, embraced the concept from the outset and gave me the freedom I needed to carry out the research. I am very grateful to the university board, in particular to rector Anne De Paepe and vice-rector Freddy Mortier, for entrusting me with this important task.

It was extremely enriching, both as a historian and as a human being, to be able to spend the past two years immersing myself in the history of my alma mater. I consulted the archives, library and image banks of the University Archives and University Library extensively. Many thanks to Hendrik Defoort, Elienne Langendries, Isabel Rotthier, Erica ten Hove and Sylvia Van Peteghem, who helped me in my quest with advice and assistance. The staff of Amsab-ISG, the Ghent University Museum, the Royal Library of Belgium, the Letterenhuis, the Liberal Archive and the municipal archives of Ghent were also very helpful in searching for and providing visual material. The Baekeland and Thiery families, Carl De Keyzer, Walter De Mulder, Paul De Paepe, Fritz Derom, Michiel Hendryckx, Alain Platel, Patrick Sorgeloos, Saskia Vanderstichele, Marc Van Montagu, Marc Verschooris, Patricia Vervenne and Patrick Vuylsteek provided photos from their own collections. The fruitful collaboration with Lars De Jaegher, Christine De Weerdt and Kristin Van Damme as part of the STAM exhibition *Stad en Universiteit. Sinds 1817* only strengthened both projects.

I might not have been able to understand the university's 'genius loci' so well without interviewing a wide range of privileged witnesses to recent history: rector Anne De Paepe and vice-rector Freddy Mortier, former rectors André De Leenheer, Paul Van Cauwenberge and Jacques Willems, former vice-rectors Marc De Clercq, Luc Moens and Etienne Vermeersch; government commissioner Yannick De Clercq; academic manager Koen Goethals and logistics manager Jeroen Vanden Berghe; research director Ignace Lemahieu, former education director Kries Versluys and director of student services Marc Bracke; deans and former deans Marc Boone, Herwig Dejonghe, Geert De Soete, Ruddy Doom, Anne-Marie Musschoot, Walter Prevenier, Herwig Reynaert, Marcel Storme, Michel Tison, Guy Vanderstraeten, Rik Van de Walle and Herman Van Langenhove; emeritus professors Fritz Derom, Alexander Evrard, Walter Fiers, Patrick Sorgeloos, Marc Van Montagu and Willy Verstraete; colleagues Eva Brems, Ann Buysse, Claude Libert, Mieke Van Houtte, Marleen Temmerman and Peter Vandenabeele, and, last but not least, honorary doctor and UGent alumnus Peter Piot. Fien Danniau interviewed environmental co-ordinator Riet Van de Velde.

A well-chosen editorial committee has read all chapters in advance and provided expert commentary with a great deal of goodwill and thoroughness. I would like to thank Herman Balthazar, Frank Cotman, Fien Danniau, Hendrik Defoort, Dirk Heirbaut, Ruben Mantels, Hilde Symoens, Christophe Verbruggen and Anne-Marie Van der Meersch for their critical eyes and pleasant encouragement along the way. My informants have also read the texts, and like Jean-Jacques Amy, Thomas Buerman, Walter Buylaert, Pierre De Clercq, Petra De Sutter, Bruno De Wever, Lieve Gheysen, Danny Praet, Jan Vandersmissen, Dominique Van Der Straeten, Patrick Van Oostveldt, Paul Verhaeghe, Marc Verschooris and Antoon Vrints have dotted a few i's and crossed a few t's.

I am very grateful to Ronny Gobyn for his unconditional 'yes' to publishing the book and for the bibliophilic care with which he and his team at Uitgeverij Tijdsbeeld supervised its production.

Thanks to Gert Dooreman, *From the Ivory Tower* has become a gem. Not coincidentally, the typeface Nobel adorning the cover dates back to the time when Henry Van de Velde designed the Book Tower. It was a pleasure to be able to work with an artist like Dooreman and to see text and images taking shape as an organic whole.

The collaboration with the equally acclaimed UGentMemorie team also ran like clockwork. Fien Danniau and Davy Verbeke, in particular, provided invaluable services, both in terms of content and in practical terms, in bringing about the provisional crowning glory of nearly ten years of work by UGentMemorie.

As always, Marc Cosyns was my most critical reader. Our story writes itself in Perpetua. Whether Casper and Quinten Rommens will let themselves be carried away by their mother's passion for writing against the clock is more difficult to say. Now that Quinten is studying at UGent, I hope that the book will stimulate his interest in the antecedents of what will become his alma mater in a few years' time. If the students of his generation read the jubilee book, I will have succeeded in fulfilling my task. They are the future of the history that was written at our university.

Gita Deneckere, August 2017

# USEFUL ACRONYMS

AAP-ers (Assisterend Academisch Personeel) Assisting Academic Personnel
ABN (Algemeen Beschaafd Nederlands) Standard Dutch
ABOS (Algemeen Bestuur voor Ontwikkelingssamenwerking) General Board for Development Cooperation
ABVV (Algemeen Belgisch Vakverbond) Belgian Socialist Union
AGS Advanced Genetic Sciences
AKO (Actiegroep Kritisch Onderwijs) Action Group for Critical Education
ALSK (Algemene Spaar- en Lijfrentekas) General Savings and Annuity Fund
Amsab-ISG (Archief en Museum van de Socialische Arbeidersbeweging – Instituut voor Sociale Geschiedenis) Archive and Museum of the Socialist Workers Movement – Institute for Social History
ANV (Algemeen Nederlands Verbond) General Dutch Association
APSS (Association Internationale pour le Progrès de Sciences Sociales) International Association for the Progress of the Social Sciences
ASO (Algemeen Secundair Onderwijs) General Secondary Education
ATP-ers (Administratief en Technisch Personeel) Administrative and Technical Personnel
AU Gent (Associatie Universiteit Gent) University Association of Ghent
AVHV (Algemeen Vlaams Hoogstudenten Verbond) General Flemish University Students Association
AVRUG (Africa Verbond Rijksuniversiteit Gent) Africa Association of Ghent University
AZ (Academisch Ziekenhuis) Academic Hospital
BOF (Bijzonder Onderzoeksfonds) Special Research Fund
BRIC nations: Brazil, Russia, India, China
BRT (Belgische Radio en Televisie) Belgian Radio and Television
B.R.U.G. (Begunstigers van de Rijksuniversiteit Gent) Beneficiaries of Ghent University
BSP (Belgische Socialistische Partij) Belgian Socialist Party
BVSV (Belgische Vereniging voor Seksuele Voorlichting) Belgian Association for Sexual Education
CAVAZ (College van Architecten voor het Academisch Ziekenhuis) College of Architects for the Academic Hospital
CBGS (Centrum voor Bevolkings- en Gezinsstudiën) Centre for Population and Family Studies
CCI (Comité Central Industriel) Central Industrial Committee
CGSO (Centra voor Geboorteregeling en Seksuele Opvoeding) Centres for Birth Control and Sexual Education
CLBs (Centra voor Leerlingenbegeleiding) Centres for Student Counselling
CMET Centre for Microbial Ecology and Technology
COPC Community Oriented Primary Care
CuDos Research Group Cultural Diversity: Opportunities and Socialisation
CVP (Christelijke Volkspartij) Christian People's Party
DIRV (Derde Industriële Revolutie in Vlaanderen) Third Industrial Revolution in Flanders
EWI (Economie, Wetenschap en Innovatie) Department of Economy, Science and Innovation
FLM Field Liberation Movement
FNRS (Fonds de la Recherche Scientifique) Research Foundation – French-speaking Belgium
FWO (Fonds voor Wetenschappelijk Onderzoek – Vlaanderen) Research Foundation – Flanders
GAP (Gents Afrikaplatform) Ghent Africa Platform
Gembir (Gentse milieubewuste ingenieurs) Environmentally Conscious Engineers of Ghent
GIMV (Gewestelijke Investeringsmaatschappij voor Vlaanderen) Regional Investment Company for Flanders
GSC (Gentsch Studenten Corps) Ghent Student Corpus
GSV (Gents Studenten Verbond) Ghent Student Alliance
GUM (Gentse Universitaire Musea) Ghent University Museums
GUSB (Gentse Universitaire Sportbond) Ghent University Sports Association
HIKO (Hoger Instituut voor Kunstgeschiedenis en Oudheidkunde) Higher Institute for Art History and Archaeology
HILO (Hoger Instituut voor Lichamelijke Opvoeding) Higher Institute for Physical Education
HIO (Hoger Instituut voor Opvoedkundige Wetenschappen) Higher Institute for Educational Sciences
HSV (Humanistisch Studenten Verbond) Humanist Students Association
HV (Humanistisch Verbond) Humanist Association
IBBT (Instituut voor Breedband Technologie) Institute for Broadband Technology
ICE International Centre for Eremology
ILVO (Instituut voor Landbouw-, Visserij- en Voedingsonderzoek) Research Institute for Agriculture, Fisheries and Food
Imec Interuniversity Micro-Electronics Centre
IOF (Industrieel Onderzoeksfonds) Industrial Research Fund
IPBO International Plant Biotechnology Outreach
IWONL (Instituut tot Aanmoediging van het Wetenschappelijk Onderzoek in Nijverheid en Landbouw) Institute for the Advancement of Scientific Research in Industry and Agriculture
IWT (Agentschap voor Innovatie door Wetenschap en Technologie) Agency for Innovation through Science and Technology
KAC (Kollektief Anticonceptie) Collective Anticonception
KANTL (Koninklijke Academie voor Nederlandse Taal en Letterkunde) Royal Academy for Dutch Language and Literature
KRAPP (Kritische Actiegroep Psychologie en Pedagogie) Critical Action Group Psychology and Pedagogy
KRO (Katholieke Radio Omroep) Catholic Radio Broadcasting
KULeuven (Katholieke Universiteit Leuven) Catholic University Leuven
KVAB (Koninklijke Vlaamse Academie voor Wetenschappen en Kunsten van België) Royal Flemish Academy for Arts and Sciences of Belgium
KVHV (Katholiek Vlaams Hoogstudenten Verbond) Catholic Flemish University Students Association
KVIV (Koninklijke Vlaamse Ingenieursvereniging) Royal Flemish Engineers Association
LEF (Levensbeschouwing, Ethiek en Filosofie) Ideology, Ethics and Philosophy
LVSV (Liberaal Vlaams Studentenverbond) Liberal Flemish Students Association
MAS (Museum aan de Stroom) MAS. A river of tales
MSK (Museum voor Schone Kunsten) Museum of Fine Arts
NFWO (Nationaal Fonds voor Wetenschappelijke Onderzoek) National Research Foundation
NRWB (Nationale Raad voor Wetenschapsbeleid) National Council of Science Policy
NSG (Nationale Studentegroepering) National Student Group
NVLC (Nationale Landbouw- en Voedingscorporatie) National Agriculture and Nutrition Corporation
OECD Organisation for Cooperation and Development
PAS (Psychologisch Advies aan Studenten) Psychological Advice for Students
PC (Pedagogisch Centrum) Pedagogical Centre
PMS (Psycho-medisch-sociale centra) Psycho-Medical Social Centres
PPW (Psychologische en Pedagogische Wetenschappen) Faculty of Psychological and Pedagogical Sciences
PVDA (Partij van de Arbeid) Labour Party

RCMG Renard Centre of Marine Geology
RIZIV (Rijksinstituut voor Ziekte- en Invaliditeitsverzekering) State Institute for Health and Disability Insurance
RUCA (Rijksuniversitair Centrum Antwerpen) University Centre of Antwerp
RWS (Recht op Waardig Sterven) Right to Die with Dignity
SASHA Sweet Potato Action for Security and Health in Africa
SBO (Strategisch Basisonderzoek) Strategic Fundamental Research
SISS (Stedelijk Instituut voor Sociale Studiën) Municipal Institute for Social Studies
SKHV (Secretariaat der Katholieke Vlaamse Hoogstudenten) Secretariat of Catholic Flemish University Students
S.M.A.K. (Stedelijk Museum voor Actuele Kunst) Museum for Contemporary Art
SMW (Socio-Medicale Werkgroep) Socio-Medical Workgroup
SOCs (Strategische Onderzoekscentra) Strategic Research Centres
Sowege (Sociale Werkgroep Geschiedenis) Social Workgroup on History
SVB (Studentenvakbeweging) Student Union Movement
SVSB (Socialistische Vlaamse Studenten Beweging) Socialist Flemish Students Movement
UA (Universiteit Antwerpen) University of Antwerp
ULB (Université Libre de Bruxelles) Free University of Brussels
UNIKO–Ganda (Universitaire Koöperatie Overzee–Ganda) University Cooperation Oversees–Ghent
UNR (Université Nationale du Ruanda) National University of Rwanda
UZ (Universitair Ziekenhuis) University Hospital
VABB (Vlaams Academisch Bibliografisch Bestand) Flemish Academic Bibliography
VBO (Verbond van Belgische Ondernemingen) Union of Belgian Companies
VEV (Vlaams Economisch Verbond) Flemish Economic Union
VGK (Vlaams Geneeskundige Kring) Flemish Medical Circle
VGK (Vlaamsche Geschiedkundige Kring) Flemish History Circle
VIB (Vlaams Instituut voor Biotechnologie) Flemish Institute for Biotechnology
VITO (Vlaams Instituut voor Technologisch Onderzoek) Flemish Institute for Technological Research
VLAB (Vlaams Actieprogramma Biotechnologie) Flemish Biotechnology Action Programme
VLAIO (Vlaams Agentschap Innoveren en Ondernemen) Flemish Agency for Innovation and Enterprise
VLD (Vlaamse Liberalen en Democraten) Flemish Liberal Democratic Party
VLIR (Vlaamse Interuniversitaire Raad) Flemish Interuniversity Council
VNV (Vlaams-Nationaal Verbond) Flemish National Alliance
VNVV (Vlaams Nationaal Vrouwen Verbond) Flemish National Women's Alliance
VTM (Vlaamse Televisie Maatschappij) Flemish Television Company
VU (Volksunie) Flemish Nationalist Party
VUB (Vrije University Brussel) Free University of Brussels
VVS (Verbond van Vlaamsche Studenten) Flemish Students Alliance
Wela (Werkgroep Landbouw) Agriculture Workgroup
WGCs (Wijkgezondheidscentra) Neighbourhood Health Centres
WIM (Werkgroep Ingenieur en Maatschappij) Workgroup on Engineers and Society
ZAP-ers (Zelfstandig Academisch Personeel) Independent Academic Personnel

# INDEX OF NAMES
Pages numbers in italics refer to captions of illustrations.

## A
Agirdag, Orhan  229
Albert I of Belgium  37, *37*, 38, 70, 174, 176, *177*, 188, 268, 265, *265*
Alexander, Martin  296
Alexander of Belgium  134
Amy, Jean-Jacques  240, 245, 246
Andries, Charles  29, 96, *96*, 124
Anseele, Edward  102
Anseele, Edward Jr.,  102, 321
Apostel, Leo  56, 57, 70, 71, *71*, 74-79, *78*, 80-81, 88, 137, 246, 328
Asser, Tobias  186
Astrid of Belgium  265
Attenborough, Richard  295

## B
Baekeland, Leo  98, 99, 100, *100*, 101, 111, 290
Baert, Stijn  51
Baets, Roel  110, 111
Bakker, Nienke  *231*
Balthazar, Herman  85, 137, 324
Basse, Maurits  214
Baudouin of Belgium  40, *40*, 180, *247*, 271, 280, 298
Baur, Frank  196
Beatty, David  193
Beke, Frank  *53*, 324
Bell, Alexander  100
Bellens, Rein  137, 245, 247
Benedict XV, pope  191
Benoit, Yves  137
Berg, Paul  310
Bergmann, Tony  61, 167
Bergsma, Cornelis A.  93, 94, 146
Bernard, Claude  29
Berners-Lee, Tim  41
Bessemans, Albert  178, *179*
Bia, Lucien  262, 263, *263*
Bidez, Joseph  191, 192, 327
Billiet, Valère  197, 206, 269
Blancquaert, Anna  134, 256
Blancquaert, Edgard  45, 168, 256
Bloch, Marc  199
Block, Thomas  317
Blockmans, Frans  205
Blommaert, Jan  282
Boas, Franz  266
Boddaert, Gustave  123, *123*, 124, 128
Boddaert, Richard  29, *123*
Boehm, Rudolf  71, 79, 223
Bolton, Ralph  249
Bonaparte, Louis-Napoleon  185
Bonaparte, Napoleon  11, 12, 64, 116
Boon, Nico  298
Boone, Marc  199

Borginon, Hendrik  *189*
Borms, August  176, *196*
Bosmans, Marleen  282
Bossuyt, Marc  207
Bouckaert, Jean-Jacques  40, 42, 43, *43*, 44, 45, 52, 77, 135, *210*, 222, 269, 271, 326, 327
Bouckaert, Jos  310, 311
Boudin, Emmanuel  96, *96*, 98
Boulvin, Jules  34, 96, 97
Brachet, Jean  302
Bracke, Marc  219, 221, 227
Braeckman, Johan  82
Brasseur, Hubert  60, 61-65
Braun, Emile  129, 175, 235
Brems, Eva  208, 209, 258, 315
Brenner, Sidney  310
Broeckx, Jan  221
Broekaert, Eric  160, 161
Brouhon, Gaby  *177*
Brutsaert, Herman  162, 256, *277*
Bultinck, John  221
Burggraeve, Adolphe  115, 118, 119, *119*, 124, 149, 150
Burke, Kenneth  57
Bursens, Laurent  160
Burssens, Amaat  265, 266, 267, *267*, *268*, 271, 281
Burssens, Gaston  267
Burssens, Herman  266, 281
Bury, Jo  312, 313
Buysse, Ann  247, 252, 253, *247*, *248*, 257, 258
Buysse, Cyriel  168, *168*

## C
Cailliau, Robert  41
Calewaert, Willy  156, 157, 223, 241, 256, 310
Callier, Albert  23, 25, 26, 31, 63, 64, 170, 213
Callier, Alexis  152
Callier, Gustave  63, *64*, 146, 151, 152
Callier, Hippolyte  64
Cardijn, Jozef  216
Carlier, Bob  247-250
Carnap, Rudolf  71
Carnegie, Andrew  37
Cattier, Félicien  38
Cerulus, Armand  133
Chandler, Charles  100
Chantrenne, Hubert  306
Claes, Tobie  263
Claeys, Arthur  204
Claparède, Edouard  159
Claus, Hugo  *81*
Clemenceau, Georges  193
Cliquet, Robert  162, 241, 245

Cloquet, Jean-Norbert  102, 103, 133, 323
Cloquet, Louis  103, 127, 287, 290, *290*
Cnops, Jan  269, *270*
Coenegrachts, Kris  160
Cogen, Eugeen  118
Collard, François  190
Colle, Gaston  71
Collen, Désiré  310-312
Collin, Fernand  314
Collin, Georges  103
Collumbien, Eliane  137, 245
Comhaire, Adalbert  140, *140*
Comte, Auguste  65, 145
Conti, Leonardo  201, *201*, 202
Conti, Nanna  201
Conway, Edward  *21*
Corijn, Herman  204
Cornet, Jules  262, *262*, 263, *263*
Correns, Carl  34
Cosyns, Marc  80, 246, 247
Cousteau, Jacques-Yves  295
Crawford, Joan  122
Crevits, Hilde  228
Crick, Francis  288, 310, 327
Crocq, Jean  122
Cruyl, Leopold  118
Cumont, Franz  33, 68, 69, *69*, 70
Curie, Marie  36, 189
Curie, Pierre  36
Cuvelier, Claude  137, 157

## D
Daels, Frans  39, 133, 178, 179, 189, *189*, 195, *196*, 198, 200-202, *202*, 203, 204, 238, 239, 250
Daem, Hilde  325
Damiaan of Molokai  274
Damrong of Siam (Rama V)  261
Dams, Richard  295
Darwin, Charles  33, 34, 65, 66, 265, 287
Dauge, Félix  98
Dawkins, Richard  82
De Backer, Franz  168
De Bast, Martin  12, 13
De Batist, Marc  68
De Batselier, Steven  245, 248
De Bens, Els  *256*, 256, *281*
Debeuckelaere, Adiel  *171*, *189*, 189
Debeuckelaere, Willem  158
De Beule, Fritz  130, *131*
Debevere, Johan  106
De Bie, Maria  161
De Bock, Gerda  161, *161*, 254, 256, *256*
De Boever, Jan  141
De Boodt, Marcel  276
De Bosschere, Koen  229
De Brabandere, Victor  193
De Bruycker, Cesar  *169*, 173, 193
De Bruyne, Camille  167, 170, 263, 265, *291*

De Bruyne, Edgar  70-72, *72*, 269
de Burlet, Jules  98
De Busscher, Jacques  122, 123, 160
De Ceuleneer, Adolf  69, 169, 214
De Cleene, Natalis  269
De Clerck, Karel  85
De Clercq, Alfred  206
De Clercq, Staf  200
De Clercq, Willy  53
De Clercq, Yannick  45
De Coninck, Lucien  76, 168, 205, 206, 223, 242, 271, 291, 292, *292*, 293, 304, 305, 314
De Cooman, Elisabeth  256
Decorte, Tom  157
De Coster, William  76, *154*, 162, 242, *271*
Decroly, Ovide  155, 159
De Decker, Josué  173
De Decker, Pieter  61-63
De Geest-Materne, Thérèse  *244*
de Gerlache, Adrien  66-68, *68*
De Groodt, Arthur  *195*, 306
De Groodt, Marie  45, 123, 309
De Gucht, Karel  51
De Guchtenaere, Rosa  232
De Haene, Canon  244, *244*
de Haulleville, Prosper  63
De Heem, Frans  201
de Hemptinne, Felix  148
de Hoon, Judocus  118
de Kerchove de Denterghem, Charles  63
De Keyser, Paul  169
Dekeyser, Rudy  312
De Lannoy, Charles  265
Delatte, Eugène  324
de la Vallée-Poussin, Louis  99, 190
de Laveleye, Emile  146, 187, 262
Delcour, Charles  25, 213, 232
Delebecque, Ludovicus  61, 62, 64, 150
De Leenheer, André  39, 52, *53*, 324
De Leenheer, Louis  218
De Lens, Philippe  14, 16, 93
De Ley, Jozef  292, 297, 300, 301, 309, 310, 312
De Leye, Gaston  219
Delvoye, Wim  298, *298*
De Maeseneer, Jan  136, 138-140, 224, 229, 246
De Man, Hendrik  170
De Mey, Marc  328
De Meyer, Armand  162
De Meyer, Leon  47, 48, 85, 142, 219, 248, 280, 282, 328, 330
De Moor, Marysa  257
De Moor, Piet  178
De Muelenaere, Felix  204
De Munck, Guido  243
Deneckere, Annie  304
Deneffe, Victor  117
De Nobele, Jules  35, *35*, 36
De Paepe, Anne  47, 86, 87, *87*, 141, 231, 253, 254, 258, 259, *285*
Depage, Antoine  190
De Picker, Anna  313

346

de Pillecyn, Filip  189
De Potter, Rudy  218
Deprez, Ada  *168*
Dept, Gaston  205
De Raet, Lodewijk  171
De Ridder, Leo  275
De Ridder, Remi  152, 153
De Ridder, Ri  243
Derom, Emile  131, *131*
De Rom, Firmin  242, 244
Derom, Fritz  131, 134, 135, *135*, 136
Derote, Philippe  60
De Ruyver, Brice  157
Derycke, Erik  280
De Ryckere, Pierre  17
De Saeger, Sarah  87
Descamps, Edouard  68, 70
De Schaepdryver, André  142, 273
Deseure, Yvonne  *235*
Desirant, Yvonne  254
De Smedt, Emile  77
Desmet, August  104, 133
De Smet, Guillaume  198, *201*, 202, 203
De Smet, René  139, 246
De Sutter, Petra  250, 251, *251*, 252, 253
De Taeye, Augusta  237, 238, 247, 290
De Vigne, Julius  167
Devisch, Ignaas  82
De Visscher, Charles  35, 194
De Vleeschauwer, Albert  105, 106
De Vleeschauwer, Herman  198, 203, 283
De Vogelaere, Marcel  155
De Vreese, Willem  173, 193,
De Vries, Hugo  34
De Vriese, Bertha  235, 236, *236*, 237, 254, 258, 301
De Vroey, Paul  251
Dewaele, Alexis  253
De Waele, Alfred  200, *201*, 203, 203, 206
De Wever, Bruno  53
De Wilde, Lode  268, 269, 276, 281
De Wildeman, Emile  264
d'Hane, Jean-Baptiste  60
Dhondt, Jan  70, 71, 200, 205, 245, 269, *269*
Dhondt, Paula  *81*
Dhont, Marc  240, 250, 251
Dillemans, Roger  49, 50
Domela Nieuwenhuis, Ferdinand  290
Donny, François  27, *28*, 93
Doom, Ruddy  277, *277*, 317
Dosfel, Lodewijk  173
Drory, Stephanie  29
Du Moulin, Nicolas  23, 24, 119, 124
Ducpétiaux, Edouard  120
Dufranne, Adolphe  167
Dumont, Alexis  118

## E

Ecker, Friedrich  191
Eco, Umberto  72, *72*

Edison, Thomas  100, 101
Eeman, Eugène  175, 215
Einstein, Albert  39, 194, 195
Einstein, Elsa  195
Elaut, Leon  198, 201
Elisabeth of Belgium  35, 36, 196
Elwes, Mabel  238, 238
Engelbrecht, Eric  143
Epsteins, Falk  197, 197, 203, 204
Erauw, Johan  158, 208
Evrard, Alexander  122, 130
Eyskens, Gaston  107

## F

Fabiola of Belgium  40
Fabre, Jan  *10*, 329, *331*
Faché, Willy  161
Fautrez, Julien  *234*, 277
Febvre, Lucien  199
Fiers, Walter  42, *113*, 288, 299, 302-304, *304*, 304-306, 309, 310, 311, 312
Filip van België  42
Flam, Leopold  305
Foch, Ferdinand  193
Franck, Louis  *164*, 171
Franco, Francisco  156, 178
François, Jules  122
Francqui, Emile  36, 38, 102, 262, 263, *263*
Franklin, Benjamin  100
Franklin, Rosalind  288
Fransen, Jan Frans  215
Fredericq, Cesar  118, 168
Fredericq, Louis  180, 203, 215, 322
Fredericq, Paul  33, 146, 167, 168, *168*, 169, 171, 189, 191, *191*, 192, 193, 198, 214
Freinet, Célestin  155, 159
Frère-Orban, Walthère  29, 30, 64, 68, 231
Freud, Sigmund  122
Frimout, Dirk  *41*, 42
Fröschel, Paul  202
Funke, George  202, 204, 265

## G

Galtung, Johan  277
Ganshof van der Meersch, Walter  200
Ganshof, François-Louis  199, 200, 205
Gatti de Gamond, Isabelle  231, 234
Gaus, Helmut  277
Geens, Gaston  46, 108, 109, *109*
Geldof, Bob  276, 317
Gentil, Louis  264
Gerlo, Aloïs  45
Gezelle, Guido  173
Gheysen, Lieve  314
Ghysbrecht, Paul  83, 157, 223
Gleesener, Valérie  100
Godin, Jean-Baptiste  150
Goethals, Koen  308, 317
Gommaerts, Florent  127, 129, *129*
Goormaghtigh, Norbert  132, 219
Goossenaerts, Jozef  179

Goossens, Hector  201
Gore, Al  292
Goubau, René  196-198, 201, 202, 302
Govaere, Inge  207
Govaert, Firmin  301
Grégoire, Henri  197
Grooten, Johan  72
Guequier, Jules  100
Guislain, Joseph  22, *23*, 115, 120, 121
Gunzburg, Nico  156, *156*, *161*, 204

## H

Hacquaert, Armand  265, 269
Haerens, Ernest  193
Hallet, Paule  235
Hallyn, Fernand  328
Hamelinck, Maurice  122, 159
Handovsky, Hans  204
Harmel, Pierre  272
Haus, Jacques-Joseph  17, *17*, 59, 64, 65, *186*
Hayes, Bill  305
Hebberecht, Patrick  157
Heene, Johan  85
Heindryckx, Ronald  295
Hellebaut, Angélique  186
Hellebaut, Jean-Baptiste  186, *186*
Hendrickx, Hendrik  106
Henriet, Jean-Pierre  68
Heremans, Jacob  146, 167, *167*, 168
Herman-Michielsens, Lucienne  247, *247*
Herrel, Jean  162
Heyerick, Luc  162
Heyman, Jules  146, 148-150
Heymans, Corneel  *126*, 127, 140, 179, 185, 196, 201, 202, 204, 301
Heymans, Jan-Frans  127
Himmler, Heinrich  201
Hitler, Adolf  178, 195, 197, 204
Hoffmann, Peter  169, 170, 173, *173*, 193, 232
Hooft, Carlos  133, 202, 256, 275
Hoover, Herbert  36
Horta, Victor  67
Hoste, Julien  90, 224, 226, 311
Howard, John  157
Houzeau de Lehaie, Auguste  235
Hubinont, Pierre-Olivier  245
Hublé, Arthur  293
Hublé, Jan  293, *293*, 294, *294*, 295
Huet, Batilde  168
Huet, François  60, 145, 146, 162, 168
Hulin de Loo, Georges  177
Hulin, Charles  118
Huyghebaert, André  106
Huysmans, Camille  153, *164*, 171, 180
Hymans, Paul  194
Hynderyckx, Yvonne  255
Hyppolite, Jean  72

## I

Illich, Ivan  277
Inzé, Dirk  313

## J

Jaequemyns, Edouard  94, 186
Jaequemyns, Emilie  186
Janssen, Paul  140
Janssens, Armand  71, 79
Janssens, Pieter Gustaaf  271, 273, 274
Jaspar, Henri  176, 177
Jaurès, Jean  152
Jellicoe, John  193
Jenner, Edward  116, 119
Joffre, Joseph  193
Jonckheere, Koen  329

## K

Kabuta, Ngo  281
Kasavubu, Joseph  272
Kaufman, Jean Marc  137
Kayibanda, Grégoire  274
Keelhoff, Ferdinand  101
Kekulé, August  26, 27, *27*, 29, 68, 99, 301, 303
Kenis, Paul  170, 187
Kesteloot, Jacob Lodewijk  17, 116, 166
Khan, Irene  209
Khorana, Har Gobind  303, 310
Kickx, Jean-Jacques  *169*
Kinsey, Alfred C.  244
Kint, André  246
Kissinger, Henry  107, 272
Klein, Karen  243
Kluyskens, Albert  *171*
Kluyskens, Joseph  116, 237
Knapen, Paul  295
Koch, Robert  124
Kooyman, Mil  158, 159, 317
Kropotkin, Pyotr  290
Kropotkin, Sofia  290
Kruithof, Jaap  57, 70, 71, *71*, 72-74, 74, 75-81, *81*, 82, *82*, 223, 228, 243, 244, *244*, 245-247
Kuijken, Eckhart  294
Kuliasko, Frederik  207

## L

Lados, Alexis  237
Lahousse, Emile  193
Lallemand, Roger  247
Lambrecht, Bart  313
Lambrechts, Pieter  108, 188, 271, 281
Lamprecht, Karl  190
Lanoye, Tom  *81*, 181
Laurent, Caroline  64
Laurent, François  60, 61, 63, 64, *64*, 65, *144*, 146, 151, 156, 161, 162, 187
Laurent, Marie  64
Lebocq, Georges  236
Lebocq, Hector  36, 235, 236
Lebocq, Marguerite  301
Lebrocquy, Pierre  166
Leclerq, Emma  233
Lefèvre, Theo  42, 43, 107, 108
Lemaire, Jean-François  93, 94
Leman, Gérard  193

Leopold I of Saxe-Coburg  20, 21, *21*, 62, 146
Leopold II of Saxe-Coburg  64, 99, 127, 187, 261, 262-264, 271
Leopold III of Belgium  134, 176, 196, 197, 200, 264, 265
Lepoutre, Lucien  304
Libbrecht, Willem  302
Lieten, Ingrid  113
Lilian of Belgium  134, *135*
Lister, Joseph  124
Lloyd George, David  193
Lodish, Harvey  310
Lombroso, Cesare  156
Loobuyck, Patrick  76
Lorein, Melanie  237
Loveling, Pauline  168
Loveling, Rosalie  168
Loveling, Virginie  168, *168*, 172, 173, 192
Lumumba, Patrice  271, 272
Lundberg, Anna  129
Luwel, Marc  51
Luysterman, Arthur  51

**M**

Mac Leod, Aimé  173
Mac Leod, Julius  34, *168*, 169, *169*, 170-173, 178, 179, 197, 214, 237, 252, 287, 289, *289*, 290, *291*, 292, 301, 325, 326, 328, 329
Maertens, Albert  205
Maertens, Fanny  290, 292
Maes, Nelly  81
Maeterlinck, Maurice  174, 238
Magnel, Gustave  101, *101*, 102, *102*, 103, *107*, 133, 190, 206, 324
Mahaim, Ernest  152
Mak, Ruud  249
Mansion, Paul  66, 67
Mareska, Daniel  146, 148-150
Martens, Adriaan  173, 198, *201*
Martens, Ludo  222
Martens, Wilfried  46, 143
Marx, Karl  79
Masereel, Frans  290
Massart, Lucien  42, 45, 299, 301, 302, 305
Matthys, Dirk  137
Matton-Van Leuven, Maria  254
Matton, Guido  254
Mazijn, Bernard  317
Mechelynck, Albert  68, 70
Meirsman-Roobroeck, Gaby  131
Mélot, Ernest  119
Mendel, Gregor  33, 34, 287
Merchiers, Laurent  235
Merchiers, Yvette  *235*, 256, *256*
Mercier, Désiré-Joseph  172, 193, 238
Merkel, Angela  41
Merleau-Ponty, Maurice  72
Mertes, Heidi  82
Mesnil, Jacques  294
Metdepenningen, Hippolyte  20
Meuwissen, Jules  34
Michaelis, Georg  192

Miele, Adolphe  236
Minnaert, Marcel  *169*, 172, 173
Mobutu, Joseph Désiré  272, 274
Moens, Luc  87, 111
Moens, Roger  136
Moerman, Fientje  86, 258, 324
Moreira da Silva, Paolo  278
Morren, Charles  94
Morris, William  238
Mortier, Freddy  57, *73*, *73*, 76, 81, 82, 86, *87*, 87
Moynier, Gustave  187
Moyson, Emile  167
Murray, John  66, *67*
Mussche, 'Ma'  219
Musschoot, Anne-Marie  *168*, 180, 256, *256*
Mussen, Maurice  129
Muyters, Philippe  113

**N**

Nihoul, Emile  136, 137, 303
Nolf, Pierre  38, 175, 176, 197
Noppius, Lambert  31
Nussbaum, Martha  8
Nyerere, Julius  277
Nyssen, René  159, 160

**O**

Obrie, Julius  193
Olbrechts, Frans  260, 266, *266*, 267, 269
Oosterlinck, André  50, 51
Orban, Maurice  204

**P**

Page, Hillary  277
Palfijn, Jan  237
Pannier, Jean-Louis  80
Pasteur, Louis  119
Pattyn, Piet  275
Pauli, Adolphe  31, *115*, 118, 121, 127
Peers, Willy  242
Peeters, Jozef  175
Penninck, Jacqueline  134
Pennings, Guido  252
Persoone, Guido  278, 295, *298*
Petri, Franz  198, 200, 203
Piaget, Jean  71
Picard, Hein  157, 223, 226, 246
Picard, Leo  170, 173
Pien, Armand  95
Pieruccini, Nora  155, 197, *197*, 204, 206
Pinel, Philippe  120
Pinxten, Rik  222
Piot, Peter  136, 137, 209, 245, 273-275, 281
Pirenne, Henri  33, 36, 37, 171, 173, 176, 185, *185*, 191, *191*, 192, 193, 199, 200, 292, 327
Pirenne, Jacques  175
Pirenne, Pierre  *185*, 190
Pirmez, Eudore  232
Pius IX  62, 64, 65
Plateau, Felix  291, 292, *326*
Plateau, Joseph  22, *23*, *24*, 33, 95, 111

Platel, Alain  130, 161
Podgaetzki, Nora  206, 293
Podgaetzki, Suzanne  206
Poelman, Charles  27
Poirier, Etienne  232, 233
Polderman, Fabrice  204
Polk, Philip  76, 293
Poma, Karel  76, 202, 205
Popelin, Marie  235, *235*
Poppe, August  103
Poulain, Norbert  324
Prevenier, Walter  83-85
Prins, Adolphe  156
Pyfferoen, Oscar  214
Pylyser, Rik  158

**Q**

Quételet, Adolphe  20, 145, *145*, 155, 161, 162, *165*, 169

**R**

Rabaey, Korneel  298
Raes, Koen  *73*, 82, 159
Ramaekers, Jef  309
Ramos de Azevedo, Francisco de Paula  98
Rappaport, Jacob  202
Reeder, Eggert  *201*
Renard, Alphonse  39, 65, 66, *66*, 67, *67*, 68, *68*, 70, *70*, 262
Repelaer van Driel, Ocker  13, 14, *15*, 211
Reynebeau, Marc  77
Ringoir, Severin  134
Robberechts, Daniël  222
Robbrecht, Paul  325
Rockefeller, John  37
Roelandt, Louis  15, 95
Roels, Frank  292, 293
Roels, Wilfried  158, 223
Roersch, Alphonse  70
Rogier, Charles  26, 27, 60, 61, 63, 146
Rolin-Jaequemyns, Gustave  150, 186, *186*, 187, 261, 262
Rolin, Albéric  165, 172, 186, *186*, 187, 194
Rolin, Hippolyte  186
Rommelaere, Willem  127
Romsée, Gerard  *201*
Röntgen, Wilhelm Conrad  35
Roosens, Heli  204
Roscam, Guido  244
Rosseel, Mong ('Vuile Mong')  160
Rostovtzeff, Michael  69
Roulez, Joseph  29
Rouneau, Christine  137, 245
Rubbrecht, Oswald  140, 190
Ruskin, John  238
Ruys, Tom  207
Ruysch, Frederik  118
Ruyssen, Romain  140, 168
Ryckbosch, Dirk  40
Ryelandt, Paul  242

**S**

Sabbe, Julius  167
Saeys, Frida  277
Saroléa, Charles  192
Sarton, George  7, 70, 170, 194, 237, 238, *238*, 290, 325, 326, 328, 330
Schauvlieghe, Madeleine  235, *235*
Schell, Jeff  42, *113*, 288, 293, *304*, 305, *305*, 306, 308-312
Scheuermann, Dietrich  309
Schmitterlöw, Georg  129
Schoentjes, Henri  35, 188, 191
Schoep, Alfred  133, 197, *201*, 254, 264
Schollaert, Frans  70
Schrant, Johannes  17, *17*
Schrijnen, Joseph  190
Schröder van der Kolk, Jacob  118
Schrödinger, Erwin  194
Schuurmans Stekhoven, J.H.  292
Sebruyns, Marcel  306, 308, 309
Sémer, Paula  240, 244, *244*, 245
Semmelweis, Ignaz  124
Serrure, Constant  61
Sharp, Phillip  310
Simon, Jules  156
Singer, André  324
Sinsheimer, Robert  303
Slembrouck, Stef  282
Snacken, Frans  292
Snellaert, Ferdinand  118, *167*
Snow, C.P.  327
Soenen, Roger  200, 201, *201*
Soetaert, Wim  106
Soete, Frank  137
Soete, Luc  50
Solvay, Ernest  67
Sorgeloos, Patrick  277, *277*, 278-280, 283, 284, 310
Soupart, Floribert  104, 123, 124
Speleers, Reimond  173, 198, 201
Staes, Gustave  214
Sterckx, Sigrid  82
Stöber, Franz  193
Stopes, Marie  240
Storme, Jules  *171*, 196, 201
Storme, Marcel  72, 79, 83, 85, 159
Suy, Raf  275
Swarts, Céline  99-101
Swarts, Frédéric  98, 258
Swarts, Théodore  29, 68, 99, 301

**T**

T'Sjoen, Guy  253
T'Sjoen, Yves  181
Tavernier, Jan  313
Tavernier, René  269, 276
Teirlinck, Herman  176, 180
Temmerman, Marleen  240, 246, 274, 281, 282, *282*
Thiery, Herman  242, 297
Thiery, Leo  242
Thiery, Leo-Michel  238, 247, 290, 291, *291*, 292, 293
Thiery, Michel  238, 239, 240, 241, *241*, 245, 246, 247, 328
Thiry, Urbain  123

Thomas, Frédéric  136, 157, 201
Thomas, Paul  187
Thorbecke, Johan  18, *18*
Timperman, Jacques  157
Tindemans, Leo  309
Tison, Michel  208
Tolstoy, Leo  238
Tordeur, Vera  237
Trasenster, Jean-Louis  233
Trenteseau, Jules  290
Triest, Petrus-Jozef  120
Trimbos, Kees  245
Trubetzkoy, Nicolai  327
Tshombe, Moïse  271, 272
Tutu, Desmond  283

## U

Uyttenhove, Pieter  282

## V

Van Acker, Achiel  269
Van Acker, Hans  45
Van Acker, Karel  122
Van Bambeke, Charles  235, 287
Van Beeumen, Jozef  305
Van Bendegem, Jean Paul  315
Van Beveren, Edmond  216
Van Beveren, Irène  216
Van Biervliet, Jules  122
Van Bilsen, Jef  272, *272*, 273, 276, 277
Van Bogaert, Elie  207
Van Caenegem, Raoul  156
Van Camp, Wim  111
Van Cauwelaert, Frans  *164*, 171, 180
Van Cauwenberge, Paul  *48*, 140
Van Cauwenberghe, Charles  233
Van Crombrugge, Lucie  246, 247
Van Crombrugghe, Joseph  20, *21*
Vande Lanotte, Johan  159
Vandekerckhove, Dirk  239, 240, 250
Vandekerckhove, Joël  306
Vanden Berghe, Herman  312
Vanden Berghe, Jeroen  221, 227, 328
Vandenabeele, Peter  141, 304, 309, 312
Van den Bossche, Georges  35, 176
Van den Bossche, Luc  49-51, 76
Van den Brande, August  277
Van den Brande, Luc  312
Vandenbroeck, Michel  166
Vandenbroucke, Frank  53, *53*
Vandendriessche, Laurent  45, 204, 273, 288, 299, 301, 302, *302*, 304, 305
Van den Enden, Hugo  79-81, 245
Vandenhoute, Pieter Jan  260
Van de Peer, Yves  313
Vandepitte, Daniel  79, 223
Vandeputte, Georges  134
Vander Beken, Tom  157
Van der Bracht, Irène  129, *129*, 234, *234*, 254
Vanderlinden, Jean  236
Van der Pas, Harry  241

Vanderpoorten, Herman  242
Vanderpoorten, Marleen  51
Vanderstegen, Alfons  196
Van der Straeten, Etienne  271, *271*
Vander Stricht, André  *301*, 301
Vandervelde, Emile  70
Van de Sompel, Herbert  325
Van De Sype, Lambert  *241*
Van de Velde, Albert Jacques Joseph  *301*, 301, 326, 328
Van de Velde, Henriette  206, 207
Van de Velde, Henry  133, *180*, 321, 322, *322*, 323, 324
Van de Velde, Jean-Jacques  206, 207, 301
Van de Velde, Riet  318
Van de Vyvere, Aloys  36
Van de Walle, Rik  87, 88, 110
Van de Wiele, Tom  298
Van de Woestijne, Karel  180, *180*
Van Dierendonck, André  258
Van Diest, Isala  232, 233
Van Durme, Paul  264
Van Duyse, Daniël  35, 327
Van Duyse, Prudens  181
Van Dyck, Barbara  314
Van Dyck, Maarten  328
Van Eeckhaut, Piet  161, 223, 250
Van Elslande, Renaat  77
Van Elslander, Antonin  *168*, 223
Van Ermengem, Emile  124, 126, 127, 130
Van Espen-Van Doorne, Yvonne  306
Van Espen, Walter  219
Van Gehuchten, Arthur  130
Van Gobbelschroy, Henriette  66
Vangramberen, Victor  189
Van Heesvelde, Eric  158
Van Herreweghe, Marie-Louise  159
Van Herreweghe, Mieke  87, 88
Van Hooland, Bob  277
Van Houtte, Mieke  162, 163, 229
Van Hove, Geert  161
Van Hove, Wilhelmine  238
Van Hulle, Hubert  289
Van Hulthem, Charles  14, *14*, 116
Van Humbeeck, Pierre  29, 30, 64, 231
Van Huylenbroeck, Guido  87
Vankenhove, Nadia  293
Vankenhove, Richard  33
Van Kets, Hendrik  241
Van Keymeulen, Jacques  181
Van Langenhove, Herman  106, 112
Van Langenhove, Lieva  86
Van Lerberghe, Wim  137
Van Meerhaeghe, Marcel  283
Van Miegroet, Marcel  294, 295
Van Miert, Karel  207
van Moffaert, Myriam  157
Van Monckhoven, Désiré  26, 95
Van Montagu, Marc  42, *44*, 111, 113, 179, 207, 216, 217, *217*, 218, *286*, 288, 293, 299, 301-304, *304*, 305, *305*, 306, *307*, 308, *308*, 309, 310, 312-316

Van Oost, Paulette  257
Van Oppen, Jeanine  243
van Ostaijen, Paul  267
Van Overbergh, Cyrille  70, 129
Van Oye, Eugeen  173, 201
Van Oye, Mieke  206
Van Oye, Paul  170, 197, 198, 203, 204, 206, 238, 265
Van Parys, Guido  256
Van Peteghem, Leonce  78, 79
Van Peteghem, Sylvia  324
Van Poucke, Willy  256
Van Praet, Jules  21
Van Roosbroeck, Rob  200
Van Rotterdam, Jan  15, 116
Van Rysselberghe, François  34
Van Severen, Joris  179, 272
Van Spaandonck, Marcel  281
Van Steirteghem, André  251
Van Straelen, Victor  265, *265*, 269
Van Ussel, Jos  244, 245, 247
Van Waeyenberge, Camille  105, 106
Van Werveke, Hans  200, 205
Varlez, Louis  153, *153*, 194, *194*
Varoujean, Daniel  188, 189
Vauthier, Maurice  176, 177
Verbeeck, Frans  116, 118
Verbist, Richard  155, 165, 242
Vercauteren, Erna  242
Vercoullie, Jozef  167, 168, 214
Vereecken, Alois  134, 135, *135*
Vereecken, Cecilia  256
Verhaeghe, Julien  39, 40
Verhaeghe, Paul  83, *83*
Verhaeren, Emile  238
Verhellen, Eugeen  161
Verhelst, Sidonie  231, 234
Verheyen, Jozef  153, *154*, 155
Verhofstadt, Guy  80
Verhofstadt, Koen  243
Verhulst, Adriaan  200
Verlat, Karel  206
Vermeersch, Etienne  71, 72, 73, 76, 79-82, 85, 86, 137, 221, 222, 224, 245, 246, 250, 317
Vermeersch, Hans  162
Vermeulen, Alex  250
Vermeylen, August  55, 165, 176, 177, *177*, 178, 180, *180*, 183, *183*, 194, 204, 223, 290, 327
Vermeylen, Piet  45, 46
Verne, Jules  187
Verschaeve, Cyriel  189, 195, 239
Verschaffelt, Jules  38, 39, *39*, 40, 170, 179, 194, 195, 206
Versichelen-Terryn, Marthe  254, 256
Versluys, Kries  182, 282
Verstraete, Willy  107, 217, 218, 295, 296, *296*, 297-299, 305
Vervenne, Frans (Loecki)  320, 321, 329
Victoria of Great Britain  21
Vincke, John  249, 253
Vlaeyen, Numa  136, *136*
Vlassenroot, Koen  277
Vlerick, André  107, *107*, 108, 269, 283

Voets, Jules  295-297
Voituron, Paul  146
von Baeyer, Adolph  27, 29
von Bethmann-Hollweg, Theobald  190
von Bismarck, Otto  185
von Bissing, Moritz  191, 196, 203
von Falkenhausen, Ludwig  192
von Humboldt, Wilhelm  6, 24, 55, 92
von Saxe-Coburg, Albert  21
von Saxe-Coburg, Ernst  21
von Tschermak-Seysenegg, Erich  34, 287, 288
Voorhoof, Dirk  159, 277, 315
Vranckx, Alfons  241
Vuylsteek, Karel  115, *136*, 136, 137, 138, 243, 246, 273, 295
Vuylsteke, Julius  61, 167

## W

Wagener, August  30, 60, 61, 64, 65, 69, 100, 146, 152, 213
Walgraeve, Irma  293
Watson, James  288, 327
Waxweiler, Emile  152
Weil, Erich  72
Wells, Thomas Spencer  124
Wens, Maria  159, 160, *160*, 161
Westlake, John  186
Wilkins, Maurice  288
Willem, Victor  232, 291, 292
Willems, Dominique  256, *256*
Willems, Jacques  51, 52, 85, 86, 207
Willems, Jean  40
William I of Orange  11-14, 16-19, *19*, 20, 21, 21, 22, 57, 58, *58*, 59, 92, 93, 116, 165, 166, 212, 236
William Frederick of Orange (William II)  14, 15
Willockx, Renaat  223
Wilson, Woodrow  191, 193
Woeste, Charles  238
Wolters, Gustave  96, *97*
Wundt, Wilhelm  122

## Z

Zabeau, Marc  111, 311
Zander, Jonas  127
Zola, Emile  100

INSTITUUT ⟷ VOOR
PUBLIEKSGESCHIEDENIS

With the support of **UNIVERSITEIT GENT**

Publisher
    TIJDSBEELD Publishing, Ghent

Picture research
    Fien Danniau, Gita Deneckere, Ruben Mantels
    and Davy Verbeke (UGentMemorie)

Translation
    Irene Schaudies

Design
    Dooreman

Typesetting
    Griet Van Haute

Image correction
    Stijn Dams

Printing and binding
    Graphius, Ghent

Paper
    Gardapat Kiara 135 g

© 2018 The illustrations were made available
    to the publisher by UGentMemorie
© 2018 SOFAM: Christian Kirchner and Focus
© 2018 Tijdsbeeld & Pièce Montée and the author

ISBN 978 94 9088 019 4
D/2018/9045/2

www.piecemontee.be
www.ugentmemorie.be
www.ipg.ugent.be

Cover
    The Book Tower, 1997,
    photo Carl De Keyzer

Author photo
    Dries Luyten

Endpapers
    The Book Tower, 1955,
    photo Walter De Mulder

Distribution in bookshops by
    Exhibitions International
    www.exhibitionsinternational.be

No part of this publication may be reproduced
or published by means of print, photocopy,
microfilm or in any other way without
the prior written permission of the publisher.

Illustration credits
    The photos and illustrations were provided
    by the following institutions and individuals:

Institutions:
Amsab-Instituut voor Sociale Geschiedenis Ghent, Archive of the Royal Palace Brussels, Canon Sociaal Werk, Centrum voor Academische en Vrijzinnige Archieven Brussels, De Maakbare Mens vzw, Gents Universiteitsmuseum (Ghent University Museum), Historische Huizen Ghent, Huis van Alijn Ghent, Letterenhuis Antwerp, Liberaal Archief Ghent, Museum aan de Stroom Antwerp, Museum Dr. Guislain Ghent, Nationaal Archief The Hague, Rijksmuseum Amsterdam, Royal Institute for Cultural Heritage (KIK-IRPA) Brussels, Royal Library of Belgium Brussels, Stadsarchief (Municipal archives) Ghent, Universiteitsarchief (University Archives) Ghent, Universiteitsbibliotheek (University Library) Ghent, Vlaams Instituut voor Biotechnologie Ghent, VRT-Beeldarchief Brussels, Yale University Art Gallery New Haven CT.

Individuals:
Baekeland family, family of Benn Deceuninck, Steven Degryse (Lectrr), Carl De Keyzer, Walter De Mulder, Paul De Paepe, Fritz Derom, Michiel Hendryckx, Geert Lenssens, Yvette Merchiers, Alain Platel, Patrick Sorgeloos, Thiery family, Saskia Vanderstichele, Stephan Vanfleteren, Marc Van Montagu, Marc Verschooris, Patricia Vervenne, Patrick Vuylsteek.

The list below only contains information concerning copyright or the origin of illustrations not mentioned in the captions. UGentMemorie has endeavoured to comply with the legal requirements concerning copyright. Anyone who still wishes to assert rights is requested to contact UGentMemorie.

Historische Huizen Ghent: p. 58
(© www.lukasweb.be - Art in Flanders vzw)
Nationaal Archief The Hague: p. 196 right (© Spaarnestad)

Universiteitsbibliotheek (University Library) Ghent:
    Collection 'beeldarchief': p. 102 right (© Fotobureau
    Focus Antwerp), p. 126 and 188 (© Heymansinstituut),
    p. 171 right (© Jeanine Schoone), p. 225 (© Yvette
    Merchiers), p. 297 (© Nadia Hublé-Vankenhove),
    p. 302 left (© Studio Claerhout)

All illustrations from the Universiteitsarchief (University Archives) are from the Collection 'beeldarchief' except:
Collection 'Huldeadressen en Guldenboeken': p. 21 right
Collection 'Studententijdschriften': p. 137
Reeks Beleidsdossiers 'Academische Aangelegenheden', 1940-2000: p. 270 above
Collection 'Plannen': p. 290